AF697697

Jerusalem in the Achaemenid Period

Jerusalem in the Achaemenid Period

The Relationship between Temple and Agriculture in the Book of Haggai

Jieun Kim

PETER LANG
Oxford • Bern • Berlin • Bruxelles • Frankfurt am Main • New York • Wien

Bibliographic information published by Die Deutsche Nationalbibliothek.
Die Deutsche Nationalbibliothek lists this publication in the Deutsche Nationalbibliografie; detailed bibliographic data is available on the Internet at http://dnb.d-nb.de.

A catalogue record for this book is available from the British Library.

Library of Congress Control Number: 2016931849

Cover image: כפר נחום (Capernaum) by עומר מרקובסקי. Available at https://commons.wikimedia.org/wiki/File:%D7%9B%D7%A4%D7%A8_%D7%A0%D7%97%D7%95%D7%9D_8.jpg under a Creative Commons Attribution-Share Alike 4.0 International Licence. Full terms at https://creativecommons.org/licenses/by-sa/4.0/legalcode

ISBN 978-3-0343-2210-2 (print)
ISBN 978-3-0353-0812-9 (eBook)

© Peter Lang AG, International Academic Publishers, Bern 2016
Hochfeldstrasse 32, CH-3012 Bern, Switzerland
info@peterlang.com, www.peterlang.com, www.peterlang.net

All rights reserved.
All parts of this publication are protected by copyright.
Any utilisation outside the strict limits of the copyright law, without the permission of the publisher, is forbidden and liable to prosecution.
This applies in particular to reproductions, translations, microfilming, and storage and processing in electronic retrieval systems.

This publication has been peer reviewed.

Printed in Germany

Dedicated to my late parents

Contents

Abbreviations

AB	Anchor Bible
ABD	*Anchor Bible Dictionary*
ABSA	*Annual of the British School at Athens*
ABL	*Assyrian and Babylonian Letters*
Ael., *NA*	Aelianus, *De Natura Animalium.*
AH	*Achaemenid History*
ANET	*Ancient Near Eastern Texts Relating to the Old Testament*
AnOr	Analecta Orientalia
AOAT	Alter Orient und Altes Testament
AOS	American Oriental Series
AOTC	Abingdon Old Testament Commentary
AP	Arthur Ernest Cowley. *Aramaic Papyri of the Fifth Century BC*
Ar	*Archaeology*
ASOR	American Schools of Oriental Research
BA	*Biblical Archaeologist*
BAR	*Biblical Archaeology Review*
BASOR	*Bulletin of the American Schools of Oriental Research*
BCLS	Bohn's Classical Library Series
BE X	Albert Tobias Clay. *Business Documents of Murashu Sons of Nippur Dated in the Reign of Darius II (424–404 BC)*
BEATAJ	Beiträge zur Erforschung vom Alten Testaments und Antiken Judentums

Bertin	Unpublished Bertin Copies of Babylonian Tablets in the Collection of the British Museum
BHQ	Biblia Hebraica Quinta
BHS	Biblia Hebraica Stuttgartensia
Bib	*Biblica*
BM	British Museum
BT	*The Bible Translator*
BWANT	Beiträge zur Wissenschaft vom Alten und Neuen Testament
CAH	*The Cambridge Ancient History*
CANE	*Civilizations of the Ancient Near East*
CBC	Cambridge Bible Commentary
CBQ	*Catholic Biblical Quarterly*
CC	A Continental Commentary
CHI	*The Cambridge History of Iran*
CHJ	*The Cambridge History of Judaism*
CMa	Inscription of Cyrus II from Murghab (a)
CMb	Inscription of Cyrus II from Murghab (b)
CMc	Inscription of Cyrus II from Murghab (c)
Colloq	*Colloquium*
CT	*Cuneiform Texts from Babylonian Tablets in the British museum*
Cyr.	Xenophon, *Cyropaedia*
DAE	Pierre Grelot, *Documents araméens d'Égypte*
Dar.	Johann Nepomuk Strassmaier, *Inschriften von Darius, König von Babylon*
DB	Darius Behistun Inscription
DCH	*The Dictionary of Classical Hebrew*
DE	Darius inscription from Mount Elvand

Diod.	Diodorus
DNa	Darius inscription from Naqš-e Rustam (a)
DSab	Darius inscription from Susa (ab)
DSe	Darius inscription from Susa (e)
DSf	Inscription F of Darius I at Susa
DZc	Darius inscription from the Red Sea Canal (c)
EI	*Encyclopaedia of Islam*
EncJud	*Encyclopaedia Judaica*
FAT	Forschungen zum Alten Testament
FGrH	Felix Jacoby. *Die Fragmente der griechischen Historiker*
GCCI II	Raymond Philip Dougherty. *Goucher college cuneiform Inscriptions II: Archives from Erech, Neo-Babylonian and Persian Periods*
GN	Geographical Name
GSCS	Grammar School Classics Series
HALOT	Ludwig Koehler, Walter Baumgartner and Johann Jacob Stamm. *The Hebrew and Aramaic Lexicon of the Old Testament*
Hist.	Herodotus, *Histories*
H-E	Historia-Einzelschriften
Her	Hermeneia
H-fS	Historisk-filosofiske Skrifter
HSM	Harvard Semitic Monographs
HUCA	*Hebrew Union College Annual*
IEJ	*Israel Exploration Journal*
Int	*Interpretation*
IR	*Iliff Review*
ITC	International Theological Commentary
JAOS	*Journal of the American Oriental Society*

JBL	*Journal of Biblical Literature*
JBQ	*Jewish Bible Quarterly*
JHS	*Journal of Hebrew Scripture*
JNES	*Journal of Near Eastern Studies*
JPSTC	Jewish Publication Society Torah Commentary
JSJSup	Supplements to the Journal for the Study of Judaism
JSOT	*Journal for the Study of the Old Testament*
JSOTSup	Journal for the Study of the Old Testament: Supplement
JSPSup	Journal for the Study of the Pseudepigrapha Supplement
Justin	Marcus Junianus Justinus, *Epitome of the Philippic History of Pompeius Trogus*
KAV	*Keilschrifttexte aus Assur verschiedenen Inhalts*
LAPO	Littérature Ancienne du Proche-Orient
LAS	*Letters from Assyrian Scholars to the Kings Esarhaddon and Assurbanipal*
LACTOR	London Association of Classical Teachers – Original Records
LHB/OTS	Library of Hebrew Bible/Old Testament Studies
LSTS	Library of Second Temple Studies
LXX	The Septuagint
MIA	Monographs of the Institute of Archaeology
ML	Russel Meiggs and David Malcolm Lewis, eds. *A Selection of Greek Historical Inscriptions*
MMA	Monographs in Mediterranean Archaeology
MT	The Masoretic Text
NBC	A New Biblical Commentary
NC	*The Numismatic Chronicle*

NCBC	The New Century Bible Commentary
NEA	*Near Eastern Archaeology*
NEAEHL	*The New Encyclopedia of Archaeological Excavations in the Holy Land*
NICOT	New International Commentary on the Old Testament
OEANE	*The Oxford Encyclopedia of Archaeology in the Near East*
OLA	Orientalia Lovaniensia Analecta
Or	*Orientalia*
OTG	Old Testament Guides
OTL	Old Testament Library
OTLS	Old Testament Library Series
PBerlin	Berlin Papyri
PEQ	*Palestine Exploration Quarterly*
PCS	Penguin Classics Series
PF	Persepolis Fortification Tablets
PN	Personal Name
PT	Persepolis Treasury Tablets
RAI	Rencontre Assyriologique Internationale
RB	*Revue Biblique*
RHAW	Routledge History of the Ancient World
RE	*Review Expositor*
SAA	State Archives of Assyria
SAM	Babylonian Tablets in the Collection of the South African Cultural History Museum
SBL	Society of Biblical Literature
SHCANE	Studies in the History and Culture of the Ancient Near East
SJOT	*Scandinavian Journal of the Old Testament*
Strabo	Strabo, *Geography*

SWBA	The Social World of Biblical Antiquity
TA	*Tel Aviv*
TCL	Texts cunéiformes. Musée du Louvre
TOTC	Tyndale Old Testament Commentaries
TLJS	Taubmen Lectures in Jewish Studies
Trans	*Transeuphratène*
TynBul	*Tyndale Bulletin*
UCOIP	The University of Chicago Oriental Institute Publications
USQR	*Union Seminary Quarterly Review*
VGT	Veröffentlichungen Gesellschaft für Theologie
VS VI	A. Ungnad. Neubabylonische und achämenidische Urkunden (Vorderasiatische Schriftdenkmäler der Königlichen Museen zu Berlin 6)
VT	*Vetus Testamentum*
VTSup	Supplements to Vetus Testamentum
WBC	Word Biblical Commentary
YBT	Yale Babylonian Texts
YOS	Yale Oriental Series, Texts
ZAW	*Zeitschrift für die alttestamentliche Wissenschaft*

Introduction: Restoration of the Jerusalem Temple

This study deals with the relationship between the restoration of the Jerusalem temple and agriculture in the Book of Haggai. The problem is twofold: firstly, I want to look into the nature of agriculture in Judah in general; secondly, I intend to relate the agricultural activities to the prophetic exhortations to rebuild the temple in Jerusalem.[1] The corpus texts I have chosen are Hag 1:2, 5–6, 7–8, 9–11, 12–14; 2:3, 8–9, 15–19.[2]

Particularly in Hag 1:5–6, 9–11; 2:15–19, Haggai focuses above all on agricultural activities that are related to the rebuilding of the Jerusalem temple. It is a major issue in the Book of Haggai that the state of Judean economy in general depended on a well functioning temple economy in Jerusalem. For this reason, quite a large portion of Haggai proclaims that the current economic disaster in Judah results from the ruined state of the Jerusalem temple (Hag 1:3–4, 9–11; 2:11–14). Thus, the text itself indicates the importance of the relationship between the temple and a larger agricultural industry.

The book of Haggai is dated to the second year of Darius. It is commonly assumed that the king in question is Darius I (522–486 BCE). From a historical viewpoint, the Book of Haggai should be read as reflecting Darius's early reign. According to the text, the rebuilding of the Jerusalem temple

1 In this thesis, the term "agriculture" is used to describe the broad array of economic activities on the land whereby human communities exploit plants, animals and metals to produce food and other products useful to sustain life and culture. Thus, the term "agriculture" can primarily be replaced with "land economy," "agricultural industry," "agricultural pursuits," "agricultural activities," or "agricultural business." These are not technical terms.

2 The text that I use for Haggai is *Biblia Hebraica Stuttgartensia* (4th ed. Edited by K. Elliger and W. Rudolph. Stuttgart: Deutsche Bibelgesellschaft, 1987). Translations into English are on my own. For some biblical passages, however, I use the *RSV*. I also provide detailed explanations on Hebrew words, considering readers who have no Hebrew.

was claimed in the time of Darius. Historians in general assume that this was common Achaemenid imperial policy.[3] Haggai emphasised that the renovated Jerusalem temple would be crucial to improving Judean economy, enabling the country to fulfil its economic duties toward the empire (Hag 1:4; 2:3, 8–9).[4] Judah had to be able to support the upcoming deployment of a huge imperial army in response to the rebellion in Egypt in 519 BCE.[5] The study of the temple rebuilding project, consequently, gives important information on Jerusalem as one of many administrative centres in the Achaemenid Empire. Darius ruled all conquered territories throughout his reign in the same manner: Judah was but one province in this huge empire.

Haggai's description of the relationship between temple and agriculture reminds us of a commonly known phenomenon. Deities all over the ancient Near East would provide blessing and prosperity if they were worshipped according to prescribed rules and regulations. However, if gods were disobeyed, they would punish.[6] Behind this "punishment" theology

3 Geo Widengren, "The Persian Period," in *Israelite and Judean History* (ed. John Haralson Hayes and J. Maxwell Miller; Philadelphia: Fortress, 1977), 489–538; Amelie Kuhrt, "The Cyrus Cylinder and Achaemenid Imperial Policy," *JSOT* 25 (1983): 83–97; Hayim Tadmor, "Judah," in *CAH*, Vol. 6, *The Fourth Century B.C.* (ed. David M. Lewis, John Boardman, Simon Hornblower, and Martin Ostwald; Cambridge: Cambridge University Press, 1994), 261–96; Pierre Briant, *From Cyrus to Alexander: A History of the Persian Empire* (trans. Peter T. Daniels; Winona Lake, IN: Eisenbrauns, 2002), 204–54; Lester L. Grabbe, *A History of the Jews and Judaism in the Second Temple Period*. Vol. 1, *Yehud: A History of the Persian Province of Judah* (LSTS; London; New York: T & T Clark, 2004), 215–16.

4 For a detailed exegesis, see Chapters 4 and 5 below.

5 Kenneth G. Hoglund, "The Achaemenid Context," in *Second Temple Studies*. Vol. 1, *Persian Period* (ed. Philip R. Davies; JSOTSup 117; Sheffield: JSOT, 1991), Kenneth G. Hoglund, *Achaemenid Imperial Administration in Syria-Palestine and the Missions of Ezra and Nehemiah* (SBL Dissertation Series 125; Atlanta: Scholars Press, 1992), 29–36, 54–68, 208–25; Jon L. Berquist, *Judaism in Persia's Shadow: A Social and Historical Approach* (Minneapolis: Fortress, 1995), 53; John Kessler, "Persia's Loyal Yahwists: Power Identity and Ethnicity in Achaemenid Yehud," in *Judah and the Judeans in the Persian Period* (eds, Oded Lipschits and Manfred Oeming; Winona Lake, IN: Eisenbrauns, 2006), 91–122. See further Chapter 2 below.

6 Jean-Claude Margueron, "Mesopotamian Temples," in *OEANE*, Vol. 3 (ed. Eric M. Meyers; New York: Oxford: Oxford University Press, 1997), 165.

is the wider understanding that the created world is good and created by gods that provide everything humans need. However, occasionally humans experienced drought or famine or defeat in the battlefields: when catastrophes occurred, they were always understood as punishment from the deities. My thesis is not so much a study of the "common theology of the ancient Near East." Rather, I want to pay attention to the role of temples within the macroeconomic system of the ancient Near East.

In centralised political entities in the ancient Near East, we find temples as cultural, religious, and economic major institutions. Further, temples were not only engaged in all sorts of agricultural pursuits, including animal husbandry, but also large-scale manufacture of goods based on agricultural products, including trade.[7] In particular, in the Neo-Babylonian and Achaemenid Empires, temples were controlled directly by kings, and played a leading role in the imperial economy.[8] Furthermore, the state of temple economic prosperity mirrored the economy of the empire. Consequently, the economic importance of temples cannot be exaggerated.

Research History

Critical analyses of the rebuilding of the Jerusalem temple during the Achaemenid rule over Judah commonly focus on its purpose and role in a political and social context. This relates the temple to the social, economic and administrative organisation of that time. However, too little attention has been paid to the importance of agriculture, which was fundamental to

7 For further details, see Chapter 1 below.

8 Theophilus G. Pinches, *Neo-Babylonian and Achaemenid Economic Texts, Cuneiform Texts from Babylonian Tablets in the British Museum Parts 55, 56, 57* (London: British Museum, 1982); Paul-Alain Beaulieu, *The Reign of Nabonidus King of Babylon 556–539 B.C.* (New Haven; London: Yale University Press, 1989); A. Martirossian, "Notes Concerning the Economic Activity of the Babylonian Temples in the First Millennium BC," *Iraq* 45 (1983): 128–30.

the economy of Judah. The Book of Haggai is primarily concerned with agriculture and the temple, therefore an analysis of Haggai should include an examination of the temple's reconstruction during the Achaemenid period.

It is widely accepted that the Book of Haggai is dated back to the early period of the Achaemenids, but the attempt to detect redactional layers in the text has been examined in various approaches and perspectives. I shall survey these literary critiques before I proceed with an exegesis of the text of Haggai. In this research survey, I shall give a small sample of those which illustrate my point about the relationship between the temple and economy: in doing so, I shall assert my conviction that a study of Haggai is essential when examining the temple rebuilding project in Achaemenid Judah.

Scholarly debates on the political status of Judah can be traced to the argument that Judah was annexed to the province of Samaria after the fall of the Judean kingdom.[9] In their view, Judah existed in sub-province of Samaria until the arrival of Nehemiah in 445 BCE. Yet, Judah enjoyed a

9 See Albrecht Alt, "Die Rolle Samarias bei der Entstehung des Judentums," in *Festschrift Otto Proksch zum 60. Geburtstag* (ed, Albrecht Alt; Leipzig: Hinrichs, 1934), 5–28; Kurt Galling, "The 'Gola-List' according to Ezra 2//Nehemiah 7," *JBL* 70 (1951): 149–58; Kurt Galling, *Die Bücher der Chronik. Ezra, Nehemiah* (Göttingen: Vandenhoeck & Ruprecht, 1954); Julian Morgenstern, "Jerusalem — 485BC," *HUCA* 27 (1956); 101–79; Julian Morgenstern, "Jerusalem — 485BC," *HUCA* 28 (1957); 15–47; Julian Morgenstern, "Jerusalem — 485BC," *HUCA* 31 (1960); 1–29; Martin Noth, *The History of Israel* (London: Harper & Row, 1960), 306–10; E. A. Speiser, "Background and Function of the Biblical nāśī," *CBQ* 25 (1963): 111–17; David L. Petersen, "Zerubbabel and Jerusalem Temple Reconstruction," *CBQ* 36 (1974): 366–72; Siegfried Herrmann, *A History of Israel in Old Testament Times* (London: SCM, 1975), 299–301; Sean E. McEvenue, "The Political Structure in Judah from Cyrus to Nehemiah," *CBQ* 43 (1981): 353–64; Ephraim Stern, "The Persian Empire and the Political and Social History of Palestine in the Persian Period," in *CHJ*, Vol. 1, *Introduction: The Persian Period* (ed. William David Davies and Louis Finkelstein; Cambridge: Cambridge University Press, 1984), 72–4; David L. Petersen, *Haggai, Zechariah 1–8: A Commentary* (OTL; London: SCM, 1985), 26–7; Daniel L. Smith, *The Religion of the Landless: The Social Context of the Babylonian Exile* (Bloomington: Meyer-Stone, 1989), 106–14; Joseph Blenkinsopp, "Temple and Society in Achaemenid Judah," in *Second Temple Studies*. Vol. 1, *Persian Period* (ed. Philip R. Davies; JSOTSup 117; Sheffield: Sheffield Academic Press, 1991), 22–53; Joel P. Weinberg, *The Citizen-Temple Community* (trans. Daniel L. Smith-Christopher;

brief period of independence as a province during the time of its governor Zerubbabel. This short spell of independence seems to have been in the time of Darius, when the Jerusalem temple rebuilding was demanded of Zerubbabel. This rebuilding project was for Judah's provincial administration, comparable in this respect to other provinces such as Samaria. For Judah's national self-definition as a province, the imperial government encouraged the establishment of a dominant elite of proven loyalty within Judah, politically sensitive region because of its proximity to Egypt. This new political level was made up of the returnees from Babylonia who were considered most likely to be a faithful allies to Darius.

However, the claim that Judah was included in the province of Samaria does not fully understand the role of Judean governor Zerubbabel. Judah evidently existed as a province of the Achaemenids under the rule of an uninterrupted line of Jewish governors from Sheshbazzar to Nehemiah and beyond.[10] Considering all the evidence available—such as imperial

---

JSOTSup 151; Sheffield: Sheffield Academic Press, 1992), 105–26; Joseph Blenkinsopp, "The Social Roles of Prophets in Early Achaemenid Judah," *JSOT* (2001): 39–58.

10 See Nahman Avigad, *Bullae and Seals from a Post-Exilic Judean Archive* (Qedem 4; Jerusalem: Hebrew University Press, 1976; Widengren, "The Persian Period," 509–11(1977); Sara Japhet, "Sheshbazzar and Zerubbabel: Against the Background of the Historical and Religious Tendencies of Ezra-Nehemiah," *ZAW* 94 (1982): 66–98; Peter Runham Ackroyd, "Archaeology, Politics and Religion: The Persian Period," *IR* 39 (1982): 8–13; Sara Japhet, "Sheshbazzar and Zerubbabel: Against the Background of the Historical and Religious Tendencies of Ezra-Nahemiah, Part II," *ZAW* 95 (1984): 218–29; Hugh Godfrey Maturin Williamson, *Ezra, Nehemiah* (WBC, Vol. 16; Waco, TX: Word, 1985), 242–4; John Wilson Betlyon, "The Provincial Government of Persian Period Judea and the Yehud Coins," *JBL* 105 (1986): 633–42; Hugh Godfrey Maturin Williamson, "The Governors of Judah under the Persians," *TynBul* 39 (1988): 59–82; Ya'akov Meshorer, "The Mints of Ashdod and Ascalon during the Late Persian Period," *EI* 20 (1989): 287–91; Haim Gilter, "New Fourth Century BC coins from Ascalon," *The Numismatic Chronicle* 156 (1990): 1–6; Sara Japhet, "The Temple in the Restoration Period: Reality and Ideology," *USQR* 44 (1991): 195–251; Hoglund, *Achaemenid Imperial Administration in Syria-Palestine and the Missions of Ezra and Nehemiah*, 69–86; Israel Eph'al, "Changes in Palestine during the Persian Period in Light of Epigraphic Sources," *IEJ* 48 (1998): 106–19; Israel Eph'al, "Syria-Palestine under Achaemenid Rule," in *CAH*, Vol. 4, *Persia, Greece and the Western Mediterranean c. 525–479 B.C.* (ed. John Boardman, David Malcolm

policies, the term פחה, stamp impressions and coins – it appears most likely that Judah in fact constituted a province of the Achaemenids. The political reality of Judah as an independent province is also assumed during the Neo-Babylonian rule.

Social and political life in the province Judah in the early Achaemenid period is marked by social conflict in various accounts. Variants of this paradigm are fundamentally bounded to the Jerusalem temple rebuilding project, wherein two issues are explored: the role of the temple rebuilding and the identity of a cultic community or theocracy in the rebuilt temple. For many debates the conflict is between the returnees from Babylonia and those who had lived in Judah during the exile in the Books of Ezra and Nehemiah.[11] Both texts unquestionably deal with the building of the temple, but very little of this would have any direct bearing on the function of the temple in the political and social context of Achaemenid Judah.

This controversial scheme also involves a monarchical concept of the Jerusalem temple in the Judean kingdom. Its emphasis is placed on prophetic texts wherein Judah's future is envisaged with the restoration of the Judean kingdom through Zerubbabel of the Davidic lineage at the time

---

Lewis, Nicholas Goeffrey Lempriere Hammond, and Ostwald Martin; Cambridge: Cambridge University Press, 1988), 151–6; Hugh Godfrey Maturin Williamson, "Judah and the Jews," in *AH*, Vol. 11, *Studies in Persian history: Essays in Memory of David M. Lewis* (eds, Maria Brosius and Amelie Kuhrt; Leiden: Nederlands Instituut voor het Nabije Oosten, 1998), 152–3; Hans M. Barstad, "After the 'Myth of the Empty Land': Major Challenges in the Study of Neo-Babylonian Judah," in Lipschits and Blenkinsopp, eds, *Judah and the Judeans in the Neo-Babylonian Period*, 3–4; Grabbe, *A History of the Jews and Judaism in the Second Temple Period*. Vol. 1, *Yehud*, 140–42. Smith, *The Religion of the Landless*, 11–42, 62–74; Morton Smith, *Palestinian Parties and Politics that Shaped the Old Testament* (London: SCM, 1987), 193–201.

11 See Wilhelm Rudolph, "Problems of the Books of Chronicles," *VT* 4 (1954): 401–9; John Bright, *A History of Israel* (3rd ed.; OTL; Philadelphia: Westminster, 1981); Gösta Werner Ahlström, *Who were the Israelites*? (Winona Lake, IN: Elsenbrauns, 1986), 101–18; Smith, *Palestinian Parties and Politics that Shaped the Old Testament*, 75–146; Shemaryahu Talmon, "The Emergence of Jewish Sectarianism in the Early Second Temple Period," in *Ancient Israelite Religion: Essays in Honor of Frank Moor Cross* (ed. Paul D. Hanson and S Dean McBride; Philadelphia: Fortress, 1987), 587–616.

of rebuilding the temple. This view of Judean restoration is developed by the notion of the kingship of YHWH in the rebuilt Jerusalem temple and is commonly termed "eschatology."[12] However, this eschatological view of Judean restoration does not give full understanding to the role of Zerubbabel; likewise, in debates on the political status of Achaemenid Judah.

Paul D. Hanson's work could be representative of the distinction in the division of Judean society. Hanson has found two groups with competing notions of how the kingship of YHWH should rule within the rebuilt Jerusalem temple.[13] One group, termed "hierocratic party" (theocratists), envisaged the rule of YHWH in his rebuilt temple, based on Ezekiel's vision: YHWH's sovereignty over his people was manifested through his presence in the cult. Visualising the rule of YHWH himself, this group accordingly encouraged the temple rebuilding, wherein Joshua the high priest of the Zadokite priests who had gained the support of the Achaemenid government was content to collaborate with the Achaemenids, since they believed that this political order had been established by YHWH.[14] In his view, Haggai is considered as belonging to the "hierocratic party" due to his focus on the temple rebuilding.[15]

The competing group, termed "visionaries" (eschatologists), which was excluded from the Jerusalem cult, regarded YHWH's kingship in Achaemenid Judah to be a miraculous divine undertaking against the temple

12 See David Noel Freedman, "The Chronicler's Purpose," *CBQ* 23 (1961): 436–42; Otto Plöger, *Theocracy and Eschatology* (2nd ed.; Translated by S. Rudman; Oxford: Blackwell, 1968), 96–109; Frank Moore Cross, "A reconstruction of the Judean Restoration," *JBL* 94 (1975): 4–18; James D. Newsome, "Toward a New Understanding of the Chronicler and His Purpose," *JBL* 94 (1975): 201–17; Hugh Godfrey Maturin Williamson, "Eschatology in Chronicles," *TynBul* 29 (1979): 120–33.

13 Paul D. Hanson, *The Dawn of Apocalyptic: The Historical and Sociological Roots of Jewish Apocalyptic Eschatology* (Philadelphia: Fortress, 1975), 32–380. See also Paul D. Hanson, *A People Called: The Growth of Community in the Bible* (San Francisco: Harper and Row, 1987), 215–311; Paul D. Hanson, "Israelite Religion in the Early Postexilic Period," in Hanson and McBride eds, *Ancient Israelite Religion*, 485–508.

14 Hanson, *The Dawn of Apocalyptic*, 209–79.

15 Hanson, *The Dawn of Apocalyptic*, 240–62.

reconstruction through Isa 40–55, 56–66 and Zech 9–14:[16] YHWH's existence in Zion (Jerusalem) as his earthly abode was to reassert his kingship over the nations. Zion would then be maintained by Judean kings over all his nations and peoples and serve the ideological and administrative needs of YHWH's sovereignty. This hope for YHWH's vindication in the context of their disenfranchisement gave rise to apocalyptic eschatology which embraced a universal vision of YHWH's sovereignty.

Hanson's understanding of the social conflict in Achaemenid Judah is based on the various definitions of prophecy and apocalyptic.[17] Hanson surely conceives of Judean kings' ruling authority in favour of YHWH in the hope of the visionary group but there is little place for the restoration of the monarchy. This may be due to Hanson's aim of establishing a social context for the rise of apocalyptic eschatology.

An alternative interpretation of the purpose of the temple rebuilding and social context in which it was taken can be found in Peter Ross Bedford. Adapting motifs such as YHWH being king of the earth and nations, the divine warrior, and the cosmic renewal from the Zion psalms (Ps 46, 48, 76) and the יהוה מלך psalms (Ps 47, 93, 96–99), Bedford focuses on both the title פחה (Hag 1:1, 14; 2:2, 21) and the uses of the term יהוה צבאות (Hag 1:2, 5, 7, 14; 2:4, 6–9, 11, 23) in Haggai which dealt with the rebuilding of the temple.[18]

Bedford has indisputably developed the intervention of the divine warrior and the cosmic renewal in the exegesis of Haggai as the assault of the nations: YHWH's portrayals in his kingship and enthronement are given to the occurrence of the motif of the shaking of the earth and nations (Hag 2:6–7). Being king of both of these, YHWH did indeed judge and

16 Hanson, *The Dawn of Apocalyptic*, 32–208.

17 On doubt of Hanson's definitions of prophecy and apocalyptic, see Lester L. Grabbe, "Prophetic and Apocalyptic: Time for New Definitions and New Thinking," in *Knowing the End from the Beginning: The Prophetic, the Apocalyptic and their Relationships* (ed. Lester L. Grabbe and Robert D. Haak; JSPSup 46; London: T & T Clark, 2003), 107–33.

18 Peter Ross Bedford, *Temple Restoration in Early Achaemenid Judah* (JSJSup 65; Leiden: Brill, 2001), 183–240.

chastise nations (Hag 2:4–5), then used funds drawn from them to make Judah glorious (Hag 2:3, 8–9).[19] For Haggai the temple rebuilding was for the expression of YHWH's return to Jerusalem and YHWH's kingship in Jerusalem, as the temple in the monarchical period.

Bedford then draws attention to the restoration of the Davidic dynasty. In his view of the monarchical temple, the temple project contributed to the restoration of the Davidic dynasty. This is evident in Haggai's intentional use of בית instead of היכל (Hag 1:4 and 9). YHWH thus declared that Zerubbabel was his servant and signet, which would be connected to the future restoration of Judah (Hag 2:20–23). However, Haggai understood "that day" to restore Judean kingship to be coming "very soon" (Hag 2:6, 23).[20] This is the way that Haggai made the eschatological claim on Zerubbabel, acknowledging the realities of Achaemenid authority but also affirming YHWH's promise of Judah's future.

This eschatological ideology of the Judean kingdom in YHWH's supremacy accompanying YHWH's return to the rebuilt Jerusalem temple legitimised the temple rebuilding among the Judean people. This acknowledgement led to the integration of society which had been in conflict for control over the temple with different groups pursuing their vision of its function. At this point, Bedford holds that rebuilding the temple was initiated by the Judean people due to the monarchical concept of the temple as evidenced in Haggai, although this rebuilding work was later granted by the Achaemenid government (Ezra 5–6). The temple rebuilding in Judah thus never challenged Achaemenid sovereignty.[21] In Bedford's reading of Haggai it is likely that the figure of Zerubbabel was promoted, such as in a monarchical institution. However, his interpretation of Haggai against the backdrop of Achaemenid Judah, as such, does no more than focus on the ideological role of the temple within Judean society.

19 Bedford, *Temple Restoration in Early Achaemenid Judah*, 194–206, 215–27.

20 Bedford, *Temple Restoration in Early Achaemenid Judah*, 206, 241–5. On eschatological hope of Judah, see also Peter A. Verhoef, *The Book of Haggai and Malachi* (NICOT; Grand Rapids: Eerdmans, 1987); Petersen, *Haggai, Zechariah 1–8*.

21 Bedford, *Temple Restoration in Early Achaemenid Judah*, 215–27.

Attempts to relate the temple rebuilding to an Achaemenid policy to establish imperial administration has been done in various studies. Joel P. Weinberg, for example, has developed "the citizen-temple community" by comparative data drawn from his previous work which is related to "temple communities" in Mesopotamia and Asia Minor.[22]

Attention in this study has above all been given to the role of the Jerusalem temple as an agrarian institution. Weinberg has studied the agrarian structure and nature of the postexilic Judean community based on social status and authority structures, concentrating on how the missions of Ezra and Nehemiah have become the focus of considerable interest in economic aspects of postexilic Judean society.[23] He has propounded the view that the Jerusalem temple was built as a result of Achaemenid administrative policy which had as its goal the formation of a self-determining institution within Judah: the Zion returnees formed בית אב as a basic social unit in postexilic Judean society, which later developed into בית אבות, a unique social institution that was composed of socio-economic units as recorded in Ezra-Nehemiah. This community of בית אבות definitely established the citizen-temple community.[24] The status of the temple members was accordingly dependent on their connection with the existence or nonexistence of temple property.

Weinberg further points out that after the missions of Ezra and Nehemiah, due to the members' acceptance of the local, non-deported population of Judah into the community, the membership of the citizen-temple community rapidly rose from only 20 per cent to 70 per cent of the population of Judah.[25] Among the emergent population, three major centres were situated in the Central Hill country around Jerusalem, in the Coastal Plain and in the Jordan Valley. Here, Haggai helped the citizen-temple community that had already begun to establish itself become more realistic and concrete while supporting the Davidic Zerubbabel and the Zadokite Joshua in his promulgation.

22 Weinberg, *The Citizen-Temple Community*, 17–33.

23 Weinberg, *The Citizen-Temple Community*, 105–38.

24 Weinberg, *The Citizen-Temple Community*, 98–104.

25 Weinberg, *The Citizen-Temple Community*, 115–21.

To redefine the postexilic community in Judah, however, Weinberg does not take into consideration the real social context, despite studying socio-economic development in postexilic Judah. Notwithstanding this, his argumentation on the missions of Ezra and Nehemiah has led to great interest in Judah's national self-definition as a province, as well as in how the Jerusalem temple generated income for the Achaemenid Empire. There are some views in this area that arouse a great deal of interest in the role of the Jerusalem temple as the economic and administrative centre of Achaemenid Judah.[26]

One important study of the temple's role within the social, political, and economic context of Achaemenid Judah has been done by Eric M. Meyers and Carol L. Meyers. Through their commentary on Haggai, Meyers and Meyers stress that the rebuilt Jerusalem temple would function as the mainstay of the economy long enough to establish the independent sub-province within the Achaemenid Empire.[27] When rebuilt, the temple in Jerusalem would become a major economic and administrative centre through its control over the annual budget of the province and management of Judah's agricultural economy.[28] Accordingly, Judah could only reap economic benefits once an administrative and economic centre had been built.

On this point, Meyers and Meyers give us an exciting new socio-economic reading of Haggai. However, Haggai's insistence that the people rebuild the temple is not examined in terms of a true appraisal of the central importance of the temple in any ancient Near Eastern society for

26 See Robert P. Carroll, "So What Do We Know about the Temple? The Temple in the Prophets," in *Second Temple Studies*. Vol. 2, *Temple Community in the Persian Period* (ed. Tamara C. Eskenazi and Kent H. Richards; JSOTSup 175; Sheffield: Sheffield Academic Press, 1994), 34–51; David J. A. Clines, "Haggai's Temple Constructed, Deconstructed and Reconstructed," in Eskenazi and Richards, eds, *Second Temple Studies*. Vol. 2, *Temple Community in the Persian Period*, 60–5; Hoglund, *Achaemenid Imperial Administration in Syria-Palestine and the Missions of Ezra and Nehemiah*, 51–91, 165–205, 207–40; Hoglund, "The Achaemenid Context," 54–72, esp. 64; Berquist, *Judaism in Persia's Shadow*, 59–68.

27 Eric M. Meyers and Carol L. Meyers, *Haggai, Zechariah 1–8* (AB, Vol. 25B; New York: Doubleday, 1987), 20–44, 195–6, 390.

28 Meyers and Meyers, *Haggai, Zechariah 1–8*, 1–8, 39–43, 220–1.

the economic health of the community as a whole. They focus on the temple rebuilding programme, but offer very little in relation to the wider socio-economic context of the temple. They devalue the importance of the temple reconstruction with regard to the reality of the people's dire economic situation (Hag 1:5–6, 9–11; 2:15–19). Accordingly, the need for the exegetical studies on Haggai based on the agricultural activities which are fundamental to the land economy are taken for granted.

A similar emphasis on the political and economic role of the temple lies in the work of John Kessler. In his commentary on Haggai, Kessler points out that the temple reconstruction would encourage the repopulation and economic redevelopment of Jerusalem, promoting a self-sufficient Judean economy.[29] This was connected to Achaemenid policy of making Judah a semi-autonomous ethnic and political province, and utilising the temple as a fiscal administrative centre for the empire unquestionably increased taxes.

When considering the economic aspect of the temple, Kessler contends that calls to rebuild the temple appear to have been rejected by the largely agricultural community, composed mainly of the non-exiled who owed their land holdings and economic stability to the land redistribution undertaken by Neo-Babylonia.[30] There may have been conflict between this land-owning community and the returnees over land tenure issues or political allegiances. Notwithstanding this, the temple as a financial centre had to be built by both groups while imperial policies were in force. In the Book of Haggai, however, the word "remnant" (שְׁארית) was never intended to invoke any conflict between the exiled and the non-exiled (Hag 1:12; 2:2). This item simply refers to the community as a collective identity, all unnamed except Zerubbabel and Joshua (see chapters 4 and 5 below).

Meyers and Meyers, and Kessler go on to contend that the governor Zerubbabel, who took charge of relations as the official agent between Judah and the Achaemenids, was responsible to the king for returning

29 Kessler, *The Book of Haggai*, 80–96, 114–22, 259–61.

30 Kessler, *The Book of Haggai*, 97–102, 122–7, 140–8, 164, 203–6, 243–58.

tribute and tax payments from the province.[31] They maintain that Haggai justified the building in the current political circumstances by reference to Zerubbabel's royal lineage, and guaranteed the possibility of change in the political status of Achaemenid Judah. In this view, the vital expression "my signet ring" (חותם) has particular royal significance, and the verb "choose" (בחר) is crucial within the Davidic election tradition (Hag 2:20–23). In this exaltation of Zerubbabel, Haggai made messianic claims of him. For Haggai, the Davidic line of Zerubbabel was not rejected, and the precise nature of Zerubbabel's future role with the "signet ring" was kept intentionally open-ended (2:23).

In the exaltation of Zerubbabel, Meyers and Meyers, and Kessler undoubtedly envisage Judah's future as lying in the restoration of the Judean kingdom under a Davidic king. All of them evidently keep messianic claims for Zerubbabel in Haggai. However, Zerubbabel's role should be acknowledged both within the political and administrative realities of Achaemenid Judah.

Since Haggai's text is one of the necessary sources for the study of Achaemenid Judah, Meyers and Meyers, and Kessler have examined Haggai in terms of the social, political, and economic role of the Jerusalem temple in Achaemenid Judah. However, too little attention has been paid to the economic importance of agricultural produce in Judah. Nor do they offer much direct bearing on the wider socio-economic context of the temple. Haggai focuses clearly on the centrality of the Judean agricultural activities which were fundamental to the land economy in relation to the temple. The topic, the reconstructed Jerusalem temple as an administrative economic centre, has been severely under-estimated.

Therefore, my study on the relationship between the temple and agriculture in the Book of Haggai has evidentiary value for analysis of the role of the rebuilt temple within the social, political, and economic context of Achaemenid Judah. The foremost objective of my research is to examine the Jerusalem temple rebuilding project in terms of its central importance within the economic and administrative organisation of the Achaemenids.

31 Meyers and Meyers, *Haggai, Zechariah 1–8*, xxxix, 1–8, 39–41, 195–6; Kessler, "Persia's Loyal Yahwists, 91–122; Kessler, *The Book of Haggai*, 114–22, 241–75.

Method and Organisation

In order to fill the described lacuna in Haggai research, this study will perform an exegesis of the Book of Haggai. I will concentrate on the purpose for rebuilding the Jerusalem temple within the larger land economy of Judah in the Achaemenid period.

My exegetical work will be economically and historically oriented. Archaeological reports will be used for evidence of agricultural activities in Judah. Historical documents on the Achaemenids, as well as secondary literature, are my sources for the study of Achaemenid administrative policy.

Chapter 1 will explore how much the ancient Near East regions had cooperated with each other in their economic structures, so to provide a background for the investigation of Judean economic abilities within a larger international context. In Chapter 1, I will also look into the role of temples for the economy throughout the ancient Near East. I will conclude that temples played a huge role for the political, economic, administrative, and military realities of the Near East.

In Chapter 2, I will undertake a historical survey of Darius's rule in Judah. The main purpose of this part is to understand the role of the Jerusalem temple within the imperial administrative system. I will look into how the various provinces were organised, and investigate the role of local leaders. Moreover, I will examine Judah's wider obligations within the administrative, economic, and military structure of the Achaemenid Empire. This will shed light upon the claim that the reconstruction of the temple in Jerusalem was intended to enhance imperial activities.

Building upon Chapters 1 and 2, Chapter 3 will survey historical and economic circumstances of Judah during the Neo-Babylonian and Achaemenid periods, paying above all attention to the material culture in Judah. I will ask if Judean industries had been sustained throughout the Babylonian exile, and also what sort of economic strategies existed in Judah under Darius. Was Darius's imperial policy carried out effectively in Judah? Since the Achaemenid Empire had few natural resources of her own, accumulation of wealth totally depended on the economy of the provinces.

Chapters 4 and 5 provide a critical exegesis on the Book of Haggai. My exegesis will demonstrate the need for a new reading of Haggai from a historical point of view. Also, I will look at the Book of Haggai as a complete and coherent work, particularly looking into the role of the Jerusalem temple rebuilding in relation to agriculture. In doing so, I will have reached a more fully informed understanding of the relationship between the temple and agriculture in the Book of Haggai, and in general of the role of agriculture for the economy of Judah.

Bibliography

Ackroyd, Peter Runham. "Archaeology, Politics and Religion: The Persian Period." *IR* 39 (1982): 8–13.

Ahlström, Gösta Werner. "Wine Presses and Cup-Marks of the Jenin-Megiddo Survey." *BASOR* 231 (1978): 19–49.

Alt, Albrecht. "Die Rolle Samarias bei der Entstehung des Judentums." Pages 5–28 in Alt, ed., *Festschrift Otto Proksch zum 60. Geburtstag.*

——. eds. *Festschrift Otto Proksch zum 60. Geburtstag.* Leipzig: Hinrichs, 1934.

Avigad, Nahman. *Bullae and Seals from a Post-Exilic Judean Archive.* Qedem 4: Institute of Archaeology. Jerusalem: The Hebrew University of Jerusalem Press, 1976.

Barstad, Hans M. "After the 'Myth of the Empty Land': Major Challenges in the Study of Neo-Babylonian Judah." Pages 3–20 in Lipschits and Blenkinsopp, eds, *Judah and the Judeans in the Neo-Babylonian Period.*

Beaulieu, Paul-Alian. *The Reign of Nabonidus King of Babylon 556–539 B.C.* New Haven; London: Yale University Press, 1989.

Bedford, Peter Ross. *Temple Restoration in Early Achaemenid Judah.* JSJSup 65. Leiden: Brill, 2001.

Berquist, Jon L. *Judaism in Persia's Shadow: A Social and Historical Approach.* Minneapolis: Fortress, 1995.

Betlyon, John Wilson. "The Provincial Government of Persian Period Judea and the Yehud Coins." JBL 105 (1986): 633–42.

Biblia Hebraica Stuttgartensia. 4th ed. Edited by K. Elliger and W. Rudolph. Stuttgart: Deutsche Bibelgesellschaft, 1987. [=BHS]

Blenkinsopp, Joseph. "The Social Roles of Prophets in Early Achaemenid Judah." *JSOT* (2001): 39–58.

——. "Temple and Society in Achaemenid Judah." Pages 22–53 in Davies, ed., *Second Temple Studies*. Vol. 1, *Persian Period*.

Boardman, John, David Malcolm Lewis, Nicholas Goeffrey Lempriere Hammond, and Ostwald Martin, eds. *The Cambridge Ancient History*. Vol. 4, *Persia, Greece and the Western Mediterranean c. 525–479 B.C.* Cambridge: Cambridge University Press, 1988. [=*CAH*]

Briant, Pierre. *From Cyrus to Alexander: A History of the Persian Empire*. Translated by Peter T. Daniels. Winona Lake, IN: Eisenbrauns, 2002.

Bright, John. *A History of Israel*. 3rd ed. OTL; Philadelphia: Westminster, 1981.

Brosius, Maria. and Amelie Kuhrt, eds. *Achaemenid History*. Vol. 11, *Studies in Persian History: Essays in Memory of David M. Lewis*. Leiden: Nederlands Instituut voor het Nabije Oosten, 1998. [=*AH*]

Carroll, Robert P. "So What Do We Know about the Temple? The Temple in the Prophets." Pages 34–51 in Eskenazi and Richards, eds, *Second Temple Studies*. Vol. 2, *Temple Community in the Persian Period*.

Clines, David J. A. "Haggai's Temple Constructed, Deconstructed and Reconstructed." Pages 60–87 in Eskenazi and Richards eds, *Second Temple Studies*. Vol. 2, *Temple Community in the Persian Period*.

Cross, Frank Moore. "A reconstruction of the Judean Restoration." *JBL* 94 (1975): 4–18.

Davies, Philip R. and John M. Halligan, eds. *Second Temple Studies*. Vol. 3, *Studies in Politics, Class and Material Culture*. JSOTSup 340. Sheffield: Sheffield Academic Press, 2002.

Eph'al, Israel. "Changes in Palestine during the Persian Period in Light of Epigraphic Sources." *IEJ* 48 (1998): 106–19.

——. "Syria-Palestine under Achaemenid Rule." Pages 139–64 in Boardman, Lewis, Hammond, and Martin, eds, *CAH*. Vol. 4, *Persia, Greece and the Western Mediterranean c. 525–479 B.C.*

Eskenazi, Tamara C. and Kent H. Richards, eds. *Second Temple Studies*. Vol. 2, *Temple Community in the Persian Period*. JSOTSup 175. Sheffield: JSOT, 1999.

Freedman, David Noel, ed. *Anchor Bible Dictionary*. 6 Vols. New York; London, Doubleday, 1992. [=ABD]

Galling, Kurt. *Die Bücher der Chronik. Ezra, Nehemiah*. Göttingen: Vandenhoeck & Ruprecht, 1954.

——. "The 'Gola-List' according to Ezra 2//Nehemiah 7." *JBL* 70 (1951): 149–58.

Gilter, Haim. "New Fourth-Century BC Coins from Ascalon." *NC* 156 (1990): 1–6.

Grabbe, Lester L. "Prophetic and Apocalyptic: Time for New Definitions and New Thinking." Pages 4–18 in Grabbe and Haak, eds, *Knowing the End from the Beginning*.

_____. *A History of the Jews and Judaism in the Second Temple Period*. Vol. 1, *Yehud: A History of the Persian Province of Judah*. LSTS. London; New York: T & T Clark, 2004.

_____ and Robert D. Haak, eds. *Knowing the End from the Beginning: The Prophetic, the Apocalyptic and their Relationships*. JSPSup 46; London: T & T Clark, 2003.

Hanson, Paul D. *The Dawn of Apocalyptic: The Historical and Sociological Roots of Jewish Apocalyptic Eschatology*. Philadelphia: Fortress, 1975.

_____. *A People Called: The Growth of Community in the Bible*. San Francisco: Harper & Row, 1987.

_____. "Israelite Religion in the Early Postexilic Period." Pages 485–508 in Hanson and McBride eds, *Ancient Israelite Religion*.

_____ and S Dean McBride, eds. *Ancient Israelite Religion: Essays in Honor of Frank Moor Cross*. Philadelphia: Fortress, 1987.

Hayes, John Haralson and J. Maxwell Miller. *Israelite and Judean History*. Philadelphia: Fortress, 1977.

Herrmann, Siegfried. *A History of Israel in Old Testament Times*. London: SCM, 1975.

Hoglund, Kenneth G. *Achaemenid Imperial Administration in Syria-Palestine and the Missions of Ezra and Nehemiah*. SBL Dissertation Series 125. Atlanta, GA: Scholars Press, 1992.

——. "The Achaemenid Context." Pages 54–72 in Davies, ed., *Second Temple Studies*. Vol. 1, *Persian Period*.

Japhet, Sara. "The Temple in the Restoration Period: Reality and Ideology." *USQR* 44 (1991): 195–251.

——. "Sheshbazzar and Zerubbabel: Against the Background of the Historical and Religious Tendencies of Ezra-Nehemiah, Part II." *ZAW* 95 (1984): 218–29.

——. "Sheshbazzar and Zerubbabel: Against the Background of the Historical and Religious Tendencies of Ezra-Nehemiah." *ZAW* 94 (1982): 66–98.

Kessler, John. "Persia's Loyal Yahwists: Power Identity and Ethnicity in Achaemenid Yehud." Pages 91–122 in Lipschits and Oeming eds, *Judah and the Judeans in the Persian Period*.

Kuhrt, Amelie. "The Cyrus Cylinder and Achaemenid Imperial Policy." *JSOT* 25 (1983): 83–97.

Lewis, David Malcolm. "The Persepolis Fortification Texts." Pages 1–6 in Sancisi-Weerdenburg and Kuhrt, eds, *AH*. Vol. 4, *Centre and Periphery*.

Lipschits, Oded. and Manfred Oeming, eds. *Judah and the Judeans in the Persian Period*. Winona Lake, IN: Eisenbrauns, 2006.

—— and Joseph Blenkinsopp, eds. *Judah and the Judeans in the Neo-Babylonian Period*. Winona Lake, IN: Eisenbrauns, 2003.

McEvenue, Sean E. "The Political Structure in Judah from Cyrus to Nehemiah." *CBQ* 43 (1981): 353–64.

Margueron, Jean-Claude. "Mesopotamian Temples." Pages 165–9 in Meyers, ed., *OEANE*. Vol. 3.

Martirossian, A. "Notes Concerning the Economic Activity of the Babylonian Temples in the First Millennium BC." *Iraq* 45 (1983): 128–130.

Meshorer, Ya'akov. "The Mints of Ashdod and Ascalon during the Late Persian Period." *EI* 20 (1989): 287–91.

Meyers, Eric M. ed. *The Oxford Encyclopedia of Archaeology in the Near East*. 5 Vols. New York; Oxford: Oxford University Press, 1997. [=*ONANE*]

—— and Carol L. Meyers. *Haggai, Zechariah 1–8*. AB. Vol. 25B. New York: Doubleday, 1987.

Morgenstern, Julian. "Jerusalem — 485BC." *HUCA* 27 (1956); 101–79.

——. "Jerusalem — 485BC." *HUCA* 28 (1957); 15–47.

——. "Jerusalem — 485BC." *HUCA* 31 (1960); 1–29.

Newsome, James D. "Toward a New Understanding of the Chronicler and His Purpose." *JBL* 94 (1975): 201–17.

Noth, Martin. *The History of Israel*. London: Harper & Row, 1960.

Petersen, David L. *Haggai, Zechariah 1–8: A Commentary*. OTL. London: SCM, 1985.

——. "Zerubbabel and Jerusalem Temple Reconstruction." *CBQ* 36 (1974): 366–72.

Pinches, G. Theophilus. *Neo-Babylonian and Achaemenid Economic Texts, Cuneiform Texts from Babylonian Tablets in the British Museum Parts 55, 56, 57*. London: British Museum, 1982.

Plöger, Otto. *Theocracy and Eschatology*. 2nd ed. Translated by S. Rudman. Oxford: Blackwell, 1968.

Rudolph, Wilhelm. "Problems of the Books of Chronicles." *VT* 4 (1954): 401–9.

Smith, Daniel L. *The Religion of the Landless: The Social Context of the Babylonian Exile*. Bloomington: Meyer-Stone, 1989.

Smith, Morton. *Palestinian Parties and Politics that Shaped the Old Testament*. London: SCM, 1987.

Speiser, E. A. "Background and Function of the Biblical nāśī." *CBQ* 25 (1963): 111–17.

Stern, Ephraim. "The Persian Empire and the Political and Social History of Palestine in the Persian Period." Pages 7–87 in Finkelstein and Davies, eds, *CHJ*. Vol. 1, *Introduction*.

Tadmor, Hayim. "Judah." Pages 261–96 in Boardman, Lewis, Hornblower, and Ostwald, eds, *CAH*. Vol. 6, *The Fourth Century BC*.

Talmon, Shemaryahu. "The Emergence of Jewish Sectarianism in the Early Second Temple Period." Pages 587–616 in Hanson and McBride, eds, *Ancient Israelite Religion.*

Verhoef, Peter A. *The Book of Haggai and Malachi.* NICOT. Grand Rapids: Eerdmans, 1987.

Weinberg, Joel P. *The Citizen-Temple Community.* Translated by Daniel L. Smith-Christopher. JSOTSup 151. Sheffield: Sheffield Academic Press, 1992.

Widengren, Geo. "The Persian Period." Pages 489–538 in Hayes and Miller, eds, *Israelite and Judean History.*

Williamson, Hugh Godfrey Maturin. "Judah and the Jews." Pages 145–63 in Brosius and Kuhrt, eds, *AH.* Vol. 11, *Studies in Persian History.*

——. "The Governors of Judah under the Persians." *TynBul* 39 (1988): 59–82.

——. *Ezra, Nehemiah,* WBC. Vol. 16. Waco, TX: Word, 1985.

——. "Eschatology in Chronicles." *TynBul* 29 (1979): 120–33.

CHAPTER 1

Agriculture and Economy in the Ancient Near East

Background

In this chapter, I will survey the agricultural activities of the ancient Near East. My survey will concern archaeological records on the above areas from the Upper Paleolithic period (between 40,000 and 10,000 years ago) to the Achaemenid period (circa fifth century BCE), even though the key concern is agricultural economy during the Achaemenid period. This historical survey will provide the necessary background on the agricultural economy of the ancient Near East, because agricultural economy in one region would not usually be changed and rather further developed throughout the ancient Near Eastern history. Therefore, the foraging Age should be considered part and even the very foundation of the ancient Near Eastern agriculture.

By way of introduction it is worth highlighting that, from the imperial period of the first millennium BCE, the agricultural economies of the Mesopotamian Empires and Israel were closely related. Mesopotamian central powers depended upon their peripheries for the many natural resources required for sustenance and prosperity. Israel demonstrated disproportionately large agricultural production, though she represented a geographically small portion of the Near East. As a result, the agricultural economy of ancient Israel contributed together with numerous other subordinates to that of the Mesopotamian empires.

The imperial administrative system which controlled taxes and trade constitutes the larger economic context for understanding the agricultural activities in the Near East at that time. Turning to the survey itself, it is necessary to take into consideration Judean patronage in the larger economic structure of the Achaemenids. Historical support for the existence of this system is provided by the Book of Haggai. The Book of Haggai is important to give a lot of information about ancient Israelite agriculture. In addition, Haggai describes Darius I (522–486 BCE) reconstructing the imperial administrative system to boost his financial power.

Agriculture in the Ancient Near East: A Short Survey

Plant Husbandry

Around 40,000 years ago, groups of people in the ancient Near East lived as gathers of wild plants, migrating regularly to pursue sources of food. Einkorn, the wild species of wheat (*Triticum boeoticum*) was their mainstay though they also depended on wild rye.[1] As groups of foragers continued congregating around the limited resources, the increased competition for food resulted in conflict. To ensure abundant harvest, the mobile foragers became sedentary and began domesticating the wild cereals between 14,000 and 10,000 years ago (Epipaleolithic).[2]

Examples of the domestication of wild cereals are available from the area surrounding the Zagros Mountains running south-eastwards from eastern Turkey and north-west Iran to the Persian Gulf and forming the Iraq-Iran border for most of their length. There, groups of foragers deliberately practised the domestication of wild crops in their natural environments, using agricultural equipments such as grinding stones and flint sickle blades

1 Daniel Zohary and Maria Hopf, *Domestication of Plants in the Old World: The Origin and Spread of Cultivated Plants in West Asia, Europe, and the Nile Valley* (2nd ed.; Oxford: Oxford University Press, 1994), 19–42.

2 See Donald O. Henry, *From Foraging to Agriculture: The Levant at the End of the Ice Age* (Philadelphia: University of Pennsylvania Press, 1989); Graeme Barker, *The Agricultural Revolution in Prehistory: Why Did Foragers Become Farmers?* (Oxford: Oxford University Press, 2006).

for grain produce.[3] Subsequently, complex foraging resulted in the settlement of the region. Remains of the domesticated form of wheat (*Triticum monococcum*) have been found at Syrian locations including Abu Hureyra and Mureybit, which provide archaeological support for these claims.[4]

A long association between wild plants and domesticated cereals informed the foragers understanding of which crops were available, which were able to be stored and which were the most productive. Foragers studied the cycles of crop productivity. This knowledge resulted in an agricultural pattern, which begins with the early rains that soften the ground for ploughing and sowing in November and culminates in the harvest.[5]

These agricultural practises were applied on increasingly large areas of land, extending into the forest-steppe areas in the Zagros region. Though steppe lands are slightly arid, they were adapted for growing wild cereals through the development of irrigation techniques such as ditches, walls, and terraces.[6] Upon generating an increase in produce, surplus was stored in underground pits and in silos at Abu Hureyra and Mureybit.[7] With a reliable food supply, these early plant-cultivating families multiplied rapidly in their settlements.

3 Barker, *Agricultural Revolution*, 73–131; Naomi F. Miller, "The Origins of Plant Cultivation in the Near East," in *The Origins of Agriculture: An International Perspective* (ed. C Wesley Cowan and Patty Jo Watson; Washington; London: Smithsonian, 1992), 41–2.

4 Barker, *Agricultural Revolution*, 106; Zohary and Hopf, *Domestication of Plants*, 38–42.

5 Annual amounts of precipitation of up to 1,000 mm are enough to cultivate agriculture. See Christopher J. Eyre, "The Agricultural Cycle, Farming, and Water Management in the Ancient Near East," in *CANE*, Vol. 1 (ed. Jack M. Sasson; New York: Scribner, 1995), 177; Daniel C. Snell, *Life in the Ancient Near East: 3100–332 BCE* (New Haven; London: Yale University Press, 1997), 123–5.

6 Oded Borowski, "Irrigation" in Meyers, ed., *OEANE*, Vol. 3, 182; Karl W. Butzer, "Environmental Change in the Near East and Human Impact on the Land," in Sasson, ed., *CANE*, Vol. 1, 142.

7 Barker, *Agricultural Revolution*, 116–18.

Archaeological evidence suggests that people cultivated emmer wheat (*Triticum dicoccum*) from 9400 BCE (pre-pottery Neolithic A).[8] Full-scale farming was first found at Çayönü in Turkey, Ali Kosh in Iran, Magzaliya, Jarmo, and Magzaliya all of which are in Iraq, and Abu Hureyra.[9] Bread wheat husbandry in Aswad and Ghoraife, both of which are in Syria, and Can Hasan III in Turkey was reported in 8500 BCE (pre-pottery Neolithic B).[10] Barley in a two-row or six-row form was cultivated at Iranian Ali Kosh and Ganj Dareh, and Turkish Can Hasan III.[11] As for legumes, the cultivation of lentils was noted at Syrian locations including Abu Hureyra, Aswad, Mureybit, and Bouqras, and at Jarmo, Magzaliya, Ali Kosh, Ganj Dareh, and Çayönü.[12]

In the Neolithic period from 6500 BCE, the cultivation of einkorn and emmer wheat was thriving at Bouqras and Hacilar, both of which are in Turkey.[13] These regions also featured barley cultivation. Their advances in produce would keep pace with Ali Kosh.[14] Bread wheat was growing well at Syrian Bouqras, Ramad, and Ras Shamra.[15] As for other crops, flax was cultivated at Mureybit, Ramad, and Ras Shamra throughout the periods.[16]

These agricultural developments influenced profound changes in human society. The surplus of one group of people opened up new pathways to food resources through bartering and sale. Agricultural work created a demand for specialised smiths, potters, weavers, carpenters, and

8 Emmer wheats are hulled wheats with tough husks that tightly enclose grains. Miller, "Origins," 43–4.

9 Barker, *Agricultural Revolution*, 131–46; Miller, "Origins," 45.

10 Miller, "Origins," 45; Zohary and Hopf, *Domestication of Plants*, 51–7.

11 Augusta McMahon, "From Sedentism to States, 10,000–3000 BCE," in *A Companion to the Ancient Near East* (ed. Daniel C. Snell; Oxford: Blackwell, 2005; 2007), 22–3; David C. Hopkins, "Cereals" in Meyers, ed., *OEANE*, Vol. 1, 480; Zohary and Hopf, *Domestication of Plants*, 59.

12 David C. Hopkins, "Agriculture," in Meyers, ed., *OEANE*, Vol. 1, 23; Miller, "Origins," 44–5.

13 Miller, "Origins," 45; Zohary and Hopf, *Domestication of Plants*, 41.

14 Zohary and Hopf, *Domestication of Plants*, 61–7.

15 Miller, "Origins," 45.

16 Miller, "Origins," 45; Zohary and Hopf, *Domestication of Plants*, 126–31.

stone toolmakers. These specialised jobs led to a need for regulation and management to ensure better coordination in production and more efficient distribution of products.[17] Agricultural developments were the stimulus for the centralised politics of the time even though this centralised redistribution concomitantly required the payment of tax or tribute to supply food to warriors, officers, and kings.[18]

One well-developed example of a centralised state is the city of Uruk. Between 3500–2800 BCE, the authorities of Uruk developed irrigation systems including reservoirs and canals.[19] They also developed agricultural instruments such as "clay sickles" and threshing sledges, and used animals for ploughing and delivery.[20] As a result of these efforts, Uruk's agricultural production of barley increased by tenfold, due to improved storage facilities.[21]

Noticeably, agricultural and manufacturing developments enhanced Uruk's ability to trade with neighbouring regions. According to the sale records of the land in ancient Kudurrus,[22] around 3000 BCE, the purchase price for fields and any other objects was paid in a wide variety of agricultural produce.[23] In addition to agricultural resources, the Uruk government developed a large scale of manufacturing of goods and a highly advanced textile

17 Elizabeth Caecilia Stone, "Mesopotamian Cities and Countryside," in Snell, ed., *A Companion to the Ancient Near East*, 158–9; Karen Rhea Nemet-Nejat, *Daily Life in Ancient Mesopotamia* (2nd ed.; Peabody: Hendrickson, 2008), 17–46.

18 Norman Yoffee, "The Economy of Ancient Western Asia," in Sasson, ed., *CANE*, Vol. 3, 1387–1400.

19 Mario Liverani, "Historical Overview," in Snell, ed., *A Companion to the Ancient Near East*, 5–7.

20 Liverani, "Historical Overview," 5.

21 Liverani, "Historical Overview," 5–6.

22 See Ignace J. Gelb, Piotr Steinkeller, and Robert M. Whiting Jr., *Earliest Land Tenure Systems in the Near East: Ancient Kadurrus* (UCOIP 104; Chicago: The Oriental Institute, 1991).

23 Ignace J. Gelb, "Household and Family in Early Mesopotamia," in *State and Temple Economy in the Ancient Near East*, Vol. 1, *of the International Conference organized by the Katholieke Universiteit Leuven from the 10th to the 14th of April 1978* (ed. Edward Lipinski; OLA 5; Leuven: Department Oriëntalistiek, 1979), 4–11; Gelb, Steinkeller, and Whiting, *Earliest Land Tenure Systems in the Near East*), 1–2, 281–98.

industry.[24] Through trading these goods, the inhabitants of Uruk secured wine, timber, metals, and precious stones, none of which occurred naturally in their region.[25] These agricultural and manufacturing developments resulted in large-scale trade networks in the Ur III period between 2112–2004 BCE.

To appreciate the agricultural and textile industries, it is worth attending to their composite parts, their pertinent crops. Barley was the leading crop.[26] It was followed by emmer wheat. From emmer wheat and barley, people made bread and beer. Beer was an important part of the diet.[27] Yet, true wheat was a rare luxury because of the lack of precipitation. The next crop, flax was woven into linen, which was fundamental to developing a textile industry.[28]

Fruits such as dates, pomegranates, apples, figs, apricots, and vines were grown. Of these, the fruit of date palms provided the greatest nutritional value and featured the desirable quality of being storable. The date's position of importance could be compared to the olive in Mediterranean lands.[29] Grapes were grown as a fruit tree. Yet, with low yields, they were usually used for fresh or dried fruits rather than for wine.[30]

Vegetables were probably grown in gardens rather than fields because they required well-developed systems of irrigation.[31] There were beetroot, turnips, leeks, onions, cress, mustard, radishes, lettuce, fennel, coriander, marjoram, rue, mint, rosemary, fenugreek, sesame, cucumbers, and garlic.[32] In addition, lentils, peas, grass peas, small broad beans, and bitter vetch were

24 David A. Warburton, "Working," in Snell, ed., *A Companion to the Ancient Near East*, 185–98; Liverani, "Historical Overview," 5–10.

25 Mark Chavalas, "The Age of Empires, 3000–900 BCE," in Snell, ed., *A Companion to the Ancient Near East*, 34–47.

26 Rosemary Ellison, "Diet in Mesopotamia: The evidence of the Barley Ration Texts (c. 3000–1400 B.C.)," *Iraq* 43 (1981), 35–45.

27 Jane Margaret Renfrew, "Vegetables in the Ancient Near Eastern Diet," in Sasson, ed., *CANE*, Vol. 1, 197.

28 Carol Bier, "Textile Arts in Ancient Western Asia" in Sasson, ed., *CANE*, Vol. 3, 1567–88.

29 Hopkins, "Farmsteads," in Meyers, ed., *OEANE*, Vol. 2, 306–7; Hopkins, "Agriculture," 24–25; Zohary and Hopf, *Domestication of Plants*, 142–72.

30 Renfrew, "Vegetables," 199–200.

31 Hopkins, "Agriculture," 25; Renfrew, "Vegetables," 193.

32 Zohary and Hopf, *Domestication of Plants*, 192–207.

cultivated. Legumes not only contributed protein to the diet but were also farmed for animal fodder.[33]

Concerning nuts, particularly around the steppe zone of the Zagros Mountains, pistachios and almonds were cultivated as a naturalised source of high-energy food. In addition to which, the wood from pines, oaks, willow, poplar, tamarisk, and maple tree were used for furniture.[34] Archaeologically retrieved remains of wooden furniture and charcoal support the prevalence and uses of these trees.[35]

So far this survey of the agricultural development in the ancient Near East has shown that, after a long history of foraging, groups of people were confronted with population expansion and its resulting stress on resources. This stress led to the domestication of cereals around 10,000 years ago. Archaeological evidence of cultivated plants has mainly been found in the Zagros area. This evidence indicates the development of reliable food sources through irrigating increasingly large areas of arable land and developing agricultural tools. Agricultural success required a centralised government for efficient management. From the time of 3500 BCE onwards, political authorities administered over agriculture and the resulting trade business. Barley was grown as a key crop. As for fruits, date palms and pomegranates were produced. Shrubs and trees were also cultivated for food, timber and sculptural materials.

Animal Husbandry

In early history, for subsistence, people certainly hunted animals. From the Epipaleolithic period, goats, sheep, gazelles, and asses inhabited the Zagros Mountains.[36] Deer, cattle, donkeys, foxes, lions, leopards, and hares

33 Eyre, "Agricultural Cycle," 183; Miller, "Origins," 50–2; Renfrew, "Vegetables," 193.

34 Allan S. Gilbert, "The Flora and Fauna of the Ancient Near East," in Sasson, ed., *CANE*, Vol. 1, 153–9; Eliazbeth Simpson, "Furniture in Ancient Western Asia," in Sasson, ed., *CANE*, Vol. 3, 1647–72.

35 Miller, "Origins," 49.

36 Barker, *Agricultural Revolution*, 136.

were also there. One can see the fossilised remains of them at Ganj Dareh, Qermez Dereh, M'lefaat, and Asiab all of which are in Iran.[37] Since then, larger settlements for hunting and slaying animals for their meat began to develop in Syrian locations including Abu Hureyra, Bouqras, and El Kowm, and in Iranian locations including Eshkaft-e Gavi, Nemrik, Çayönü, and Maghzaliya.[38] In addition to meats, products of milk, yoghurt, cheese, and butter were in high demand.[39] For wool, hair, and leather, geometric microliths, pointed arrowheads, axes, and tempered steel tools are also used.[40]

As with cereals, the population's rising demand put pressure on the natural resources, causing animals to be slaughtered in increasing numbers. As a result, animal husbandry was brought into the plant farming areas. Massive stalks of cereals after the harvest were undoubtedly useful for animal fodder. A combination of animal excrement and rotting straw used for livestock bedding then fertilised the soil.

A multitude of evidence for the herding of sheep and goats has been found at the site of the settlement of Ganj Dareh.[41] Flattened horn cores of goats, goat footprints, and deciduous teeth of sheep were preserved in mud bricks. These preserved remnants suggest the domestication of both sheep and goats at the settlements. Widespread similar evidence has been found at Syrian Abu Hureyra, Mureybit, and Jerf el-Ahmar, at Turkish Çayönü, Çatalhöyük, Göbekli Tepe, Gritille, and Hallan Çemi, at Iraqi Maghzaliya, Shanidar, Zawi Chemi Shanidar, Jarmo, Zarzi, and Umm Dabaghiyah, and at Iranian Asiab, Ali Kosh, M'lefaat, Qermez Dereh, and Pa Sangar, suggesting the prevalence of flock herding.[42]

37 Barker, *Agricultural Revolution*, 136–7.

38 Barker, *Agricultural Revolution*, 137–41.

39 Gerald A. Klingbeil, "Methods and Daily Life: Understanding the Use of Animals in Daily Life in a Multi-disciplinary Framework," in *Life and Culture in the Ancient Near East* (eds, Richard E. Averbeck, Mark W. Chavalas, and David B. Weisberg; Bethesda, MD: CDL, 2003), 413–21.

40 Brian Hesse, "Animal Husbandry and Human Diet in the Ancient Near East," in Sasson, ed., *CANE*, Vol. 1, 204–10.

41 Barker, *Agricultural Revolution*, 139.

42 Barker, *Agricultural Revolution*, 137–43; Melinda A. Zeder, *Feeding: Specialized Animal Economy in the Ancient Near East* (Washington; London: Smithsonian,

The rush to exploit animal resources was restricted by the need to regulate the slaughter of animals.[43] Not only was the slaughter of animals restricted by the demands of sustainability, but also by the limited storage available for meat. In the mixed farming areas, the crop structure provided further limitations, as it was divided to provide food for humans in addition to the livestock. For these reasons, village based animal husbandry started to be developed in areas nearby but outside of human residences. As with the agricultural developments, the developments in animal husbandry resulted in centralised political and economical control to improve coordination and distribution of animal products.

Between 2112–2004 BCE, in the Ur III dynasty, a specialised animal economy became well developed in the Kur River Basin in southwest highland Iran.[44] Tal-e Malyan, ancient Anshan played a specialised and centralised administrative role for this animal economy.[45] Although the process of identifying animal bones is not easy, the faunal remains in Malyan suggest the presence of sheep, goats, cattle, asses, dogs, gazelles, and wild pigs. Among them, sheep and goats were in the highest demand, due to the large demand for milk, wool, and hair products.[46] Sheep flocks were more numerous than goat flocks, counted together, though during the Uruk period, the ratio of sheep and goats to humans would have been about four to one.[47]

Meat distribution also took into consideration the animals' age and sex. For the most part, male sheep and goats between six months and two years would be butchered.[48] By contrast, in the other age groups, males and females were shepherded equally. In this specialised animal economy,

1991), 59–61.

43 Liverani, "Historical Overview," 5–19.

44 Zeder, *Feeding*, 13–17, 23–55, 71–2.

45 Especially, this period is called Qaleh phase at which highly structured urban system seriously begins to break down. It would be connected to dominant struggles for political power. Chavalas, "The Age of Empires, 3000–900 BCE," 45–6; Zeder, *Feeding*, 71–3.

46 Zeder, *Feeding*, 75–118.

47 Melinda A. Zeder, "Sheep and Goats" in Meyers, ed., *OEANE*, Vol. 5, 23–5; Liverani, "Historical Overview," 5–10; McMahon, "From Sedentism to States," 20–33.

48 Zeder, *Feeding*, 40–2, 141–8, 161–8.

milk was not handled administratively. Instead, milk production and distribution were the direct responsibility of regions themselves.[49] This was more appropriate, more just, because it supported milk production that met local needs for subsistence.

According to the records in Kudurrus, the purchase price for fields was paid in animals and animal products: sheep, goats, lambs, rams, ewes, cows, bulls, oxen, Lions, lions' heads, horses, donkeys, mules, asses, pigs, falcons' heads, birds, chickens, doves, ducks, geese, pigeons, fowls, rodents, fish, dried fish, turtles, cowries, milk, cream, ghee, butter, sheep oil, lard, wool, and leather.[50] They were also used for the payment of tax and tribute to kings, court officials, the military, temples, professional groups of architects, scribes, and various craftsmen.[51] Ivory from elephants is levied for a craft material.[52] Increased use of animals as items of trade, tribute, and tax resulted in the further development of animal husbandry to optimise market value.[53]

Of other applicable animals for husbandry, the few cattle were tamed as household animals because cattle are much harder to sustain both in terms of food requirements and their water consumption.[54] A single cow provided far more meat, manure, and milk than a single goat or sheep. In addition to which, cows were used to pull ploughs and deliver the harvest. For transporting people and heavier goods, though, mules and

49 Zeder, *Feeding*, 33–40.

50 Gelb, Steinkeller, and Whiting, *Earliest Land Tenure Systems*, 281–98.

51 William W. Hallo, "God, King, and Man at Yale," in Lipinski, ed., *State and Temple Economy*, 1, 99–112.

52 Albert Kirk Grayson, "Assyrian Civilization," in *CAH*, Vol. 3, Part 2, *The Assyrian and Babylonian Empires and other States of the Near East, from the Eighth to the Sixth Centuries B.C.* (ed. John Boardman, Iorwreth Eiddon Stephen Edwards, and Nicholas Goeffrey Lempriere Hammond; Cambridge: Cambridge University Press, 1991), 213–5; Gilbert, "Flora," 170.

53 Stephanie Dalley, "Ancient Mesopotamian Military Organization" in Sasson, ed., *CANE*, Vol. 1, 413–4.

54 Barker, *Agricultural Revolution*, 143–6; McMahon, "From Sedentism to States," 22–3.

donkeys were usually employed.[55] Horses were seen as a luxury animal for authorities.

Pigs would be specialised for meat production in Near Eastern societies because of the high yield in terms of meat.[56] However, pigs failed to play a major role in the Near Eastern subsistence economy. The numerous possible explanations range from ecological to psycho-ideological theories.[57] Among them, a noteworthy explanation is that large-scale pig rearing required close supervision to prevent the harm of agricultural areas when the pigs were foraging for food. Thus, only small-scale pig herding was undertaking in some regions, such as in Iraqi locations including Tell ed-Der, al-Hiba, and Sakheri Sughir, where pigs were an important resource.[58]

A variety of fish were found in coastal and river-line areas, such as at al-Hiba.[59] However, fishing practices were not specialised, even though fresh fish was eaten and dried fish provided a year-round resource.

Above, I have surveyed the development of animal husbandry in the ancient Near East, showing that people domesticated animals such as sheep and goats for sustainable provisions. Increased demand for animal resources resulted in the regulation of the slaughter of animals by numbers, species, age, and sex. Then, the administrative distribution of one region for specialised animal economy was established at Malyan. Widespread acknowledgement of the market value of animals and animal products inspired continued investment in the development of animal husbandry. Moreover, the use of animals for ploughing, threshing, and transporting led to the domestication of cattle, donkeys, mules, and horses.

55 Gilbert, "Flora," 163–4; Hesse, "Animal Husbandry and Human Diet," 209–10, 217–20.

56 Zeder, *Feeding*, 30–2.

57 Brian Hesse, "Animal Husbandry," in Meyers, ed., *OEANE*, Vol. 1, 140–3; Hesse, "Animal Husbandry and Human Diet," 204, 215.

58 Hesse, "Animal Husbandry," 140–1.

59 Gilbert, "Flora," 163.

Agriculture in Ancient Israel

Agricultural Industries

Ancient Israel shared the economic transition from foraging to food production. As in the ancient Near East, evidence dating back 40,000 years has been found in the Carmel Caves, supporting the prevalence of foraging practices, including the collection of wild barley, wild emmer wheat, wild nuts, oak, almond, and pistachio. Evidence for development in food production, similar to those in the Near East, has been found along Mount Carmel, Mount Hermon, Galilee, the Golan Plains, and in the cave of Shukbah in the Judean Hills.[60] Fish and crustaceans served as staple foods for those inhabiting the region between Lake Hula in east of Galilee and Wadi Judayid in the Jordan Valley.[61] Sparsely populated, the hilly Highlands of the Negev region were relatively favourable for herding animals.[62] Faunal remains from environs near settlements indicate the presence of goats, sheep, cattle, pigs, deer, gazelles, birds, and reptiles. Similar remains at Ein Gev in east of Galilee, Hayonim Cave in west of Galilee and Ein Aqev in the Negev date back 18,000 years ago, and similar remains at Hayonim Cave B, Hayonim Terrace, and Rosh Horesha three of which are in the Negev date back 13,000 years ago.[63]

Evidence has been found demonstrating the emergence of sedentary communities during the period of transition from foraging to agriculture. Crops were domesticated for a reliable source of food. Agricultural instruments were developed, including sickle blades, microburins, geometric

60 Barker, *Agricultural Revolution*, 116–28.

61 Henry, *From Foraging to Agriculture*, 21.

62 Benjamin Mazar, "The Early Israelite Settlement in the Hill Country," *BASOR* 241 (1981): 75–85; Edward Bruce Banning, "Highlands and Lowlands: Problems and Survey Frameworks for Rural Archaeology in the Near East," *BASOR* 301 (1996): 25–45; Moshe Avnimelech, "Influence of Geological Conditions on the Development of Jerusalem," *BASOR* 181 (1966): 24–31.

63 Henry, *From Foraging to Agriculture*, 6–7, 16–20.

microliths, and grinding stones.[64] Emmer wheat was the first cereal domesticated at Jericho.[65] 'Ain Ghazal and Iraq ed-Dubb both of which are in the Jordan Valley proved suitable for wheat cultivation, and both regions also became associated with barley and legumes farming. Barley farming also took place in Netiv Hagdud in the Jordan Valley and Lagama North in the Negev. Peas, lentils, almonds, figs, and pistachios were naturalised at Jericho and Nahal Hemar, southwest of the Dead Sea.

Similar assemblages of early farming have been found at ʿAin Mallaha in the north of Galilee, Hayonim and Ohalo in southwest of Galilee, Mugharet el Wad in south of Carmel, Nahal Oren in north of Carmel, Shukbah, El Wad, and Erq el Ahmar in the Judean Hills, Azraq, Iraq ed-Dubb, Netiv Hagdud, and Wadi Hammeh in the Jordan Valley, Gezer, and Beidha, Dhra', Nahal Hamar, Rosh Horesha, Rosh Zin, and Wadi Judayid in the Negev.[66]

The beginning of the third millennium BCE (Bronze Age) coincided with the first attempts to cultivate grapes, olives, dates, and pomegranates in the Levant.[67] The earliest remains of cultivated grapes have been found at Bene-Bereq and Taʿannek in the Judean hills, Babedh-Dhraʿ and Numeira in the Jordan Valley, Jericho and Lachish.[68] Remains of olives have been discovered at Megiddo, Afula, Taʿannek, Aphek, and Tell Halif in the Judean Hills, Beth-Yerah and Beth-Shean in south of Galilee, Teleilat Ghassul in the Jordan Valley, Tell Mashosh near Beersheba, Lachish, Gezer, the Arad

64 Jennie R. Ebeling, "Archaeological Remains of Every Activities: Ground Stone Tools in Bronze and Iron Age Palestine," in Averbeck, Chavalas, and Weisberg, eds, *Life and Culture in the Ancient Near East*, 311–26.

65 Miller, "Origins," 45.

66 Barker, *Agricultural Revolution*, 131–40; Henry, *From Foraging to Agriculture*, 35–8, 79–228.

67 Among these early settlements, Jericho presents a well-developed settlement which is enclosed by a substantial wall. Frank S. Frick, "Cities: An Overview," in Meyers, ed., *OEANE*, Vol. 2, 14–19.

68 Oded Borowski, *Agriculture in Iron Age Israel* (Winona Lake, IN: Eisenbrauns, 1987), 102–14, 117–28; Carey Ellen Walsh, *The Fruit of the Vine: Viticulture in Ancient Israel* (HSM 60; Winona Lake, IN: Eisenbrauns, 2000), 12–21.

Valley, and the Cave of Treasure in the Negev.[69] Archaeological remains of dates have been found at Jericho and Teleilat Ghassul in the Jordan Valley, and the Cave of Treasure and 'Elim in the Negev.[70] Archaeological remains of domesticated pomegranate have been found at Tell Halif and Tell Qiri in the Judean Hills, Gezer, Jericho and Arad.[71]

Due to water irrigation systems, the areas between Arad and Kadesh Barnea also attracted agricultural and pastoral populations.[72] They domesticated sheep, goats, deer, donkeys, and cattle, and they farmed barley and emmer wheat.[73] From the second millennium BCE onwards, with the development of desert routes, significant numbers of donkeys and camels appeared in the region. Camels provided the advantage of being able to reach distant water sources during the dry summers, in addition to their usefulness for ploughing. Camels also produced milk and provided meat. In contrast to the prevalence of camel remains found in the region, few remains of cattle have been found due to their impractical pasture and water requirements.[74]

Irrigation systems played a crucial role in enlarging agricultural fields. Using the primary water sources such as streams, springs, and rainfall, ancient Israel developed wells, cisterns, and reservoirs. Wells were ordinarily cut through rock in order to reach the ground water which came from the underground water system. In the fifteenth or fourteenth century BCE, Gezer constructed wells which were connected to the springs at

69 Lawrence E. Stager, "The Firstfruits of Civilisation," in *Palestine in the Bronze and Iron Ages* (ed. Jonathan N. Tubb; London: Institute of Archaeology, 1985), 172–8.

70 Stager, "The Firstfruits of Civilisation," 180–8.

71 Borowski, *Agriculture in Iron Age Israel*, 171.

72 Grinding stones, mortars, stone basins and sickle blades are found at most excavated sites in Negev. Israel Finkelstein, *Living on the Fringe: The Archaeology and History of the Negev, Sinai and Neighbouring Regions in the Bronze and Iron Ages* (MMA 6; Sheffield: Sheffield Academic Press, 1995), 23–30.

73 Barker, *Agricultural Revolution*, 144–6; Finkelstein, *Living on the Fringe*, 103–13, 118–26.

74 Finkelstein argues that although the dominant species in animal herding of arid areas change significantly, the fauna, wild and domesticated alike, by and large, do not change. Finkelstein, *Living on the* Fringe, 62–3.

Hazor, Megiddo, El-Jib northwest of Jerusalem, and Jerusalem.[75] Ashkelon included more than a hundred wells dating from the settlement of the Philistines.[76] Cisterns cut into bedrock collected and conserved runoff water from roofs and courtyards (1 Kgs 22:38). They are very necessary for settlements lacking natural springs or other water sources. Fifty cisterns have been unearthed at Tell en-Nasbeh in the northwest of Jerusalem.[77] The largest and most elaborate underground reservoir uncovered to date is at Beth-Shemesh; while in use, its capacity was about 800 cubic metres (Ezek 31:15).[78]

In the tenth century BCE, well-developed channels conducted water from the Gihon spring of Jerusalem to the Kidron valley, for irrigation.[79] In fact, remains of water-collection and distribution facilities dating to the Iron Age have been found at Buqeiʿa in northwest of Galilee, Ramat

75 Amnon Ben-Tor, "Hazor: Fifth Season of Excavations (1968–1969)," in *NEAEHL*, Vol. 2 (ed. Ephraim Stern; New York; London etc: The Israel Explaration Society Carta, Jerusalem, 1993), 604–5; Lawrence E. Stager, "The Archaeology of the East Slope of Jerusalem and the Terraces of the Kidron," *JNES* 41 (1982): 111–21; Yigael Yadin, "Hazor," in Stern, ed., *NEAEHL*, Vol. 2, 599; Yohanan Aharoni, "Megiddo," in Stern, ed., *NEAEHL*, Vol. 3, 1022–3; William G. Dever, "Gezer," in Stern, ed., *NEAEHL*, Vol. 2, 500–1.

76 Lawrence E. Stager, "Ashkelon," in Stern, ed., *NEAEHL*, Vol. 1, 103–12; Philip J. King and Lawrence E. Stager, *Life in Biblical Israel* (Louisville, KY: Westminster John Knox, 2002), 126–7; Tsvika Tsuk, "Cisterns," in Meyers, ed., *OEANE*, Vol. 2, 12–3.

77 Dever, "Gezer," 500. However, Zorn states that there is no need of cistern because the water is well supplied through eight drain channels. Jeffrey Ralph Zorn, "Nasbeh, Tell En-," in Stern, ed., *NEAEHL*, Vol. 3, 1101.

78 Shelomoh Bunimovitz and Zvi Lederman, "Beth-Shemesh: Culture Conflict on Judah's Frontier," *BAR* 23 (1997): 46–7.

79 For excavations in Jerusalem, see Kathleen M. Kenyon, *Jerusalem: Excavating 3000 Years of History* (London: Thames & Hudson, 1967). Fortresses around Jerusalem and its vicinity are related to the protection of the economic industries in Jerusalem. Gabriel Barkay, Alexander Fantalkin, and Oren Tal, "A Late Iron Age Fortress North of Jerusalem," *BASOR* 328 (2002): 49–71.

Matred in northeast of Jerusalem, and Arad, Horvat Haluqim, and Mishor ha-Ruah in the Negev.[80]

In hilly regions, the techniques developed to conserve and control water included terracing and runoff farming strategies.[81] Certainly, these helped to achieve a more stable and productive agricultural system, which, in turn, enabled ancient Israel to establish a complete agricultural calendar.[82] Engaging this set of strategies, Israel's agricultural economy began to thrive, as is indicated by the many archaeological remains of granaries (ערמה, Hag 2:16 or מסכנות, 1 Kgs 9:19; 2 Chr 32:27–29) and silos or barns (מגורה, Hag 2:19; Jer 50:26; Joel 1:17, מגדל, Isa 5:2; or סכה, Isa 1:8) used for grain, wine, and oil storage. Many remains of storage structures have been found at Tel Hadar in the northeast of Galilee, ʿAin Mallaha, Tell en-Nasbeh, Megiddo, Tell Jemmeh in south of Gaza, Tell Beit Mirsim in southwest of Hebron,

80 Oded Borowski, "Irrigation" in Meyers, ed., *OEANE*, Vol. 3, 182; Borowski, *Agriculture in Iron Age Israel*, 1–20; Ephraim Stern, Oded Lipschits, and David Vanderhooft, "New Yehud Stamp Impressions from En Gedi," *TA* 34 (2007): 66–73; Lily Singer-Avitz, "Arad: The Iron Age Pottery Assemblages," *TA* 29 (2002): 110–214; Rudolf Cohen, "Middle Bronze Age I and Iron Age II Sites in the Negev Hills," in Stern, ed., *NEAEHL*, Vol. 3, 1126; Ze'ev Herzog and Lily Singer-Avitz, "Redefining the Centre: The Emergence of State in Judah," *TA* 31 (2004): 209–44.

81 Avraham Faust, "Israelite Village: Cultural Conservatism and Technological Innovation," *TA* 32 (2005): 204–19; BenJamin Mazar, "The Early Israelite Settlement in the Hill Country," *BASOR* 241 (1981); 75–85; David C. Hopkins, *The Highlands of Canaan: Agricultural Life in the Early Iron Age* (SWBAS 3; Almond: JSOT, 1985), 96–7; Jack Pastor, *Land and Economy in Ancient Palestine* (London: Routledge, 1997), 1–3; Magen Broshi and Israel Finkelstein, "The Population of Palestine in Iron Age II," *BASOR* 287 (1992): 47–60; Magen Broshi and Ram Gophna, "The Settlements and Population of Palestine during the Early Bronze Age II–III," *BASOR* 253 (1984): 41–53; Oded Borowski, "Agriculture" in *ABD*, Vol. 1 (ed. David Noel Freedman; New York; London, Doubleday, 1992), 96; Rica Gonen, "Urban Canaan in the Late Bronze Period," *BASOR* 253 (1984): 61–73.

82 The Gezer Calendar contained a seven-line inscription on a small limestone slab, with three letters. The reverse side shows signs of an earlier inscription which was scraped off. The date of the inscription would be established from 925 B.C.E. roughly. Ian Young, "The Style of the Gezer Calendar and Some 'Archaic Biblical Hebrew' Passage," *VT* 42 (1992): 362–75.

Beth-Shemesh, Lachish, Jericho and Rosh Zin in the Negev.[83] That granaries or silos at Beth-Yerah and Arad could hold 2,250 cubic meters of grain is an impressive indication of Israel's agricultural success.[84]

Both the Hebrew Bible and archaeological remains provide evidence that farmers were cultivating barley (שְׂעֹרה, Deut 8:8), wheat (חטה, Jer 12:13), millet (דחן, Ezek 4:9), legumes, including lentils (עדשה), vetch (קלי), chick-peas (חמיין), and peas (פול, 2 Sam 23:11–12; Isa 30:24).[85] The Hebrew Bible additionally records that farmers were cultivating cucumbers (קִשֻּׁאָה), watermelons (אבטיח), leeks (חציר), onions (בצל), and garlic (שׁוּמִים) as vegetables (Num 11:5; Isa 37:27; Ps 129:6). Furthermore, farmers had naturalised grapevines (גפן, the fruit ענב, Isa 5:2; 17:10; Hag 2:19), olives (זית, Jer 11:17; Hag 2:19), figs (תאנה, Hag 2:19; Deut 8:8), pomegranates (רמון, Hag 2:19; Song 6:11; 7:13), and dates (תמר, Joel 1:12; Judg 4:5; 2 Chr 28:15). Other cultivated plants included flax (פִּשְׁתּ, Exod 9:31; Isa 19:9), sesame (תסמן, Isa 28:25), cumin (כמן, Isa 28:25, 27), and coriander (גד, Exod 16:31; Num 11:7).

This survey has demonstrated that the agricultural developments in ancient Israel unquestionably started with gathering and hunting as foragers. Through a long period of transitional agriculture, the Israelites developed crop farming and animal husbandry. The Israelite further devised a wide-ranging and elaborate irrigation system, and maximised the use of their land with terracing and runoff farming. As a result, Israel obtained agricultural prosperity and agriculture became immensely important to Israel's economy. Archaeological excavations and surveys have unearthed considerable material culture suggesting that agriculture in Israel extended throughout every cultivatable part of the territory.

83 Oded Borowski, "Granaries and Silos," in Meyers, ed., *OEANE*, Vol. 2, 431–3; Borowski, *Agriculture in Iron Age Israel*, 78–9.

84 Barker, *Agricultural Revolution*, 116–18; Edward Bruce Banning, "Towers," in Freedman, ed., *ABD*, Vol. 6, 622–4.

85 Agricultural activities would vary from locale to locale because of differences in natural conditions. Oded Borowski, *Daily Life in Biblical Times* (Atlanta, GA: SBL, 2003); Robert D. Miller, "Modeling the Farm Community in Iron I Israel," in Averbeck, Chavalas, and Weisberg, eds, *Life and Culture in the Ancient Near East*, 289–310.

Olive and Vine

Extending more concentrated attention on a survey of agricultural products, I shall first discuss two exceedingly important products, olive oil and wine (Deut 8:8; Jer 40:10; 41:8; Ezek 16:13, 19). Olive oil and wine were of the greatest economic value in the ancient Near Eastern economy, because they were not cultivated in Mesopotamia in spite of the suitability of the Syrian area (Upper Mesopotamia), to the cultivation of both olive trees and grapevines. Consequently, there was a large demand in Mesopotamia for olive oil and wine imported from ancient Israel.[86]

The production of olive oil thrived in ancient Israel. Olive oil, the main product of the olive tree, had a prominent place in cultic life as a libation (Deut 7:13; 11:14; 12:17; 14:23; 18:4; 28:51). It was used to anoint prophets, kings, priests, and the Tabernacle (Exod 28:41; 29:7; Judg 9:8; 1 Sam 16:1–13; 1 Kgs 19:16; 2 Kgs 9:1–3). Olive oil is also used as a healing ointment (Isa 1:6).[87] In the production of perfumes, olive oil was used in lamps to illuminate houses (Exod 25:6; 35:14; 39:37; Num 4:16) and temples (1 Kgs 17:12, 14, 16; 19:6). It was also used in food preparation, such as frying (Ezek 16:13; 2 Kgs 4:1–7).

The cultivation of olives sharply increased throughout the Bronze Age and continued to be in high demand during the Iron Age. Considerable research, spanning 200 archaeological sites, indicates that Israel produced 5,500 tons of olive oil a year during the Late Bronze Age.[88] Evidence of its massive quantity of production includes material remains from a great variety of lever presses. In addition to which, beam weights from the late Bronze Age have been found at Jerusalem, Lachish, Megiddo, Gezer, Bene-Beraq in southwest of Carmel, Horvat Rosh Zayit, Beth-Yerah, Beth-Shean, and

86 Hans M. Barstad, *History and the Hebrew Bible: Studies in Ancient Israelite and Ancient Near Eastern Historiography* (FAT 61; Archaeology and Biblical Studies 5; Tübingen: Mohr Siebeck, 2008), 153–4.

87 Borowski, "Agriculture," 97–98; Borowski, *Agriculture in Iron Age Israel*, 117–26.

88 Rafael Frankel, *Wine and Oil Production in Antiquity in Israel and Other Mediterranean Countries* (JSOT/ASOR 10; Sheffield: Sheffield Academic Press, 1999), 38–9.

Afula all of which are in the Judean Hills, and Tell Halif in the Negev.[89] More beam weights dated from the Iron Age have been found at Dan and Qala both of which are in north of Golan, ʿAvdon in northeast of Carmel, Tell Balata and Tel Beit-Mirsim both of which are in the Judean Hills, and Beth-Shemesh.[90]

Archaeological evidence suggests that Tell en-Nasbeh produced vast amounts of olive oil. As a result, the great offset-inset wall was built for economic security, which would be destroyed under the Omride dynasty of the ninth century BCE (1 Kgs 15:22).[91] At Tell en-Nasbeh, archaeologists have uncovered many hundreds of jars with the למלך seal impressions dated to the period of Hezekiah,[92] and below-ground storage vats, or cellars, dated from the monarchic period.[93] These archaeological findings indicate that olive oil production in Tell en-Nasbeh not only continued to exist but also flourished during the Neo-Babylonian period. To protect the olive industry, the Babylonians commissioned military armies at this site (2 Kgs 25:24–25; Jer 41:3).[94] Supporting modifications to the fortification of Tell en-Nasbeh's have been archaeologically dated to the sixth century BCE.

89 Zvi Gal, "Rosh Zayit, Horvat," in Stern, ed., *NEAEHL*, Vol. 4, 1289–91.

90 David Ilan, "Dan," in Meyers, ed., *OEANE*, Vol. 2, 107–12; Frankel, *Wine and Oil Production*, 29, 56–8, 63, 113–14, 118; Lawrence E. Stager and Samuel R. Wolff, "Production and Commerce in Temple Courtyards: An Olive Press in the Sacred Precinct at Tel Dan," *BASOR* 243 (1981): 95–102.

91 Jeffrey Ralph Zorn, "A Note on the Date of the 'Great Wall' of Tell en-Nesbeh: A Rejoinder," *TA* 26 (1999): 147–8. However, Katz states that the olive presses at best only indicate the existence, not the construction, of Tel en-Nesbeh in the eighth century BCE. Hayah Katz, "A Note on the Date of the 'Great Wall' of Tel en-Nesbeh," *TA* 25 (1998): 131–3.

92 The mark of למלך has a variety interpretation. For royal vineyards, see Anson Rainey, "Wine from Royal Vineyards," *BASOR* 251 (1982): 57–62. For royal property or administrative centre, see Nadav Na'aman, "Hezekiah's Fortified Cities and the LMLK Stamps," *BASOR* 261 (1986): 5–21.

93 Diana Edelman, "Gibeon and the Gibeonites Revisited," in *Judah and the Judeans in the Neo–Babylonian Period* (eds, Oded Lipschits and Joseph Blenkinsopp; Winona Lake, IN: Eisenbrauns, 2003), 153–67.

94 David Vanderhooft and Wayne Horowitz, "The Cuneiform Inscription from Tell en-Nasbeh: The Demise of an Unknown King," *TA* 29 (2002): 318–27.

These reinforcements continued to function as defensive features of the offset-inset wall through the end of the fifth century BCE (Neh 3:7; 7:25; 1 Chr 8:29–40; 9:35–44).[95]

Philistine sites of Tel Miqne and Tel Batash in the Shephela offer considerable evidence for the production of olive oil. Remarkably, in Tel Miqne, 161 installations from the Iron Age have been found with an average capacity for producing at least 1000 tons of olive oil a year.[96] Further evidence of the large-scale olive oil producing at Miqne includes spacious basins, dozens of large-sized loom weights and more than 600 heavier weights.

The other major industry in ancient Israel was the production of wine. Archaeological evidence of several hundred winepresses reflects the massive scale of wine production. Its economic importance may even have been equal to that of olive production. Thus, vineyards were surrounded with stone walls for protection (Ps 62:4; Prov 24:31; Isa 5:5). Interesting calculations suggest that the amount of wine consumed with daily meals, in ancient Israel ranged from 330 to 694 litres per household, per year.[97] If the population of the Judean kingdom in the Iron Age was nearly 110,000,[98] then the estimated total of wine consumed would range from 8,150 tons to 17,350 tons.[99] Ancient Israel's ability to produce such gargantuan quantities of wine is quite astonishing.

This feat required a multitude of grapes to be grown. Juice (תִּירוֹשׁ) from grapes was released through the wine press (Hos 2:11),[100] and collected into

95 David Ussishkin, "Lachish," in Stern, ed., *NEAEHL*, Vol. 3, 897–911; Jeffrey Ralph Zorn, "Tell en-Nesbeh and the Problem of the Material Culture of the Sixth Century," in Lipschits and Blenkinsopp, eds, *Judah and the Judeans in the Neo-Babylonian Period*, 413–50.

96 Trude Dothan and Saymour Gitin, "Miqne, Tel," in Stern, ed., *NEAEHL*, 1051–9; Trude Dothan and Saymour Gitin, "Miqne, Tel" in Meyers, ed., *OEANE*, 30–5.

97 Walsh, *Fruit of the Vine*, 12–21, 210–47.

98 Broshi and Finkelstein, "The Population of Palestine," 51–2.

99 The average family size per household is normally four. See Lawrence E. Stager, "The Archaeology of the Family in Ancient Israel," *BASOR* 260 (1985): 1–35.

100 Wineries and oil presses share machinery but, from the Iron Age II onwards, they become clearly distinguishable. In the winery, there is a treading floor with a comparatively large collecting vat, while in the oil press, there was an olive crushing device

large jars. Most of this fresh juice was fermented for wine (יין, Isa 16:9–10). Both wine and grapes were used in ritualistic contexts though (Deut 12:17; 14:23; Isa 24:7; Jer 31:11). Besides תירוש and יין, there are different kinds of wine which are designated with other words, usually used with the term יין in the Hebrew Bible: לבנון (Hos 14:8), חלבון (Ezek 27:18), רקח (Song 8:2) and חמר (Deut 32:14; Ps 75:9).[101] Fresh grapes and a variety of wine were also consumed with meals. Dried grapes (raisins) were important for daily food; they were pressed into cakes (אשישה, 2 Sam 6:19 // 1 Chr 16:3; Isa 16:7; Hos 3:1) and used for provisions on a long journeys (צמק, 1 Sam 25:18; 30:12). Vinegar (חמץ, Ruth 2:14) and syrup (משרת ענבים, Num 6:3) as a condiment were also made from grapes.

Particular mention should be made of El-Jib in northwest of Jerusalem, which was a region of great wine production. In addition to ten winepresses dated from 1200–1000 BCE, impressive installations have been discovered at El-Jib, indicating that its wine industry continued thriving through the eighth and seventh centuries BCE.[102] Dated to around the seventh century BCE, sixty-three rock-cut storage cellars have been found, which were able to maintain a constant temperature of eighteen degrees for storing wine. These cellars suggest a capacity for storing 95,000 litres of wine. Furthermore, the recovery of twenty-three jar handles inscribed with the city name demonstrates that El-Jib was indeed a leading wine export centre.

Cellars occurring in association with winepresses have also been discovered at Beth-Shemesh, Khirbet er-Ras in the Jordan Valley, and Deir Daqleh and Qarawat Beni Hasan both of which are in the Judean Hills.[103] In the area surrounding Jerusalem, installations for pressing wine have been found at Ras Abu Maʿaruf and Mevasseret Yerushalayim.[104] Winepress remnants have also been found at Ramat Rahel, Beit Safafa, Manahat, and

---

and a comparatively small collecting vat without a treading floor. Frankel, *Wine and Oil Production*, 140–59.

101 Borowski, "Agriculture," 112–3.

102 James B. Pritchard, "Gibeon," in Stern, ed., *NEAEHL*, Vol. 2, 511–4.

103 King and Stager, *Life in Biblical Israel*, 62.

104 Walsh, *Fruit of the Vine*, 154–5.

Rogem Gannim all of which are in south of Jerusalem, Tell en-Nasbeh, and Nahal Refa'im in the Judean Hills.[105]

In the Samarian region, 300 winepresses have been discovered. A particularly large winepress was excavated at Hirbet Jemin.[106] Most of the pottery found at the site dates from the eighth and the seventh centuries BCE,[107] which relates it to the Assyrian reign. This suggests that, after the conquest in 722 BCE, the region's population continued to increases and stabilise, in spite of the many people exiled by the Assyrians (2 Kgs 17:5–23). At Kh. Merajjim, Jellamet Wusta, kh. Umm Qatan, the el-Qaʿadeh Camp, Kh. Meras ed-Din, Tel Michal, Khirbet Qeiyafa, Tel Beit Nattif, Hirbet Hamad and Tzur Nathan, press complexes have been dug up.[108] Another 117 winepresses have been uncovered in the area spanning from Jenin to Megiddo, which indicates vigorous economic activities in the Samarian region.[109]

Moreover, archaeological evidence suggests that Tel Batash and Ashkelon in the Philistine region were lucrative production centres with numerous winepresses dating from the eighth and the seventh centuries

105 Raphel Greenberg and Gilad Cinamon, "Stamped and Incised Jar Handles from Rogem Gannim and Their Implications for the Political Economy of Jerusalem: Late 8th –Early 4th Centuries BCE," *TA* 33 (2006): 229–43. Nebi Samwil located on the main road leading from the city to the Shephelah can be identified with Biblical Mizpah in the Achaemenid period. See Yitzhak Magen and Benny Har-Even, "Persian Period Stamp Impressions from Nebi Samwil," *TA* 34 (2007): 38–58.

106 Shimon Dar, *Landscape and Pattern: An Archaeological Survey of Samaria 800 BCE–636 CE* (Oxford: B.A.R. International Series, 1986), esp 147–64.

107 Adam Zertal, "The Province of Samaria (Assyrian Samerina) in the Late Iron Age (Iron Age III)," in Lipschits and Blenkinsopp, eds, *Judah and the Judeans in the Neo-Babylonian Period*, 377–412.

108 Adam Zertal, "The Wedge-Shaped Decorated Bowl and the Origin of the Samaritans," *BASOR* 276 (1989): 77–84; Walsh, *Fruit of the Vine*, 154–7.

109 Gösta Werner Ahlström, "Wine Presses and Cup-Marks of the Jenin-Megiddo Survey," *BASOR* 231 (1978): 19–49; Yigal Shiloh, "Meggido, City: The Iron Age," in Stern, ed., *NEAEHL*, Vol. 3, 1012–24.

BCE.[110] So, it follows that the wine industry contributed significantly to the Neo-Assyrian economy.[111]

This chapter's survey of olive and grape farming has demonstrated that ancient Israel consistently produced more olive oil and wine than could be used internally. Many hundreds of installations for olive oil and wine production have been excavated and described in the Biblical record, clearly reflecting the massive scale of production. Israel's agricultural surpluses had high economic value in Mesopotamia. Due to their economic importance, olive and grape fields were carefully protected by stone walls. Tell en-Nasbeh and Tel Miqne should be particularly mentioned as the production centres of olive oil, whereas El-Jib, the areas surrounding Jerusalem and the Samarian region were known centres for wine production.

Other Products

Another important agricultural product for ancient Israel was wheat. Wheat was used to make bread and porridge (לחם, Exod 29:2; Ezek 4:9).[112] It was consumed both parched (קלי, Lev 23:14) and raw (כרמל, 2 Kgs 4:42). Together with vines and olives, it also had crucial and competitive economic value because true wheat was a rare luxury in Mesopotamia. Thus, references to wheat often recurs alongside references to vines and olives, as grain-wine-oil (דגן, תירוש, יצרוש), a combination which functions as a symbol for valuable commodities in ancient Israel (Deut 28:5; Hag 1:11). One instance of this is Solomon's payment of oil, wine, and wheat to Hiram of Tyre in exchange for cedar wood (1 Kgs 5:25; 2 Chr 2:9, 14).

110 David Schloen, "Ashkelon," in Meyers, ed., *OEANE*, Vol. 1, 220–3; Lawrence E. Stager, "The Fury of Babylon: Ashkelon and the Archaeology of Destruction," *BAR* 22 (1996): 56–69.

111 In the Late Bronze period, ancient Israel supplies 95,000 litres of wine to Egypt as taxes. Shmuel Ahituv, "Economic Factors in the Egyptian Conquest of Canaan," *IEJ* 28 (1978), 104.

112 Borowski, *Agriculture in Iron Age Israel*, 89–90.

One wheat silo found at Megiddo, dated to a time when the city was under Assyrian rule, had a capacity for 346 tons of wheat, an amount of wheat which could sustain 1,178 people for a year.[113] Similar granaries used for wheat grains have been also excavated at Hazor, Beth-Shemesh, Beth-Yerah, Tell el-Hesi near Lachish, and Tel Sheva near Beersheba.[114]

Three other mainstays of Israel's agricultural economy were figs (תאנה), dates (תמר), and pomegranates (רמון). Figs were used for juice or wine.[115] They were also dried, to be made into cakes (דבלה, 1 Sam 30:12; 1 Chr 12:40). Dried figs (קיץ) are also consumed during the winter time (2 Sam 16:1–2; Isa 16:9; Jer 40:10, 12; 48:32; Amos 8:1–2; Mic 7:1). Fresh juice or wine was extracted from pomegranates (עסים, Song 8:2; Joel 1:5),[116] while pomegranate seeds were eaten fresh, dried, and stored or even made into syrup. Furthermore, due to the beautiful shapes of the flower and fruit, pomegranates served as models for decorating the high priests' garments, Solomon's temple and Solomon's crown.

The date palm was also of great importance for ancient Israel. Jericho was described as the city of palm trees in records dating back to the early period (Deut 34:3). The irrigation system at En Gedi enabled dense date palm growth, gaining Elim its fame for date production (Exod 15:27; Num 33:9). Dates had the benefit of being a storable crop of great nutritional value as such in cakes (אשׁפר) and their usefulness in healing skin infections (שׁחין, 2 Kgs 20:7; Isa 25:18).[117] Honey was another valued product of the date palms (דבשׁ, Exod 3:8). Also, palm branches were used in the celebration of Tabernacles (סכות, Lev 23:40; Neh 8:15). Palm leaves were woven into mats and baskets, and their fibrous sheaths were used for making ropes, pillows, and mattresses.

113 Aharoni, "Megiddo," 1023.

114 Yadin, "Hazor," 594–5; Bunimovitz and Lederman, "Beth-Shemesh," in Stern, ed., *NEAEHL*, Vol. 1, 250–1; Valerie M. Fargo, "Hesi, Tell El-," in Stern, ed., *NEAEHL*, Vol. 2, 630–4; Valerie M. Fargo, "Hesi, Tell El-," in Meyers, ed., *OEANE*, Vol. 3, 22.

115 Borowski, *Agriculture in Iron Age Israel*, 114–7.

116 Borowski, *Agriculture in Iron Age Israel*, 117.

117 Borowski, *Agriculture in Iron Age Israel*, 127.

In addition to these agricultural products, animal husbandry created a daily source of milk (חָלָב), cheese (חֵלֶב), curd, and butter (חמאה) from sheep (צאן) and goats (עתוד), sometimes even from cows (בָקָר, Gen 18:8; Deut 32:14; Judg 5:25; 1 Sam 17:18; Isa 55:1).[118] As a sustainable source of meat (ר'שב), the people of ancient Israel raised rams (כר, Gen 31:38), lambs (כר), calves (בן־בקר, Amos 6:4), cows (בקר, Gen 41:4), fish (דגה, Num 11:5), and birds (עוף, Deut 14:20) are eaten. In Tell Jemmeh, the ostrich was also served as food.[119]

In agricultural activities, oxen (פר) and cows were identified with ploughing the land and threshing the harvest. Meanwhile, donkeys (חמור), mules (פרד), and camels (גמל) were normally used for the burden of local and regional transport (Gen 12:16; 1 Sam 9:3; 2 Sam 18:9; 1 Kgs 1:38).[120] As in the Near East, camels opened the way for intensive overland travel, and the trade of inland goods to coastline cities.[121] The camel's ability to survive on periodic drinking had an especially strong effect on long-distance Arabian trade where the main commodity was incense.[122] Archaeologists have found copious remains of camels at Tell Jemmeh, which date from the seventh century BCE and appear to have been used in the caravan trade.[123]

Agricultural produce was crucial to the textile industry, which relied on wool (צמר), flax (פשת), and cotton (בגד, Lev 14:47).[124] Sheep were primarily raised for their wool, which was a valuable commodity in commerce.[125] Goat hides were generally valued for tent making and clothing, and goat

118 Nathan MacDonald, *Not Bread Alone: The Use of Food in the Old Testament* (Oxford: Oxford University Press, 2008), 50.

119 Hesse, "Animal Husbandry and Human Diet," 204–5, 220.

120 Aharon Sasson, "The Pastoral Component in the Economy of Hill Country Sites during the Intermediate Bronze and Iron Ages: Archaeo-Ethnographic Case Study," *TA* 25 (1998): 3–63.

121 Finkelstein, *Living on the Fringe*, 120–3.

122 Sasson, "Pastoral Component in the Economy of Hill Country Sites," 5–23.

123 Finkelstein, *Living on the Fringe*, 144–9.

124 Douglas R. Edwards, "Dress and Ornamentation," in Freedman, ed., *ABD*, Vol. 2, 232–8.

125 Zeder, *Feeding*, 23–5.

hair was used in the manufacturing of sacks and tent cloth.[126] Flax was usually grown in the Negev region. Remains of flax from the early period have been found in the Nahal Hemar Cave in the Judean Desert and in Nahal Mishmar near the Dead Sea.[127] Horvat ʿUza in the Negev have found material remains of cotton.[128] Due to the high demand, flax and cotton were usually imported from Egypt. The success of Israel's wool industry, though, was comparable to Egypt's flax industry. Also, records indicate that ancient Israel cultivated black mulberry (משׁי) for feeding silkworms (Ezek 16:10, 13; 2 Sam 5:23 // 1 Chr 14:14–15; Ps 84:7).

Agricultural developments also enabled the cultivation of timber for small construction, though for large-scale construction, cedar wood (ארז) from Lebanon was imported (1 Kgs 5). Cypress (ברושׁ, Isa 41:19; 55:13; 60:13) and sycamore trees (שׁקמה, 1 Chr 27:28; 2 Chr 9:27; Ps 78:47; Isa 9:9) were cultivated for use in the Jerusalem temple under Solomon (1 Kgs 5:22; 2 Chr 3:5).[129] Pine (תדהר, 1 Kgs 5:22; Isa 41:19; Ezek 31:8; Ps 104:17) too was used in Solomon's temple, for flooring, doors and ceilings.[130] The fruit trees used in the temple included olive wood as a building material (עץ־שׁמן, 1 Kgs 6:31–33; 10:27; 2 Chr 1:15; Isa 41:19; Neh 8:15), and date palm (תמרה) in temple ornaments (1 Kgs 6:32). Almond wood (אגוז) was used for constructing the fortress at Gibeah.[131]

The survey of ancient Israel's agricultural products has demonstrated that wheat was a crucial and competitive commodity in Israelite economy. Wheat production flourished in Israel, particularly in the regions of Galilee and the Judean Hills. Israel's other important agricultural produce included figs, dates, and pomegranates. Jericho and the Judean Hills were particularly associated with the farming of these fruit trees. Though, because of its

126 King and Stager, *Life in Biblical Israel*, 113–4.

127 Tsvika Tsuk and Avi Gopher, "Nahal Hemar Cave," in Stern, ed., *NEAEHL*, Vol. 3, 1082–8.

128 Cotton is not attested earlier than the eighth –seventh century BCE. Itzhaq Beit-Arieh, "ʿUza, Horvat," in Stern, ed., *NEAEHL*, Vol. 4, 1495–7.

129 Irene Jacob and Water Jacob, "Flora," in Freedman, ed., *ABD*, Vol. 2, 805.

130 It is also utilised for shipbuilding and musical instruments. Nili Liphschitz and Gideon Biger, "The Timber Trade in Ancient Palestine," *TA* 22 (1995): 121–7.

131 Borowski, *Agriculture in Iron Age Israel*, 132.

successful irrigation system, the En Gedi is very well known for cultivating the date palm. In addition to which, in the Levant region Israel moderately developed animal husbandry and enjoyed animal products. These products included wool, which was successfully used in textiles. In all of these ways Israel was agriculturally self-sufficient, however, Israel's timber industry was constrained to cultivating small trees requiring continued dependence on Near Eastern societies for large timber, especially cedar.

Economy in the Ancient Near East

Imperial Administrative System

As I have surveyed above, both Israel and Mesopotamia were agricultural societies. In an agrarian society, land is the most fundamental economic resource. Thus, once a centralised political entity had developed in Mesopotamia, land ownership became linked to political power.[132] Kings consistently owned the biggest portion of land and assigned the farming of their land to tenants or local communities via temples.

The priests of temples supported by these kings managed everything from land leases to the large scale manufacturing of goods.[133] They even

132 For the temple management in the economy, see Johannes Renger, "Interaction of Temple, Palace, and 'Private Enterprise' in the Old Babylonian Economy," in Lipinski, ed., *State and Temple Economy in the Ancient Near East*, Vol. 1, 249–50; John H. Walton, *Ancient Near Eastern Thought and the Old Testament: Introducing the Conceptual World of the Hebrew Bible* (Norton: Apollos, 2007), 113–23; Anson Rainey, "Aspects of Life in Ancient Israel," in Averbeck, Chavalas, and Weisberg, eds, *Life and Culture in the Ancient Near East*, 253–68; Grabbe, *A History of the Jews and Judaism in the Second Temple Period*. Vol. 1, *Yehud*, 207–8.

133 The term household includes social groups covering from a small family household living under one roof to a large socio-economic community. It may consist of owners, managers, labour force, domestic animals and residential houses, storages as well as fields, orchards, pastures and forests. Gelb, "Household and Family," 1–11.

oversaw the trade of agricultural produce. Afterwards, the priests extracted taxes through a land tenure system, which contributed to the economic wealth of the palace. From an economic point of view, priests can be understood as having carried out administrative roles. In the period between 2800–2000 BCE, Uruk, Ebla, Eridu, Umma, Lagash, Adab, Fara, Kish Shuruppak, Eshnunna, and Akshak all organised the temple household.[134]

As political entities became increasing centralised, polio-economic relations became increasingly strained within the Mesopotamian Empires.[135] This was in part a result of decreased agricultural production in Mesopotamia.[136] Limited local resources caused the Mesopotamian Empires to depend on external sources for food, timber, metals, and stone.[137] This led to Mesopotamian expansionism. The expansion of the Mesopotamian Empires not only extended their cultivated lands, but also intensified the demands for agricultural contributions for increasing the economic and military power.[138] Political incentives stimulated surplus production and provided the necessary security. With the same methods employed in Israel's temple administration, an imperial administrative system governed Mesopotamian lands. These were the material foundations of civilisation that endured, and further developed throughout the Mesopotamian Empires.

In Neo-Assyrian times, land ownership was evidently exclusive to the royal class, and cultivation rights were allotted to tenants (*ilku*) via the temples. Those who were allocated farmland had to fulfil the *ilku* obligations

134 Renger, "Interaction of Temple," 250–2.

135 Renger, "Interaction of Temple," 252.

136 Due to increased salinisation, the land environments gradually degraded. It led to the abandonment of wheat cultivation in upper Mesopotamian area. It further forced usable areas for normal cultivation to the abandonment. Butzer, "Environmental Change," 142; Carlos E. Cordova, "The Degradation of the Ancient Near Eastern Environment," in Snell, ed., *A Companion to the Ancient Near East*, 125–41.

137 Barstad, *History and the Hebrew Bible*, 144–5.

138 Paul-Alain Beaulieu, "World Hegemony, 900–300 BCE," in Snell, ed., *A Companion to the Ancient Near East*, 48–61; Liverani, "Historical Overview," 15–6.

to pay taxes.[139] In a similar way, the Babylonians governed the land through temples. One fine case can be seen in the time of Nabonidus (555–539 BCE):

> Given the need for land lease contracts, Sum-ukin and Kalbaia, descendants of previous tenants, Bel-zeri and Iqisaia who cultivated only 6,000 kurs of arable land, renew them through the Eanna, temple of the goddess Ishtar in Uruk. Also, for the temple household, Nabonidus, from Cilicia, over 900 kg of iron and several hundred kilograms of iron and copper from Yaman are brought in. It is likewise that Nebuchadnezzar (605–562 BCE) conveyed over 2 kg of Ionian blue-purple wool for producing garments to the temple of Eanna. Then, they similarly deliver not only 25,000 kurs of best quality barley and 10,000 kurs of choice dates that their fathers paid as the rental payment. In this lease contraction, the palace gives instructions to the officials of the Eanna temple with respect to rental payment in barley.[140]

139 John Nicholas Postgate, "*Ilku* and Land Tenure in the Middle Assyrian Kingdom: A Second Attempt," in *The Land of Assur & the Yoke of Assur: Studies on Assyria: 1971–2005* (ed. John Nicholas Postgate; Oxford: Oxbows, 2007), 112–22; Postgate, "Land Tenure in the Middle Assyrian Period: A Reconstruction," in Postgate, ed., *The Land of Assur*, 2–26; Nicholas Sekunda, "Achaemenid Settlement in Caria, Lycia and Greater Phryia," in *Achaemenid History*, Vol. 6, *Asia Minor and Egypt: Old Culture in a New Empire* (ed. Heleen Sancisi-Weerdenburg and Amelie Kuhrt; Leiden: Nederland Instituut voor het Nabije Oosten, 1991), 83–143.

140 YOS VI, 6, sourced from Paul-Alain Beaulieu, *The Reign of Nabonidus King of Babylon 556–539 B.C.* (New Haven; London: Yale University Press, 1989), 119; YOS VI, 11, sourced from Beaulieu, *The Reign of Nabonidus King of Babylon 556–539 B.C.*, 117; YOS VI, 103, sourced from Beaulieu, *The Reign of Nabonidus King of Babylon 556–539 B.C.*, 196; YOS VI, 131, sourced from Beaulieu, *The Reign of Nabonidus King of Babylon 556–539 B.C.*, 194; YOS VI, 150, sourced from Beaulieu, *The Reign of Nabonidus King of Babylon 556–539 B.C.*, 150; YOS VI, 155, sourced from Beaulieu, *The Reign of Nabonidus King of Babylon 556–539 B.C.*, 194. Joannes explains that 1 kur of barley is equal to 180 litres and 1 kur of cultivated l and 1.5 hectares. See Francis Joannes, *The Age of Empires: Mesopotamia in the First Millennium BC* (Edinburgh: Edinburgh University Press, 2004), 170–4. For secondary document of temple economy in the Neo-Babylonian period, see Muhammad A. Dandamaev, "State and Temple in Babylonia in the First Millennium B.C.," *in State and Temple Economy in the Ancient Near East*, Vol. 2, 591–2; Muhammad A. Dandamaev, "Neo-Babylonian Society and Economy," in Boardman, Edwards, and Hammond, eds, *CAH*, Vol. 3, *The Assyrian and Babylonian Empires and Other States of the Near East*, 267–8; A. Martirossian, "Notes Concerning the Economic Activity of the Babylonian Temples in the First Millennium BC," *Iraq* 45 (1983), 130.

A land tenure system based on family-owned property was applied through contracts with local temples that were usually long-term and remained binding for multiple generations. Some tenants leased large assets and functioned as intermediary tenants by hiring farm-workers of their own.[141] Tenants, being in control of agricultural affairs, could also engage in commerce with their agricultural products and make great fortunes.[142]

In the Achaemenid period, the relationship between the palace economy and the temple household became even more intertwined. The temples continued managing the land and continued to raise the imperial economy through taxation. Also, the Achaemenids further developed family-based-businesses, which yielded greater profits for the palace.[143] In general, the prices for agricultural production varied seasonally by 30–50 per cent.[144] This fluctuation in prices corresponded to supply and demand, so prices were highest before the harvest of a given crop and lowest immediately after. For example, barley was regularly harvested in late April, so from May to June, while barley was most abundantly available barley prices were very low. Starting around September, the price of barley gradually increased obtaining its most expensive prices during the three or four months before the next barley harvest.

Of the few powerful business houses, the Egibi house provides a fine case of the interregional trading from the late eighth century BCE

141 Govert van Driel, "Agricultural Entrepreneurs in Mesopotamia," in *Landwirtschaft im Alten Orient: Ausgewählte Vorträge der XLI* (ed. Horst Klengel and Johannes Renger; RAI Berlin, 4.–8.7. 1994; Berlin: Berliner Beitrge zum Vorderen Orient 18, 1999), 214–7.

142 Liverani, "Historical Overview," 16–9.

143 Andreau comments that it is a contrast to the statement of Finley who argues that the vital industry of the ancient Near East is agriculture and there is no need to make a trade but for only luxury goods with the high cost of transport cost. Jean Andreau, "Twenty Years after Moses I. Finley's the Ancient Economy," in *The Ancient Economy* (ed. Walter Scheidel and Sitta von Reden; trans. Antonia Nevill; Edinburgh: Edinburgh University Press, 2002), 33–4.

144 Peter Vargyas, "Agrarkrisen und Umfang der Agrarproduktion im Babylonien des 1. Jahrtausends," in Klengel and Renger, eds, *Landwirtschaft im Alten Orient*, 189–96.

onwards.[145] The Egibis gained access to the temple's land income. During the Neo-Babylonian period, through internal trade, the Egibis purchased large quantities of grain, dates, onions, and wool from temples in the countryside surrounding Babylon, and transported the goods by boat to the markets in the capital.[146] They did this because Nebuchadnezzar needed to feed the many craftsmen, artisans and other state-controlled workers involved in the enormous building projects he sanctioned.

However, the Egibis were not content to be mere middlemen and would not concede to be limited to making profits solely with the purchase of part of the temples' produce.[147] These entrepreneurs knew that land and its agriculture were the prime source of wealth and investment, yet, small scale arable agriculture was not profitable beyond subsistence purposes. Therefore, granting larger and larger land leases was vitally important for the running of a professional business. They leased large estates of high officials or royal family members.[148] To benefit their business, they maintained good political connections.[149]

These entrepreneurs themselves supervised the cultivation of their subjugators and agricultural management of land. To ensure effective competitiveness in an annually fluctuating grain market, they rather invested in the manufacture by which raw materials were converted into market-ready goods for houses.[150] Here, the Egibis could make profits with which, they buy even more of their own arable land.

However, the thing is, in this economic structure, the part apportioned to land personnel from the land income was not enough, for entrepreneurs never want to make a loss. Compared with entrepreneurs who made fortunes, land subjugators had trouble making a living in their subsistence

145 Kathleen Abraham, *Business and Politics under the Persian Empire: The Financial Dealings of Marduk-nāsir-apli of the House of Egibi (521–487 B.C.E)* (Bethesda, MD: CDL, 2004), 9–11.

146 Abraham, *Business and Politics*, 11–3.

147 Driel, "Agricultural Entrepreneurs," 215.

148 Vargyas, "Agrarkrisen und Umfang," 191–4.

149 Driel, "Agricultural Entrepreneurs," 215–7.

150 Vargyas, "Agrarkrisen und Umfang," 191–4.

and got relegated merely to the labour force of the land. In these tricky circumstances, the Egibis began to lend money as a long-term loan at a standard rate and proceed to enjoy the financial benefits.[151] Eventually, they firmly established the banking system, accepting deposits, issuing and receiving promissory notes, paying the debts of their clients, and financing or founding commercial businesses interests.

In the Achaemenid period, Marduk-nasir-apli, who belonged to the fourth generation of the Egibis, ran the business.[152] During the reign of King Darius, Marduk-nasir-apli acquired the rights to the temples of the Babylonian god Marduk in the countryside south of Babylon, including temples at Esagil,[153] Nergal,[154] E'igikalamma,[155] and

151 Dandamaev, "State and Temple in Babylonia in the First Millennium B.C.," 272–3; Daniel C. Snell, "Methods of Exchange and Coinage in Ancient Western Asia," in Sasson, ed., *CANE*, Vol. 3, 1487–97; Francis Joannes, "Private Commerce and Banking in Achaemenid Babylon," in Sasson, ed., *CANE*, Vol. 3, 1480–4.

152 See Abraham, *Business and Politics*, 17–32.

153 Dar 315, cited from Abraham, *Business and Politics*, 401–3; Dar 342, cited from Abraham, *Business and Politics*, 409–10; Dar 359, cited from Abraham, *Business and Politics*, 415–6; Dar 390, cited from Abraham, *Business and Politics*, 418–9; Dar 437, cited from Abraham, *Business and Politics*, 428–9; BM 30233, cited from Abraham, *Business and Politics*, 202–8; BM 30747, cited from Abraham, *Business and Politics*, 240–1; BM 31018, cited from Abraham, *Business and Politics*, 264–5; BM 33122, cited from Abraham, *Business and Politics*, 234–7; BM 33935, cited from Abraham, *Business and Politics*, 344–7; BM 33959, cited from Abraham, *Business and Politics*, 353–5; BM 33972, cited from Abraham, *Business and Politics*, 358–60. For Abraham's examination of Esagil temple, see Abraham, *Business and Politics*, 143–54.

154 Dar 338, sourced from Abraham, *Business and Politics*, 406–9; Dar 527, sourced from Abraham, *Business and Politics*, 443–4; Dar 541, sourced from Abraham, *Business and Politics*, 445–6; Dar 552, sourced from Abraham, *Business and Politics*, 450–2; BM 31976, sourced from Abraham, *Business and Politics*, 318–20; BM 33112, sourced from Abraham, *Business and Politics*, 331–2; BM 33930, sourced from Abraham, *Business and Politics*, 341–4. For Abraham's work of Nergal temple, see Abraham, *Business and Politics*, 154–9.

155 Dar 182, referred to from Abraham, *Business and Politics*, 385–6; Dar 338, referred to from Abraham, *Business and Politics*, 406–9; BM 31018, referred to from Abraham, *Business and Politics*, 264–5. For Abraham's survey of E'igikalamma temple, see Abraham, *Business and Politics*, 159–60.

Ehursag.[156] Through taxes, these temples raised between one-third and one-fourth of the total harvest from their leased land. These taxes supplied the E'igikalamma temple with wool, the Esagil temple with onions and dates, and both the Nergal and the Ehursag temples with dates.[157] Excluding the royal treasury, which should have been sent to the kings, these gains were then drafted to the Egibis. In exchange for access to the temples' harvest, the Egibis would pay the Esagil temple forty-two and a half minas of silver.[158]

Another entrepreneurial family, the Murashu of Nippur, was contracted by the palace primarily to ensure the supply of military equipment.[159] They were guaranteed by the royal authority and then permitted to cultivate farther farmlands and practice animal husbandry. The cultivation of vast arable land permitted the Murashu to enjoy bountiful agricultural production. Also, the management of canals enabled them to raise money from the tolls paid by users of canals.

As I have shown in studies of the Mesopotamian imperial economic administration, centralised political authorities retained exclusive rights to land ownership. Land ownership provided ongoing access to the resources necessary for maintaining power. Thus, faced with a shortage of natural resources, the Mesopotamian Empires sent out military campaigns for territorial expansion. These expanded lands, and their agricultural produce, were administered by local temples. The palace economy and temple households are undoubtedly connected with each other. The temples sponsored by kings

156 Dar 405, sourced from Abraham, *Business and Politics*, 421–2; BM 30965, sourced from Abraham, *Business and Politics*, 259–61. For Abraham's work of Ehursag temple, see Abraham, *Business and Politics*, 160–1.

157 Dar 315, sourced from Abraham, *Business and Politics*, 401–3; Dar 405, sourced from Abraham, *Business and Politics*, 421–2; BM 33930, sourced from Abraham, *Business and Politics*, 341–4.

158 Dar 315 is referred to from Abraham, *Business and Politics*, 401–3.

159 The business of Murashu family is from the archives dating from Artaxerxes I (486–465 BCE) to Darius II (465–405 BCE), or of certain archives from Ur, dated in the reign of Artaxerxes II (405–359 BCE). See Albert Tobias Clay, *Business Documents of Murashu Sons of Nippur Dated in the Reign of Darius II (424–404 BC)* (Philadelphia: The University of Pennsylvania Press, 1904); Joannes, "Private Commerce and Banking," 1475–6, 1480–4; Briant, *From Cyrus to Alexander*, 458–61.

carried out leading role in kings' economy and were the backborn of the imperial economy entire. The major temples such as Esagila in Babylon and Eanna in Uruk continued to recognise the privileged status of the empires. In addition to which, the empires employed specialised entrepreneurs to engage in trade with other regions. The most celebrated beneficiaries of this great fortune were the Egibi house first mentioned in the late eighth century BCE and the Murashu family of the Achaemenid period.

Trade in the Achaemenid Empire

In order to secure tributes from conquered territories, the Mesopotamian Empires created networks of roads. The roads also played an important role in trade. The major interregional transport network was called the Way of the Sea. It originated in the Nile Delta, followed Phoenician and Syrian coastal roads, turned inland at the Carmel Range, crossed the Plain of Jezreel at Megiddo, then headed to and through Hazor and Damascus, and finally terminated in Mesopotamia (Isa 8:23; 23:1–17; 60:9; Ezek 23:1–17; 27:12; Exod 13:17).[160] Another main road, the King's Highway, originated at the Gulf of Aqab, crossed Edom, Moab, Ammon and Gilead, and finally connected with the road north to Damascus (Num 20:17).[161]

Through their conquest of Greece, the Achaemenids continued consolidating the Assyrian-Babylonian trade system. Trading posts connecting Phoenicia to Greece extended inlands from the Cypriot cities of Phaselis, on the coast of Lycia: Naukratis, on the Canopic branch of the Nile; and Tell el-Kheleifeh, at the head of the Gulf of Aqabah.[162] At these cities,

160 David A. Dorsey, "Transportation," in Meyers, ed., *OEANE*, Vol. 5, 243–4.

161 Michael Czernichow Astour, "Overland Trade Route in Ancient Asia," in Sasson, ed., *CANE*, Vol. 3, 1416–17.

162 Elat states that there are professional traders even in the international commerce in ancient Israel. Moshe Elat, "Trade in Ancient Israel," in Lipinski, ed., *State and Temple Economy*, Vol. 2, 527–46. See also more Daniel T. Potts, "Distant Shores: Ancient Near Eastern Trade with South Asia and Northeast Africa," in Sasson, ed., *CANE*, Vol. 3, 1451–63; Michael Vickers, "Interactions between Greeks and Persians," in Sancisi-Weerdenburg and Kuhrt, eds, *AH*, Vol. 4, *Centre and Periphery*, 253–62;

Uluburun ship would exchange Egyptian goods for raw materials including gold, silver and copper.[163] The Scythians (in Iran), who had a reputation for being strong, nomadic equestrian warriors, were hired to ensure the security of the trade routes.

Through taxation and legislation, the Achaemenids required conquered populations to cultivate produce that could be exported and was in high demand.[164] In general, the goods viewed as luxury commodities were not indigenous to the empire. Given the imperial economic structure, it was quite conceivable that Judah, one of their subordinates, would be required to increase the production of such luxury crops as olive oil, wine, and wheat. A process of repopulation and resettlement, resulting in the abandonment of many regions throughout the Babylonian period reflect the stringent imperial requirements for agricultural production. Special imperial attention was given to Jerusalem and the surrounding areas, with the hope of restoring their capacities for economic contribution.[165] A similar historical phenomenon is recorded in the book of Haggai, which deals with the restoration of the Jerusalem temple in the period of Darius I (522–486 BCE).[166]

Geographically, Israel forms a land bridge between Egypt and Mesopotamia, linking Greece, Anatolia, and Africa via military and trade routes.[167] During the monarchical times, Israel bartered or sold any surplus

---

Robert Morkot, "Nubia and Achaemenid Persia: Sources and Problems," in Sancisi-Weerdenburg and Kuhrt, eds, *AH*, Vol. 6, *Asia Minor and Egypt*, 321–36.

163 Eric H. Cline and Assaf Yasur-Landau, "Musings from a Distant Shore: The Nature and Destination of the Uluburun Hip and Its Cargo," *TA* 34 (2007): 125–41.

164 Grayson, "Assyrian Civilization," 213–15.

165 Oded Lipschits, *The Fall and Rise of Jerusalem: Judah under Babylonian Rule* (Winona Lake, IN: Eisenbrauns, 2005), 134–45; Lipschits, "Judah, Jerusalem and the Temple (586–539 B.C.E.)," *Trans* 26(2001): 129–42.

166 I will discuss this issue in Chapters 2 and 4 below.

167 Astour, "Overland Trade Route," 1401–20; C. Roebuck, "Trade," in Boardman, Lewis, Hammond, and Martin, eds, *CAH*, Vol. 4, *Persia, Greece and the Western Mediterranean*, 446–60; Josette Elayi and Jean Sapin, *Beyond the River: New Perspectives on Transeuphratene* (trans. J. Edward Crowley; JSOTSup 250; Sheffield: Sheffield Academic Press, 1998), 110–12.

from the harvest at Ezion-Geber centred on the northern shore of the Gulf of Aqaba.[168] This suggested the probability that with luxury goods, Achaemenid Judah would have played a vital role within the imperial economic system through which the Achaemenids obtained important commodities from the Phoenicians, the Philistines, and Arabian traders, as in Neo-Assyria and Neo-Babylonia.[169] Greek vessels of various types at Tell en-Nasbeh, dating from circa 540 BCE to the second half of the fifth century, give evidence of active trade under Achaemenid control.[170]

According to Ezek 27, Tyre in Phoenicia traded with Israel for agricultural commodities. Israel primarily traded wheat, millet, honey, oil, and balm, but in Tyre one could also procure fir trees from Senir near mountain Hermon, oaks from Bashan, cypresses from Cyprus, linen from Egypt, blue and purple dye from Elishah in the Phoenician region, and cedars from Lebanon. Cedars were in high demand in Egypt, Mesopotamia, the Aegean,

168 According to biblical tradition, Solomon runs commercial fleets called ships of Tarshish. And he levies customs charges on merchandise passing through Israel, which provides a boost to the economy through this trade covering from the Red Sea eastward to Africa and Arabia (1 Kgs 9:26, 28; 10:10). After Solomon, Jehoshaphat (873–849 BCE) of Judah continues to run Tarshish ships at Ezion-Geber for travel to Ophir, but this business ends in shipwreck (1 Kgs 22:48–49; 2 Chr 20:35–37). Alan Ralph Millard, "Does the Bible Exaggerate King Solomon's Wealth?" *BAR* 15 (1989): 20–34; Daniel C. Snell, "Trade and Commerce," in Freedman, ed., *ABD*, Vol. 6, 625–9; King and Stager, *Life in Biblical Israel*, 183, 194.

169 Mogens Trolle Larsen, "The City-States of the Early Neo-Babylonian Period," in *A Comparative Study of Thirty-State Cultures: An Investigation Conducted by the Copenhagen Polis Centre* (ed. Mogens Herman Hansen; H-fS 21; Copenhagen: C. A. Reitzels Forlag, 2000), 120–1; Spencer P. Harrington, "Royal Treasures of Nimru," *Ar* 43 (1990): 48–53; Vadim S. Jigoulov, "Administration of Achaemenid Phoenicia: A Case for Managed Autonomy," in *Exile and Restoration Revised: Essays on the Babylonian and Persian Periods in Memory of Peter Runham Ackroyd* (ed. Lester L. Grabbe and Gary N. Knoppers; LSTS 73/JSPSup; London: T & T Clark, 2009), 138–52.

170 Charles E. Carter, *The Emergence of Yehud in the Persian Period: A Social and Demographic Study* (JSOTSup 294; Sheffield: Sheffield Academic Press, 1999), 126–32. On pottery and seals reflecting Judean trade with areas from the Neo-Babylonian through the Achaemenid periods, see also Chapter 3 below.

Anatolia and the Athens, and were therefore of particular value.[171] Using Israelite goods, Tyre was able to trade for silver, iron, tin, and lead from Cyprus; humans (slaves) and bronze vessels of Javan, Tubal and Meshech in the Ionians: the horses, steeds, and mules of Togamah; the ivory tusks and ebony of Dedan in Anatolia; and the emeralds, purple, embroidery, fine linen, corals, and rubies of Syria. Other goods traded through Tyre included: wine from Helbon; white wool from Suhru in Damascus; iron, cassia, and cane from Uzal in Yemen; saddlecloths for riding, lambs, rams and goats from Arabia and Kedar in Arabia; perfumes and all kinds of precious stones and gold from Sheba and Raamah in Arabia; and purple clothes, embroidered garments, multicoloured carpets, and sturdy woven cords from Haran, Canneh, Eden, and Chilmad in northern Syria. So, Tyre provided Israel with the opportunity to export their three main agricultural products and import gold, precious stones, metals, horses, and chariots.[172]

Concerning the trade of Judean olive produce, special mention should be made of the Philistine site Tel Miqne. The enormous quantities of olives came from Judean Shephelah sites, especially Gezer, Beth-Shemesh, and Tell Beit Mirsim.[173] This is because Miqne had the double benefit: Miqne itself had the capacity to mass olive oil produce; the site Miqne was located

171 Diana Edelman, "Tyrian Trade in Yehud under Artaxerxes I: Real or Fictional? Independent or Crown Endorsed?" in Lipschits and Oeming, eds, *Judah and the Judeans in the Persian Period*, 207–46; Hans Georg Niemeyer, "The Early Phoenician City-States on the Mediterranean. Archaeological Element for their Description," in Hansen, ed., *Comparative Study of Thirty-State Cultures*, 104–6; Hayah Katz, "Commercial Activity in the Kingdoms of Judah and Israel," *TA* 31 (2004): 268–77; Ignor Mikhailovich Dyakonov, "The Naval Power and Trade of Tyre," *IEJ* 42 (1992): 168–93; Shulamit Geva, "Archaeological Evidence for the Trade between Israel and Tyre?" *BASOR* 248 (1982): 69–72.

172 Avner Raban and Robert R. Stieglitz, "The Sea Peoples and Their Contributions to Civilization," *BAR* 17 (1991): 34–42.

173 Israel Finkelstein, "The Archaeology of the Days of Manasseh," in *Scripture and Other Artifacts: Essays on the Bible and Archaeology in Honor of Philip J. King* (ed. Michael D. Coogan, Exum J. Cheryl, and Lawrence E. Stager; Westminster: John Knox, 1994), 169–87; Seymour Gitin, "The Neo-Assyrian Empire and Its Western Periphery: The Levant, with a Focus on Philistine Ekron," in *Assyria 1995: Proceedings of the 10th Anniversary Symposium of the Neo-Assyrian Text Corpus Project, Helsinki,*

close to the coast. In the imperial economy, thus, this site would have been specialised as a world-wide distribution centre of olives and olive oil from the neo-Assyrian period.[174] Its silver caches are consistent with the increased use of silver as currency during the Neo-Assyrian period.[175]

Of the major seaports in the Philistine region, Gaza, Ashdod, and Ashkelon were the hubs for Arabian trade.[176] Gaza facilitated trade between the Assyrians and the Egyptians. Ashdod became a centre for pottery production, providing up to 30 per cent of the store jars found at Miqne. Ashkelon prospered as a great administrative centre, probably exporting the wool and wine of Ashkelon, the olive oil and wine of Ashdod, and the wheat and wine of Israel, while importing fish and grains from Egypt and copper from Anatolia or the Aegean.[177] Lachish and Tel Yacoz located near Gezer facilitated trade with the coastal plain and the northern Shephelah.[178]

September 7–11, 1995 (ed. Simo Parpola and Robert Whiting; Helsinki: Neo-Assyrian Text Corpus Project, 1997), 77–103.

174 Seymour Gitin, "New Philistine Finds at Tel Miqne-Ekron," *BA* 59 (1996), 70; Seymour Gitin and Trude Dothan, "The Rise and Fall of Ekron of the Philistines: Recent Excavations at an Urban Border Site," *BA* 50 (1987): 197–222.

175 David Ben-Shlomo, Itzhaq Shai, and Aren M. Maeir, "Late Philistine Decorated Ware ('Ashdod Ware'): Typology, Chronology and Production Centers," *BASOR* 335 (2004): 1–35; John Strange, "The Philistine City-States," in Hansen, ed., *Comparative Study of Thirty-State Cultures*, 134; Nadav Na'aman, "Ekron under the Assyrian and Egyptian Empires," *BASOR* 332 (2003): 81–91. On economic continuity throughout the Mesopotamian empires, see Joannes, *The Age of Empires*, 78–174, 203–25.

176 Avraham Faust and Ehud Weiss, "Judah, Philistia and the Mediterranean World: Reconstructing the Economic System of the Seventh Century B.C.E," *BASOR* 338 (2005):71–92; David Ben-Shlomo "The Iron Age Sequence of Tel Ashdod: A Rejoinder to 'Ashdod Revisited' by I. Finkelstein; L. Singer-Avitz," *TA* 30 (2003): 83–107.

177 Daniel M. Master, "Trade and Politics: Ashkelon's Balancing Act in the Seventh Century BCE," *BASOR* 330 (2003): 47–64.

178 Alexander Fantalkin and Oren Tal, "Redating Lachish Level I: Identifying Achaemenid Imperial Policy at the Southern Frontier of the Fifth Satrapy," in Lipschits and Oeming, eds, *Judah and the Judeans in the Persian Period*, 167–98; Moshe Fischer, Israel Roll, and Oren Tal, "Persian and Hellenistic Remains at Tel Yacoz," *TA* 35 (2008): 123–63.

From late in the sixth and the fifth centuries BCE, the Arabs additionally secured an important position in the caravan trade to supplement the maritime routes.[179] Their main advantage was their use of camels, whose ability to store sufficient water allowed traders to cross much larger tracts of desert than could be crossed by donkey.[180] This in turn opened up safe inland routes through the desert to Egypt, enabling caravan trade between Mesopotamia and the Philistine ports, including Gaza and Ashkelon.[181]

The textile industry and the dyeing business were important to the ancient Near East's interregional trade. Garment colours and qualities functioned as signs of social status. Wool was one of the most important commodities in textiles, and while white wool was uncompetitively priced, purple wool was in high demand and very expensive. So, the dyeing industry in Israel was very marketable as is evidenced by the large numbers of dyeing establishments excavated throughout ancient Israel.[182] Tell Beit Mirsim, also had a burgeoning dyeing trade in the eighth century BCE.[183] Yet, the dyeing industry was made all the more lucrative with the importing of purple colour from Phoenicia and blue from the Aegean.

The Phoenicians were particularly famous for their purple dye industry from 2000 BCE onwards. Large quantities of alum were brought from Egypt to Babylon for bleaching wool, for use in clothing and for medical purposes. Egyptian linen was in high demand because of its high quality.

Metal industry also flourished in Israel, according to the records of numerous craftsmen exiled to Neo-Babylonia (2 Kgs 24:16). In the

179 Jørgen Bæk Simonsen, "Mecca and Medina: Arab City-States or Arab Caravan-Cities?" in Hansen, ed., *Comparative Study of Thirty-State Cultures*, 241–3.

180 Paula Wapnish, "Camels," in Meyers, ed., *OEANE*, Vol. 1, 407–8.

181 Michael C. A. Macdonald, "North Arabia in the First Millennium B.C.E.," in Sasson, ed., *CANE*, Vol. 2, 1355–69; Robert Barnett, "Lachish, Ashkelon and the Carmel: A Discussion of Its Use in Southern Palestine," in Tubb, ed., *Palestine in the Bronze and Iron Ages*, 15–28; Ryan Byrne, "Early Assyrian Contacts with Arabs and the Impact on Levantine Vassal Tribute," *BASOR* 331 (2003): 11–25.

182 Barstad, *History and the Hebrew Bible*, 146; Edwards, "Dress," 235; Jacob and Jacob, "Flora," 807.

183 Elizabeth J. Wayland Barber, "Textiles of the Neolithic through Iron age," in Meyers, ed., *OEANE*, Vol. 5, 190–5.

monarchical period, every three years, gold and silver were imported (1 Kgs 10:22).[184] Afterwards, gold was imported via the Arabian merchants from the Nubian deserts, Havilah and Ophir.[185] The extraordinary quantity of imported gold was reflected in a hoard of gold jewellery found in tombs at Gaza, Beth-Shemesh, Megiddo, Beth-Shean, and Ketef Hinnom in southwest of Jerusalem.[186] Also, silver was brought from Attica and Thrace in the Aegean.[187]

Copper was naturalised at Arabah, Khirbet en-Nahas, Arad, Timnaʿ, Fenan, Punon, and Nahal Mishmar all of which are in the Negev.[188] It was usually smelted and used to produce bronze, an alloy of copper, and tin. A well-developed copper industry was then established in Dan.[189] Strong archaeological evidence has been found at Tel Masos in Arabia of both copper production and copper trades with the Philistines.[190] Cypriot copper ores were primarily exchanged with Mesopotamia and Egypt.[191]

184 Peter Roger Stuart Moorey, *Ancient Mesopotamian Materials and Industries: The Archaeological Evidence* (Oxford: Clarendon, 1994), 223–4, 232–40.

185 Benjamin Mazar, "Two Hebrew Ostraca from Tell Qasîle," *JNES* 10 (1951): 265–7.

186 Ernst Badian and John Moors, "Alexander in Iran," in *CHI*, Vol. 2, *The Median and Achaemenid Periods* (ed. Ilya Gershevitch; Cambridge: Cambridge University Press, 1985), 462; Max Mallowan, "Cyrus the Great (558–529 CE)," in Gershevitch, ed., *CHI*. Vol. 2, *The Median and Achaemenid Periods*, 405; P. M. Michele Daviau and Paul-Eujene Dion, "Economy-Related Finds from Khirbat al-Mudayna (Wadi ath-Thamad, Jordan)," *BASOR* 328 (2002): 31–48.

187 Under the Achaemenids, Uluburun ship succeeds in exchanging requested gold, silver and copper in the Aegean for Egyptian goods. Arthur Bernard Knapp, "Island Cultures: Crete, Thera, Cyprus, Rhodes and Sardinia," in Sasson, ed., *CANE*, Vol. 3, 1433–50; Cline and Yasur-Landau, "Musings from a Distant Shore," 125–41.

188 Israel Finkelstein, "Khirbet en-Nahas, Edom and Biblical History," *TA* 32 (2005): 119–25; James David Muhly, "Metals: Typology and Technology," in Meyers, ed., *OEANE*, Vol. 4, 1–5; Thomas E. Levy and Mohammad Najjar, "Some Thoughts on Khirbet en-Nahas, Edom, Biblical History and Anthropology: A Response to Israel Finkelstein," *TA* 33 (2006): 3–17.

189 Avraham Biran, "Dan," in Stern, ed., *NEAEHL*, Vol. 1, 331.

190 Finkelstein, *Living on the Fringe*, 103–26.

191 Hopkins, "Agriculture," 25; Wolf-Dietrich Niemeier, "Greek Merchants at Tel Kabri and Other Sites in the Levant," *TA* 29 (2002): 328–31.

With regard to iron, major deposits of iron ore were discovered at Mugharat el Wardeh in east of the Jordan Valley and Abu Thawab in west of the Jordan Valley.[192] Mugharat el Wardeh in particular would have been the administrative centre for the iron industry in Gilead. Iron workshops were also found at Syrian Tell Deir ʿalla, Tell Qasile near Tel Aviv and Tell Jemmeh.[193] Iron was also imported from Cyprus and Asia Minor.[194]

Perfumes, one of the luxury items, were also successfully traded in Israel.[195] At Jericho, besides four winepresses for dates, two or three unique installations were discovered which had been used in the production of perfumes and medicines from raw materials (Prov 27:9; Esth 2:12; 2 Sam 12:20; Ps 45:9; 2 Kgs 20:13; Jer 6:20; Exod 30:23–25, 34–35; 37:29).[196]

In this survey of trades in the Achaemenids, I have demonstrated that the empire developed a highly advanced economic structure by developing the network of roads. Through taxation, the empire secured luxury goods specific to a variety of regions and control over the interregional exchange throughout the conquered territories. Seaports in the Phoenicians, the Philistinians, and Anatolia played significant roles in the imperial maritime economy. The Arabs and the Scythians, with their camels and armies, were crucial to protecting the trade. In this larger economic structure of the Achaemenids, Judah supplied the majority of oil and wine (Ezek 27), and contributed to the wool, metal, and perfume industries. Meanwhile alum for bleaching textiles was uniquely successful in Egypt, purple and blue wool were in high demand in Phoenicia and the Aegean, respectively. Cedar in Phoenicia was undoubtedly in high demand as timber and metals was supplied exclusively by Asia Minor, Cilicia, and Cyprus.

192 Robert A. Coughenour, "A Search for Mahanaim," *BASOR* 273 (1989): 57–66.

193 King and Stager, *Life in Biblical Israel*, 168–9.

194 Roebuck, "Trade," 446–7.

195 Victor H. Matthew, "Perfumes and Spices," in Freedman, ed., *ABD*, Vol. 5, 226–8.

196 Ehud Netzer, "Did Any Perfume Industry Exist at 'Ein Feshkha?" *IEJ* 55 (2005): 97–100.

Conclusions

In this chapter, I have shown that the economy of the ancient Near East was above all agrarian. Though early in history the population of the Near East survived primarily through foraging, they later developed elaborate agricultural practices that generated a great surplus of food. And, trading their agricultural surplus led to prosperity. Meanwhile barley and emmer wheat were the key crops in Mesopotamia, ancient Israel showed a high agricultural competitiveness through their cultivation of olives and the vine. In particular, olive oil and wine of ancient Israel retained considerable economic value as cash crops throughout the period.

The development of agricultural economies in the Near East, and the resulting demands for economic management led to the development of centralised political power. And then, political authorities paid great attention to the cultivation of land which was essential to creating sufficient resources to sustain the structures of power. In particular, the economy of the Mesopotamian Empires, having few natural resources of their own, turned to military expansionism to increase their prosperity. The Mesopotamian authorities forcedly exploited their conquered territories' most marketable commodities to boost royal revenues.

Certainly, the empires transformed the economic structure of conquered regions through imposing the imperial economic system. This was especially evident through the temple fiscal administration, which managed the agricultural economy within the conquered regions. This temple economy in the Near East goes back to the Uruk reign from 3500 BCE.

The flourishing income of the empires was also reflected in trade. Interregional trade may extend back to the Neo-Assyrian period from the eighth century BCE, but the expanse of these trade routes was unparalleled, extending to Asia Minor, Cyprus, Crete, Anatolia, and even the Aegean. The Achaemenids established this trade network through the conquest of Greece. In the larger economic market, the Achaemenids exclusively employed and advanced the professional entrepreneurs from the Egibi house of Babylon and the Murashu family of Nippur. Well-structured road networks greatly contributed to the Achaemenids' economic success.

Due to its agricultural success, ancient Israel actively engaged in a broad interregional trade system. Judah in particular was lauded for having increased the production of olive oil and wine, products which were in great demand as luxury items. Accordingly, these products were used as cash commodities for trading (Ezek 27). They were traded for metals in Asia Minor and Cyprus, for linen in Egypt, for wool and dyeing materials in the Phoenicians. Judean goods were also traded for cedar in Tyre, precious stones in Anatolia and Syria, and animals in Arabia. Likewise, Judah played a vital role in the much bigger economic system.

Bibliography

Abraham, Kathleen. *Business and Politics under the Persian Empire: The Financial Dealings of Marduk-nāsir-apli of the House of Egibi (521–487 B.C.E).* Bethesda, MD: CDL, 2004.

Aharoni, Yohanan. "Megiddo." Pages 1003–12 in Stern, ed., *NEAEHL*. Vol. 3.

Ah"ituv, Shmuel. "Economic Factors in the Egyptian Conquest of Canaan." *IEJ* 28 (1978): 93–108.

Ahlström, Gösta Werner. "Wine Presses and Cup-Marks of the Jenin-Megiddo Survey." *BASOR* 231 (1978): 19–49.

Andreau, Jean. "Twenty Years after Moses I. Finley's the Ancient Economy." Pages 33–52 in Scheidel and von Reden, eds, *The Ancient Economy*.

Astour, Michael Czernichow. "Overland Trade Route in Ancient Western Asia." Pages 1401–20 in Sasson, ed., *CANE*. Vol. 3.

Averbeck, Richard E., Mark W. Chavalas, and David B. Weisberg, eds. *Life and Culture in the Ancient Near East*. Bethesda, MD: CDL, 2003.

Avnimelech, Moshe A. "Influence of Geological Conditions on the Development of Jerusalem." *BASOR* 181 (1966): 24–31.

Badian, Ernst and John Moors. "Alexander in Iran." Pages 420–501 in Gershevitch, ed., *CHI*. Vol. 2, *The Median and Achaemenid Periods*.

Banning, Edward Bruce. "Highlands and Lowlands: Problems and Survey Frameworks for Rural Archaeology in the Near East." *BASOR* 301 (1996): 25–45.

Barber, Elizabeth J. Wayland. "Textiles of the Neolithic through Iron age." Pages 190–95 in Meyers, ed., *OEANE*. Vol. 5.

Barker, Graeme. *The Agricultural Revolution in Prehistory: Why Did Foragers Become Farmers?* Oxford: Oxford University Press, 2006.

Barkay, Gabriel. Alexander Fantalkin, and Oren Tal. "A Late Iron Age Fortress North of Jerusalem." *BASOR* 328 (2002): 49–71.

Barnett, Robert. "Lachish, Ashkelon and the Carmel: A Discussion of Its Use in Southern Palestine." Pages 15–30 in Tubb, ed., *Palestine in the Bronze and Iron Ages: Papers in Honour of Olga Tufnell.*

Barstad, Hans M. *History and the Hebrew Bible: Studies in Ancient Israelite and Ancient Near Eastern Historiography*, FAT 61. Archaeology and Biblical Studies 5. Tübingen: Mohr Siebeck, 2008.

Beaulieu, Paul-Alian. "World Hegemony, 900–300 BCE." Pages 48–61 in Snell ed., *A Companion to the Ancient Near East.*

——. *The Reign of Nabonidus King of Babylon 556–539 B.C.* New Haven; London: Yale University Press, 1989.

Beit-Arieh, Itzhaq. "'Uza, Horvat." Pages 1495–97 in Stern, ed., *NEAEHL*. Vol. 4.

Ben-Shlomo, David. "The Iron Age Sequence of Tel Ashdod: A Rejoinder to 'Ashdod Revisited' by I. Finkelstein; L. Singer-Avitz." *TA* 30 (2003): 83–107.

——, Itzhaq Shai, and Aren M. Maeir, "Late Philistine Decorated Ware ('Ashdod Ware'): Typology, Chronology and Production Centers." *BASOR* 335 (2004): 1–35.

Ben-Tor, Amnon. "Hazor: Fifth Season of Excavations (1968–1969)." Pages 604–5 in Stern, ed., *NEAEHL*. Vol. 2.

Bier, Carol. "Textile Arts in Ancient Western Asia." Pages 1567–88 in Sasson, ed., *CANE*. Vol. 3.

Biran, Avraham. "Dan." Pages 323–32 in Stern, ed., *NEAEHL*. Vol. 1.

Boardman, John, David M. Iorwerth Eiddon Stephen Edwards, and Nicholas Goeffrey Lempriere Hammond, eds. *The Cambridge Ancient History*. Vol. 3, Part 2, *The Assyrian and Babylonian Empires and other States of the Near East, from the Eighth to the Sixth Centuries B.C.* 2nd ed. Cambridge: Cambridge University Press, 1991. [=*CAH*]

Borowski, Oded. *Daily Life in Biblical Times*. Atlanta, GA: SBL, 2003.

——. "Irrigation." Pages 181–84 in Meyers, ed., *OEANE*. Vol. 3.

——. "Agriculture." Pages 95–98 in Freedman, ed., *ABD*. Vol. 1.

——. *Agriculture in Iron Age Israel: The Evidence from Archaeology and the Bible.* Winona Lake, IN: Eisenbrauns, 1987.

Broshi, Magen and Israel Finkelstein. "The Population of Palestine in Iron Age II." *BASOR* 287 (1992): 47–60.

—— and Ram Gophna. "The Settlements and Population of Palestine during the Early Bronze Age II–III." *BASOR* 253 (1984): 41–53.

Bunimovitz, Shelomoh and Zvi Lederman, "Beth-Shemesh: Culture Conflict on Judah's Frontier." *BAR* 23 (1997): 46–47.

Butzer, Karl W. "Environmental Change in the Near East and Human Impact on the Land." Pages 123–52 in Sasson, ed., *CANE*. Vol. 1.

Byrne, Ryan. "Early Assyrian Contacts with Arabs and the Impact on Levantine Vassal Tribute." *BASOR* 331 (2003): 11–25.

Carter, Charles E. *The Emergence of Yehud in the Persian Period: A Social and Demographic Study*. JSOTSup 294. Sheffield: Sheffield Academic Press, 1999.

Chavalas, Mark. "The Age of Empires, 3000–900 BCE." Pages 34–47 in Snell ed., *A Companion to the Ancient Near East*.

Clay, Albert Tobias. *Business Documents of Murashu Sons of Nippur Dated in the Reign of Darius II (424–404 BC)*. Philadelphia: The University of Pennsylvania Press, 1904. [=*BE X*]

Cline, Eric H. and Assaf Yasur-Landau, "Musings from a Distant Shore: The Nature and Destination of the Uluburun Hip and Its Cargo." *TA* 34 (2007): 125–41.

Cohen, Rudolf. "Middle Bronze Age I and Iron Age II Sites in the Negev Hills." Pages 1123–33 in Stern, ed., *NEAEHL*. Vol. 3.

Coogan, Michael D., Exum J. Cheryl, and Stager E. Lawrence, eds. *Scripture and Other Artifacts: Essays on the Bible and Archaeology in Honor of Philip J. King*. Westminster: John Knox, 1994.

Cordova, Carlos E. "The Degradation of the Ancient Near Eastern Environment." Pages 125–41 in Snell ed., *A Companion to the Ancient Near East*.

Coughenour, Robert A. "A Search for Mahanaim." *BASOR* 273 (1989): 57–66.

Cowan, Wesley C. and Patty Jo Watson, eds. *The Origins of Agriculture: An International Perspective*. Washington; London: Smithsonian, 1992.

Dalley, Stephanie. "Ancient Mesopotamian Military Organization." Pages 413–22 in Sasson, ed., *CANE*. Vol. 1.

Dandamaev, Muhammad A. "Neo-Babylonian Society and Economy." Pages 252–75 in Boardman, Edwards, and Hammond, eds, *CAH*. Vol. 3, Part 2, *The Assyrian and Babylonian Empires and other States of the Near East*.

——. "State and Temple in Babylonia in the First Millennium B.C." Pages 589–96 in Lipinski ed., *State and Temple Economy in the Ancient Near East*. Vol. 2.

Dar, Shimon. *Landscape and Pattern: An Archaeological Survey of Samaria 800 BCE–636 CE*. Oxford: B.A.R. International Series, 1986.

Daviau, P. Michele M., and Paul-Eugene Dion. "Economy-Related Finds from Khirbat al-Mudayna (Wadi ath-Thamad, Jordan)." *BASOR* 328 (2002): 31–48.

Dever, William G. "Gezer." Pages 496–506 in Stern, ed., *NEAEHL*. Vol. 2.

Dorsey, David A. "Transportation." Pages 243–44 in Meyers, ed., *OEANE*. Vol. 5.

Dothan, Trude, and Seymour Gitin, "Miqne, Tel (Ekron)." Pages 1051–59 in Stern, ed., *NEAEHL*. Vol. 3.

——. "Miqne, Tel." Pages 30–35 in Meyers, ed., *OEANE*. Vol. 4.

Driel, Govert van. "Agricultural Entrepreneurs in Mesopotamia." Pages 213–23 in Klengel and Renger, eds, *Landwirtschaft im Alten Orient*.

Dyakonov, Ignor Mikhailovich. "The Naval Power and Trade of Tyre." *IEJ* 42 (1992): 168–93.

Ebeling, Jennie R. "Archaeological Remains of Everyday Activities: Ground Stone Tools in Bronze and Iron Age Palestine." Pages 311–26 in Averbeck, Chavalas, and Weisberg eds, *Life and Culture in the Ancient Near East*.

Edelman, Diana. "Tyrian Trade in Yehud under Artaxerxes I: Real or Fictional? Independent or Crown Endorsed?" Pages 207–46 in Lipschits and Oeming, eds, *Judah and the Judeans in the Persian Period*.

——. "Gibeon and the Gibeonites Revisited." Pages 153–67 in Lipschits and Blenkinsopp eds, *Judah and the Judeans in the Neo-Babylonian Period*.

Edwards, Douglas R. "Dress and Ornamentation." Pages 232–38 in Freedman, ed., *ABD*. Vol. 2.

Elat, Moshe. "Trade in Ancient Israel." Pages 527–46 in Lipinski ed., *State and Temple Economy in the Ancient Near East*.

Elayi, Josette. and Jean Sapin, *Beyond the River: New Perspectives on Transeuphratene*. Translated by J. Edward Crowley. JSOTSup 250. Sheffield: Sheffield Academic Press, 1998.

Ellison, Rosemary. "Diet in Mesopotamia: The evidence of the Barley Ration Texts (c. 3000–1400 B.C.)." *Iraq* 43 (1981), 35–45.

Eyre, Christopher J. "The Agricultural Cycle, Farming, and Water Management in the Ancient Near East." Pages 175–90 in Sasson, ed., *CANE*. Vol. 1.

Fantalkin, Alexander and Oren Tal. "Re-Dating Lachish Level I: Identifying Achaemenid Imperial Policy at the Southern Frontier of the Fifth Satrapy." Pages 167–98 in Lipschits and Oeming, eds, *Judah and the Judeans in the Persian Period*.

Fargo, Valerie M. "Hesi, Tell El-." Pages 630–34 in Stern, ed., *NEAEHL*. Vol. 2.

——. "Hesi, Tell El-." Page 22 in Meyers, ed., *OEANE*. Vol. 3.

Faust, Avraham. "Israelite Village: Cultural Conservatism and Technological Innovation." *TA* 32 (2005): 204–19.

—— and Ehud Weiss, "Judah, Philistia and the Mediterranean World: Reconstructing the Economic System of the Seventh Century B.C.E." *BASOR* 338 (2005):71–92.

Finkelstein, Israel. "Khirbet en-Nahas, Edom and Biblical History." *TA* 32 (2005): 119–25.

——. *Living on the Fringe: The Archaeology and History of the Negev, Sinai and Neighbouring Regions in the Bronze and Iron Ages*. MMA 6. Sheffield: Sheffield Academic Press, 1995.

——. "The Archaeology of the Days of Manasseh." Pages 169–87 in Coogan, Exum, and Stager, eds, *Scripture and Other Artifacts*.

Fischer, Moshe, Israel Roll, and Oren Tal. "Persian and Hellenistic Remains at Tel Yacoz." *TA* 35 (2008): 123–63.

Frankel, Rafael. *Wine and Oil Production in Antiquity in Israel and Other Mediterranean Countries*, JSOT/ASOR 10. Sheffield: Sheffield Academic Press, 1999.

Freedman, David Noel, ed. *Anchor Bible Dictionary*. 6 Vols. New York; London, Doubleday, 1992. [=ABD]

Frick, Frank S. "Cities, An Overview." Pages 14–19 in Meyers, ed., *OEANE*. Vol. 2.

Gal, Zvi. "Rosh Zayit, Horvat." Pages 1289–91 in Stern, ed., *NEAEHL*. Vol. 4.

Gelb, Ignace J. "Household and Family in Early Mesopotamia." Pages 1–98 in Lipinski, ed., *State and Temple Economy in the Ancient Near East*.

——, Piotr Steinkeller, and Robert M. Whiting Jr. *Earliest Land Tenure Systems in the Near East: Ancient Kadurrus*, UCOIP 104. Chicago, IL: The Oriental Institute, 1991.

Geva, Shulamit. "Archaeological Evidence for the Trade between Israel and Tyre?" *BASOR* 248 (1982); 69–72.

Gilbert, Allan S. "The Flora and Fauna of the Ancient Near East." Pages 153–74 in Sasson, ed., *CANE*. Vol. 1.

Gitin, Seymour. "The Neo-Assyrian Empire and Its Western Periphery: The Levant, with a Focus on Philistine Ekron." Pages 77–103 in Parpola and Whiting, eds, *Assyria 1995: Proceeding of the 10th Anniversary Symposium of the Neo-Assyrian Text Corpus Project*.

——. "New Philistine Finds at Tel Miqne-Ekron." *BA* 59 (1996): 70.

—— and Trude Dothan. "The Rise and Fall of Ekron of the Philistines: Recent Excavations at an Urban Border Site." *BA* 50 (1987): 197–222.

Gonen, Rica. "Urban Canaan in the Late Bronze Period." *BASOR* 253 (1984): 61–73.

Grabbe, Lester L. and Gary N. Knoppers, eds. *Exile and Restoration Revised: Essays on the Babylonian and Persian Periods in Memory of Peter R. Ackroyd*. LSTS 73/JSPSup; London: T & T Clark, 2009.

Grayson, Albert Kirk. "Assyrian Civilization." Pages 194–228 in Boardman, Edwards, and Hammond, eds, *CAH*. Vol. 3, Part 2, *The Assyrian and Babylonian Empires and other States of the Near East*.

Greenberg, Raphel, and Gilad Cinamon. "Stamped and Incised Jar Handles from Rogem Gannim and Their Implications for the Political Economy of Jerusalem: Late 8th–Early 4th Centuries BCE." *TA* 33 (2006): 229–43.

Hallo, William. W. "God, King, and Man at Yale." Pages 99–112 in Lipinski ed., *State and Temple Economy in the Ancient Near East.*

Hansen, Mogens Herman, ed. *A Comparative Study of Thirty-State Cultures: An Investigation Conducted by the Copenhagen Polis Centre.* Historisk-filosofiske Skrifter 21. Copenhagen: C. A. Reitzels Forlag, 2000.

Harrington, Spencer P. M. "Royal Treasures of Nimru." *Ar* 43 (1990): 48–53.

Henry, Donald O. *From Foraging to Agriculture: The Levant at the End of the Ice Age.* Philedelphia: University of Pennsylvania Press, 1989.

Herzog, Ze'ev. "Beersheba." Pages 287–91 in Meyers, ed., *OEANE.* Vol. 1.

—— and Lily Singer-Avitz, "Redefining the Centre: The Emergence of State in Judah." *TA* 31 (2004): 209–44.

Hesse, Brian. "Animal Husbandry: Paleozoology." Pages 140–43 in Meyers, ed., *OEANE.* Vol. 1.

——. "Animal Husbandry and Human Diet in the Ancient Near East." Pages 203–22 in Sasson, ed., *CANE.* Vol. 1.

Hopkins, David C. "Agriculture." Pages 22–30 in Meyers, ed., *OEANE.* Vol. 1.

——. "Cereals." Pages 479–81 in Meyers, ed., *OEANE.* Vol.1.

——. *The Highlands of Canaan: Agricultural Life in the Early Iron Age.* SWBA 3. Sheffield: Almond, 1985.

Ilan, David. "Dan." Pages 107–12 in Meyers, ed., *OEANE.* Vol. 2.

Jacob, Irene and Water Jacob. "Flora." Pages 803–17 in Freedman, ed., *ABD.* Vol. 2.

Jigoulov, Vadim S. "Administration of Achaemenid Phoenicia: A Case for Managed Autonomy." Pages 138–51 in Grabbe and Knoppers, eds, *Exile and Restoration Revised.*

Joannes, Francis. *The Age of Empires: Mesopotamia in the First Millennium BC.* Edinburgh: Edinburgh University Press, 2004.

——. "Private Commerce and Banking in Achaemenid Babylon." Pages 1475–85 in Sasson, ed., *CANE.* Vol. 3.

Katz, Hayah. "Commercial Activity in the Kingdoms of Judah and Israel." *TA* 31 (2004): 268–77.

——. "A Note on the Date of the 'Great Wall' of Tel en-Nesbeh." *TA* 25 (1998): 131–33.

Kenyon, Kathleen M. *Jerusalem: Excavating 3000 Years of History.* London: Thames & Hudson, 1967.

King, Philip J. and Lawrence E. Stager. *Life in Biblical Israel.* Louisville, KY; London: Westminster John Knox, 2002.

Klengel, Horst and Johannes Renger, eds. *Landwirtschaft im Alten Orient: Ausgewählte Vorträge der XLI. Recontre Assyriologique Internationale Berlin, 4. –8.7. 1994.* Berlin: Berliner Beitrge zum Vorderen Orient 18, 1999.

Klingbeil, Gerald A. "Methods and Daily Life: Understanding the Use of Animals in Daily Life in a Multi-disciplinary Framework." Pages 401–34 in Averbeck, Chavalas, and Weisberg, eds, *Life and Culture in the Ancient Near East.*

Knapp, Arthur Bernard. "Island Cultures: Crete, Thera, Cyprus, Rhodes and Sardinia." Pages 1433–50 in Sasson, ed., *CANE.* Vol. 3.

Larsen, Mogens Trolle. "The City-States of the Early Neo-Babylonian Period." Pages 117–28 in Hansen, ed., *A Comparative Study of Thirty-State Cultures.*

Levy, Thomas E. and Mohammad Najjar, "Some Thoughts on Khirbet en-Nahas, Edom, Biblical History and Anthropology: A Response to Israel Finkelstein." *TA* 33 (2006): 3–17.

Liphschitz, Nili and Gideon Biger. "The Timber Trade in Ancient Palestine." *TA* 22 (1995): 121–27.

Lipinski, Edward, ed. *State and Temple Economy in the Ancient Near East.* Vols. 1–2, *of the International Conference Organized by the Katholieke Universiteit Leuven from the 10th to the 14th of April 1978.* OLA 5. Leuven: Department Oriëntalistiek, 1979.

Lipschits, Oded. *The Fall and Rise of Jerusalem: Judah under Babylonian Rule.* Winona Lake, IN: Eisenbrauns, 2005.

—— and Joseph Blenkinsopp, eds. *Judah and the Judeans in the Neo-Babylonian Period.* Winona Lake, IN: Eisenbrauns, 2003.

Liverani, Mario. "Historical Overview." Pages 3–19 in Snell, ed., *A Companion to the Ancient Near East.*

Macdonald, Michael C. A. "North Arabia in the First Millennium B.C.E." Pages 1355–69 in Sasson, ed., *CANE.* Vol. 2.

MacDonald, Nathan, *Not Bread Alone: The Use of Food in the Old Testament.* Oxford: Oxford University Press, 2008.

McMahon, Augusta. "From Sedentism to States, 10,000–3000 BCE." Pages 20–33 in Snell, ed., *A Companion to the Ancient Near East.*

Magen, Yitzhak and Benny Har-Even. "Persian Period Stamp Impressions from Nebi Samwil." *TA* 34 (2007): 38–58.

Mallowan, Max. "Cyrus the Great (558–529 CE)." Pages 392–419 in Gershevitch, ed., *CHI.* Vol. 2, *The Median and Achaemenid Periods.*

Martirossian, A. "Notes Concerning the Economic Activity of the Babylonian Temples in the First Millennium BC." *Iraq* 45 (1983): 128–130.

Master, Daniel M. "Trade and Politics: Ashkelon's Balancing Act in the Seventh Century BCE." *BASOR* 330 (2003): 47–64.

Matthew, Victor H. "Perfumes and Spices." Pages 226–8 in Freedman, ed., *ABD.* Vol. 5.

Mazar, Benjamin. "The Early Israelite Settlement in the Hill Country." *BASOR* 241 (1981): 75– 85.

——. "Two Hebrew Ostraca from Tell Qasîle." *JNES* 10 (1951): 265–67.

Millard, Allan Ralph. "Does the Bible Exaggerate King Solomon's Wealth?" *BAR* 15 (1989): 20–34.

Miller, Naomi F. "The Origins of Plant Cultivation in the Near East." Pages 39–58 in Cowan and Watson, eds, *The Origins of Agriculture: An International Perspective*.

Miller, Robert D. "Modeling the Farm Community in Iron I Israel." Pages 289–310 in Averbeck, Chavalas, and Weisberg, eds, *Life and Culture in the Ancient Near East*.

Moorey, Peter Roger Stuart. *Ancient Mesopotamian Materials and Industries: The Archaeological Evidence*. Oxford: Clarendon, 1994.

Morkot, Robert. "Nubia and Achaemenid Persia: Sources and Problems." Pages 321–36 in Sancisi-Weerdenburg and Kuhrt, eds, *AH*. Vol. 6, *Asia Minor and Egypt*.

Muhly, James David. "Metals: Typology and Technology." Pages 1–5 in Meyers, ed., *OEANE*. Vol. 4.

Na'aman, Nadav. "Ekron under the Assyrian and Egyptian Empires." *BASOR* 332 (2003): 81–91.

——. "Hezekiah's Fortified Cities and the LMLK Stamps." *BASOR* 261 (1986): 5–21.

Nemet-Nejat, Karen Rhea. *Daily Life in Ancient Mesopotamia*. 2nd ed. Peabody: Hendrickson, 2008.

Netzer, Ehud. "Did Any Perfume Industry Exist at 'Ein Feshkha?" *IEJ* 55 (2005): 97–100.

Niemeier, Wolf-Dietrich. "Greek Merchants at Tel Kabri and Other Sites in the Levant." *TA* 29 (2002): 328–31.

Niemeyer, Hans Georg. "The Early Phoenician City-States on the Mediterranean. Archaeological Element for their Description." Pages 89–116 in Hansen ed., *A Comparative Study of Thirty-State Cultures*.

Parpola, Simo. and Robert Whiting, eds. *Assyria 1995: Proceedings of the 10th Anniversary Symposium of the Neo-Assyrian Text Corpus Project, Helsinki, September 7–11, 1995*. SAA 12. Helsinki: Helsinki University Press, 1997.

Pastor, Jack. *Land and Economy in Ancient Palestine*. London: Routledge, 1997.

Postgate, John Nicholas. "*Ilku* and Land Tenure in the Middle Assyrian Kingdom: A Second Attempt." Pages 112–22 in Postgate, ed., *The Land of Assur*.

——. "Land Tenure in the Middle Assyrian Period: A Reconstruction." Pages 2–26 in Postgate, ed., *The Land of Assur*.

——, ed. *The Land of Assur & the Yoke of Assur: Studies on Assyria: 1971–2005*. Oxford: Oxbow Books, 2007.

Potts, Daniel T. "Distant Shores: Ancient Near Eastern Trade with South Asia and Northeast Africa." Pages 1451–63 in Sasson, ed., *CANE*. Vol. 3.

Pritchard, James Bennett. "Gibeon." Pages 511–14 in Stern, ed., *NEAEHL*. Vol. 2.

Raban, Avner and Robert R. Stieglitz, "The Sea Peoples and Their Contributions to Civilization." *BAR* 17 (1991): 34–42.

Rainey, Anson. "Aspects of Life in Ancient Israel." Pages 253–68 in Averbeck, Chavalas, and Weisberg, eds, *Life and Culture in the Ancient Near East.*
——. "Wine from Royal Vineyards." *BASOR* 245 (1982): 57–62.
Renger, Johannes. "Interaction of Temple, Palace, and 'Private Enterprise' in the Old Babylonian Economy." Pages 249–56 in Lipinski, ed., *State and Temple Economy in the Ancient Near East.* Vol. 1.
Renfrew, Jane Margaret. "Vegetables in the Ancient Near Eastern Diet." Pages 191–202 in Sasson, ed., *CANE.* Vol. 1.
Roebuck, C. "Trade." Pages 446–60 in Boardman, Lewis, Hammond, and Martin, eds, *CAH.* Vol. 4, *Persia, Greece and the Western Mediterranean c. 525–479 B.C.*
Sancisi-Weerdenburg, Heleen. "The Quest for an Elusive Empire." Pages 263–74 in Sancisi-Weerdenburg and Kuhrt, eds, *AH.* Vol. 4, *Centre and Periphery.*
—— and Amelie Kuhrt eds. *Achaemenid History.* Vol. 4, *Centre and Periphery.* Leiden: Nederlands Instituut voor het Nabije Oosten, 1990. [=*AH*]
Sasson, Aharon. "The Pastoral Component in the Economy of Hill Country Sites during the Intermediate Bronze and Iron Ages: Archaeo-Ethnographic Case Study." *TA* 25 (1998): 3–51.
Sasson, Jack M, ed. *Civilizations of the Ancient Near East.* 4 Vols. New York: Scribner, 1995. [=*CANE*]
Scheidel, Walter and Sitta von Reden eds. *The Ancient Economy.* Translated by Antonia Nevill. Edinburgh: Edinburgh University Press, 2002.
Schloen, David. "Ashkelon." Pages 220–23 in Meyers, ed., *OEANE.* Vol. 1.
Sekunda, Nicholas. "Achaemenid Settlement in Caria, Lycia and Greater Phryia." Pages 83–143 in Sancisi-Weerdenburg and Kuhrt, eds, *AH.* Vol. 6, *Asia Minor and Egypt.*
Shiloh, Yigal. "Meggido, City: The Iron Age." Pages 1012–14 in Stern, ed., *NEAEHL.* Vol. 3.
Simonsen, Jørgen Bæk. "Mecca and Medina. Arab City-States or Arab Caravan-Cities?" Pages 241–50 in Hansen ed., *A Comparative Study of Thirty-State.*
Simpson, Eliazbeth. "Furniture in Ancient Western Aisa." Pages 1647–72 in Sasson, ed., *CANE.* Vol. 3.
Singer-Avitz, Lily. "Arad: The Iron Age Pottery Assemblages." *TA* 29 (2002): 110–214.
Snell, Daniel C. *Life in the Ancient Near East: 3100–332 BCE.* New Haven; London: Yale University Press, 1997.
——. "Trade and Commerce." Pages 625–29 in Freedman, ed., *ABD.* Vol. 6.
——. "Methods of Exchange and Coinage in Ancient Western Asia." Pages 1487–97 in Sasson, ed., *CANE.* Vol. 3.
——, ed. *A Companion to the Ancient Near East.* Oxford: Blackwell, 2005; 2007.
Speiser, E. A. "Background and Function of the Biblical nāśī." *CBQ* 25 (1963): 111–17.

Stager, Lawrence E. "The Fury of Babylon: Ashkelon and the Archaeology of Destruction." *BAR* 22 (1996): 56–69.

——. "Ashkelon." Pages 103–12 in Stern, ed., *NEAEHL*. Vol. 1.

——. "The Firstfruits of Civilisation." Pages 172–88 in Tubb, ed., *Palestine in the Bronze and Iron Ages*.

——. "The Archaeology of the Family in Ancient Israel." *BASOR* 260 (1985): 1–35.

——. "The Archaeology of the East Slope of Jerusalem and the Terraces of the Kidron." *JNES* 41 (1982): 111–21.

—— and Samuel R. Wolff. "Production and Commerce in Temple Courtyards: An Olive Press in the Sacred Precinct at Tel Dan." *BASOR* 243 (1981): 95–102.

Stern, Ephraim. ed. *The New Encyclopedia of Archaeological Excavations in the Holy Land*. 5 Vols. New York; London; Tronto etc: The Israel Exploration Society & Carta, Jerusalem, 1993. [=*NEAEHL*]

——, Oded Lipschits, and David Vanderhooft, "New Yehud Stamp Impressions from En Gedi." *TA* 34 (2007): 66–73.

Stone, Elizabeth Caecilia. "Mesopotamian Cities and Countryside." Pages 157–70 in Snell, ed., *A Companion to the Ancient Near East*.

Strange, John. "The Philistine City-States." Pages 129–40 in Hansen, ed., *A Comparative Study of Thirty-State Cultures*.

Tsuk, Tsvika. "Cisterns." Pages 12–13 in Meyers, ed., *OEANE*. Vol. 2.

—— and Avi Gopher, "Nahal Hemar Cave." Pages 1082–88 in Stern, ed., *NEAEHL*. Vol. 3.

Ussishkin, David. "Lachish." Pages 897–911 in Stern, ed., *NEAEHL*. Vol. 3.

Vanderhooft, David. and Wayne Horowitz, "The Cuneiform Inscription from Tell en-Nasbeh: The Demise of an Unknown King." *TA* 29 (2002): 318–27.

Vargyas, Peter. "Agrarkrisen und Umfang der Agrarproduktion im Babylonien des 1. Jahrtausends." Pages 189–96 in Klengel and Renger, eds, *Landwirtschaft im Alten Orient*.

Vickers, Michael. "Interactions between Greeks and Persians." Pages 253–62 in Sancisi-Weerdenburg and Kuhrt, eds, *AH*. Vol. 4, *Centre and Periphery*.

Walsh, Carey Ellen. *The Fruit of the Vine: Viticulture in Ancient Israel*. HSM 60. Winona Lake, IN: Eisenbrauns, 2000.

Walton, John H. *Ancient Near Eastern Thought and the Old Testament: Introducing the Conceptual World of the Hebrew Bible*. Norton: Apollos, 2007.

Warburton, David A. "Working." Pages 185–98 in Snell, ed., *A Companion to the Ancient Near East*.

Wapnish, Paula. "Camels." Pages 407–8 in Meyers, ed., *OEANE*. Vol. 1.

Yadin, Yigael. "Hazor." Pages 594–603 in Stern, ed., *NEAEHL*. Vol. 2.

Yoffee, Norman. "The Economy of Ancient Western Asia." Pages 1387–1400 in Sasson, ed., *CANE*. Vol. 3.

Young, Ian. "The Style of the Gezer Calendar and Some 'Archaic Biblical Hebrew' Passage." *VT* 42 (1992): 362–75.

Zeder, Melinda A. "Sheep and Goats." Pages 23–25 in Meyers, ed., *OEANE*. Vol. 5.

——. *Feeding: Specialized Animal Economy in the Ancient Near East*. Washington; London: Smithsonian, 1991.

Zertal, Adam. "The Province of Samaria (Assyrian Samerina) in the Late Iron Age (Iron Age III)." Pages 377–411 in Lipschits and Blenkinsopp, eds, *Judah and the Judeans in the Neo-Babylonian Period*.

——. "The Wedge-Shaped Decorated Bowl and the Origin of the Samaritans." *BASOR* 276 (1989): 77–84.

Zohary, Daniel and Maria Hopf. *Domestication of Plants in the Old World: The Origin and Spread of Cultivated Plants in West Asia, Europe, and the Nile Valley*. 2nd ed. Oxford: Oxford University Press, 1994.

Zorn, Jeffrey Ralph. "Tell en-Nesbeh and the Problem of the Material Culture of the Sixth Century." Pages 413–50 in Lipschits and Blenkinsopp, eds, *Judah and the Judeans in the Neo-Babylonian Period*.

——. "A Note on the Date of the 'Great Wall' of Tell en-Nesbeh: A Rejoinder." *TA* 26 (1999): 146–50.

——. "Nasbeh, Tell en-." Pages 1098–1102 in Stern, ed., *NEAEHL*. Vol. 3.

CHAPTER 2

Darius and the Achaemenid Empire

Background

The purpose of this chapter is to explore the extent to which, in the political, military, and economic aspects, Darius I (522–486 BCE)'s policies developed and were imposed on all his subordinates. The necessity of historical survey on Darius and his empire is that Judah formed a part of Darius's empire and was obliged to submit to Darius's administrative policies. Also, the Book of Haggai speaks to the historical reconstruction of political and economic systems during Darius's reign.

Very soon after Darius ascended the Persian throne, he was faced with a series of revolts by subordinates within his territories. Those revolts which broke out on Darius's accession seriously threatened the fundamental cohesion of the empire, and the crisis in Darius's kingship might provide an opportunity for subjugated peoples to make a bid for independence. The numerous revolts against Darius were due to a suspicion at the time of accession to the throne. Accordingly, it is necessary to investigate Darius's seizure of the Persian throne.

Throughout the unrest, Darius needed ideological legitimacy for his authority in order to put down rebellions and any resistance. In relation to territorial expansion, the imposition of his propaganda needed to be sufficient to ensure the successful pacification of subordinates. This is because the ability to expand the territory rested in secure military power. Thus, I look at how Darius set in motion his propaganda to gain full control over subordinates among the various regional-ethnic grounds within his dominion.

Afterwards, I will examine how Darius executed an imperial administrative reorganisation to ensure the compulsory collaboration from conquered territories, especially in terms of taxation. This is very important because both imperial military power and imperial administrative policy were designed for the sole purpose of a constant exploitation of resources from conquered territories. Accordingly, it is also necessary to look into how, in the administrative, economic, and military system of Darius, Judah was expected to contribute with her forced charges, whether economic or military.

The Rise of the Achaemenids

Darius's Succession

The fall of the Neo-Babylonian Empire (626–539 BCE) to an army alleged to be under the command of Cyrus (559–530 BCE) in 539 BCE opened a new extension of Persian control to the west.[1] The Persian Empire inherited the territorial scope enjoyed by the Babylonian power which spanned the region of Syria-Palestine and the Assyrian heartland. The accession of Cambyses (530–522 BCE) to the throne brought about little change in the imperial western territories. Egypt, which could be capable of being a threat to the Persians, was finally conquered by Cambyses.[2] The Persians

1 For Achaemenid regnal years, see Christopher Walker, "Achaemenid Chronology and the Babylonian Source," in *Mesopotamia and Iran in the Persian Period: Conquest and Imperialism 539–331 BC: Proceedings of a Seminar in Memory of Vladimir G. Lukonin* (ed. John E. Curtis; London: British Museum, 1997), 17–25; Elias Joseph Bickerman, "Calendar and Chronology," in *CHJ*, Vol. 1, *Introduction*, 60–2.

2 Amelie Kuhrt, *The Ancient Near East c. 3000–330 B.C.* (RHAW 2; London; New York: Routledge, 1995), 661–4; Briant, *From Cyrus to Alexander*, 50–61; Richard Nelson Frye, *The History of Ancient Iran* (Munich: Beck, 1984), 126; T. Cuyler Young Jr, "The Early History of the Medes and the Persians and the Achaemenid Empire

apparently re-asserted and consolidated their control up to, and beyond the Neo-Babylonian territories.

Afterwards, Darius I (522–486 BCE) became the third king of Achaemenid Persia, dealing first with the rebellion of Gaumata (Bardiya/Smerdis). In relation to the rise of Darius, however, some doubts were raised concerning the events of Cambyses's death, Bardiya's revolt and Gaumata's identity. As reported by Babylonian documents, Bardiya, a satrap of the eastern part of the empire was given a Babylonian royal title, "king of Babylon, king of lands" in 522 BCE.[3] It denotes that Bardiya rebelled against his brother Cambyses; however, he failed and was killed.[4] Shortly after, Cambyses was again confronted, this time by Gaumata, a Median priest, who pretended to be Bardiya, and was killed by a group of nobles headed by Darius.[5] Within the confusion surrounding Bardiya, there could be a fairly plausible argument that once Bardiya ascended the throne after Cambyses, Darius rebelled against Bardiya and made up the story about Gaumata to cover his tracks.[6] Regardless of whether the usurper was the pretender Gaumata or imaginary Gaumata, there was clearly more than a palace coup taking place in Darius's rule.[7]

---

to the Death of Cambyses," in Boardman, Lewis, Hammond and Martin, eds, *CAH*, Vol. 4, *Persia, Greece and the Western Mediterranean*, 47–52.

3 Xenophon, *The Cyropaedia of Xenophon* (GSCS; Noted by George Martyn Gorham from the Text of L. Dinfort; London: Whittaker, 1856), 8.7.11.

4 Darius Behistun Inscription I: §10. I use the translation by Maria Brosius, *The Persian Empire from Cyrus II to Artaxerxes I* (LACTOR 16; Kingston: The London Association of Classical Teachers, 2000), 22.

5 DB I: §§11–15, sourced from Brosius, *The Persian Empire from Cyrus II to Artaxerxes I*, 23–24; Herodotus, *The Histories* (PCS; trans. Aubrey de Selincourt; Harmondsworth: Penguin, 1954), III.61–67.3; 70; 78.4–5.

6 *Hist.* III, 70–3; 76–9, 83–84.2.

7 John Manuel Cook, "The Rise of the Achaemenids and Establishment of their Empire," in Gershevitch, ed., *CHI*, Vol. 2, *The Median and Achaemenid Periods*, 201–9; Josef Wiesehöfer, *Ancient Persia: From 550 BC to 650 AD* (trans. A. Azodi; London: New York: Tauris, 1996), 13–14, 29–30; T. Cuyler Young Jr, "The Consolidation of the Empire and Its Limits of Growth under Darius and Xerxes," in Boardman, Lewis, Hammond and Martin, eds, *CAH*, Vol. 4, *Persia, Greece and the Western*

Concerning the kingship, Cambyses's brother Bardiya, the next in line to the throne after Cambyses, was killed without leaving any male heir. Thus, the Persian throne could be contested by any member of the extended royal family, or indeed of the Persian nobility. Then, as the chief conspirator from the nobility, Darius finally seized power.[8] In fact, he was not an immediate member of the royal family but of the Ariaramnes branch of the Achaemenid line. Doubts about his genuine right to succeed to the throne made him claim to be descended from a line of kings.[9] Darius traced his ancestral line back to a Persian called Achaemenes, whom he presented as the father of Teispes. This led to a familial link between his family and that of Cyrus. None of the earliest records, including the Cyrus Cylinder, mentioned Achaemenes.

It is well-attested that Darius added "Cyrus the great king, the Achaemenids" into Cyrus's inscriptions concerning the Achaemenid line in Old Persian, Elamite and Akkadian at Pasargadae.[10] Herodotus recorded this almost a hundred years later.[11] In order to prevent any future

---

Mediterranean, 54–5; Lester L. Grabbe, *Judaism from Cyrus to Hadrian* (London: SCM, 1992), 124–5.

8 DB I: §11–15, referred to from Brosius, *The Persian Empire from Cyrus II to Artaxerxes I*, 23–4; *Hist.* I, 209–10; III, 68–9; 74–5; 84.3–87; 88.2–3.

9 Heleen Sancisi-Weerdenburg, "Darius I and the Persian Empire," in Sasson, ed., *CANE*, Vol. 2, 1035–9;
David Stronach, "Anshan and Persia: Early Achaemenid History, Art and Architecture on the Iranian Plateau," in Curtis, ed., *Mesopotamia and Iran in the Persian Period*, 1997; Richard Nelson Frye, "Cyrus the Mede and Darius the Achaemenid?" in *The World of Achaemenid Persia: History, Art and Society in Iran and the Ancient Near East* (ed. John Curtis and St John Simpson; Proceedings of a Conference at the British Museum 29th September – 1st October 2003; London; New York: Tauris, 2010), 18–19.

10 CMa = DMa; CMb = DMb; CMc = CMc. These texts are cited from Amelie Kuhrt, *The Persian Empire: A Corpus of Sources from the Achaemenid Persian* (London: Routledge, 2008), 177.

11 Peter Calmeyer, "Greek Historiography and Achaemenid Reliefs," in *AH*, Vol. 2, *Greek Sources: Proceedings of the Groningen 1984 Achaemenid History Workshop* (ed. Heleen Sancisi-Weerdenburg and Amelie Kuhrt; Leiden: Nederlands Instituut voor het Nabije Oosten, 1987), 11–26.

competition for the throne Darius concluded a series of marriage alliances with all surviving royal daughters. He even contracted with the conspirators' and nobles' daughters, even though the nobles themselves were married to sisters of Darius.[12]

From the above survey, I have shown that in 539 BCE Cyrus opened up the Persian Empire. The following king, Cambyses expanded the imperial western territory towards Egypt. He was then confronted with the rebellion of Gaumata (Bardiya/Smerdis). Some doubts from the two different stories of DB and Herodotus were raised in Cambyses's death, Bardiya's revolt and Gaumata's identity. Regardless of who the usurper was, after Cambyses was killed, the kingship was handed over to Darius in 522 BCE by a group of nobles headed by Darius. And then, the family line of Achaemenes of Darius soon went back to Cyrus. Eventually, he established the Achaemenid kingship and became the third king of Achaemenid Persia.

Darius's Crisis

The confusion surrounding Darius's power undoubtedly provided the background for widespread rebellion in the first year of Darius's reign. Elam and Babylon in the eastern part of the empire rebelled first. In Elam, AÇina, son of Upadarma seized power but was quickly subdued by Darius.[13] Nidintu-bel was recognised as the new king in Babylonia, where the revolt took place, presenting himself as the son of Nabonidus. Darius quickly suppressed it but Nidintu-bel returned with an army against Darius. Darius, leading the army, inflicted a second successive defeat and eventually killed him.[14]

12 *Hist.* III, 88.2–3.

13 DB I: §§16–17, cited from Brosius, *The Persian Empire from Cyrus II to Artaxerxes I*, 31–2.

14 DB I: §§18–II: 20, sourced from Brosius, *The Persian Empire from Cyrus II to Artaxerxes I*, 32.

In 521 BCE, Babylon rebelled again under the rule of Arkha who took the title of King of Babylon, but was also overrun.[15]

Subsequent revolts happened in the eastern part of the empire, especially Media, Assyria, Parthia, Margiana (or Bactria), Sattagydia, and Scythia. They likewise claimed the legitimacy to the throne and attempted to revive the former kingdoms.[16] Fravartiš of Media resisted for five months, the loss of men amounted to 3,827 killed and 4,329 captured.[17] A man named Vahyzdata, notably claiming to be Bardiya, son of Cyrus became a king in Persia.[18] Vahyzdata's revolt was defeated by the army that Darius sent. Nevertheless, he successfully assembled a second army and rebelled again.

Egypt rose up against Darius. The governor of Egypt, Aryandes, who was appointed by Cambyses, tried to make himself the equal of Darius.[19] He minted coins for Darius with gold, but also minted some for himself with silver. Darius's elimination of Aryandes reflected his revolts against

15 DB II: §21, referred to from Brosius, *The Persian Empire from Cyrus II to Artaxerxes I*, 32. For secondary source, see Briant, *From Cyrus to Alexander*, 116–17; Amelie Kuhrt, "Achaemenid Babylonia: Sources and Problems," in *AH*, Vol. 4, *Centre and Periphery* (ed. Heleen Sancisi-Weerdenburg and Amelie Kuhrt; Leiden: Nederlands Instituut voor het Nabije Oosten, 1990), 177–94.

16 DB II: §§21–IV 54, sourced from Brosius, *The Persian Empire from Cyrus II to Artaxerxes I*, 32–7; *Hist.* III, 118–99; 126–8; IV, 166. For secondary source, see Stuart C. Brown, "Media in the Achaemenid Period: The Late Iron Age in the Central West Iran," in Sancisi-Weerdenburg and Kuhrt, eds, *AH*, Vol. 4, *Centre and Periphery*, 63–76.

17 DB II: §25, cited from Brosius, *The Persian Empire from Cyrus II to Artaxerxes I*, 32–3. For secondary source, see Briant, *From Cyrus to Alexander*, 118; Muhammad A. Dandamaev, *A Political History of the Achaemenid Empire* (trans. W. J. Vogelsang; Leiden: Brill, 1989), 118–20.

18 DB I: §§16–II: 23 in Brosius, *The Persian Empire from Cyrus II to Artaxerxes I*, 31–2. As for secondary source, see Briant, *From Cyrus to Alexander*, 115–16, 120–1.

19 *Hist.* III, 14–15, IV, 166–7, 200, 203; DB II: §20, cited from Brosius, *The Persian Empire from Cyrus II to Artaxerxes I*, 32; Polyaenus VII.1.7, sourced from Briant, *From Cyrus to Alexander*, 121; Aelianus, *De Natura Animalium* (ed. Manuela Garcia Valdes, Luis Alfonso Liera Fueyo, and Lucia Rodriguez-Noriega Guillen; Berolini; Novi Eboraci: De Gruyter, 2009), 12.21.

Darius's authority.[20] Darius held Egypt. This can be reflected by inscriptions of Darius's statues, wherein he is addressed with the royal titles supported by Egyptian deities.[21] Although the control of Egypt was of great importance as a practical and tactical region in maintaining the western border, it was not until 519 BCE that Darius launched a military campaign against Egypt.[22] The reason was that he had to concentrate on recurrence of revolts in the more crucial region of the empire, Babylon. Also, it took a long time for Darius to gain the reliable allegiance of surrounding subordinates in a pervading time of revolts.[23]

Judah also took advantage of the chaotically rebellious conditions of Darius and rallied around a royal plot, similar to the plots that had arisen elsewhere, especially amid the continuous Egyptian revolts.[24] The people in Judah intrigued to rouse to the throne in Jerusalem a descendant of David, Zerubbabel (Hag 1:4, 9; 2:20–23). Darius had granted permission to Zerubbabel to return to Jerusalem in order to rebuild the temple, and had appointed Zerubbabel to the governor of Judah. Just seventeen or so years after the Judean return from Babylon, however, Zerubbabel, the governor of Judah, was enough to contemplate seriously the restoration of the

20 *Hist.* IV, 166. As for secondary sources of Egyptian revolts, see Briant, *From Cyrus to Alexander*, 115–16, 120–1; Kuhrt, *The Ancient Near East c. 3000–330 B.C.*, 668; Jack Martin Balcer, *Herodotus & Bisitun: Problems in Ancient Persian Historiography* (H-E 49; Stuttgart: Steiner-Verlag-Wiesbaden-GmbH, 1987), 145–6.

21 DSab, cited from Brosius, *The Persian Empire from Cyrus II to Artaxerxes I*, 44–5; "Hieroglyphic inscription on the base of Darius's statue from Susa," sourced from Brosius, *The Persian Empire from Cyrus II to Artaxerxes I*, 45; DSab and "Hieroglyphic text" are also found in Kuhrt, *The Persian Empire*, 477–8; *Hist.* IV, 166.

22 Briant, *From Cyrus to Alexander*, 115–16; Kuhrt, *The Ancient Near East c. 3000–330 B.C.*, 668; Frye, *The History of Ancient Iran*, 126; Balcer, *Herodotus & Bisitun*, 145–6; Hans M. Barstad, "Haggai Among the Prophets: An Example of Prophetic Continuity in the Hebrew Bible," in *Shai le-Sara Japhet: Studies in the Bible, its Exegesis and its Language* (ed. Bar-Asher, Moshe, Dalit Rom-Shiloni, Emanuel Tov, and Nili Wazana; Jerusalem: The Bialik Institute, 2007), 265–83.

23 Dandamaev, *A Political History of the Achaemenid Empire*, 122–7; Berquist, *Judaism in Persia's Shadow*, 51–8; Ephraim Stern, *Material Culture of the Land of the Bible in the Persian Period 538–332 B.C.* (Warminster: Aris & Phillips, 1982), 229, 247–9.

24 Balcer, *Herodotus & Bisitun*, 149–52.

monarchy.[25] The effort to restore the Davidic kingdom through Zerubbabel was in the same manner that most rebels throughout his territories took a regnal name individually that permitted them to connect with the local dynasty. The people in Judah certainly contested Achaemenid authority (Hag 1:4, 9; 2:4, 6–7).

A similar enmity in Judah in the power balance between Egypt and the Mesopotamian empires can be seen in Josiah's battle in 2 Chr 35:20–24.[26] On the eve of the war between Egypt and Neo-Babylonia, Josiah was in the middle of repairing the temple. He went out to intervene in the war between the Egyptians and the Neo-Babylonians but he was slain by the Egyptian force. Haggai, like a message from YHWH in the time of Josiah, warned that Judah should not interfere with this battle (Hag 2:4, 6–7). Judean contention against Darius could only result in a political catastrophe, as with Josiah.

As I have shown above, the suspicion of Darius's usurpation of the Persian throne generated revolts from every subordinate ruler in the first and second periods of his reign. Especially, the recurrence of revolts in Babylon and Egypt was crucial as it could disturb the empire, as they could play a great role in the integration of conquered territories into Darius's dominion. Throughout the time of overall revolts against Darius, troubles arose in Judah. Judah was seized by the conspiracy of Judean independence led by Zerubbabel. This pressing historical backdrop fitted with the critical message of the book of Haggai.

Darius's Territorial Expansion

Following the successful suppression of the multiple uprisings, Darius turned to further expansion to reinforce his imperial authority.[27] From

25 See exegeses of those passages in Chapters 4 and 5 below.

26 Throughout her history, Judah has been dominated by geopolitical strategies of the Egyptian and Neo-Assyrian, and Neo-Babylonian powers. See James M. Trotter, *Reading Hosea in Achaemenid Yehud* (JSOTSup 328; Sheffield: Sheffield Academic Press, 2001), 52; Lipschits, *The Fall and Rise of Jerusalem*, 25–9.

27 *Hist.* III, 135.1; 136; 138–47; 149. For Achaemenid imperial armies, see H. T. Wallinga, "Polycrates and Egypt: The Testimony of the Samaina," in Sancisi-Weerdenburg

Asia, such as Punjab (India), he advanced the eastern border established by Cyrus (520–513 BCE).[28] He captured the Ionian islands (517 BCE)[29] and defeated the Scythians who lived a nomadic life moving along the northern coast of the Black Sea.[30] Thrace (by the Balkan Mountains on the north, the Aegean Sea on the south, and by the Black Sea on the east) and most of the northern Aegean were captured in around 513 BCE.

In 499 BCE, peace in the west was disturbed by the Ionian revolt.[31] It was connected to Darius's unsuccessful expedition against Naxos which was supported by Athens.[32] By 493 BCE, Darius restored the power throughout the Ionian cities and Cyprus. In response to Athenian support for the Ionians, Darius decided to invade Athens in 491 BCE but he only lost the battle at Marathon.[33] He intended to prepare a renewed attack on Athens, but he died in 486 BCE before he could retake Athens.[34]

To sum up, after the suppression of extensive revolts, Darius concentrated his efforts at further expansion to reinforce the imperial authority. His extended imperial dominion covered the mainland to the Aegean

---

and Kuhrt, eds, *AH*, Vol. 4, *Centre and Periphery*, 179–97; Maria Brosius, *Persians: An Introduction* (London: Routledge, 2006), 44; T. Cuyler Young Jr, "Persian," in Meyers, ed., *OEANE*, Vol. 4, 298.

28 *Hist.* IV, 44. For Darius's conquest in India, see Willem Vogelsang, "The Achaemenids and India," in Sancisi-Weerdenburg and Kuhrt, eds, *AH*, Vol. 4, *Centre and Periphery*, 93–110.

29 *Hist.* IV, 165; 167; 200–4.

30 *Hist.* IV, 1; 83; 85.1; 87; 89; 91–3; 97–8; 102; 120–8; 131–138.1; 140.3; 141; 142.1; 143.1.

31 *Hist.* IV, 43–5; 144; V, 1–2; 11; 14–6; 17.1; 18.1; 21.2–22.1; 23.2; 25.1; 26; 73; 98.1; VI, 46; 47.2; VII, 25.2; 59.1; 105.1; 110–111.1; 112; VI, 59.2–4.

32 *Hist.* V, 28; 30–8; 49–51; 55.1; 96–7; 99.1; 100–5.1; 108–116.1; 117–24; VI, 1–11.1; 18; 19.3–20; 21.2–22.1; 25–6; 28–30.1; 31–3; 41.1–2; 42–3. For Greek situations during the Achaemenid rule, see Jack Martin Balcer, "The East Greek under Persian Rule: A Reassesment," in *AH*, Vol. 6, *Asia Minor and Egypt: Old Culture in a New Empire* (ed. Heleen Sancisi-Weerdenburg and Amelie Kuhrt; Leiden: Nederlands Instituut voor het Nabije Oosten, 1991), 57–65.

33 *Hist.* VI, 48–49.1; 94–7; 98.1; 99–102; 107.2; 112–3; 115–6; 118; 119.1–2, 4.

34 *Hist.* VII, 1.1; 4. For historical accounts of Darius's wars against Greek, see Kuhrt, *The Persian Empire*, 177; Michael Vickers, "Interactions between Greeks and Persians," in Sancisi-Weerdenburg and Kuhrt, eds, *AH*, Vol. 4, *Centre and Periphery*, 253–62.

Islands, incorporating the conquest of Cyrus and furthermore the taking of Egypt under Cambyses. From then on, there was no further territorial expansion in the Achaemenids. Efforts were only directed towards tightening and adjusting the imperial administration.

Achaemenid Administrative Systems

Administrative Principles

In the aftermath of turmoil of his beginning (522–521 BCE), Darius needed to tighten and exalt his power so as to stabilise and expand his territory. It forced him to devise a highly sophisticated and efficient system of propaganda that would allow various peoples to function within the confines of the imperial authority.[35] It began with the restoration of the sanctuaries which Gaumata had destroyed. Darius then returned confiscated private property and reestablished the people in their homelands, both in Persia and Media, and in the other provinces.[36] The purpose of this building project in each subordinate was to recognise Darius as the representative that each deity chose for religious and political leadership. Subsequently, every region was required, in the name of each local deity, to build or rebuild his temple.

Above all, this recognition of Darius had political connotations connected to his territorial campaigns. It meant that, although a variety of religions were practised in the Achaemenids, in several of Darius's inscriptions,

35 The extraordinary elaboration of the royal centre at Pasargadae would be an example of this. Elspeth R. M. Dusinberre, *Aspect of Empire in Achaemenid Sardis* (Cambridge: Cambridge University Press, 2002), 1–4; Young, "The Consolidation of the Empire," 99–103; Wiesehöfer, *Ancient Persia*, 21.

36 DB I: §14, sourced from Brosius, *The Persian Empire from Cyrus II to Artaxerxes I*, 23; DB V: §§ 71–2, sourced from Brosius, *The Persian Empire from Cyrus II to Artaxerxes I*, 39.

Ahura Mazda was the supreme.[37] In fact, Ahura Mazda was an Iranian deity but was by necessity elevated to a royal religious cult on the eve of his eastern campaigns.[38] Then, as Ahura Mazda's representative on earth, Darius merely accomplished the divine work under the god's guidance.[39] This led to Darius's supremacy.

For similar reasons, Darius made great efforts to accept and support the gods of subordinates.[40] He restored the cult of Marduk in Babylon.[41] He also adopted divine kingship in Egypt, where the pharaoh, by the authority of office, was a god. Thus, he performed the necessary official duties for the burial of the Apis bull that died.[42] Darius was even commemorated as the

37 DSf, cited from Brosius, *The Persian Empire from Cyrus II to Artaxerxes I*, 40–1; DSe, cited from Brosius, *The Persian Empire from Cyrus II to Artaxerxes I*, 41–2; DE, cited from Brosius, *The Persian Empire from Cyrus II to Artaxerxes I*, 42; DNa, cited from Brosius, *The Persian Empire from Cyrus II to Artaxerxes I*, 42–4.

38 DB I: §§5, 9, referred to from Brosius, *The Persian Empire from Cyrus II to Artaxerxes I*, 30. For secondary literature, Briant, *From Cyrus to Alexander*, 63, 175–8.

39 Briant, *From Cyrus to Alexander*, 165–203; Root Cool Magaret, "From the Heart: Powerful Persianisms in the Art of the Western Empire," in Sancisi-Weerdenburg and Kuhrt, eds, *AH*, Vol. 6, *Asia Minor and Egypt*, 1–29; Edwin MaseoYamauchi, *Persia and the Bible* (Grand Rapids, MI: Baker, 1990), 149–51; Robert Morkot, "Nubia and Achaemenid Persia: Sources and Problems," in Sancisi-Weerdenburg and Kuhrt, eds, *AH*, Vol. 6, *Asia Minor and Egypt*, 321–36.

40 According to Gadatas inscription (ML 12), Darius demonstrated his respect for the Greek god Apollo by reprimanding his Magnesian satrap Gadatas for collecting taxes from the temple land. Yet later this inscription has proved a creation of the Hellenistic period. This text is found in Brosius, *The Persian Empire from Cyrus II to Artaxerxes I*, 93. For comments of this text, see Grabbe, *A History of the Jews and Judaism in the Second Temple Period*. Vol. 1, *Yehud*, 116–17; Briant, *From Cyrus to Alexander*, 401–2.

41 Brosius, *Persians*, 71; Young, "The Consolidation of the Empire and Its Limits of Growth under Darius and Xerxes," 99–103.

42 "Apis Bull Inscription," cited from Brosius, *The Persian Empire from Cyrus II to Artaxerxes I*, 45–6 and Kuhrt, *The Persian Empire*, 122–4; *Hist*. III, 27–30.1. For secondary literature, see Briant, *From Cyrus to Alexander*, 687–8; Grabbe, *A History of the Jews and Judaism in the Second Temple Period*. Vol. 1, *Yehud*, 268.

restorer of the temple of the Egyptian goddess, Neith in the city of Sais, and as the restorer of the temple of Amun-Re at El-Khargeh.[43]

The temple rebuilding project is seen in the Hebrew Bible. Judah was allowed in the name of YHWH to rebuild the temple in Jerusalem which had been destroyed in the Babylonian raid (Ezra 1:1–11; 6:1–8). This decision has usually been regarded as a particularly generous act of the Persian king which confirms the special status of Judah.[44] However, it has nothing to do with a particular concern for the Judean religion. Rather, it is just an example of imperial policy of controlling other peoples and religions (Hag 1:1, 15; 2:8–9).[45] The ruined temple seemed sufficient to Judah (Hag 1:2, 3–4), but was not for Darius in terms of imperial administration (Hag 2:3, 8–9).[46] In accord with Darius's military strategy of the campaign against Egypt looming, the rebuilt Jerusalem temple would promptly enhance the produce of agriculture and devote supplies for the imperial army as it passes nearby.[47]

Along with restoring temples and their deities in locals, Darius also employed their own laws as administrative principles. This was developed through scribes *tupšar Ebabbar*, who were commissioned by the imperial kings.[48] The significance of scribes might go back to Cambyses. While in

43 "Hieroglyphic Inscription of Udjahorresnet," sourced from Brosius, *The Persian Empire from Cyrus II to Artaxerxes I*, 47–8 and Grabbe, *A History of the Jews and Judaism in the Second Temple Period*. Vol. 1, *Yehud*, 113. For secondary literature, see Briant, *From Cyrus to Alexander*, 478.

44 Peter Runham Ackroyd, "The Biblical Portrayal of a Ruler," in *AH*, Vol. 5, *The Root of the European Tradition* (ed. Heleen Sancisi-Weerdenburg and Jan Willem Drijvers; Leiden: Nederlands Instituut voor het Nabije Oosten, 1990), 5:1–16; Widengren, "The Persian Period," 489–538; Tadmor, "Judah," 261–96.

45 Wiesehöfer, *Ancient Persia*, 63–4. On imperial religious policy, see Grabbe, *A History of the Jews and Judaism in the Second Temple Period*. Vol. 1, *Yehud*, 209–37.

46 For exegeses on those verses, see Chapters 4 and 5 below.

47 Berquist, *Judaism in Persia's Shadow*, 53, 59–63.

48 CT 22,51, cited from C. V. M. Bongenaar, *The Neo-Babylonian Ebabbar Temple at Sippar: Its Administration and Its Prosopography* (Leiden: Nederlands Historisch-Archaeologisch Instituut te Istanbul, 1997), 60–1; CT 56,463, cited from Bongenaar, *The Neo-Babylonian Ebabbar Temple at Sippar*, 62–3; CT 55,627, cited from Bongenaar, *The Neo-Babylonian Ebabbar Temple at Sippar*, 63–4; SAM 1581, cited

Egypt, he destroyed some temples, and mocked Egyptian laws and custom which had been sacred.[49] This caused uproar in the entire land of Egypt. It made him name the Egyptian Udjahorresnet as a collaborator in order to quash this unrest. In the reign of Darius, Udjahorresnet continued to codify the laws that were in effect in Egypt and successfully emphasised Darius's fulfilment of the traditional ideals of Egyptian kingship.[50] Within Judah, the Kings Law in Ezra 7:26 was probably an indicator of the laws that were in place in Judah as a result of imperial codification.[51] This law presumably reflected earlier Judean traditions but was rendered into its final form by scribes in the service of imperial policies.

In the religious strategies of the temple rebuilding and the law codification, Darius followed strict protocol in foreign policies. The loyalty of subordinates was best procured if their cultural and religious environments which were linked with political issues were left undisturbed.[52] Evidence showed that things changed drastically when this loyalty was not given. An instance of revolts against Darius's rule was not only answered with military force, but its effects rippled into people's lives as well, such as in Naxos 507 BCE.[53]

---

from Bongenaar, *The Neo-Babylonian Ebabbar Temple at Sippar*, 64–6. According to Bongenaar, temple scribes generally assist temple administrators (*šatammu*) and mainly keep records in the temple archives in the Babylonian Eanna temple. See Bongenaar, *The Neo-Babylonian Ebabbar Temple at Sippar*, 56–68.

49 Strabo, *The Geography of Strabo* (Bohn's Classical Library Series; trans H. C. Hamilton; London: Bell, 1854–1857), XVII. 1.27, 46.

50 Bresciani states that the codification of Egypt's laws does not occur until 495 BCE. See Edda Bresciani, "The Persian Occupation of Egypt," in Gershevitch ed., *CHI*, Vol. 2, *The Median and Achaemenid Periods*, 502–28. Blenkinsopp drew this text to examine the activities of Ezra and Nehemiah. See Joseph Blenkinsopp, "The Mission of Udjahorresnet and Those of Ezra and Nehemiah," *JBL* 106 (1987): 409–21.

51 Gregor Ahn, "Toleranz und Reglement: Die Signifikanz Achaimenidischer Religionspolitik für den jüdisch-persischen Kulturkontakt," in *Religion und Religionskontakte im Zeitalter der Achämeniden* (ed. Reinhard Gregor Kratz; VGT 22; Gütersloh: Gütersloher Verlagshaus, 2002),195–206.

52 Heleen Sancisi-Weerdenburg, "The Quest for an Elusive Empire," in Sancisi-Weerdenburg and Kuhrt, eds, *AH*, Vol. 4, *Centre and Periphery*, 264–6.

53 *Hist.* VI, 94–6.

As I have surveyed above, Darius exalted his power effectively to govern every conquered region. As expressed in a number of temple restorations in the names of subordinates' deities. The temple rebuilding project was capable of demonstrating the religious and political image of Darius as the representative of local deities. By using religion as a political ruse, Darius even utilised the conceit of religious laws and ordered as controlling principles. Scribes (*tupšar Ebabbar*) who also served as imperial administrative delegates in the temple carried them out.

Temple Administration

The temple reconstruction projects among subordinates were also utilised to boost the financial powers of the empire. It was related to the fact that, as I have examined in Chapter 1 concerning the imperial economic structure, newly constructed temples organised the temple household in their regions respectively by managing land tenants and controlling agricultural affairs. The purpose of temple household was to enhance locals' riches and improve their welfare. Subsequently, the temples made great fortunes, inclusive of various kinds of taxes. Then, temples' treasuries were to be handed over to the great king as the local deities' representative.[54] Thus, the rebuilt temples managed local economies and carried out administrative centres in an economic manner.[55] Through this temple administrative strategy, Darius exercised the governance over the temple finances of locals and administered a huge quantity of imperial economic resources.

Examples of temple administration in the Neo-Babylonian period are available in the Eanna temple of Uruk, which was dedicated to the goddess Inanna-Ištar, the "Lady of Uruk." At the Eanna temple in the Neo-Babylonian period the *šatammu* (or *šangû*) administered the Eanna

54 Dandamaev, "State and Temple in Babylonia in the First Millennium B.C.," 272–3; Abraham, Business and Politics; Joachim Schaper, "The Temple Treasury Committee in the Times of Nehemiah and Ezra," *VT* 47 (1997): 200–6.

55 Briant, *From Cyrus to Alexander*, 70–6; Dandamaev, *A Political History of the Achaemenid Empire*, 103–77; Berquist, *Judaism in Persia's Shadow*, 51–8.

temple. The temple officer *šatammu* was in control of vast agricultural areas irrigated by a sophisticated system of canals in a network along the Euphrates. The Eanna dedicated itself primarily to growing barley and dates.[56] The other was the royal administrator, the *qīpu* who played a role of the imperial king's eyes and ears. The royal director *qīpu* had responsibility for the management of the royal treasury in the temple. His particular duty was to deliver the temple treasuries to the imperial kings. Likewise, the top administrators managed agricultural production including the sales of surpluses, and supervised the temple's possessions and personnel.[57]

One well-developed example of temple's administration can be taken in the Neo-Babylonian Ebabbar temple at Sippar:

> Letter of Nabû-balassu-iqbi, the temple administrator of Sippar, Bēl-iddina and Usallissu-Gula, the scribes to Ibna, who is in charge of the rent of Šamaš, our brother. May Bēl and Nabû ordain the health and life of our brother! Give 7;4.4.0 *kor* (=ca. 1448 1.) of barley and 0;2.5.0 *kor* (=ca. 102 1.) of emmer for the offering of the bakers of the first month of the 27th year to Ribâta, the performer of Nabû-balassu-iqbi.[58]

56 Joannes, *The Age of Empires*, 160–4; Martirossian, "Notes Concerning the Economic Activity of the Babylonian Temples in the First Millennium BC," 128–30. For Neo-Babylonian Agriculture, see Govert van Driel, "Neo-Babylonian Agriculture." *Annual of the British School at Athens* 83 (1988): 121–59; Govert van Driel, "Neo-Babylonian Sheep and Goats." *Annual of the British School at Athens* 88 (1993): 219–58.

57 YOS VI, 11, sourced from Beaulieu, *The Reign of Nabonidus King of Babylon 556–539 B.C.*, 117; YOS VI, 103, sourced from Beaulieu, *The Reign of Nabonidus King of Babylon 556–539 B.C.*, 196; YOS VI, 150, sourced from Beaulieu, *The Reign of Nabonidus King of Babylon 556–539 B.C.*, 193; YOS VI, 155, sourced from Beaulieu, *The Reign of Nabonidus King of Babylon 556–539 B.C.*, 194. For Neo-Babylonian legal documents, see Alfred Pohl, *Neubabylonische Rechtsurkunden aus den Berliner Staatlichen Museen I* (AnOr 8; Roma: Pontificio Istituto Biblico, 1933). As for secondary literature, see Joannes, *The Age of Empires*, 161–74; Briant, *From Cyrus to Alexander*, 72–3; Muhammad A. Dandamaev, "Neo-Babylonian and Achaemenid State Administration," in Lipschits and Oeming, eds, *Judah and the Judeans in the Persian Period*, 389–95.

58 CT 55, 32, sourced from Bongenaar, *The Neo-Babylonian Ebabbar Temple at Sippar*, 16–17. For other texts related to the temple administrator in Ebabbar, *Dar.* 281, sourced from Bongenaar, *The Neo-Babylonian Ebabbar Temple at Sippar*, 18–19; BM 75779, sourced from Bongenaar, *The Neo-Babylonian Ebabbar Temple at Sippar*,

The above letter is for the issue of barley for future offerings to be made by the bakers. For this, the temple administrator of Sippar and two scribes of Ebabbar sent a letter to Ibnâ who was in charge of the rent on temple land. The land tenant then handed over the barley and emmer.

The *qīpu* of Ebabbar can also be seen in the texts: the *qīpu* was involved in the management of the property of the temple, witnessed the leasing of land, organised tax delivery, and supervised temple personnel.[59] In this manner, the *qīpu* played a relative role of governor in the administrative authority. And he received a double portion of food supply per month:

> 66 *kor* (=ca. 11,800 1.) of barley and 66 *kor* (=ca. 11,800 1.) of dates, food rations for fifty workmen, two carpenters, one smith, ten guards, two food rations for *qīpu* and one for the chief of the oblates for th first and the second month is given to Bēl-ahhē-iqīša, the *qīpu* of Ebabbar, and the headmen. In toto 132 *kor* (=ca. 23,760 1.) of barley and dates went out of the big storehouse on the Euphrates.[60]

The economic affairs of the temples in the Achaemenids continued in much the same way as it had done during the Neo-Babylonian period.[61] In its agriculture, the temple administrator supervised an agricultural calendar and assessed the standing crops for the coming year.[62] Afterwards, the temple

---

19–20. For Bongenaar's examination of these texts, see Bongenaar, *The Neo-Babylonian Ebabbar Temple at Sippar*, 11–25. As another source for Ebabbar temple, see John MacGinnis, *Letter Orders from Sippar and the Administration of the Ebabbara in the Late-Babylonian Period* (Poznan: Bonami, 1995).

59 Bertin 1231, cited from Bongenaar, *The Neo-Babylonian Ebabbar Temple at Sippar*, 38–40; CT 56,610, cited from Bongenaar, *The Neo-Babylonian Ebabbar Temple at Sippar*, 42–3. For Bongenaar's survey on *qīpu*, see Bongenaar, *The Neo-Babylonian Ebabbar Temple at Sippar*, 34–46.

60 CT 56,633, cited from Bongenaar, *The Neo-Babylonian Ebabbar Temple at Sippar*, 35–8.

61 The officials, *šatammu* and *qīpu*, are firmly attested from the time of Cyrus and Cambyses. In Cyrus' years, Gurabu is given the position of governor of "Babylon and Beyond the River" (535 BCE). Oreotes is still in office in Sardis as the governor at the accession of Darius (*Hist.* III, 120, 126). As for Egypt, Cambyses appoints Aryandes as the governor. See Briant, *From Cyrus to Alexander*, 63–4.

62 YBT VII,168, cited from translated in Briant, *From Cyrus to Alexander*, 74; TCL XIII.150, cited from Briant, *From Cyrus to Alexander*, 74; YOS VII,128, cited from Briant, *From Cyrus to Alexander*, 74.

administrator calculated and drew the temple's revenues which were related to the imperial taxation from the land. Two imperial commissioners took charge of temple economy. In the reign of Cyrus, the imperial authorities *šatammu* and *qīpu* were commissioned to work exclusively on the reconstruction of the ruined Eanna temple and both delegates worked for the governance of the temple. As the high priest in the religious authority, the duty of the *šatammu* was to work exclusively on the project of economic restoration at the rebuilt Eanna temple.[63] There is no doubt that the temples took charge of not only financial affairs but also administrative businesses in the Achaemenids.

As taxes, the temple administrator collected silver, barley, dates, sweet date beer, goats, lambs, and oxen.[64] Then, those treasuries were passed over to the imperial court. Generally, the temples in the season of harvest extracted taxes from both their region and their inhabitants. Also, the temples repeatedly sent labourers to do building work at the royal palaces or to supply raw materials like wood and bricks for royal buildings.[65] They also furnished the royal administration with soldiers, at least providing campaign equipment for cavalry soldiers.[66]

63 Briant, *From Cyrus to Alexander*, 63–4, 71–6.

64 *Dar.* 156, sourced from Abraham, *Business and Politics*, 377–8; *Dar.* 206, sourced from Abraham, *Business and Politics*, 386–7; *Dar.* 268, sourced from Abraham, *Business and Politics*, 392–3; *Dar.* 315, sourced from Abraham, *Business and Politics*, 401–3; *Dar.* 342, sourced from Abraham, *Business and Politics*, 409–10; *Dar.* 359, sourced from Abraham, *Business and Politics*, 415–6; *Dar.* 390, sourced from Abraham, *Business and Politics*, 418–19; *Dar.* 437, sourced from Abraham, *Business and Politics*, 428–9; BM 30233, sourced from Abraham, *Business and Politics*, 206–8; BM 30591, sourced from Abraham, *Business and Politics*, 232–3; BM 30629, sourced from Abraham, *Business and Politics*, 234–5; BM 30639, sourced from Abraham, *Business and Politics*, 235–6; BM 30747, sourced from Abraham, *Business and Politics*, 240–1; BM 31347, sourced from Abraham, *Business and Politics*, 282–4; BM 31393, sourced from Abraham, *Business and Politics*, 287–9; BM 31572, sourced from Abraham, *Business and Politics*, 301–3; BM 32891, sourced from Abraham, *Business and Politics*, 328–9; BM 33112, sourced from Abraham, *Business and Politics*, 331–2; BM 33928, sourced from Abraham, *Business and Politics*, 339–41.

65 Briant, *From Cyrus to Alexander*, 73–4.

66 PF 1797 is referred to from Kuhrt, *The Persian Empire*, 627–8.

Obviously, the Jerusalem temple was financed by treasuries stocked enough for it to take the role of fiscal centre. When the Babylonian Judeans returned to Jerusalem, thus, Cyrus ordered the treasurer Mithradata, who might be charged with the management of the income and expenditure, by the king's order, to return the sacred vessels that Nebuchadnezzar took (Ezra 1:7–11; 5:14–15).[67] In a similar manner, Darius helped to build the Jerusalem temple with the royal treasury, concurrently charging them with returning his temple treasuries (Ezra 6:3–5).

According to Haggai, for this, Darius commissioned the governor (פחה) and the high priest (ןהכה לודגה, Hag 1:1, 12, 14).[68] Both of them were certainly involved in the temple restoration. There might be no doubt that the rebuilt Jerusalem temple was involved in economic affluence for the empire. Storerooms (לִשׁכה, Neh 10:4; 13:4) in the Jerusalem temple could be used to stock up with oil, wine, wheat, barley, fruits, sheep, goats and silver (Neh 10:32–39).[69] This suggests something of the temple economy of the Jerusalem temple.[70]

From the above survey, I have shown that the temple reconstruction project was devoted to the maximisation of imperial income. As a result, the restored temples controlled all agriculture activities from land tenants to trades throughout agricultural productions and made great fortunes consequently. This wealth was then transferred to the great king by various kinds of taxes. For the fiscal management of the temples, two imperial administrators, the *šatammu* and the *qīpu* were duly delegated to the temples that served as royal patrons. In relation to the Jerusalem temple rebuilding, roles similar to the *šatammu* and the *qīpu* could be seen in the governor (פחה) and the high priest (הכהן הגדול).

67 For the discussion on authenticity of Ezra 1:7–11; 5:14–15, see Lester L. Grabbe, *An Introduction to First Judaism: Jewish Religion and History in the Second Temple Period* (Edinburgh: T & T Clark, 1996), 1–2; Grabbe, *Judaism from Cyrus to Hadrian*, 126–9.

68 This will be discussed in Chapter 4 below.

69 Joachim Schaper, "The Jerusalem Temple as an Instrument of the Achaemenid Fiscal Administration," *VT* 45 (1995), 530–4.

70 See Chapters 4 and 5 below.

Administrative Reorganisation

The administrative reorganisation was exerted for the purpose of taxation. This administration was also used to fund the military exploits from subordinates.[71] Darius, by neighbouring region arrangement, first structured the whole territory into twenty administrative and military satrapies (אחשדרפן).[72] Considering different ethnic groups, he further divided satrapies into one hundred and twenty seven regions (מדינה, Esth 3:8, 12). This regional-ethnic group administration clearly continued but further developed the administrative system established by the Neo-Assyrians and the Neo-Babylonians. Already, at an early stage of the empires, conquered territories were subdivided into provincial districts for collecting various imperial taxes and for insuring the conscription of troops.[73]

To boost the royal treasury, Darius again assessed subordinates based on the importance of political and territorial advantages.[74] Then, they were classified into states, city-states or provinces which were obviously applied to different kinds of taxes. In correspondence, a satrap פחה was appointed to each satrapy (Ezra 5:3; Esth 3:12) and a semi-autonomous city-state king or a sub-governor פחה to each province. Despite both being called the same term פחה, the administrative functions of the satrap and the governor were completely different.[75] In this administrative organisation,

71 Grabbe, *A History of the Jews and Judaism in the Second Temple Period*. Vol. 1, *Yehud*, 260.

72 *Hist*. III, 89; Pierre Briant, "History of the Persian Empire 550–330 BC," in *Forgotten Empire: The World of Ancient Persia* (ed. John E. Curtis and Nigel Tallis; London: The Trustees of the British Museum, 2005), 15; Briant, *From Cyrus to Alexander*, 390–1.

73 Hoglund, *Achaemenid Imperial Administration*, 5–6, 29–36, 54–68, 208–25.

74 DB §7, sourced from Brosius, *The Persian Empire from Cyrus II to Artaxerxes I*, 30; *Hist*. III, 67; Marcus Junianus Justinus, *Justin: Epitome of the Philippic History of Pompeius Trogus* (Clarendon Ancient History Series; trans J. C. Yardly; Oxford: Clarendon, 1997), I, 9.12.

75 Amelie Kuhrt, "Babylonia from Cyrus to Xerxes," in Boardman, Lewis, Hammond, and Martin, eds, Vol. 4. *Persia, Greece and the Western Mediterranean*, 138; Israel Eph'al, "Changes in Palestine during the Persian Period in Light of Epigraphic

it is true that Judah was allotted as a politically small province having sub-governor (פחה) under the satrap (פחה) of "Beyond the River." Through biblical accounts, Judean governors of Sheshbazzar (during Cyrus reign, Ezra 5:15), Zerubbabel (520 BCE, Hag 1:1, 14; 2:2) and Nehemiah (445 BCE, Neh 5:14; 12:26) are seen.[76]

In terms of administration, the satrap functioned as the king's eyes and ears. He travelled within his regions and reported directly to the imperial kings. In the event of politically severe unrest in a province, however, its satrap reported it to the king, and he could order the satraps of the neighbouring satrapies to levy troops and quash the rebellion.[77] A satrap made political decisions at the regional level, but he had to consult with the king on any major issues.

Also, local leaders under the satrap had to report their issues to their satrap, who then reported to the emperor. This was likely the case with Tattenai, the satrap of "Beyond the River." He dealt with the disputes that broke out between the governors of provinces and reported to the king Darius. Then, Darius issued an order to investigate them (Ezra 5–6).

As local governors, Darius, considering maximum possible effectiveness, appointed an existing local royal lineage to its leader with allowance for the interests of local groups.[78] Among locals who had local royal leaders, states or city-states could enjoy and exercise the power and privileges delegated to them. This was not, however, an indication of provincial independence. The status of city-states depended on allegiance to imperial kings, including collection of taxes and mustering of military forces. On the provincial level the governor was merely responsible for collecting the

---

Sources," *IEJ* 48 (1998): 106–19; Israel Eph'al, "Syria-Palestine under Achaemenid Rule," in Boardman, Lewis, Hammond, and Martin, eds, *CAH*, Vol. 4, *Persia, Greece and the Western Mediterranean*, 151–6.

76 To fill the gap between Zerubbabel and Nehemiah, Avigad adds Elhanan, Yehoyezer, and *'ah'zai* based on impressions at Ramath Rahel. See Avigad, *Bullae and Seals from a Post-Exilic Judean Archive*.

77 The translation of an Aramaic document, DAE 67, is referred to from Briant, *From Cyrus to Alexander*, 364. For satrapal authorisation, see Brosius, *Persians*, 47–8; Eph'al, "Syria-Palestine under Achaemenid Rule," 153–6.

78 Berquist, *Judaism in Persia's Shadow*, 63–5; Brosius, *Persians*, 48.

taxes connected with the land.[79] It meant that, although some could have their own governmental structures in terms of political activities, all subordinates were substantially controlled and repressed by the imperial power.

By looking at administrative organisation in his territories, Darius maximised taxation for subordinates, and conducted military exploits through them. It led to the administration of one hundred and twenty seven regions (מדינה) of twenty satrapies (אחשדרפן) based on regional-ethnic groups. Subsequently, different kinds of taxes were applied to subordinates by the classification of regions. Judah was designated a province. For administrative efficiency, each satrapy was ruled by a satrap (פחה) and each local was managed by a governor (פחה). Satrap and sub-governor used the same term פחה but their function was entirely different. Notwithstanding this, unfailing loyalty was expected from all representatives. Thus, all of the king's delegates were usually appointed from among the royal families or among existing locals with royal lineages.

Achaemenid Economy

Fiscal Taxation

In accord with the administrative and military assessment, every subordinate was required to comply with the taxation of tribute (מדה), land tax (הלך) and poll tax (בלו, Ezra 4:13, 20; 7:24) which was of utmost importance to imperial treasuries.[80] In Persepolis monthly accounts are made on the basis of individual receipts, and are subsequently checked by a royal accountant. These administrative processes reflect a sophisticated system

79 Wiesehöfer, *Ancient Persia*, 63.

80 *Hist.* III, 89; Briant, *From Cyrus to Alexander*, 67–70, 393–4; Kuhrt, *The Persian Empire*, 672–3.

of record-keeping which ultimately derived from a centuries-old archival tradition of the Near East.[81]

Compulsory tribute (*mandattu* in Akkadian) was imposed on dependencies that Darius saw as having comparatively less political and military strength.[82] After fixing the tribute which subjects were to pay, Darius sent for the leading men of the provinces and asked them whether the tribute was not too onerous. Sometimes, Darius had the tribute decided by his satraps in order to see who set them at an exorbitant amount and then reduced their dues by half.[83] However, it was nothing but a taxation trick.

As taxes, poll tax (*biltu* in Akkadian) was of a portioned, fixed amount per individual in accordance with the census as opposed to a percentage of income.[84] Hence, poll taxes were one of the important sources of the royal treasury. There were references to poll tax in Judah (Ezra 4:13; 7:24 and Neh 5:15).[85] This tax was also required for the imperial campaign and ambitious construction project such as palaces and temples. Subjects had to provide military equipment and travel provisions for royal soldiers when they passed their territories.[86]

81 Some PF and PT texts in the reign of Darius are found in Kuhrt, *The Persian Empire*, 627–8, 641–4. The Persepolis Fortification Tablets (PF) record the allocation of food rations for feeding workers, supplying travellers to and from the palaces, as well as of donations to various gods. The Persepolis Treasury Tablets (PT) concern payments from the royal treasury. For more explanation of texts, see David Malcolm Lewis, "The Persepolis Fortification Texts," in Sancisi-Weerdenburg and Kuhrt, eds, *AH*, Vol. 4, *Centre and Periphery*, 1–6; Pierre Briant, Amelie Kuhrt, Margaret Cool Root, Heleen Sancisi-Weerdenburg, and Josef Wiesehöfer, eds, *AH*, Vol. 9, *Persepolis Seal Studies*. Leiden: Nederlands Instituut voor het Nabije Oosten, 1996/8.

82 *DCH*, Vol. 5, 176.

83 Plutarch, Moralia 172f; Polyaenus VII, 11.3, both of which are referred to from Kuhrt, *The Persian Empire*, 677.

84 *DCH*, Vol. 2, 143–4.

85 Williamson, *Ezra, Nehemiah*, 63, 103; Jacob Myers, *Ezra, Nehemiah* (AB, Vol. 14; Garden City, NY: Doubleday, 1965), 33–4, 37–8, 61–2. However, there is some uncertainty about what 40 shekels of silver signified. For this, see Williamson, *Ezra, Nehemiah*, 242–4; Myers, *Ezra, Nehemiah*, 133; Grabbe, *A History of the Jews and Judaism in the Second Temple Period*. Vol. 1, *Yehud*, 173, 303.

86 *Hist.* VII, 96; 118–9.

In Judah, there was a well-built road connecting Egypt with the centre of the empire via Jerusalem and Damascus. One route of this road led north toward Asia Minor and another east to Media.[87] Consequently, Judah had to contribute the essential provision to imperial armies who passing nearby Judah.[88] To do this well, Judah had to be able to produce a high amount of produce in advance of the army's arrival. Thus, through the Jerusalem temple reconstruction, Judah was asked to increase the produce of agriculture.

The land tax (*ilku* in Akkadian) comprised plant produce, animal produce and market dues which were applied to the cultivation of the land.[89] Every land holder had to pay the field tax or land revenue levied on every agricultural activity including manufacturing and commerce. This is because land belonged to the kings and was only allocated for maintenance of subordinates under the approval of their deities.[90] Subsequently, the assessment of crops became vitally important for the calculation of the fiscal gross in the imperial economy.

Minerals specific to regions were also imposed as the land tax. Silver came from India, Mede, and Babylon.[91] There was gold in Syspiritis in Anatolia, Niriz and Bactria both of which are in Iran, and Lydia in Asia Minor.[92] Iron deposits existed at Niriz, bitumen deposits, salt, and oil on the Euphrates,[93] and greywacke quarries in Egypt's eastern desert.[94] The copper and silver resources were in Cyprus, particularly in the realm of

87 Wiesehöfer, *Ancient Persia*, 53.

88 Berquist, *Judaism in Persia's Shadow*, 53. However, Grabbe argues that Judah would not be seen in any strategic reason. See Grabbe, *A History of the Jews and Judaism in the Second Temple Period*. Vol. 1, *Yehud*, 275.

89 Briant, *From Cyrus to Alexander*, 72–3.

90 Brosius, *Persians*, 51.

91 PT 85; PF 1342; PF 1357, all of which are sourced from Kuhrt, *The Persian Empire*, 716–9. On metals for tribute, see Briant, *From Cyrus to Alexander*, 406–10.

92 Strabo XI, 14.9; FGrH 688 F45 (26), both of which are cited from Kuhrt, *The Persian Empire*, 708.

93 *Hist.* VI, 119. 2–3.

94 "Hieroglyphic Egyptian Rock Inscription," sourced from Kuhrt, *The Persian Empire*, 707–8.

Kition.[95] Indeed, Darius's campaigns related to gold and silver in Asia Minor and Greece.[96]

Also, Darius received gifts in place of fixed tributes. Yet, it was only imposed on cooperative subjects making a great contribution towards political benefits and military campaigns.[97] Nonetheless, gifts even from provinces that paid mandatory tribute were generally sent as a gesture of loyalty. Precious and rare items or artefacts were usually sent;[98] Ethiopians on the border of Egypt provided gold, logs, five Ethiopian men, and twenty elephant tusks every two years and Colchians sent 100 boys and girls every four years.[99] The Indian king sent a tiny Indian bird whose excrement made one die painlessly, as if in one's sleep and a marvellous dye for the famous coloured textiles.[100]

On top of taxation, regions had to pay another tax to their governors. It was known as the word תרומה (Neh 10:40; 12:44; 13:5; Mal 3:8). The people in Judah paid this tax תרומה with the first fruits of all the fruit of every tree, the first-born cattle, and the first of their coarse meal, wine, and oil (Neh 5:17–18). In a depressed economy, Nehemiah emphasised that neither his servants nor he had received the food normally allotted to Judah's governor. This reveals that the תרומה could be administrated at local level by the governor.

In the survey of imperial taxation, I have shown that Darius applied a highly sophisticated taxation system for the imperial fiscal power. According to the administrative classes, subordinates had to pay the fixed tribute (מדה), land tax (הלך), poll tax (בלו), and gifts. The mandatory tribute was charged only to provinces like Judah which were politically weak. The poll tax and the land tax were levied on subject peoples who lived on or cultivated the land. Very cooperative subjects only offered arbitrary gifts of luxurious items

95 Strabo XV, 2.14.

96 Vickers, "Persian, Thracian and Greek Gold and Silver," 31, 36–7.

97 See Briant, *From Cyrus to Alexander*, 68–9, 395–9.

98 Strabo XV, 3.21.

99 *Hist.* III, 97.

100 Ael., *NA* 4.41, 46.

for the continued patronage. Apparently, these combined taxes played a great part in building up the royal treasury.

Corvee Obligation

The demand of man-power as a corvee system belonged to the הלך tax. For transport services, military services, and imperial constructions, it was one of the most ongoing and urgent government requirements. When land tenants were called up as one form of a corvee system, their land was leased out or passed on through inheritance to be worked, for land taxes were ceaselessly levied on land-workers.[101] However, all the corvee obligations could be discharged with a money payment which could be substituted with the בלו tax.[102]

When the harvest finished, grains, flour, fruits, oil, wine, beer, honey, and perfumes together with livestock of goats and sheep were offered for the royal treasury.[103] Large numbers of seedlings, possibly of fruit trees, and of animals were also issued. They were used for planting for the economy. With regard to the delivery of the products, landholders themselves had to directly carry or supply workers.[104] Alternatively, landholders would employ boat holders that the king grants as tenures.[105]

101 "Babylonian Tablet" which belongs to Darius II (423–405 BCE) at 421 BCE shows this appropriate duty. This text is found in Kuhrt, *The Persian Empire*, 722–3.

102 Ael., *NA* XV, 26; Siculus Diodorus, *Diodorus of Sicily*, Vols. 1–12 (trans C. H. Oldfather, Charles L. Sherman, C. Bradford Wells, Russel M. Geer, and F. R. Walton; Cambridge, Mass; London: Harvard University Press; Heinemann, 1933–1967), XVIII, 32.2; Babylonian tablet of VS VI, no. 160 is cited from Kuhrt, *The Persian Empire*, 708–9.

103 *Hist.* I, 192. Royal revenues from Egypt were recorded in Aramaic papyri which are found in Kuhrt, *The Persian Empire*, 681–703. Royal treasuries in Judah are in Neh 5:15; 10:40; 12:44; 13:5.

104 Borsipa, XI/21, sourced from Kuhrt, *The Persian Empire*, 708–9.

105 Arthur Ernest Cowley, *Aramaic Papyri of the Fifth Century B.C.* (Oxford: Clarendon Press, 1953), # 26.

On top of agricultural products, imperial taxation was normally delivered in coins. They were melted down again and stored in large earthenware jars in the treasuries. They were broken again and made into bullion whenever kings were in need of money.[106] Gold and silver coinages were introduced and minted according to an imperial standard. For a universal currency, Darius introduced the daric.[107]

In order to ensure a productive administration, Darius drew on an already existing road system which connected Asia Minor and Neo-Assyria. He further established the Royal Road to connect the main cities of each satrapy and royal centre across the empire.[108] It stretched about 2,700 km between Susa in southwest Persia and Sardis in western Anatolia. The building and maintenance of a road system required considerable work.[109] For this, subordinates had to repeatedly furnish the required wood and bricks, together with forced labour, for three months at least in turn.[110]

The Royal Road facilitated an effective postal system within the imperial territories.[111] It ensured the fast and safe progress of the king's

106 BE X 97, sourced from Kuhrt, *The Persian Empire*, 680–1.

107 *Hist.* VIII, 98. Apparently, Croesus of Lydia introduced gold and silver coins as state currency. Cyrus later introduces the Lydian innovation into the empire. Yet, it is Darius who first officially applies coinage as a standard transnational currency. For coinage, see Heleen Sancisi-Weerdenburg, "Darius I and the Persian Empire," in Sasson, ed., *CANE*, Vol. 2, 1042–3; Karen Farrokh, *Shadows in the Desert: Ancient Persia at War* (Oxford: Osprey, 2007), 65.

108 Diod. XIX, 19.2; *Hist.* V, 52–4. The Achaemenids maintain road stations at intervals of 24 km, which provided food and shelter for officials carrying messages to and from the king. For the Achaemenid road system, see Farrokh, *Shadows in the Desert*, 64; Gary H. Oller, "Messengers and Ambassadors in Ancient Western Asia," in Sasson, ed., *CANE*, Vol. 3, 1465–74.

109 Ael., *NA* XV, 26; Diod. XVIII, 32.2; BM 79746, sourced from Kuhrt, *The Persian Empire*, 710; VS VI, no. 160, sourced from Kuhrt, *The Persian Empire*, 708–9.

110 BM 49718, cited from Kuhrt, *The Persian Empire*, 711.

111 *Hist.* V: 52–4; Diod. XIX, 19.2. More primary sources for Achaemenid route and communication networks, see Kuhrt, *The Persian Empire*, 730–62. As for secondary document, see Andrew R. Meadows, "The Administration of the Achaemenid Empire," in Curtis and Tallis, eds, *Forgotten Empire*, 181–209; Nigel Tallis, "Transport and Warfare," in Curtis and Tallis, eds, *Forgotten Empire*, 210–35.

messengers.[112] This Road was also useful for transportation and trades.[113] Thus, it was closely monitored by the king's watchers on account of protection. Caravans were undoubtedly escorted by armed men (Neh 2:9). Ezra, fearing attack, made the same journey accompanied by many Judeans entrusted with gold and riches for the temple of YHWH (Ezra 8:22, 31). Nehemiah's travel to Judah was also protected (Neh 2:7).

Darius also exploited the naval route at the government's expense in order to discover trade routes, particularly off the eastern Mediterranean coast.[114] Another route went from the Red Sea to the Gulf of Oman and from there via the Indian Ocean to the mouth of the River Indus. He also dug a canal from the Nile River to the Red Sea,[115] and set up boat-bridges along many rivers that the Royal Road crossed.[116] Taxes were then levied on these transits. One case was on the Nile, where the Phoenician boats paid 10 per cent of each product carried (wine, wood, metals such as bronze, iron, tin, wool, clay) from Samos.[117]

In addition, subject people could at any time be summoned to the imperial army. They were usually stationed in a garrison anywhere in the empire.[118] One of these garrisons was probably the Judean garrison at Elephantine. They manned the frontier on the Nile like a considered regular army. An Aramaic text from Egypt suggests that the task of equipping the

112 *Cyr.* VIII, 6.17–18; *Hist.* VIII, 98; 239.2–3; PF 1315, sourced from Kuhrt, *The Persian Empire*, 754; PF 1335, sourced from Kuhrt, *The Persian Empire*, 755; PF 1672, sourced from Kuhrt, *The Persian Empire*, 755; BM 74463, sourced from Kuhrt, *The Persian Empire*, 709.

113 *Cyr.* VI, 2.36; *Hist.* VII, 131; PFa19; 30, sourced from Kuhrt, *The Persian Empire*, 746.

114 Potts, "Distant Shores," 1451–63; Vickers, "Interactions between Greeks and Persians," 253–62.

115 DZc §3, cited from Kuhrt, *The Persian Empire*, 485–6 and Brosius, *The Persian Empire from Cyrus II to Artaxerxes I*, 47. For imperial canal's construction, see Christopher Tuplin, "Darius's Suez Canal and Persian Imperialism," in Sancisi-Weerdenburg and Kuhrt, eds, *AH*, Vol. 6, *Asia Minor and Egypt*, 237–83.

116 *Hist.* IV, 87–8, 141; BM 74463, sourced from Kuhrt, *The Persian Empire*, 709.

117 Cowley, *Aramaic Papyri of the Fifth Century B.C.*, # 72. For comments of this text, see Briant, *From Cyrus to Alexander*, 385.

118 Young, "Persian," 298; Young, "The Consolidation of the Empire," 91–2.

garrison soldiers was very expensive: for twelve soldiers, this equipment could amount to 1 mule, 12 blankets, 12 cuirasses, 12 helmets, 12 travel bags, 12 pairs of shoes, 1 pi oil, 2 pi salt and 2 pi cress. There is no doubt that the Judean garrison at Elephantine would likewise be fed by Egypt.[119] In 410 BCE, thus, a group of Egyptians defaced the Judean temple in Elephantine.[120]

From the survey of corvee obligations, it is clear that subject peoples were quite frequently summoned through forced labours to work at continuing and compelling tasks undertaken by the imperial administration. They were used for military services, for building fields and even for tax deliveries. Even during farming season, peasants were not exempted in corvee duty. However, they could avoid this service by paying a monetary tax.

Taxation in "Beyond the River"

Darius organised his empire for taxation purposes and levied the taxation of 350 talents on "Beyond the River" separate from "Babylonia" (Ezra 6:8):

> The fifth satrapy included contains the whole of Phoenicia and that part of Syria which is called Palestine, and Cyprus, from the town of Posideium, which was founded by Amphilochus, the son of Amphiareus, on the border between the Cilicia and Syria, as far as Egypt — omitting Arabian territory, which was free of tax — came 350 talents.[121]

Notwithstanding this, the title "Babylonia and Beyond the River" appeared in Babylonian legal documents from the years 535–486 BCE. Gubaru

119 *Dar.* 253, sourced from Kuhrt, *The Persian Empire*, 715–17.

120 The translation of "a demotic papyrus at Elephantine," PBerlin 13582, sourced from Kuhrt, *The Persian Empire*, 706. For Judean garrison at Elephantine, see Reinhard G. Kratz, "The Second Temple of Jeb of Jerusalem," in Lipschits and Oeming, eds, *Judah and the Judeans in the Persian Period*, 247–64.

121 *Hist.* III, 91.

(535–525 BCE),[122] Ushtani (521–525 BCE),[123] and *Hu-ta-*[*x-*ʾ] son of *Pa-ga-ka-an-na* (486 BCE)[124] explicitly occurred as governors of "Babylonia and Beyond the River."[125] Meanwhile, Tattenai (circa 518–502 BCE), the governor of "Beyond the River" was known from Darius's reign (Ezra 5:3).[126] It looks likely that "Beyond the River" constituted a tributary subunit within the vast satrapy of "Babylonia and Beyond the River."[127] These accounts certainly show how incisive the provinces could find Darius's reform of the administrative and tributary system.[128] "Beyond the River" had its own governor again, probably instated by Xerxes (486–465 BCE) after Shamash-eriba's revolt in Babylon.[129] "Beyond the River" was later known as Coele-Syria which included all the land on the west side of the Euphrates as far as Egypt.[130]

The peoples being grouped together into "Beyond the River," according to Herodotus, were Syrians, Phoenicia, "that part of Syria which was called Palestine," and the Arabs.[131] Palestine extended from Phoenicia to the border of Gaza. Palestinian ethnicity applied largely to Judah and Samaria. However,

122 Pohl, *Neubabylonische Rechtsurkunden aus den Berliner Staatlichen Museen I*, 43; TCL XIII. 168, referred to from Eph'al, "Syria-Palestine under Achaemenid Rule," 154.

123 *Dar*. 27, sourced from Eph'al, "Syria-Palestine under Achaemenid Rule," 154.

124 BM 74554, sourced from Kuhrt, *The Persian Empire*, 815–16.

125 See Eph'al, "Syria-Palestine under Achaemenid Rule," 154; Briant, *From Cyrus to Alexander*, 393–4.

126 *Hist*. III, 91–2. For argumentation on Babylonian legal documents which bear witnesses to a governor of "Babylonia and Beyond the River" till 486 BCE, see Eph'al, "Changes in Palestine," 106–19; Eph'al, "Syria-Palestine under Achaemenid Rule," 139–64; Briant, *From Cyrus to Alexander*, 390–4.

127 See Briant, *From Cyrus to Alexander*, 393–4.

128 See Wiesehöfer, *Ancient Persia*, 63; Grabbe, *A History of the Jews and Judaism in the Second Temple Period*. Vol. 1, *Yehud*, 133–66.

129 Eph'al states that Herodotus referred to an administrative measure carried out after 486 BCE. See Eph'al, "Syria-Palestine under Achaemenid Rule," 153–5.

130 See Briant, *From Cyrus to Alexander*, 393; Grabbe, *A History of the Jews and Judaism in the Second Temple Period*. Vol. 1, *Yehud*, 134; Eph'al, "Syria-Palestine under Achaemenid Rule," 154.

131 *Hist*. II, 46–7, 104; VII, 89.

there were also peoples who were designated "Syrians" encompassing northern Sinai and the west of the Euphrates up to the Cyprus border.[132] There is an interesting claim about these "Syrians":[133] from the eighth BC century the Greeks had closely traded with Assyria, which was in immediate proximity to the south east of Syria-Palestine.[134] In a cultural similarity, this area and its indigenous population were evidently well known to the Greeks, which led to the Greeks calling the Assyrians Syrians.[135] Therefore, the term, "Syrians," in Herodotus should be applied during the Greek period.

According to the sources for the Achaemenid period "the Arabs" inhabited the area between Egypt and the Euphrates.[136] This wide expanse of the Arabs in southern Palestine and northern Sinai possessed immense strategic and economic importance in the context of the Achaemenid Empire for the control of Egypt and Arabian trade.[137] The Achaemenid authorities preferred to grant control of all the emporia along the coast, from Gaza to Ienysus, to the king of the Arabs and entrusted him with collecting the customs duty for spices.[138]

However, Gaza had been one of the cities of the Philistinians, since the Judean kingdom period in the Hebrew Bible. Gaza was constantly named a Philistine city throughout the Assyrian and Babylonian records.[139]

132 Grabbe argues that "Beyond the River" included all the land on the west side of the Euphrates as far as Egypt. See Grabbe, *A History of the Jews and Judaism in the Second Temple Period*. Vol. 1, *Yehud*, 133–66.

133 On the "Syrians" of northern Sinai, see *Hist*. III, 5; of the west of the Euphrates, see *Hist*. I. 72, 76; *Hist*. II. 104; *Hist*. III. 90; *Hist*. VII. 63.

134 Alan B. Lloyd, *Herodotus Book II: Commentary 99–182* (Leiden; New York; København; Köln: Brill, 1988), 21–5; Eph'al, "Changes in Palestine," 109–10; Eph'al, "Syria-Palestine under Achaemenid Rule," 153–5.

135 Alan B. Lloyd, *Herodotus Book II: Commentary 1–98* (Leiden: Brill, 1976), 214–9; Alan B. Lloyd, *Herodotus Book II: Introduction* (Leiden: Brill, 1975), 147–8.

136 *Hist*. III, 5 and 8.

137 See Briant, *From Cyrus to Alexander*, 45; Eph'al, "Syria-Palestine under Achaemenid Rule," 161–3.

138 *Hist*. III, 4–9; Diod. XV, 2.4; XIII, 46.6.

139 Strange, "The Philistine City-States," in Hansen, ed., *Comparative Study of Thirty-State Cultures*, 135–7; Larsen, "The City-States of the Early Neo-Babylonian Period," in Hansen, ed., *Comparative Study of Thirty-State Cultures*, 118–27.

In Darius's time, the Arabs' camel caravans crossed the vast desert area to the Palestinian coastal port, Gaza, or up to the Nile Delta.[140] The Arabs certainly profited from their role as intermediaries between Mesopotamia and the Mediterranean ports, principally Gaza.[141] Then, Gaza was largely populated by Arabs, particularly merchants, since this place was the principal outlet for Arabian trade.[142] Thus Gaza became a fortified place of great importance that was controlled by the Arabs.[143]

Within the fifth satrapy the Books of Ezra and Nehemiah mention other ethnicities: Ammon in the east (Ezra 9:1) and Moab (Ezra 2:6; 8:4; 10:30) in the southern region. However, regions of Moab and Edom were already annexed to the Arabs, and Ammon to Samaria.[144] They are merely ethnic names.

From epigraphic and material finds on Palestine and Phoenicia, the satrapy of "Beyond the River" included the Phoenicians, the Philistinians, the Arabs, Judah, and Samaria.[145] Particularly, Darius was keenly interested in the areas of the Negev, Sinai, and the former Edomite region, in hope of perpetuating the goodwill of the Arabs. They assisted the imperial army in approaching Egypt by supplying it with water.[146] They also played a great role as intermediaries between Egypt and the Euphrates.[147] The Arabs were in a like manner exempted from the assessed tribute.[148] Instead, they

140 See Briant, *From Cyrus to Alexander*, 378.

141 See Briant, *From Cyrus to Alexander*, 53–4, 717.

142 See Briant, *From Cyrus to Alexander*, 45.

143 See Briant, *From Cyrus to Alexander*, 275, 717.

144 David A. Graf, "Arabia during Achaemenid Times," in Sancisi-Weerdenburg and Kuhrt, eds, *AH*, Vol. 4, *Centre and Periphery*, 131–48; Eph'al, "Syria-Palestine under Achaemenid Rule," 163–4.

145 See Eph'al, "Changes in Palestine," 139–43, 156–64; Eph'al, "Syria-Palestine under Achaemenid Rule," 143–4, 147–8.

146 An imperial garrison is also posted in Arad. See Ephraim Stern, "The Archaeology of Persian Palestine," in *CHJ*, Vol. 1, *Introduction*, 113; Eph'al, "Syria-Palestine under Achaemenid Rule," 147–52; *Hist.* III, 5.3–7.1; Kuhrt, *The Ancient Near East*, 661–4.

147 See Eph'al, "Syria-Palestine under Achaemenid Rule," 162–3; Briant, *From Cyrus to Alexander*, 717.

148 See Briant, *From Cyrus to Alexander*, 391–3; Eph'al, "Syria-Palestine under Achaemenid Rule," 153–6.

contributed 1,000 talents of incense as "gifts" to the royal treasury for annual trade.[149] In the time of Nehemiah, we can see Geshem the Arabs (Neh 6:1).

The Phoenicians, living in Tyre, Sidon, Bylos, and Adarus, maintained their existence as vassal kingdoms.[150] They offered two warships indispensable to the Persian army, which was ill-equipped for naval warfare. In particular, when Darius invaded Greece, the participation of Phoenician fleets was of paramount importance.[151] With them and their merchantmen, the Phoenicians made full trades loaded with every luxury goods.[152] They also had granaries for the use of imperial armies.[153] With patronages in naval wars and trades, the Phoenician city-states could enjoy a unique political status, involving rule by local dynasties.

Along the Mediterranean coast Gaza, Ashdod, and Ashkelon consistently maintained their political power.[154] Gaza became a port of great importance to the Arabs, and in Judith 3:1 Ashdod is mentioned as an important city for the Phoenicians. Herodotus, however, referred to the Philistine cities Syria or Syrians of Palestine in order to separate the inhabitants of the Phoenicians.[155] Also, Gaza and Ashdod cast coins and engraved city names ע, עז, or עזה, or אשדד, אש, or א.[156] Accordingly, it may be assumed that the Philistine cities possessed administrative

149 *Hist.* III, 91.

150 D. R. ap-Thomas, "The Phoenicians," in *People of Old Testament Times* (ed. Donald John Wiseman; Oxford: Clarendon, 1973), 259–86.

151 *Hist.* III, 19; 136; V, 108; 112; VI, 6; 14. For imperial navy, see H. T. Wallinga, "The Ancient Persian Navy and Its Predecessors," in *AH*, Vol. 1, *Sources, Structures and Synthesis* (ed. Heleen Sancisi-Weerdenburg; Leiden: Nederlands Instituut voor het Nabije Oosten, 1987), 47–78; Josette Elayi, "The Phoenician Cities in the Achaemenid Period: Remarks on the Present State and Prospects of Research," in Sancisi-Weerdenburg and Kuhrt, eds, *AH*, Vol. 4, *Centre and Periphery*, 227–37.

152 See Eph'al, "Syria-Palestine under Achaemenid Rule," 156–7.

153 Diod. XV, 41.3.

154 See Eph'al, "Changes in Palestine," 139–43, 156–64; Eph'al, "Syria-Palestine under Achaemenid Rule," 143–4, 147–8.

155 *Hist.* II, 46–7, 104; VII, 89.

156 See Eph'al, "Changes in Palestine," 139–43, 156–64.

segregation within the Achaemenid ethnic-national administrative policy.[157] Certainly, Gaza, Ashdod, and Ashkelon, took control of the logistics base for the imperial army with their ships during Achaemenid rule (Neh 4:1; 13:23; Zech 9:5). Subsequently, they received equal benefits to the Phoenician city-states.[158] They co-operated with the incense trade of the Arabs who controlled the desert region between Gaza and the Egyptian border.[159]

Evidence of the existence for the provinces of Judah and Samaria can be found in their stamped coins and seal impressions which have been unearthed in various excavations.[160] However, there is no mention of services or of contributions of logistical bases, army posts, or warship providers by the provinces of Judah and Samaria. Rather, both provinces traditionally thrived on agriculture (see Chapter 1 above). With their plentiful produce, Judah and Samaria were to supply daily provisions to cavalry soldiers passing near their territories on imperial expeditions.[161] Transit roads within their regions from Sais or Memphis in Egypt to the coastline of Tyro and Damascus, meeting the road from Sardis to Susa, supported their provincial commissions.[162]

157 See Eph'al, "Changes in Palestine," 139–43, 156–64; Eph'al, "Syria-Palestine under Achaemenid Rule," 143–4, 147–8.

158 Epraim Stern, "New Evidence on the Administrative Division Palestine in the Persian Period," in Sancisi-Weerdenburg and Kuhrt, eds, *AH*, Vol. 4, *Centre and Periphery*, 221–6; H. J. Katzenstein, "Gaza in the Persian Period," *Trans* 1 (1989): 67–9. On question of the status of the Philistinians, see Grabbe, *A History of the Jews and Judaism in the Second Temple Period*. Vol. 1, *Yehud*, 34–42; 159–62.

159 Graf, "Arabia," 142–3; Kuhrt, *The Ancient Near East*, 690; Meshorer, "The Mints of Ashdod and Ascalon during the Late Persian Period," 287–91; Gitler, "New Fourth Century BC coins from Ascalon," 1–6.

160 Eph'al, "Changes in Palestine," 106–19; Eph'al, "Syria-Palestine under Achaemenid Rule," 139–64.

161 Hoglund, "The Achaemenid Context," 54–68; Hoglund, *Achaemenid Imperial Administration*, 1–28.

162 Wright states that the city wall in Achaemenid Jerusalem creates military space (Neh 2). John W. Wright, "A Tale of Three Cities: Urban Gates, Squares and Power in Iron Age II, Neo-Babylonian and Achaemenid Judah," in *Second Temple Studies*.

Concerning the tribute (מדה) of 350 silver talents per annum (Ezra 4:13; 6:8),[163] the Phoenician and the Philistine city states could support their portions of the tribute through trades between Egypt to the west and Mesopotamia to the east. The provinces Judah and Samaria were also obliged to contribute. Both provinces, traditionally agricultural regions, were evidently required to increase their agricultural produce.[164] Accordingly, they had to produce enough to sustain economic stability and enrich treasuries for their taxes.

From the study of imperial administration, it is clear that the satrapy "Beyond the River" was composed of the Phoenician city-states, the Philistinian city-states, the Arabs, Judah, and Samaria. With their warships, logistic ships, or logistic base, the Phoenicians, the Philistinians, and the Arabs were of the utmost strategic importance with regard to the Eastern Mediterranean seaboard and army posts as the focal point in monitoring Egypt. Consequently, the Arabs, the Phoenicians, and the Philistinians were legitimised and prospered, existing in the centres of the larger imperial economic structure. Meanwhile, Judah and Samaria as agrarian societies were nothing but commissary bases.

Conclusion

I have discussed in some detail both Darius and the Achaemenid Empire from a political, military, and economic point of view. Darius's accession to the Persian throne was in effect a royal coup because through it Darius and his Achaemenid family became the royal family of Persia.

Darius's lack of any prior right to become ruler of the Persians provoked the uprisings against him throughout the conquered territories.

Vol. 3, *Studies in Politics, Class and Material Culture* (ed. Philip R. Davies and John M. Halligan; JSOTSup 340; Sheffield: Sheffield Academic Press, 2002), 42–7.

163 *Hist.* III, 89–95.

164 See Chapter 3 below.

The recurring rebellions, particularly in the crucial regions of Babylon and Egypt, caused Darius tremendous troubles. Darius certainly devised propaganda which was effective enough to put the revolts down. It was founded on the temple rebuilding or restoring concept, using the religion of each subordinate as a political ruse. Darius was identified as the representative of each region's deity.

This ideological concept also worked very well in ensuring absolute loyalty from subordinates which was essential for the territorial expansion. With this allegiance, Darius added the Aegean Islands and north-west Asia Minor to his dominion.

The magnitude of Darius's achievement should also be measured by the rebuilding of temples. Throughout a temple rebuilding project, Darius activated the temple economy in which the temples being sanctioned by Darius supervised the economy of their regions and enhanced their income, and then devoted their fund to the royal income. In this temple fiscal administrative system, Darius integrated the economy of subordinates into the Achaemenid Empire. If as a well functioning economic institution the temple was in trouble, the whole economy could suffer.

Darius also set up administrative reorganisation for levying the taxes of tribute, poll tax, and land tax. One hundred and twenty seven provincial governorships within twenty satrapies were assessed each for taxes. The imperial treasury in Babylon was governed by the imperial authorities of *šatammu* and *qīpu* from the temples.

There is no doubt that the rebuilding of the Jerusalem temple was important for the imperial economic structure, as Judah functioned as a military buffer zone between Mesopotamia and Egypt. Thus, the Jerusalem temple to be rebuilt was to increase domestic income and then greatly boost the income of the royal power. The Jerusalem temple economy was to be incorporated into Darius's economy. For this purpose, Darius commissioned two imperial delegates, the governor and the high priest to oversee the work of rebuilding the Jerusalem temple (Hag 1:1, 12, 14).

For taxation, in the satrapy of "Beyond the River" the Phoenicians, the Philistinians, Judah, and Samaria were to pay the mandatory tribute of 350 silver talents every year omitting the Arab. From the Bible, the poll tax and the land tax were also applied to Judah (Ezra 4:13, 20; 7:24). In an imperial economic system, Judah was just assigned as a commissary base. Subsequently, politically weak, Judah had to be loyal to be an imperial patron both in the temple rebuilding project and in the imperial taxation system.

Bibliography

Abraham, Kathleen. *Business and Politics under the Persian Empire: The Financial Dealings of Marduk-nāsir-apli of the House of Egibi (521–487 B.C.E).* Bethesda, MD: CDL, 2004.

Ackroyd, Peter Runham. "The Biblical Portrayal of a Ruler." Pages 1–16 in Sancisi-Weerdenburg and Drijvers, eds, *AH*. Vol. 5, *The Root of the European Tradition.*

Ahn, Gregor. "Toleranz und Reglement: Die Signifikanz achaimenidischer Religionspolitik für den jüdisch-persischen Kulturkontakt." Pages 191–209 in Kratz, ed., *Religion und Religionskontakte im Zeitalter der Achämeniden.*

Ap-Thomas, D. R. "The Phoenicians." Pages 259–86 in *People of Old Testament Times.* Edited by Donald John Wiseman. Oxford: Clarendon, 1973.

Avigad, Nahman. *Bullae and Seals from a Post-Exilic Judean Archive.* Qedem 4: Institute of Archaeology. Jerusalem: The Hebrew University of Jerusalem Press, 1976.

Balcer, Jack Martin. "The East Greek under Persian Rule: A Reassesment." Pages 57–65 in Sancisi-Weerdenburg and Kuhrt, eds, *AH*. Vol. 6, *Asia Minor and Egypt.*

——. *Herodotus & Bisitun: Problems in Ancient Persian Historiography.* H-E 49. Stuttgart: Steiner-Verlag-Wiesbaden-GmbH, 1987.

Bar-Asher, Moshe, Dalit Rom-Shiloni, Emanuel Tov, and Nili Wazana, eds. *Shai le-Sara Japhet: Studies in the Bible, its Exegesis and its Language.* Jerusalem: The Bialik Institute, 2007.

Barstad, Hans M. "Haggai Among the Prophets: An Example of Prophetic Continuity in the Hebrew Bible." Pages 265–83 in Bar-Asher, Rom-Shiloni, Tov, and Wazana, eds, *Shai le-Sara Japhet: Studies in the Bible, its Exegesis and its Language.*

Beaulieu, Paul-Alian. *The Reign of Nabonidus King of Babylon 556–539 B.C.* New Haven; London: Yale University Press, 1989.

Berquist, Jon L. *Judaism in Persia's Shadow: A Social and Historical Approach.* Minneapolis: Fortress, 1995.

Bickerman, Elias Joseph. "Calendar and Chronology." Pages 60–9 in Davies and Finkelstein, eds, *CHJ*. Vol. 1, *Introduction.*

Blenkinsopp, Joseph. "The Mission of Udjahorresnet and Those of Ezra and Nehemiah." *JBL* 106 (1987): 409–21.

Bongenaar, A. C. V. M. *The Neo-Babylonian Ebabbar Temple at Sippar: Its Administration and its Prosopography*. Leiden: Nederlands Historisch-Archaeologisch Instituut Te Istanbul, 1997.

Bresciani, Edda. "The Persian Occupation of Egypt." Pages 502–28 in Gershevitch, ed., *CHI*. Vol. 2, *The Median and Achaemenid Periods*.

Briant, Pierre. "History of the Persian Empire 550–330 BC." Pages 12–17 in Curtis and Tallis, *Forgotten Empire*.

——. *From Cyrus to Alexander: A History of the Persian Empire*. Translated by Peter T. Daniels. Winona Lake, IN: Eisenbrauns, 2002.

Brosius, Maria. *Persians: An Introduction*. London: Routledge, 2006.

——. *The Persian Empire from Cyrus II to Artaxerxes I*. LACTOR 16. Kingston: The London Association of Classical Teachers, 2000.

Calmeyer, Peter. "Greek Historiography and Achaemenid Reliefs." Pages 11–26 in Sancisi-Weerdenburg and Kuhrt, eds, *AH*. Vol. 9, *Persepolis Seal Studies*.

Cook, John Manuel. "The Rise of the Achaemenids and Establishment of their Empire." Pages 200–91 in Gershevitch, ed., *CHI*. Vol. 2, *The Median and Achaemenid Periods*.

Cowley, Arthur Ernest. *Aramaic Papyri of the Fifth Centuty BC*. Oxford: Clarendon, 1923. [=*AP*]

Curtis, John E., ed. *Mesopotamia and Iran in the Persian Period: Conquest and Imperialism 539–331 BC: of a Seminar in Memory of Vladimir G. Lukonin*. London: British Museum, 1997.

—— and St John Simpson., eds. *The World of Achaemenid Persia: History, Art and Society in Iran and the Ancient Near East*. Proceedings of a Conference at the British Museum 29th September – 1st October 2003; London; New York: Tauris, 2010.

—— and Nigel Tallis., eds. *Forgotten Empire: The World of Ancient Persia*. London: The Trustees of the British Museum, 2005.

Dandamaev, Muhammad A. "Neo-Babylonian and Achaemenid State Administration." Pages 373–98 in Lipschits and Oeming, eds, *Judah and the Judeans in the Persian Period*.

——. *A Political History of the Achaemenid Empire*. Translated by W. J. Vogelsang. Leiden: Brill, 1989.

——. "State and Temple in Babylonia in the First Millennium B.C." Pages 589–96 in Lipinski ed., *State and Temple Economy in the Ancient Near East*. Vol. 2.

Diodorus, Siculus. *Diodorus of Sicily*. Vols. 1–12. Translated by C. H. Oldfather, Charles L. Sherman, C. Bradford Wells, Russel M. Geer, and F. R. Walton. Cambridge, Mass; London: Harvard University Press; Heinemann, 1933–1967. [=*Diod*]

Driel, Govert van. "Neo-Babylonian Sheep and Goats." *BSA* 88 (1993): 219–58.

——. "Neo-Babylonian Agriculture." *BSA* 83 (1988): 121–59.

Dusinberre, Elspeth R. M. *Aspect of Empire in Achaemenid Sardis*. Cambridge: Cambridge University Press, 2003.

Elayi, Josette. "The Phoenician Cities in the Achaemenid Period: Remarks on the Present State and Prospects of Research." Pages 227–37 in Sancisi-Weerdenburg and Kuhrt, eds, *AH*. Vol. 4, *Centre and Periphery*.

Eph'al, Israel. "Changes in Palestine during the Persian Period in Light of Epigraphic Sources." *IEJ* 48 (1998): 106–19.

——. "Syria-Palestine under Achaemenid Rule." Pages 139–64 in Boardman, Lewis, Hammond, and Martin, eds, *CAH*. Vol. 4, *Persia, Greece and the Western Mediterranean c. 525–479 B.C.*

Farrokh, Kaveh. *Shadows in the Desert: Ancient Persia at War*. Oxford: Osprey, 2007.

Frye, Richard Nelson. "Cyrus the Mede and Darius the Achaemenid?" Pages 17–20 in Curtis and Simpson, eds, *The World of Achaemenid Persia*.

——. *The History of Ancient Iran*. Munich: Beck, 1984.

Grabbe, Lester L. *A History of the Jews and Judaism in the Second Temple Period*. Vol. 1, *Yehud: A History of the Persian Province of Judah*. LSTS. London; New York: T & T Clark, 2004.

______. *An Introduction to First Century Judaism: Jewish Religion and History in the Second Temple Period*. Edinburgh: T & T Clark, 1996.

______. *Judaism from Cyrus to Hadrian*. London: SCM, 1992.

Graf, David A. "Arabia during Achaemenid Times." Pages 131–48 in Sancisi-Weerdenburg and Kuhrt, eds, *AH*. Vol. 4, *Centre and Periphery*.

Hansen, Mogens Herman, ed. *A Comparative Study of Thirty-State Cultures: An Investigation Conducted by the Copenhagen Polis Centre*. Historisk-filosofiske Skrifter 21. Copenhagen: C. A. Reitzels Forlag, 2000.

Hoglund, Kenneth G. *Achaemenid Imperial Administration in Syria-Palestine and the Missions of Ezra and Nehemiah*. SBL Dissertation Series 125. Atlanta, GA: Scholars Press, 1992.

——. "The Achaemenid Context." Pages 54–72 in Davies, ed., *Second Temple Studies*. Vol. 1, *Persian Period*.

Joannes, Francis. *The Age of Empires: Mesopotamia in the First Millennium BC*. Edinburgh: Edinburgh University Press, 2004.

Justinus, Marcus Junianus. *Justin: Epitome of the Philippic History of Pompeius Trogus*. Clarendon Ancient History Series. Translated by J. C. Yardly; Commented by Waldemar Hekel. Oxford: Clarendon, 1997. [=*Justin*]

Katzenstein, H. J. "Gaza in the Persian Period." *Trans* 1 (1989): 67–9.

Kratz, Reinhard Gregor. "The Second Temple of Jeb of Jerusalem." Pages 247–64 in Lipschits and Oeming, eds, *Judah and the Judeans in the Persian period.*

——, ed. *Religion und Religionskontakte im Zeitalter der Achämeniden.* Veröffentlichungen Gesellschaft für Theologie 22, Gütersloh: Gütersloher Verlagshaus, 2002.

Kuhrt, Amelie. *The Persian Empire: A Corpus of Sources from the Achaemenid Persian.* London; New York: Routledge, 2008.

——. *The Ancient Near East c. 3000–330 B.C.* Routledge History of the Ancient World 2. London: Routledge, 1995.

——. "Achaemenid Babylonia: Sources and Problems." Pages 177–94 in Sancisi-Weerdenburg and Kuhrt, eds, *AH.* Vol. 4, *Centre and Periphery.*

——. "Babylonia from Cyrus to Xerxes." Pages 112–38 in Boardman, Lewis, Hammond, and Martin, eds, *CAH.* Vol. 4, *Persia, Greece and the Western Mediterranean c. 525–479 B.C.*

Larsen, Mogens Trolle. "The City-States of the Early Neo-Babylonian Period." Pages 117–28 in Hansen, ed., *A Comparative Study of Thirty-State Cultures.*

Lewis, David Malcolm. "The Persepolis Fortification Texts." Pages 1–6 in Sancisi-Weerdenburg and Kuhrt, eds, *AH.* Vol. 4, *Centre and Periphery.*

Lipschits, Oded. *The Fall and Rise of Jerusalem: Judah under Babylonian Rule.* Winona Lake, IN: Eisenbrauns, 2005.

Lloyd, Alan B. *Herodotus Book II: Commentary 99–182.* Leiden; New York; København; Köln: Brill, 1988.

——. *Herodotus Book II: Commentary 1–98.* Leiden: Brill, 1976.

——. *Herodotus Book II: Introduction.* Leiden: Brill, 1975.

MacGinnis, John. *Letter Orders from Sippar and the Administration of the Ebabbara in the Late-Babylonian Period.* Poznan: Bonami, 1995.

Magaret, Root Cool. "From the Heart: Powerful Persianisms in the Art of the Western Empire," in Sancisi-Weerdenburg and Kuhrt, eds, *AH,* Vol. 6, *Asia Minor and Egypt.*

Martirossian, A. "Notes Concerning the Economic Activity of the Babylonian Temples in the First Millennium BC." *Iraq* 45 (1983): 128–30.

Meadows, Andrew R. "The Administration of the Achaemenid Empire." Pages 181–209 in Curtis and Tallis, *Forgotten Empire.*

Meshorer, Ya'akov. "The Mints of Ashdod and Ascalon during the Late Persian Period." *EI* 20 (1989): 287–91.

Morkot, Robert. "Nubia and Achaemenid Persia: Sources and Problems." Pages 321–36 in Sancisi-Weerdenburg and Kuhrt, eds, *AH.* Vol. 6, *Asia Minor and Egypt.*

Myers, Jacob. *Ezra, Nehemiah,* AB. Vol. 14. Garden City, NY: Doubleday, 1965.

Oller, Gary H. "Messengers and Ambassadors in Ancient Western Asia." Pages 1465–74 in Sasson, ed., *CANE.* Vol. 3.

Pohl, Alfred. *Neubabylonische Rechtsurkunden aus den Berliner Staatlichen Museen I.* AnOr 8. Roma: Pontificio Istituto Biblico, 1933.

Potts, Daniel T. "Distant Shores: Ancient Near Eastern Trade with South Asia and Northeast Africa." Pages 1451–63 in Sasson, ed., *CANE.* Vol. 3.

Sancisi-Weerdenburg, Heleen. "The Quest for an Elusive Empire." Pages 263–74 in Sancisi-Weerdenburg and Kuhrt, eds, *AH.* Vol. 4, *Centre and Periphery.*

——. "Darius I and the Persian Empire." Pages 1035–49 in Sasson, ed., *CANE.* Vol. 2.

——, ed. *Achaemenid History.* Vol. 1, *Sources, structures and Synthesis.* Leiden: Nederlands Instituut voor het Nabije Oosten, 1987. [=*AH*]

——, Pierre Briant, Root Cool Margaret, and Josef Wiesehöfer, eds *Achaemenid History.* Vol. 9, *Persepolis Seal Studies.* Leiden: Nederlands Instituut voor het Nabije Oosten, 1996/8. [=*AH*]

—— and Amelie Kuhrt, eds. *Achaemenid History.* Vol. 6, *Asia Minor and Egypt: Old Culture in a New Empire.* Leiden: Nederlands Instituut voor het Nabije Oosten, 1991. [=*AH*]

—— and Jan Willem Drijvers, eds. *Achaemenid History.* Vol. 5, *The Root of the European Tradition.* Leiden: Nederlands Instituut voor het Nabije Oosten, 1990. [=*AH*]

—— and Amelie Kuhrt, eds. *Achaemenid History.* Vol. 4, *Centre and Periphery.* Leiden: Nederlands Instituut voor het Nabije Oosten, 1990. [=*AH*]

Schaper, Joachim. "The Temple Treasury Committee in the Times of Nehemiah and Ezra." *VT* 47 (1997): 200–6.

——. "The Jerusalem Temple as an Instrument of the Achaemenid Fiscal Administration." *VT* 45 (1995): 528–39.

Strabo. *The Geography of Strabo.* BCLS. Translated by H. C. Hamilton. London: Bell, 1854–1857. [=*Strabo*]

Stern, Ephraim. "The Babylonian Gap: The Archaeological Reality." *JSOT* 28 (2004): 273–7.

——. "New Evidence on the Administrative Division Palestine in the Persian Period." Pages 221–6 in Sancisi-Weerdenburg and Kuhrt, eds, *AH.* Vol. 4, *Centre and Periphery.*

——. "The Archaeology of Persian Palestine." Pages 88–114 in Finkelstein and Davies, eds, *CHJ.* Vol. 1, *Introduction.*

——. *Material Culture of the Land of the Bible in the Persian Period 538–332 B.C.* Warminster: Aris & Phillips, 1982.

Strange, John. "The Philistine City-States." Pages 129–40 in Hansen, ed., *A Comparative Study of Thirty-State Cultures.*

Stronach, David. "Anshan and Persia: Early Achaemenid History, Art and Architecture on the Iranian Plateau." Pages 35–53 in Curtis, ed., *Mesopotamia and Iran in the Persian Period.*

Tallis, Nigel. "Transport and Warfare." Pages 210–35 in Curtis and Tallis, *Forgotten Empire*.

Trotter, James M. *Reading Hosea in Achaemenid Yehud*. JSOTSup 328. Sheffield: Sheffield Academic Press, 2001.

Tuplin, Christopher. "Darius' Suez Canal and Persian Imperialism." Pages 237–83 in Sancisi-Weerdenburg and Kuhrt, eds, *AH*. Vol. 6, *Asia Minor and Egypt*.

Vickers, Michael. "Persian, Thracian and Greek Gold and Silver: Questions of Metrology." Pages 31–9 in Sancisi-Weerdenburg and Kuhrt, eds, *AH*. Vol. 6, *Asia Minor and Egypt*.

——. "Interactions between Greeks and Persians." Pages 253–62 in Sancisi-Weerdenburg and Kuhrt, eds, *AH*. Vol. 4, *Centre and Periphery*.

Vogelsang, Willem. "The Achaemenids and India." Pages 93–110 in Sancisi-Weerdenburg and Kuhrt, eds, *AH*. Vol. 4, *Centre and Periphery*.

Walker, Christopher. "Achaemenid Chronology and the Babylonian Source." Pages 17–25 in Curtis, ed., *Mesopotamia and Iran in the Persian Period*.

Wallinga, H. T. "Polycrates and Egypt: The Testimony of the Samaina." Pages 179–97 in Sancisi-Weerdenburg and Kuhrt, eds, *AH*. Vol. 6, *Asia Minor and Egypt*.

——. "The Ancient Persian Navy and its Predecessors." Pages 47–78 in Sancisi-Weerdenburg, ed., *AH*. Vol. 1, *Sources, structures and Synthesis*.

Wiesehöfer, Josef. *Ancient Persia: From 550 BC to 650 AD*. Translated by A. Azodi. London: New York: Tauris, 1996.

Williamson, Hugh Godfrey Maturin. *Ezra, Nehemiah*, WBC. Vol. 16. Waco, TX: Word, 1985.

Wright, John W. "A Tale of Three Cities: Urban Gates, Squares and Power in Iron Age II, Neo-Babylonian and Achaemenid Judah." Pages 19–51 in Davies and Halligan, eds, *Second Temple Studies*. Vol. 3, *Studies in Politics, Class and Material Culture*.

Xenophon. *The Cyropaedia of Xenophon*. Noted by George Martyn Gorham from the Text of L. Dinfort. GSC. London: Whittaker, 1856. [=*Cyr.*]

Yamauchi, Edwin Maseo. *Persia and the Bible*. Grand Rapids, MI: Baker, 1990.

Young, T. Cuyler Jr. "Persians." Pages 295–300 in Meyers, ed., *OEANE*. Vol. 4.

——. "The Early History of the Medes and the Persians and the Achaemenid Empire to the Death of Cambyses." Pages 1–52 in Boardman, Lewis, Hammond, and Martin, eds, *CAH*. Vol. 4, *Persia, Greece and the Western Mediterranean c. 525–479 B.C.*

CHAPTER 3

Judah in the Neo-Babylonian and the Achaemenid Periods

Background

The discussion in this chapter concerns the cultural and economic circumstances of Judah under two empires: The Neo-Babylonian and the Achaemenid. The Achaemenids simply took over the Neo-Babylonian Empire, coordinated it and expanded it. Imperial policies in various regions would not usually be changed as long as they furthered profit and income for the empire. For this reason, I will discuss the history and archaeology of both Neo-Babylonian Judah and Achaemenid Judah.

The Neo-Babylonian Empire developed an advanced political and economic system. Having few natural resources of its own it had to depend upon import of all sorts of food, and luxury and building materials like metals, stone and timber from the conquered territories. Judah was well known for her agricultural products above all the vine and the olive (see Chapter 1 above). Both of these were always expensive items in the larger international economic context of Mesopotamia.

In relation to Judah, Darius utilised already existing administrative systems to maximise economic growth. Similar administrative strategies existed in all conquered territories (see Chapters 1 and 2 above). Darius controlled production and trade. For this reason, I will also investigate the administration of Achaemenid Judah. The Book of Haggai is an important historical source for Darius's administrative policy in Judah.

Destruction in Judah by Babylonian Campaigns

The Biblical account of the Babylonian campaigns against Judah is in 2 kgs 24–25. In the days of Jehoiakim (608–597 BCE), Neo-Babylonia attacked with a joint army of Arameans, Moabites, and Ammonites.[1] They destroyed Judah and put Jehoiakim's son Johoiachin (597 BCE) in his place (2 Kgs 24:1–6). Three months later, Nebuchadnezzar of Babylonia again besieged Judah and crowned Zedekiah (597/6–586 BCE) king of Judah. This time, Nebuchadnezzar carried off all the treasures from the palace and the Jerusalem temple (2 Kgs 24:8–13). The Jerusalem palace and its temple were burned down and its city wall broken down (2 Kgs 25:1–21).[2] Tell en-Nasbeh then took over Jerusalem's position (2 Kgs 25:22–24).

Also, in his campaigns, Nebuchadnezzar carried "all of Jerusalem" into exile (2 Kgs 24:14–15; 25:12; Jer 52:16). It has been claimed that Neo-Babylonian Judah was uninhabited or uninhabitable.[3] At this point, it is necessary to examine the phrase "all the people" in Biblical passages. One fine case can be found in 2 Kgs 25:26, where "all the people" went to Egypt after Gedaliah is killed. It shows that "all the people" did not mean "all the people" of Judah but just a large number of people. Therefore, it

1 On conflict in the statements in 2 Kgs 24:6; 2 Chr 36:6–7; Jer 22:18–19, see Lester L. Grabbe, "The Kingdom of Judah from Sennacherib's Invasion to the Fall of Jerusalem: If We had only the Bible...," in *Good Kings and Bad Kings* (ed. Lester L. Grabbe; LHB/OTS 393; London: T & T Clark, 2005), 108–13.

2 Amihai Mazar, *Archaeology of the Land of the Bible: 10,000–586 BCE* (New York, NY: Doubleday, 1992), 458–60; Delbert R. Hillers, *Lamentations* (AB, Vol. 7A; New York: Doubleday, 1972), XVIII; Georg Fohrer, *History of Israelite Religion* (trans. David E. Green; New York; Nashville: Abingdon, 1972), 308–9; Lipschits, *The Fall and Rise of Jerusalem*, 68–97; Walter C. Kaiser Jr, *A History of Israel: From Bronze Age through the Jewish Wars* (Nashville, TN: Broadman & Holman, 1998), 408.

3 John Wilson Betlyon, "Neo-Babylonian Military Operations Other than War," in Lipschits and Blenkinsopp, eds, *Judah and the Judeans in the Neo-Babylonian Period*, 265–8; Lisbeth S. Fried, "The Land Lay Desolate: Conquest and Restoration in the Ancient Near East," in Lipschits and Blenkinsopp, eds, *Judah and the Judeans in the Neo-Babylonian Period*, 21–54.

is plausible that the concept that the land remained desolate is hyperbole. The captives were all the princes, officials, soldiers, craftsmen, and smiths of Jerusalem (2 Kgs 24:14; 25:11).

From the standpoint of the Biblical traditions, the capital life in Jerusalem sharply declined with several deportations of the population.[4] Jer 52:28–29 lists the numbers of the people that Nebuchadnezzar carried into exile: the first deportees after the first fall of Jerusalem in the seventh year (597 BCE) amounted to 3,023; in Nebuchadnezzar's eighteenth year (586 BCE), total 832 people were deported from Jerusalem after the second fall; and in his twenty–third year (582 BCE) in response to the assassination of Gedaliah, 745 Jews were taken into exile. There were 4,600 people in all (Jer 52:30).

On the other hand, 2 Kgs mentions two different figures for the deportation of 10,000 people in 597 BCE and of 8,000 people in 586 BCE (2 Kgs 24:14–16). The third deportation is not mentioned by the writer of 2 Kgs. Thus, the exact total number of deportees is not known.[5] One can only say that this exile was a severe blow to Jerusalem (Jer 24).

According to demographic studies, it has been claimed that an estimate of the built-up area of Jerusalem at the end of Iron Age reached approximately 600–1,000 dunams.[6] Based on this estimation, the calculated

4 Bustenay Oded, "Where Is the 'Myth of the Empty Land' to Be Found? History versus Myth," in Lipschits and Blenkinsopp, eds, *Judah and the Judeans in the Neo-Babylonian Period*, 55–74; Oded Lipschits, "Demographic Changes in Judah between the Seventh and the Fifth Centuries B.C.E.," in Lipschits and Blenkinsopp, eds, *Judah and the Judeans in the Neo-Babylonian Period*, 326–34.

5 T. Raymond Hobbs, *2 Kings* (WBC, Vol. 13; Waco, TX: Word, 1985), 352–3; William Lee Holladay, *Jeremiah 2: A Commentary on the Book of the Prophet Jeremiah, Chapters 26–52* (Hermeneia: Philadelphia: Fortress, 1989), 443.

6 One way to estimate the population is to base the calculation on a fixed coefficient of twenty to twenty-five people per dunam. This makes it possible to compare the demographic data from the end of the Iron Age and the Persian period with the data from other periods in the history of ancient Israel. See Israel Finkelstein, "A Few Notes on Demographic Data from Recent Generations and Ethnoarchaeology," *PEQ* 122 (1990): 47–52; Jeffrey Ralph Zorn, "Estimating the Population Size of Ancient Settlements: Methods, Problems, Solutions and a Case Study," *BASOR* 295 (1994): 31–48; Lipschits, "Demographic Changes," 326–7, 55–6. Meanwhile, Shiloh counts

population remained from 12,000 to 25,000. It reflects that in Jerusalem occurred the sharpest decline of around 80 per cent from over 760 dunams to 230 dunams.

On the basis of the excavated remains, the Babylonian armies razed other areas near Jerusalem. Ramat Rahel which served as one of the administrative cities to supply the required tribute in the Judean kingdom was apparently broken down while Jerusalem lay in ruins.[7] Also, Tell es Sultan (historical Jericho) and Tel-Goren (historical En-Gedi) which were agricultural and industrial centres received a diminished settlement.[8]

The Babylonians further destroyed the main cities of Judah's western border, including Lachish in the southern part of Jerusalem (Jer 34:7).[9] Yet, Lachish connected the coastline as one of the supply routes. Thus, this place undertook the settlement of the other cities on the west coastline then established the Philistinian city-states.

In a similar manner, most of the Negev fortresses were destroyed in the early sixth century BCE.[10] However, there is some evidence of the settlement beginning to make incursions into the southern part of the Negev and into the Hebron hills.[11] They plainly consisted of Arabian tribes.

---

forty to fifty populations per dunam. Yigal Shiloh, "The Population of Iron Age Palestine in the Light of a Sample Analysis of Urban Plans, Areas and Population Density," *BASOR* 239 (1980): 25–35.

7 Oded Lipschits, Yuval Gadot, Manfred Oeming, and Benjamin Arubas, "The 2006 and 2007 Excavation Seasons at Ramat Rahel: Preliminary Report," *IEJ* 59 (2009): 1–20; Lester L. Grabbe, "The Kingdom of Judah from Sennacherib's Invasion to the Fall of Jerusalem," 83–4. However, Na'aman argues that this site was already abandoned after the Assyrian invasion. Nadav Na'aman, "An Assyrian Residence at Ramat Rahel?" *TA* 28 (2001): 260–80.

8 Lipschits, *The Fall and Rise of Jerusalem*, 338–9.

9 Lipschits, "Demographic Changes," 341–2.

10 Lipschits, *The Fall and Rise of Jerusalem*, 135–46, 153–4; Lipschits, "Demographic Changes," 334–7.

11 Andre Lemaire, "Nabonidus in Arabia and Judah in the Neo-Babylonian Period," in Lipschits and Blenkinsopp, eds, *Judah and the Judeans in the Neo-Babylonian Period*, 285–300; Eph'al, "Changes in Palestine," 106–19; Eph'al, "Syria-Palestine," 151–6; Ephraim Stern, "The Babylonian Gap: The Archaeological Reality," *JSOT* 28 (2004): 273–7.

Owing to the invasion of Nebuchadnezzar, the destruction of Jerusalem and its eastern environs was evidently vast. A great number of the Jerusalem population were also deported. Jerusalem lost the function of the political and administrative centre. In addition, some territories in the west and south of Jerusalem were even annexed to the Philistinian city-states and to the Arabs respectively. Relatively, the northern area of Jerusalem was little devastated. Therefore, it is unlikely that the whole land was completely rooted and unpopulated.

Continuity in Babylonian Judah

Within the Babylonian rule, Judean political status was changed to that of a minor administrative region. Considering the productive ability of Judah, however, the Judean land could not be devoid of people requiring a governing or administrative organisation.[12]

Certainly, Nebuchadnezzar left behind the people of the land to be vine-dressers and ploughmen (2 Kgs 25:12; Jer 39:10; 40:7; 52:16).[13] They were certainly peasants. Gedailiah was appointed as a governor of Judah by Nebuchadnezzar of "the people who were left in the country" (2 Kgs

12 Hans M. Barstad, *The Myth of the Empty Land: A Study in the History and Archaeology of Judah during the "Exilic" Period* (Oslo: Scandinavian University Press, 1996); Barstad, "After the 'Myth of the Empty Land,'" 3–20; Philip R. Davies, "Exile! What Exile? Whose Exile?," in *Leading Captivity Captive: "The Exile" as History and Ideology* (ed. Lester L. Grabbe: JSOTSup 278; Sheffield: Sheffield Academic Press, 1998); Robert P. Carroll, "Exile! What Exile? Deportation and the Discourse of Diaspora," in Grabbe, ed., *Leading Captivity Captive*, 62–79; Ronald H. Sack, "Nebuchadnezzar II and the Old Testament: History versus Ideology," in Lipschits and Blenkinsopp, eds, *Judah and the Judeans in the Neo-Babylonian Period*, 221–34.

13 Lipschits argues that "the people who remain in the land of Judah" is called "the poorest people of the land" by the various stages of the text formation. See Lipschits, *The Fall and Rise of Jerusalem*, 102–9, 113, 289–95.

25:22). These people were not counted amongst the "all of Jerusalem" that were taken into exile. Apparently, the reference to those "who were living in these ruins" of Ezek 33:24 was a reflection of this situation. Also, eighty men from several regions of Judah brought grain offerings, incense even to the Jerusalem temple which might not be in good state (Jer 41:5).

From an economic standpoint, the Babylonians certainly needed to exploit the lands they conquered by way of plunder (see Chapter 1 above). It was for the same reason that metal objects such as gold, silver and bronze were taken away from the Jerusalem temple and brought to Babylon together with craftsmen and smiths (2 Kgs 25:13–17). Also, the main reason behind Nebuchadnezzar's decision to move Judah's administrative city to Tell en-Nasbeh was that there were olive oil and wine industries that were of great value to the Babylonian economy.[14]

There is little doubt that the Babylonians treated the conquered Judah very much in the same way that they treated other conquered territories. Nebuchadnezzar was interested in maintaining or even increasing the existing practices of production although the destruction of Judah damaged his economy. One good case is Tell en-Nasbeh. Its site history of olive oil production goes back to the early ninth century BCE onwards (1 Kgs 15:22).[15] The economic importance of Tell en-Nasbeh was protected by constructed walls in the eighth century BCE.[16] Further fortifications were later carried out in the sixth century BCE and continued to function as a defensive feature with the offset-inset wall.[17] This suggests that olive oil even flourished during the Neo-Babylonian period.

Accordingly, the settlement in Tell en-Nasbeh continued to exist and even further increased.[18] The estimated population of Tell en-Nasbeh

14 David Vanderhooft, "Babylonian Strategies of Imperial Control in the West: Royal Practice and Rhetoric," in Lipschits and Blenkinsopp, eds, *Judah and the Judeans in the Neo-Babylonian Period*, 235–62.

15 Zorn, "A Note on the Date of the 'Great Wall' of en-Nesbeh: A Rejoinder," 147–8.

16 Katz, "A Note on the Date of the 'Great Wall' of Tel en-Nesbeh," 131–2.

17 Zorn, "Tell en-Nesbeh and the Problem," 413–50.

18 Kirsi Valkama, *Judah in the Mid-Sixth Century BCE: Archaeological Evidence for a Post-Collapse Society* (Helsinki: Bookwell, 2012), 55–71.

reached between 800 and 1,000 dunams.[19] This figure could be equalised to that of Jerusalem in the Judean kingdom period. However, the settlement of Tell en-Nasbeh demonstrated a rural form, which was in stark contrast to the urban life of Jerusalem.[20] It was related to the outcome of a planned Babylonian policy of setting aside some of the rural highland areas for agricultural purposes. It was no more than a specialised centre for oil production in the Babylonian economic structure.

However, there was the opposite argument that the northern region of Jerusalem also underwent a more moderate decrease of approximately 60 per cent from 1,150 dunams to 500 dunams.[21] From more balanced archaeological results, the northern Judean hills offered two contrasting examples of research on the continuity or discontinuity in the settlement of rural areas. In each case, one should check the continuity and discontinuity of the rural settlement according to their correspondence to the pattern of the rural settlement from both the Iron Age and the Achaemenid period. Therefore, it might be reasonable to infer that the gradual impoverishment of the settlements in that region took place at the end of the sixth and the beginning of the fifth centuries. Since, at that time, Tell en-Nasbeh was withdrawn to the core of the region. This resulted in the renewed status of Jerusalem, due to economic and security concerns, during the Achaemenid period.

A similar archaeological situation in terms of imperial economy to Tell en-Nasbeh was observed in the region of Ammon. Many farms and small villages continued to exist in those areas, characterised by many wine presses and other agricultural installations.[22] The results of Tell el-ʿUmeiri excavations demonstrated that a large area south of the capital Rabbath-Ammon

19 Zorn, "Estimating the Population Size," 44. Valkama, *Judah in the Mid-Sixth Century BCE*, 60–71.

20 Vanderhooft and Horowitz, "The Cuneiform Inscription," 318–27. On urban development of Jerusalem, see Ronny Reich and Eli Shukron, "The Urban Development of Jerusalem in the late Eight Century B.C.E.," in *Jerusalem in Bible and Archaeology: The First Temple Period* (eds, Andrew G. Vaughn and Ann E. Killebrew; SBL Symposium series 18; Atlanta: SBL, 2003), 209–18.

21 Lipschits, "Demographic Changes," 356.

22 Oded Lipschits, "The Rural Settlement in Judah in the Sixth Century B.C.E.: A Rejoinder," *PEQ* 136 (2004): 99–101.

was not destroyed by the Babylonians and even flourished throughout the Babylonian and Achaemenid periods.[23] The Babylonian rulers built Tell el ʿUmeiri in the Ammon area as the new administrative centre; it was similar to Tell en-Nasbeh in Judah.

Parallels to Tell en-Nasbeh can be made to El-Jib (historical Gibeon), Tell el Ful (historical Gibeah), Bethel, Horvat Zimri in the north of Jerusalem, Kh. er-Ras in the south of Jerusalem, and Kh. et-Tabaqa (historical Beth-Zur).[24] El-Jib showed a stratum of settlement of the Babylonian period.[25] Tell el Ful had a significant amount of pottery which was dated to the second half of the sixth century BCE.[26] A conical seal portraying worship of a Babylonian deity and the pottery group in Bethel belongs to the sixth century BCE.[27] horvat Zimri exposed ceramic remains which were similar to styles of the late Iron Age.[28] Kh. er-Ras offered sixteen winepresses with a treading part and collecting vat that were used from the late Iron Age to the Achaemenid time.[29] Kh. et-Tabaqa also showed the almost identical pattern of the rural sites throughout the sixth century BCE.[30] Even the

23 James A. Sauer, "Transjordan in the Bronze and Iron Ages: A Critique of Nelson Glueck's Synthesis," *BASOR* 263 (1986): 18.

24 Avraham Faust, "Judah in the Sixth Century B.C.E.: A Rural Perspective," *PEQ* 135 (2003): 37–53; Charles E. Carter, "Ideology and Archaeology in the Neo-Babylonian Period: Excavating Text and Tell," in Lipschits and Blenkinsopp, eds, *Judah and the Judeans in the Neo-Babylonian Period*, 301–22; Joseph Blenkinsopp, "Bethel in the Neo-Babylonian Period," in Lipschits and Blenkinsopp, eds, *Judah and the Judeans in the Neo-Babylonian Period*, 93–108; Valkama, *Judah in the Mid-Sixth Century BCE*, 71–84, 92–101, 123–4, 205–21.

25 Stern, *Material Culture*, 33; Valkama, *Judah in the Mid-Sixth Century BCE*, 95–8.

26 The storage capacity in Tell el Ful was 25,000 gallons of wine. See, James B. Pritchard, *Winery, Defences, and Soundings at Gibeon* (Philadelphia: University of Pennsylvania Press, 1964), 1–27; Valkama, *Judah in the Mid-Sixth Century BCE*, 75–81.

27 Carter, *The Emergence of Yehud in the Persian Period*, 125.

28 Carter, *The Emergence of Yehud in the Persian Period*, 132–3; Valkama, *Judah in the Mid-Sixth Century BCE*, 100–1.

29 Carter, *The Emergence of Yehud in the Persian Period*, 134; Valkama, *Judah in the Mid-Sixth Century BCE*, 123–4.

30 William Foxwell Albright and O. R. Sellers, "The First Campaign of Excavation at Beth-Zur," *BASOR* 43 (1931), 9.

west site adjacent to Jerusalem, Ketef Hinnom showed the common potteries of the sixth century BCE although these finds could, at most, only attest to the limited existence of culture during the Babylonian period.[31]

The above evidence supported the continued settlement at those sites in the years following the Babylonian invasion into Judah. Further, the burial pattern which was a distinctive feature of Judean culture was found in all of those sites.[32] Especially, they were well known for wine production throughout their history (see Chapter 1 above). Its production during the Babylonian period should be related to the wine production for imperial bureaucracies and armies.[33] It reflected that organised economic and administrative activities existed in the Babylonian province of Judah.[34]

With regard to administration, forty-two seal impressions with the word מוצה or with the vowel-letter omitted מצה should be noted.[35] They were apparently used to designate wine or oil production which was dated to the Babylonian rule in the sixth century BCE. More than 70 per cent of the total number of 42 seal impressions were found in Tell en-Nasbeh. This suggests the central position of the Babylonian province following the destruction of Jerusalem. Four additional seal impressions were also discovered in Jerusalem (10 per cent), four in El-Jib (10 per cent), two in Tell es Sultan (5 per cent), and one in Ramat-Rahel (2 per cent).

From archaeological finds at Babylonian Judah, it has been shown that a culture of the large majority of the population likely remained in Judah. Its continued material culture was considerably shown in the northern

31 Gabriel Barkey, "The Priestly Benediction on Silver Plaques from Ketef Hinnom in Jerusalem," *TA* 19 (1992): 139–92; Valkama, *Judah in the Mid-Sixth Century BCE*, 104–13.

32 Burial caves of this type are to be found nowhere else in Judah and her immediate environs. Irit Yezerski, "Burial-Cave Distribution and the Borders of the Kingdom of Judah toward the End of the Iron Age," *TA* 26 (1999): 253–70.

33 Oded Lipschits, "The History of the Benjaminite Region under Babylonian Rule," *TA* 26 (1999): 172–6.

34 Blenkinsopp, "Bethel in the Neo-Babylonian Period," 96–7; Carter, *The Emergence of Yehud in the Persian Period*, 51; Valkama, *Judah in the Mid-Sixth Century BCE*, 231–4.

35 Lipschits, *The Fall and Rise of Jerusalem*, 149–50; Stern, *Material Culture*, 229, 247–9.

region of Jerusalem. To some degree, the west and the south of Jerusalem showed the common culture of Neo-Babylonia. The Babylonian Judean sites were related to the production of olive oil and wine which were of great affluence. Among them, Tell en-Nasbeh, replacing Jerusalem with the administrative and economic centre, led industrial work and contributed to the economy of Neo-Babylonia.

Settlement of Judean Cities in the Achaemenid Policy

One of the Achaemenid foreign policies was to maximise the effectiveness and benefit that each subordinate could provide, as the Babylonian Empire had done. It promptly incited a process of resettlement in places ruined by the Babylonian raids. Therefore, the Achaemenids allowed Babylonian Judeans to let their locals return to their regions.[36] This is reflected in the lists of returnees in Ezra 2:1–67 and Neh 7:6–68.[37] Ezra stated that the whole accompanying numbers totalled 42,360, in addition to their 7,337 menservants and maid-servants, including 200 men and women singers (Ezra 2:64–65). Meanwhile, in Nehemiah, the whole assembly was 42,360, besides 7,337 menservants and maid-servants as well as 245 men and women singers (Neh 7:66–67).[38]

36 With regard to the Judean restoration, Berquist argues that Yehudite society becomes an amalgamation of divergent forms and structures having various centres of power. Jon L. Berquist, "Constructions of Identity in Postcolonial Yehud," in Lipschits and Oeming, eds, *Judah and the Judeans in the Persian Period*, 53–66.

37 Ezra 2 is dependent on Neh 7 for two main reasons. The first one is that in the continuation of the narrative the seventh month of Neh 7:72 forms an integral part of its context by the reference to the same month in Neh 8:2. The second is that Ezra 2:68–69 represents a summary of Neh 7:69–71 rather than an expansion of Ezra. Williamson, *Ezra, Nehemiah*, 28–31, 268–9.

38 Bob Becking, "'We All Returned as One!': Critical Notes on the Myth of the Mass Return," in Lipschits and Oeming, eds, *Judah and the Judeans in the Persian Period*, 3–18; Eric M. Meyers, "Exile and Restoration in Light of Recent Archaeology and

However, the actual computing number in all was 29,818 in Ezra 2 and 31,089 in Neh 7. It showed the slight difference in population numbers recorded in the respective lists. Besides, from a structural point of view, Ezra 2 and Neh 7 were mixed with the list counted by families (Ezra 2:3–19// Neh 7:8–24; Ezra 2:32–33//Neh 7:34–35) and the other list counted by towns (Ezra 2:20–29//Neh 7:25–33; Ezra 2:33–35//Neh 7:36–38). So, these lists in Ezra 2 and Neh 7 would be imposed upon diverse materials. It denotes that the resettlement together with the returnees continued to happen although such return was not the kind of large scale operation. This accorded with the imperial purpose to consolidate the economic prosperity in every conquered territory.

Another list in Neh 3:1–32 showed delegations to work on the walls of Jerusalem in Achaemenid Judah. In the list, one important find was the use of the term פלך. It generally represented "a district" or "work duty in the form of conscripted labour" (Neh 3: 9, 12, 14, 15, 16, 17, 18).[39] In every case, it formed part of the designation of an individual responsible for the repair of part of Jerusalem's wall with the formula of personal name (PN) followed by geographical name (GN): "the leaders of the half district or the district of GN." The GNs attached to the half districts included Jerusalem twice, Keilah in northwest of Kh. et-Tabaqa and Kh. et-Tabaqa.

Demographic Studies," in Grabbe and Knoppers, eds, *Exile and Restoration Revised*, 166–73; Lester L. Grabbe, "'They Shall Come Rejoicing to Zion' – Or Did They?: The Settlement of Yehud in the Early Persian Period," in Grabbe and Knoppers, eds, *Exile and Restoration Revised*, 116–27; Tamara C. Eskenazi, "From Exile and Restoration to Exile and Reconstruction," in Grabbe and Knoppers, eds, *Exile and Restoration Revised*, 78–93.

39 *DCH*, Vol. 6, 931; Aaron Demsky, "*Pelekh* in Nehemiah 3," *IEJ* 33 (1983): 242–4; Moshe Weinfeld, "*Pelekh* in Nehemiah 3," in *Studies in Historical Geography and Biblical Historiography: Presented to Zecharia Kallai* (ed. Gershon Galil and Moshe Weinfeld; VTSup 81; Leiden: Brill, 2000), 249–50. For Judean geography, see Anson Rainey, "The Biblical Shephelah of Judah," *BASOR* 251 (1983): 16–18; Anson Rainey, "Historical Geography: The Link between Historical and Archaeological Interpretation," *BA* 45 (1982): 217–23; Yohanan Aharoni, *The Land of Bible: A Historical Geography* (trans. Anson F. Rainey; London: Burns & Oates, 1967), 416.

The GNs associated with whole districts were Beth Hakkerem in southwest of Jerusalem and Tell en-Nasbeh.

In terms of realm of פלך, it should be said that there were the administrative centres within the Judean territory.[40] Jerusalem should be in charge of Jerusalem and its immediate vicinity. Tell en-Nasbeh commanded the northern region of Jerusalem. Gezer would control the west northern part of Jerusalem.[41] Tell es Sultan would cover the entire plain of Tell es Sultan. Keilah might head the plain southwest of Jerusalem. And, Beth Hakkerem could cover the area south of Jerusalem to Tekoah. The rest of the south hilly area might belong to the direction of Kh. et-Tabaqa.

Also, the list of cultic officials (Neh 11:25–36) would be a parallel to the returnees in the Jerusalem area and in the Tell en-Nasbeh region.

From the lists, one can unearth some repopulated cities in Achaemenid Judah. Approximately twenty cities were settled in: Bethlehem, Netophap, Tekoa, and Keilah in the southern Judean hills; Kirjath-Jearim, Geba, and Bethel in the northern Judean hills; Jericho and Senaah in the eastern Judean hills; Lod and Ono in the north eastern Judean hills near the coastline.[42] Jerusalem and its surrounding environs clearly regained a population.

40 Ephraim Stern, "New Evidence on the Administrative Division Palestine in the Persian Period," in Sancisi-Weerdenburg and Kuhrt, eds, *AH*, Vol. 4, *Centre and Periphery*, 221–6. About the borders of Achaemenid Judah, see John W. Wright, "Remapping Yehud: The Borders of Yehud and the Genealogies of Chronicles," in Lipschits and Oeming, eds, *Judah and the Judeans in the Persian Period*, 67–90.

41 Both Jericho and Gezer were added as centres of separate districts in the Hellenistic period. Israel Finkelstein, "Territorial Extent and Demography of Yehud/Judea in the Persian and Early Hellenistic Periods," *RB* 117 (2010): 40.

42 Descendents of former residents from some adjacent settlements are bunched into single units and counted. This applies for: Kiriath Yearim, Kephirah and Beeroth; Ramah and Geba; Bethel and Ai; Lod, Hadid and Ono. The agglomeration may indicate that as a consequence of intermarriage between families from these cities, clans from one area possessed legitimate land claims in another. For this reason, early Persian period administrators treated each unit as a single administrative subunit. Each unit would have consisted of two or more core villages of the pre-exilic period, their outlying hamlets and farmsteads, adjacent agricultural lands and pasturing areas, as well as the unclaimed land between them. Ziony Zevit, "Is there an Archaeological Case for Phantom Settlement in the Persian Period," *PEQ* 141 (2009): 125–7.

They showed a significant number of Achaemenid period finds such as being densely populated and several similar cisterns and farmsteads.[43]

However, they included cities that were certainly outside Achaemenid Judah, such as Beersheba, Lachish, Dibon in the Jordan, Yekabzeel, Yeshua, and Moladah all of which were in Arabs, Beth-Pelet and Hazar-Shual both of which were near Beersheba, and Ziklag, Meconah, En-Rimmon, and Zorah all of which were in the Negev.[44] So, it has been argued that these cities might be an idealised portrait of Judah rather than the reconstituted community of the Achaemenid period.[45] Also, it has been claimed that the lists were probably compiled in the late Hellenistic, chiefly Hasmonaean period and represented the reality of that time, around the second century BCE.[46] Especially, seven of the places appeared in the Books of Maccabees as important places in the history of the Hasmonaeans such as Beeroth in the northern Judean hills, Michmash in east of Bethel, and Hadid in west central of Jerusalem. However, it could be said that they might be

43 Charles E. Carter, "The Province of Yehud in the Post-Exilic Period: Soundings in Site Distribution and Demography," in Eskenazi and Richards, eds, *Second Temple Studies*. Vol. 2, *Temple Community in the Persian Period*, 106–45; Carter, *The Emergence of Yehud in the Persian Period*, 134–45; Eric M. Meyers and Carol L. Meyers, "Demography and Diatribes: Yehud's Population and the Prophecy of Second Zechariah," in Coogan, Exum, and Stager, eds, *Scripture and Other Artifacts: Essays on the Bible and Archaeology in Honor of Philip J. King*, 268–85; Oded Lipschits, "Persian Period Finds from Jerusalem: Facts and Interpretations," *JHS* 9 (2009): 1–30.

44 Carter, *The Emergence of Yehud in the Persian Period*, 80–1.

45 Blenkinsopp states that the list of Neh 11 represents an idealised portrait of Judah rather than the reconstituted community of the Achaemenid period. Joseph Blenkinsopp, *Ezra-Nehemiah* (OTL; Philadelphia: Fortress, 1988), 43–5, 83–7, 231–9, 328–32; Blenkinsopp, "Temple and Society," 44.

46 Samarian Lod was added to the Hasmonaean territory in 145 BCE (1 Macc 11:34). Israel Finkelstein, "Persian Period Jerusalem and Yehud: A Rejoinder," *JHS* 9 (2009): 1–13; Israel Finkelstein, "Archaeology and the List of Returnees in the Books of Ezra and Nehemiah," *PEQ* 140 (2008): 7–16; Israel Finkelstein, "Jerusalem in the Persian (and Early Hellenistic) Period and the Wall of Nehemiah," *JSOT* 32 (2008): 501–20; Finkelstein, "Territorial Extent and Demography," 40–2.

unimportant but truly function in Achaemenid Judah, at least in the fifth century BCE. That was why it incorporates those places under Nehemiah.

The settlement in Achaemenid Judah can also be estimated by Yehud seal impressions. The inscribed seals may be broadly divided into three categories: the word מוצה or with the vowel-letter omitted מצה, which was dated from Babylonian rule in the sixth century BCE, primarily from areas associated with the territory of Tell en-Nasbeh before Jerusalem regained its place as the seat of the centre of Judah;[47] the Aramaic toponym יהוה in the stamp impressions with or without the Aramaic official title פחוא;[48] and a personal name which could be dated to sometime after 586 BCE when Judah became a sub-province within a satrapy of Neo-Babylonia in the Achaemenid period (Ezra 5:8).

These variant types can be classified into three chronologically defined groups according to the Paleography: Early (late sixth through fifth centuries BCE), Middle (fourth and third centuries BCE) and Late (second century BCE).[49] From the viewpoint of the use of seals, they have been discovered in Jerusalem, Bethel, Tell en-Nasbeh, Tell el-Ful, Ramat Rahel, Tell es Sultan, Gezer, Horvat Zimri, El-Jib, Kh. et-Tabaqa, Kedef Hinnom, Mamilla in the City of David, Wadi Salim in the Jordan Valley, Tel Goren, Keilah, Kh. Er-ras, and Har Adar in west of Jerusalem. As under-exploited areas developed, populated cities expanded.

Also, numismatic evidence has given not only some indication of settlement but also of the restoration of economic business. It was not until the sixth and fifth centuries BCE that coinage was first introduced into the economic life of Judah in order to promote and maintain trade, and

47 Carter, *The Emergence of Yehud in the Persian Period*, 259–66; Jeffrey Ralph Zorn, Joseph Yellin, and John Hayes, "The *m(w)sh* Stamp Impressions and the Neo-Babylonian Period," *IEJ* 44 (1994): 161–83.

48 The יהוד seals would cease to be in use from around the second century BCE when ירצלם stamp impressions replaced them. Hillel Geva, "A Chronological Reevaluation of Yehud Stamp Impressions in Palaeo-Hebrew Script, Based on Finds from Excavations in the Jewish Quarter of the Old City of Jerusalem," *TA* 34 (2007): 92–103.

49 Oded Lipschits and David Vanderhooft, "Yehud Stamp Impressions: History of Discovery and Newly-Published Impressions," *TA* 34 (2007): 3–11.

to support the administrative taxation, although those coins were minted in Greece in the sixth century BCE.[50] There were Judean coins which were minted with the name of the governor (יחזקיה) or the priest (ידדע).[51] These were found in the City of David, Horvat Zimri, Ramat-Rahel, Tell Jemmeh in south of Gaza and Kh. et-Tabaqa, mainly in the fourth century BCE.

From the archaeological finds of Achaemenid Judah, I have shown that a process of repopulation and resettlement was applied in places ruined by the Babylonians. Judean deportees in Babylon returned to their impoverished regions from which Jerusalem and its environs clearly regained a population. For Achaemenid benefit, the settlement in the Judean territory continued to develop throughout the Achaemenid period with the emergence of the administrative districts Jerusalem, Tell en-Nasbeh, Beth-Haccerem, Kh. et-Tabaqa, and Keilah under Nehemiah.

Continuity in Achaemenid Judah

Along with the demand of the Jerusalem temple reconstruction (the Book of Haggai), the Achaemenids certainly carried out the policy to revive Jerusalem.[52] It is because Jerusalem would have available all the political, economical, and cultural systems necessary to survive as an administrative

50 Rappaport, "Numistics," 25–59; Ya'akov Meshorer, "Ancient Coinage," *BA* 56 (1993): 148–9.

51 Peter Machinist, "The First Coins of Judah and Samaria: Numismatics and History in the Achaemenid and Early Hellenistic Periods," in *Continuity and Change: Proceedings of the Last Achaemenid History Workshop, April 6–8, 1990* (ed. Heleen Sancisi-Weerdenburg, Amelie Kuhrt, and Margaret Cool Root; Leiden: Nederlands Instituut voor het Nabije Oosten, 1994), 365–79.

52 Wright states that the city wall in Achaemenid Jerusalem created military space (Neh 2). Wright, "A Tale of Three Cities," 42–7. However, Grabbe argues that Jerusalem was not in charge of an imperial garrison. Lester L. Grabbe, "Was Jerusalem a Persian Fortress," in Grabbe and Knoppers, eds, *Exile and Restoration Revised*, 128–37.

centre for the empire.[53] Moreover, there was a transit road in Jerusalem from Sais or Memphis in Egypt to the coastline of Tyro and Damascus, encountering the King's road of Sardis-Susa (see Chapter 1 above).

Nonetheless, the settlement in Jerusalem in the early Achaemenid period was quite small. Some archaeological evidence for its settlement can be found only on the eastern slope of Jerusalem and its immediate environs.[54] Ketef Hinnom continued in use throughout the sixth century BCE.[55] Kh. er-Ras in the west adjacent to Jerusalem had agricultural installations and ceramic remains.[56] To the north, Wadi Salim showed agricultural units with terraces.[57]

As the Achaemenids intended Jerusalem to re-establish its status as the administrative centre of the province, the population of Jerusalem increased and its settlements were expanded.[58] The settlement formed a rural settlement which grew on the level of agricultural farms. It was quite different to its settlement in the kingdom period. It denoted that Jerusalem ensured the enlarged areas for cultivation and that Jerusalem's immediate vicinities got densely populated.

At Beth Hakkerkem and Rogem Gannim in the southwest of Jerusalem, vineyards were there. Twenty-two stamped and incised jar handles have been found. In the farmsteads of Nahal Refa'im in south of Jerusalem which was well suited to viticulture, a number of winepresses of the basic treading floor-and-vat type that could be associated with the production of wine have been uncovered.[59] Plastered tanks and storage caves are also seen.

53 Barstad, "Haggai Among the Prophets," 269–70.

54 Yigal Shiloh, *Excavations at the City of David. I. 1978–1982, Interim Report of the First Five Seasons* (Qedem 19; Institute of Archaeology; Jerusalem: The Hebrew University of Jerusalem Press, 1984), 29.

55 Barkey, "Priestly Benediction," 139–92; Carter, *The Emergence of Yehud in the Persian Period*, 145–6.

56 Carter, *The Emergence of Yehud in the Persian Period*, 148–50.

57 Carter, *The Emergence of Yehud in the Persian Period*, 150.

58 Avraham Faust, "Rural Settlements, State Formation, and 'Bible and Archaeology'," *NEA* 70 (2007): 5; Lipschits, "The Rural Settlement in Judah," 99–100.

59 David Vanderhooft and Oded Lipschits, "A New Typology of the Yehud Stamp Impressions," *TA* 34 (2007): 12–37; Greenberg and Cinamon, "Stamped and Incised Jar Handles," 229–43.

At the north site adjacent to Jerusalem, also, evidence for a repopulation supportive to the agricultural economy of Jerusalem has been unearthed. Nebi Samwil in the north of Jerusalem which was on the main road leading to Jerusalem from the northern region continued to yield fine remains of the Achaemenids.[60] Seventeen stamp impressions are discovered.

From a total of 412 יהוה seal impressions dated to the Achaemenid period, 170 seal impressions (41.3 per cent) found in Jerusalem and its immediate environs reflect its reviving economic businesses, instead of מוצה seal impressions.[61]

In the area surrounding Jerusalem, also, Ramat Rahel was densely populated. Ramat Rahel reveals a significant number of Achaemenid finds.[62] It was quite likely that the west site adjacent to Jerusalem was restored for an administrative function in Jerusalem's agricultural economy. From 412 יהוה seal impressions, 194 impressions (47.1 per cent) are unearthed at Ramat Rahel.[63] The exploitation of Ramat Rahel definitely correlated to the sponsored measures by which Jerusalem and the Judean economy suddenly grew. Ramat Rahel took for granted the restoration of its administrative role.

Along the Dead Sea, Tel Goren was evidently expanded due to a trade route.[64] Thirty-eight impressions being dated to the early Achaemenid Judah are discovered.[65] Industrial installation such as ovens, large clay containers

60 Magen and Har-Even argue that, among seventeen stamp impressions, fourteen are marked in the form of the lion which are regarded as the official impression of the provincial administration. Thus, they claim that this site should be identified with Tell en-Nasbeh. See Magen and Har-Even, "Persian Period Stamp Impressions," 38–58.

61 Lipschits and Vanderhooft, "Yehud Stamp Impressions," 3–5; Ronny Reich and Eli Shukron, "The Yehud Stamp Impressions from the 1995–2005 City of David Excavations," *TA* 34 (2007): 59–65.

62 Lipschits, "Demographic Changes," 329–32.

63 Oded Lipschits, Yuval Gadot, Manfred Oeming, and David Vanderhooft, "Seventeen Newly-Excavated Yehud Stamp Impressions from Ramat Rahel," *TA* 34 (2007): 74–89.

64 Carter, *The Emergence of Yehud in the Persian Period*, 157–60.

65 Carter, *The Emergence of Yehud in the Persian Period*, 144–5.

and pottery vessels verified the incessant economic activities in Tel-Goren.[66] It attested to a special industry of manufacturing perfumes, an industry long associated with this locale.

Further settlements were also gradually renewed in the area from Bethlehem to Kh. et-Tabaqa.[67] Especially, the numismatic evidence of Kh. et-Tabaqa was of great importance in their economic structure.[68] The reservoir for coins at Kh. et-Tabaqa supports the notion that this place served as an economic centre in this district from the late sixth century BCE.

The re-settlement at Tell es Sultan was quite small. Yet, a variety of remains which are found at Jerusalem and its immediate environs have been discovered.[69] It indicates that this site was involved in economic activities.[70]

Obviously, the gradual increase of Jerusalem and its surroundings affected the gradual decrease of the district of Tell en-Nasbeh. It was a result of the reduced status of Tell en-Nasbeh as an economic and administrative centre during the Achaemenid period. Indeed, the process of depopulation and settlement decline in the Benjamin region was closely linked to the increase in population of the Jerusalem region.[71] From the Achaemenid period onwards, the settlement in Tell el-Ful, Bethel, and El-Jib stagnated and decreased, and was ultimately desolate by the fifth century BCE.[72]

According to settlements and population during the Achaemenid period, the number of settlements was up to 125 sites and the whole population grew to 826 dunams.[73] At this time, the population of Jerusalem was

66 Benjamin Mazar and Immanuel Dunayevsky, "En-gedi: The Third Season of Excavation." *IEJ* (1964): 121–30; Carter, *The Emergence of Yehud in the Persian Period*, 157–60.

67 Carter, *The Emergence of Yehud in the Persian Period*, 134–45; Lipschits, "Demographic Changes," 337–8, 352–3.

68 Carter, *The Emergence of Yehud in the Persian Period*, 153–7.

69 Carter, *The Emergence of Yehud in the Persian Period*, 160–2; Lipschits, *The Fall and Rise of Jerusalem*, 232–7.

70 Stern, Lipschits, and Vanderhooft, "New Yehud Stamp Impressions," 66–73.

71 Zorn, "Tell en-Nesbeh and the Problem," 413–50.

72 Carter, *The Emergence of Yehud in the Persian Period*, 122–32.

73 Carter, *The Emergence of Yehud in the Persian Period*, 224–33.

estimated at around 110 dunams.[74] And, the size of Jerusalem and its vicinities may have reached approximately 726 dunams, almost 88 per cent of the population. A very high population density in Jerusalem and its vicinities would provide evidence for the administrative activity of Jerusalem in the Judean agricultural economy.

From the cultural materials of Achaemenid Judah, it has been demonstrated that Jerusalem and its surroundings were restored from an economic and administrative point of view. In particular, sites of the south, the southwest, and the north of Jerusalem were highly specialised in the agricultural economic structure. Tell es Sultan and Tel-Goren were obviously engaged in the Jerusalem agricultural structure. Also, Kh. et-Tabaqa supported the Jerusalem economic administration in terms of finance. However, the restored economic ability of Jerusalem led to the economic contraction of Tell en-Nasbeh.

Political Reality of Achaemenid Judah

In the Achaemenid administrative structure, Judah was merely placed as a province in the satrapy of "Beyond the River." Judah was nothing but a tributary subordinate that should be loyal to imperial taxation. It is related to Judah's loss of solid barrier against Egypt. From Cambyses's conquest, Egypt became one of the imperial colonies. Afterwards, Judah was placed as a politically insignificant province in an imperial political structure.

The geopolitical strategy between Egypt and the Mesopotamian Empires in Judean history began with the king Sargon II (721–705 BCE)

74 Carter, *The Emergence of Yehud in the Persian Period*, 288; Oded Lipschits, "Achaeological Imperial Policy, Settlement Processes in Palestine, and the Status of Jerusalem in the Middle of the Fifth Century B.C.E.," in Lipschits and Oeming, eds, *Judah and the Judeans in the Persian Period*, 32. Meanwhile, Finkelstein estimates the area to consist of sixty dunams. This is less than half of the size that Carter and Lipschits advocate. See Finkelstein, "Territorial Extent and Demography," 44–5.

in Neo-Assyria. From the time when Judah became one of their subject kingdoms, Judah formed a virtually uninterrupted Neo-Assyrian block.[75] Following Sargon II's offensive in southern Palestine, Egypt fomented a revolt in Judah. It led to Sennacherib (704–681 BCE) facing an Egyptian army in support of anti-Sennacherib rebels in 701 BCE. Egypt's repeated meddling in Judah provoked Esarhaddon to extend Assyrian activity into Egypt itself (680–669 BCE). And, in 671 BCE, the Assyrian armies captured Memphis. However, the Assyrian control over Egypt, with its basically fragmented political system, was no more than the defeat of Egypt's Napatan rulers.[76]

When the Neo-Babylonians defeated the Assyrians, they took control of the territories in a way comparable to the way the Assyrian regime had. The Egyptian border now stood against the Neo-Babylonians. It was very important for Nebuchadnezzar (604–562 BCE) to tighten Babylonian power in the Levant if it was not to lose that region to Egypt.[77] Nevertheless, Egypt's meddling in Judah continued into the Nebuchadnezzar reign. In the course of tension between the two sides, Jerusalem was captured and deported by Nebuchadnezzar's campaigns (2 Kgs 24–25). Along the desert frontiers, Egyptian supported opposition was driven out. As such, Judean fate had been dominated by the geopolitical tactics between Egypt and the Mesopotamian Empires.

Judean geopolitical tactics of the Egyptians, Assyrians, and Babylonians were defeated. During Cambyses's conquest in the Persian period, Egypt was taken and even placed on the imperial border against Greece. The Egyptian hegemony over Judah was completely broken. When Darius took the throne, Egypt annoyed him with the repeated revolts.[78] These revolts undoubtedly affected Judah. Unlike the reality, Judah still took for granted her geopolitical manoeuvre at the symmetry between Egypt and the Achaemenids.

75 Lipschits, *The Fall and Rise of Jerusalem*, 25–9.
76 Kuhrt, *The Ancient Near East*, 496–501.
77 Kuhrt, *The Ancient Near East*, 590–1.
78 *Hist.* III, 14–5, IV, 166; Ael., *NA* 12.21; DB II: §21 in Brosius, *The Persian Empire from Cyrus II to Artaxerxes I*, 32.

Amid the recurring Egyptian rebellions against Darius, Judah was also ensnared by the fanciful hope that Zerubbabel of the Davidic line would reign (see Chapter 2 above). The attempt to restore the Davidic monarchy happened for the benefit of Zerubbabel, the governor of Judah. This plot itself undeniably considered the uprising against Darius.[79] This will be evidenced in the exegesis on the Book of Haggai (Hag 1:4, 9; 2:4, 6–7).[80]

Being afraid of any potential uprisings in Egypt or Egypt's meddling in its surroundings, Darius stationed imperial garrison troops at Beersheba, Kadesh Barnea, Arad, and Tell Kheleifah in the Phoenicians.[81] Fortified military posts already let the Arabs enjoy an amicable relationship with Darius.[82] Starting from Cambyses's campaign against Egypt in 525 BCE, the Arabs had proven a very reliable patron to the empire with supplying the necessary reinforcements to the Cambyses's army.[83] Lachish was evidently established as an administrative centre to respond to the changes in this area.[84]

Nevertheless, when Darius acceded his throne to Xerxes I (486–465 BCE), Egypt certainly revolted again. It was led by Megabyzus who was the leader of an army in an Egyptian army fighting against the Athenians and their allies.[85] This Egyptian uprising again stirred up the atmosphere of revolt in Judah (Ezra 4:13, 19–20) and soured Achaemenid attitudes towards the province Judah. Judah needed to be transformed as a reliable dependant for the policy of the Achaemenid administration intent on tightening control in their western territories.[86] Steps taken by Ezra and Nehemiah would fit this sort of policy.

79 See Briant, *From Cyrus to Alexander*, 115.

80 See Chapters 4 and 5 below.

81 Briant, *From Cyrus to Alexander*, 164–5; Graf, "Arabia," 142; Stern, *Material Culture*, 79–82.

82 See Chapter 2 above. See also Briant, *From Cyrus to Alexander*, 164–5; Graf, "Arabia," 142; Stern, *Material Culture*, 79–82.

83 Briant, *From Cyrus to Alexander*, 52–4; Eph'al, "Syria-Palestine," 163–4.

84 Fantalkin and Tal, "Redating Lachish," 167–98.

85 Hoglund, *Achaemenid Imperial Administration*, 96–164.

86 Kuhrt, *The Ancient Near East*, 29–49, 207–40.

Returning to the place of the Judean revolt in Darius's time, we would do well to pay particular attention to the Book of Haggai. It is because the dates described in Haggai all took place in the second year of Darius. At that time, Darius planned the campaign against the Egyptian revolts. From an economic and military point of view, Judah had to provide daily provisions to imperial armies passing nearby or through the Judean territory.[87]

From Judah's standpoint, this was the ideal time for Judah to show committed loyalty to Darius.[88] With this success, Judah could be considered significant to Darius's security. It is quite likely that small states are even more dependent upon an ally than strong states.[89] With a keen eye on exploiting this arrangement, Darius commanded the Jerusalem reconstruction business. He certainly applied the temple fiscal administration to the rebuilt Jerusalem temple. Accordingly, Judah was to make the rebuilt Jerusalem temple function as a nucleus for the Judean flourishing agriculture. In Darius's campaign against Egypt, the sole thing that Judah must do was to produce the required inventory for the imperial armies. Judah could then be assured of an imperial patron as guaranteed.

Irrespective of the imperial demand, during Darius's march on Egypt, Judah plotted the uprising with Zerubbabel. This allegation in Hag 1:4 and 9 was caused by the imperial policy to allow for the interests of local groups by appointing a local royal lineage to its representative. In the pressing time of the Jerusalem temple rebuilding, the people of Judah had an illusion of Zerubbabel in the Davidic lineage who was appointed as the governor of Judah. The status of Zerubbabel was enough to incite the desire for the restoration of the Davidic kingdom. With Zerubbabel, the people attempted to change the political status of Judah to a self-independent entity or at least as a semi-independent state in the imperial political system.

From the above survey, I have shown that Judah, with lost military tactics of virtually solid barrier against Egypt, became politically insignificant

87 Hoglund, "The Achaemenid Context," 54–68; Hoglund, *Achaemenid Imperial Administration*, 1–28.

88 Barstad, "Haggai Among the Prophets," 267–8.

89 Briant, *From Cyrus to Alexander*, 70–6; Dandamaev, *Political History*, 103–77; Kessler, "Persia's Loyal Yahwists," 104–5.

in the Achaemenid political structure. With the agricultural production ability of Judah, however, Judah remained as a vehicle for taxation within the imperial system. For that purpose, Darius deployed the Jerusalem restoration along with the temple rebuilding as a fiscal administrative centre. In accord with this development, Judah had to secure imperial patronage. However, meddling in the recurring Egyptian rebellions against Darius, Judah revolted against Darius with Zerubbabel of the Davidic line, seeking change in Judah's political status (Hag 1:4 and 9).

Economic Reality of Achaemenid Judah

Agriculture in the Judean economy was of great importance. She always ensured reliable sources of food, sustained economic stability and enriched treasuries with the more agricultural produce. The resettlement of Judah by Darius aimed at the restoration and extension of cultivated areas that Nebuchadnezzar had destroyed in order to improve Judean agriculture.[90] In the wake of the imperial campaigns against Egyptian rebellion and even territorial expansion, Darius sought Judean alliances with an adequate partner.

Thus, it would not be expected that Judah would not face a problem in the general harvest that she produced so much agricultural produce than she could use. In the second year of Darius, however, Judah had a harvest shortfall, where the people of Judah ate their meals but never felt full, nor could their thirst be quenched when they drank, and they put on clothes but nobody could get warm (Hag 1:6, 9–11; 2:15–19). They appeared disappointed as their daily provisions did not even meet their needs.

The Book of Haggai further depicts erratic climates that cause the Judean agricultural breakdown. The heavens withheld the dew (חרֹבָ, Hag 1:10–11), and the land inevitably withheld all its produce (יבול). In a drought, the produce of grain (דגן), wine (תירושׁ), and oil (יצהר), which

90 Young, "The Consolidation of the Empire," 97–9.

were the major crops in Judah, completely spoiled (Hag 1:6, 11; 2:19; Joel 2:24; Zech 8:12; 10:1; 14:17). The prolonged lack of rainfall also attacked all tree-fruits such as vines, figs, pomegranates, palms, and apples (Hag 2:16; Joel 1:11–13; Isa 17:10–11; Jer 5:24; 14:7–22; Ezek 34:26–27). People and animals suffered affliction too (Hag 1:11).

Hail (ברד) also severely affected the crop yields (Hag 2:17; Exod 9:18–35; Isa 28:2, 17; Ps 18:13; 78:47, 48).[91] When the hail was heavy and possibly accompanied by strong winds, it could completely ravage the harvest (Hag 2:17; Josh 10:17). At the agricultural harvest time, storms could lead to great loss of meagre harvest (Hag 1:9).

In addition, agricultural produce was damaged by crop diseases of "blight" (שׁדפון) and "mildew" (ירקון, Hag 2:11). Blight meant scorching or burning of leaves by one of the crop diseases, symptoms of which appeared with withering and cessation of growth. It was caused by fungus attacking cereals, mostly barley (Gen 41:6).[92] Mildew always followed the disease of "blight" when referring to a plant disease (Hag 2:17; Deut 28:22; 1 Kgs 8:37; 2 Chr 6:28; Amos 4:9). Mildew was also a fungal disease that produced spores which appeared as a whitish growth on the host surface. It prevented plants from ripening properly.[93] The common symptom was mould on stems and leaves, the effects of which changed the colour from yellow to red. It could cause a loss of up to 30 per cent of the yield by reducing the number of kernels and shivering the grain, resulting in low weight and protein content.[94]

Haggai's near contemporary, Joel deals with units of the locust attack that brings out the economic disaster. Several items such as גזם, ארבה, ילק, and חסיל appearing in Joel 1:4 and 2:25 were references to different stages

91 Kessler regards hail (ברד) as a plague in the area of the agricultural economic activities. Kessler, *The Book of Haggai*, 207–8.

92 Blight is affected by the hot east wind that sometimes blows across Palestine from the desert. Borowski, *Agriculture in Iron Age*, 158–9.

93 Mildew is caused by humidity winds. Borowski, *Agriculture in Iron Age Israel*, 159–60.

94 Verhoef, *The Book of Haggai and Malachi*, 127.

in the development of the locust.[95] Locusts destroyed the fields for grains, wine, and oil (Joel 1:10–13).

In all disasters which could happen in an agricultural area, Judah was confronted with a breakdown in the agricultural economy. Lack of food is drastically reviewed in Haggai. There was little doubt that Judah could not create the inventory for Darius's campaign against Egypt. In the bigger imperial economic system, undoubtedly Judah could not send olive produce to Tel Miqne for olive oil production nor vines to Ashdod and Ashkelon for the wine production.[96] Judean responsibility for supplies could not serve both a military force and the interregional trade market. No benefits could create with shortages of basic products.

The economic breakdown of Judah could be verified by minted coins in Judah. The standard Judean coin weighed relatively less than other coins in the satrapy of "Beyond the River."[97] This represented the economic difficulties of Judah, for the weight of coin was a marker of the value of coin. In the level of high inflation, the people could not keep up with costs (Hag 1:6). What is worse, any shortage of daily provisions led to increased demand, and subsequently a rise in value. Hence, the people were forced to pay a high price, which, in turn, led to a high cost of living. Imperial taxes that people should pay were already beyond the limits of their capacities.

There is one of the resulting complaints in Neh 5:1–5. The first group, who owned no land, was dependent on wages from labour of whatever sort and could no longer support their families. Meanwhile, some of landholders mortgaged their lands, their vineyards and their houses in order to buy grains because of the shortage of the produce. Other landholders needed to

95 ילק is the first stage; חסיל refers to the second and third stages; and גזם refers to the fourth and fifth stages. Other words are ארבה (Exod 10:4, 12–14; Lev 11:22; Nah 3:15; Job 39:20) and צלצל (Deut 28:42). Borowski, *Agriculture in Iron Age Israel*, 154–8.

96 On the capacity to mass-produce olives of the Judean Shephela, see Finkelstein, "The Archaeology of the Days of Manasseh," 169–87; Gitin, "The Neo-Assyrian Empire," 77–103. See also Chapter 1 above.

97 The province Judah would mint coins after the period of Nehemiah. Haim Gilter, "The Levant," in *A survey of Numismatic Research 1990–1995* (ed. Cecile Morrison and B. Kluge; Berlin: International Association of Professional Numismatists Special Publication, 1997), 101–13.

borrow silver for the king's tribute upon their land and vineyards.[98] When worst came to worst, this burden resulted in debt. And then, those who had already mortgaged their lands or had a heap of debts could never afford to get their land back. In some cases, this led to their children being sold into debt-slavery. The heavy debts also let tenant-peasants sell their allotments and then placed themselves as slaves for royal, temple, or private lands.

Above, I have examined that during Darius's reign, drought in Judah led to famine (Hag 1:11). The concurrent erratic climate of hail (ברד) and crop diseases of blight (שׁדפון) and mildew (ירקון) led to a breakdown in the Judean agricultural economy (Hag 1:6, 9–11; 2:16–19). It was quite the opposite of what Judah had expected and hoped for the looming campaign against Egypt. Inevitably, the cash commodities of oil (יצהר) and wine (תירושׁ) lost their competitiveness (Hag 1:11; 2:19). Also, Judah's economic status was evidently downgraded in this crisis. As a result, Judah was not only politically insignificant but also economically poor.

Conclusions

This chapter has surveyed in some detail the cultural and economic conditions in Judah in the Neo-Babylonian and the Achaemenid periods. My study is above all based on archaeological excavation reports of sites from those periods.

In my presentation, I do not deny that Judah was devastated during the Neo-Babylonian military campaigns. Nor do I ignore that several deportations took place (2 Kgs 24–25; Jer 39–40; 52:15–16). My main point is that destruction and deportations occurred mainly in Jerusalem. Many Judeans left behind by the Babylonians took up agricultural industries as their tasks (2 Kgs 25:12; Jer 39:10; 52:16). Losing the south and west borders closest to Egypt, however, converted Judah into a politically less important province.

98 Williamson, *Ezra, Nehemiah*, 236–9.

A large majority of the population still remained in Judah throughout the Babylonian period. Archaeological excavations particularly in the north of the Judean hills confirm beyond doubt a continued agricultural activity of considerable size. Tell en-Nasbeh, the new central administration of Neo-Babylonian Judah, supervised the thriving production of olive oil, wine, and other agricultural products. Tell el-Ful, Bethel, El-Jib, and Kh. et-Tabaqa supported the Tell en-Nasbeh agricultural economic administration. Clearly, Judah after the fall of Jerusalem continued to accumulate wealth for their Neo-Babylonian, and later Achaemenid overlords.

In order to maximise booty and taxes from Judah, Darius supported the Jerusalem restoration. Jerusalem was, after all, the administrative and economic centre of the province. Soon, the imperial policy of resettlement and repopulation followed throughout the Judean territory. As Jerusalem recovered, its hinterland was quickly resettled for agricultural purposes. Ramat Rahel, Kh. et-Tabaqa, Tell es Sultan, and Tel-Goren co-operated with Jerusalem's economic administration.

To judge from the Biblical accounts (Ezra 2 and Neh 3 and 7) as well as from the archaeological records, the size and population of the above regions at the end of the sixth century BCE were small. However, throughout the period, populations steadily increased. Around the fifth century BCE, they would reach a population of as much as 20,000.

In relation to Judean reality in the second year of Darius (520 BCE), from the Book of Haggai we learn that Judah attempted to seek the restoration of the Davidic kingdom with Zerubbabel being granted the title "the governor of Judah" (Hag 1:4, 9; 2:4, 6–7). However, the plan to build this dynasty through Zerubbabel never developed beyond delusive hope.

To make matters worse, Judah continued to encounter an almost complete breakdown of the agricultural systems (Hag 1:6, 11; 2:18) due to the repeated instances of drought and hail (Hag 1:10; 2:17). Crop diseases like blight and mildew (Hag 2:17), and attacks from locusts (Joel 1:4 and 2:25) also led to a breakdown of the Judean agricultural economy. Judah remained economically weak.

Bibliography

Aharoni, Yohanan. *The Land of Bible: A Historical Geography*. Translated by Anson F. Rainey. Philadelphia: Westminster, 1967.

Albright, William Foxwell and O. R. Sellers, "The First Campaign of Excavation at Beth-Zur," *BASOR* 43 (1931): 2–13.

Barkay, Gabriel. "The Priestly Benediction on Silver Plaques from Ketef Hinnom in Jerusalem." *TA* 19 (1992): 139–92.

Barstad, Hans M. "Haggai Among the Prophets: An Example of Prophetic Continuity in the Hebrew Bible." Pages 265–83 in Bar-Asher, Rom-Shiloni, Tov, and Wazana, eds, *Shai le-Sara Japhet: Studies in the Bible, its Exegesis and its Language*.

——. "After the 'Myth of the Empty Land': Major Challenges in the Study of Neo-Babylonian Judah." Pages 3–20 in Lipschits and Blenkinsopp, eds, *Judah and the Judeans in the Neo-Babylonian Period*.

——. *The Myth of the Empty Land: A Study in the History and Archaeology of Judah during the "Exilic" Period*. Oslo: Scandinavian University Press, 1996.

Becking, Bob. "'We All Returned as One!': Critical Notes on the Myth of the Mass Return." Pages 3–18 in Lipschits and Oeming, eds, *Judah and the Judeans in the Persian Period*.

Berquist, Jon L. "Constructions of Identity in Postcolonial Yehud." Pages 53–66 in Lipschits and Oeming, eds, *Judah and the Judeans in the Persian Period*.

Betlyon, John Wilson. "Neo-Babylonian Military Operations Other than War." Pages 263–84 in Lipschits and Blenkinsopp, eds, *Judah and the Judeans in the Neo-Babylonian Period*.

Blenkinsopp, Joseph. "Bethel in the Neo-Babylonian Period." Pages 93–108 in Lipschits and Blenkinsopp, eds, *Judah and the Judeans in the Neo-Babylonian Period*.

——. "Temple and Society in Achaemenid Judah." Pages 22–53 in Davies, ed., *Second Temple Studies*. Vol. 1, *Persian Period*.

——. *Ezra-Nehemiah*. OTL. Philadelphia: Fortress, 1988.

Borowski, Oded. *Agriculture in Iron Age Israel: The Evidence from Archaeology and the Bible*. Winona Lake, IN: Eisenbrauns, 1987.

Briant, Pierre. *From Cyrus to Alexander: A History of the Persian Empire*. Translated by Peter T. Daniels. Winona Lake, IN: Eisenbrauns, 2002.

Brosius, Maria. *The Persian Empire from Cyrus II to Artaxerxes I*. LACTOR 16. Kingston: The London Association of Classical Teachers, 2000.

Carroll, Robert P. "Exile! What Exile? Deportation and the Discourse of Diaspora." Pages 62–79 in Grabbe, ed., *Leading Captivity Captive*.

Carter, Charles E. "Ideology and Archaeology in the Neo-Babylonian Period: Excavating Text and Tell." Pages 301–22 in Lipschits and Blenkinsopp, eds, *Judah and the Judeans in the Neo-Babylonian Period.*

——. *The Emergence of Yehud in the Persian Period: A Social and Demographic Study.* JSOTSup 294. Sheffield: Sheffield Academic Press, 1999.

——. "The Province of Yehud in the Post-Exilic Period: Soundings in Site Distribution and Demography." Pages 106–45 in Eskenazi and Richards, eds, *Second Temple Studies.* Vol. 2, *Temple Community in the Persian Period.*

Coogan, Michael D., Exum J. Cheryl, and Stager E. Lawrence, eds. *Scripture and Other Artifacts: Essays on the Bible and Archaeology in Honor of Philip J. King.* Westminster: John Knox, 1994.

Dandamaev, Muhammad A. *A Political History of the Achaemenid Empire.* Translated by W. J. Vogelsang. Leiden: Brill, 1989.

Davies, Philip R. "Exile! What Exile? Whose Exile?" Pages 128–38 in Grabbe, ed., *Leading Captivity Captive.*

——. *In Search of "Ancient Israel".* JSOTSup 148; Sheffield: JSOT, 1992.

Demsky, Aaron. "Pelekh in Nehemiah 3." *IEJ* 33 (1983): 242–4.

Eph'al, Israel. "Changes in Palestine during the Persian Period in Light of Epigraphic Sources." *IEJ* 48 (1998): 106–19.

——. "Syria-Palestine under Achaemenid Rule." Pages 139–64 in Boardman, Lewis, Hammond, and Martin, eds, *CAH.* Vol. 4, *Persia, Greece and the Western Mediterranean c. 525–479 B.C.*

Eskenazi, Tamara C. and Kent H. Richards, eds. *Second Temple Studies.* Vol. 2, *Temple Community in the Persian Period.* JSOTSup 175. Sheffield: JSOT, 1999.

Fantalkin, Alexander and Oren Tal. "Re-Dating Lachish Level I: Identifying Achaemenid Imperial Policy at the Southern Frontier of the Fifth Satrapy." Pages 167–98 in Lipschits and Oeming, eds, *Judah and the Judeans in the Persian Period.*

Faust, Avraham. "Rural Settlements, State Formation, and 'Bible and Archaeology'." *NEA* 70 (2007): 4–9, 23–35.

——. "Judah in the Sixth Century B.C.E.: A Rural Perspective." *PEQ* 135 (2003): 37–53.

Finkelstein, Israel. "Territorial Extent and Demography of Yehud/Judea in the Persian and Early Hellenistic Periods." *RB* 117 (2010): 39–54.

——. "Persian Period Jerusalem and Yehud: A Rejoinder." *JHS* 9 (2009): 1–13.

——. "Archaeology and the List of Returnees in the Books of Ezra and Nehemiah." *PEQ* 140 (2008): 7–16.

——. "Jerusalem in the Persian (and Early Hellenistic) Period and the Wall of Nehemiah." *JSOT* 32 (2008): 501–20.

——. "The Archaeology of the Days of Manasseh." Pages 169–87 in Coogan, Exum, and Stager, eds, *Scripture and Other Artifacts.*

——. "A few Notes on Demographic Data from Recent Generations and Ethnoarchaeology." *PEQ* 122 (1990): 47–52.

Fohrer, Georg. *History of Israelite Religion*. Translated by David E. Green. New York; Nashville: Abingdon, 1972.

Fried, Lisbeth S. "The Land Lay Desolate: Conquest and Restoration in the Ancient Near East." Pages 21–54 in Lipschits and Blenkinsopp, eds, *Judah and the Judeans in the Neo-Babylonian Period*.

Galil, Gershon and Moshe Weinfeld, eds. *Studies in Historical Geography and Biblical Historiography: Presented to Zecharia Kallai*. VTSup 81. Leiden: Brill, 2000.

Geva, Hillel. "A Chronological Reevaluation of Yehud Stamp Impressions in Palaeo-Hebrew Script, Based on Finds from Excavations in the Jewish Quarter of the Old City of Jerusalem." *TA* 34 (2007): 92–103.

Gilter, Haim. "The Levant." Pages 101–13 in Morrison and Kluge, eds, *A Survey of Numismatic Research 1990–1995*.

Gitin, Seymour. "The Neo-Assyrian Empire and Its Western Periphery: The Levant, with a Focus on Philistine Ekron." Pages 77–103 in Parpola and Whiting, eds, *Assyria 1995: Proceeding of the 10th Anniversary Symposium of the Neo-Assyrian Text Corpus Project*.

Grabbe, Lester L. "'They Shall Come Rejoicing to Zion' – Or Did They?: The Settlement of Yehud in the Early Persian Period." Pages 116–27 in Grabbe and Knoppers, eds, *Exile and Restoration Revised*.

_____. "Was Jerusalem a Persian Fortress?" Pages 128–37 in Grabbe and Knoppers, eds, *Exile and Restoration Revised*.

_____. "The Kingdom of Judah from Sennacherib's Invasion to the Fall of Jerusalem: If We had only the Bible…." Pages 78–122 in Grabbe, ed., *Good Kings and Bad Kings*.

_____, ed. *Leading Captivity Captive: "The Exile" as History and Ideology*. JSOTSup 278; Sheffield: Sheffield Academic Press, 1998.

_____ and Gary N. Knoppers, eds. *Exile and Restoration Revised: Essays on the Babylonian and Persian Periods in Memory of Peter R. Ackroyd*. LSTS 73/JSPSup; London: T & T Clark, 2009.

Graf, David A. "Arabia during Achaemenid Times." Pages 131–48 in Sancisi-Weerdenburg and Kuhrt, eds, *AH*. Vol. 4, *Centre and Periphery*.

Greenberg, Raphel, and Gilad Cinamon. "Stamped and Incised Jar Handles from Rogem Gannim and Their Implications for the Political Economy of Jerusalem: Late 8th–Early 4th Centuries BCE." *TA* 33 (2006): 229–43.

Hillers, Delbert R. *Lamentations*. AB. Vol. 7A. New York: Doubleday, 1972.

Hobbs, T. Raymond. *2 Kings*. WBC. Vol. 13. Waco, Texas: Word, 1985.

Hoglund, Kenneth G. *Achaemenid Imperial Administration in Syria-Palestine and the Missions of Ezra and Nehemiah*. SBL Dissertation Series 125. Atlanta, GA: Scholars Press, 1992.

——. "The Achaemenid Context." Pages 54–72 in Davies, ed., *Second Temple Studies*. Vol. 1, *Persian Period*.

Holladay, William Lee. *Jeremiah 2: A Commentary on the Book of the Prophet Jeremiah Chapters 26–52*. Her. Philadelphia: Fortress, 1989.

Katz, Hayah. "A Note on the Date of the 'Great Wall' of Tel en-Nesbeh." *TA* 25 (1998): 131–3.

Kaiser, Walter C. Jr. *A History of Israel: From the Bronze Age through the Jewish Wars*. Nashville, TN: Broadman & Holman, 1998.

Kessler, John. "Persia's Loyal Yahwists: Power Identity and Ethnicity in Achaemenid Yehud." Pages 91–122 in Lipschits and Oeming eds, *Judah and the Judeans in the Persian Period*.

——. *The Book of Haggai: Prophecy and Society in early Persian Yehud*. VTSup 91. Leiden: Brill, 2002.

Kuhrt, Amelie. *The Ancient Near East c. 3000–330 B.C.* Routledge History of the Ancient World 2. London: Routledge, 1995.

Lemaire, Andre. "Nabonidus in Arabia and Judah in the Neo-Babylonian Period." Pages 285–300 in *Judah and the Judeans in the Neo-Babylonian Period*.

Lipschits, Oded. "Persian Period Finds from Jerusalem: Facts and Interpretations." *JHS* 9 (2009): 1–30.

——. "Achaeological Imperial Policy, Settlement Processes in Palestine, and the Status of Jerusalem in the Middle of the Fifth Century B.C.E." Pages 19–32 in Lipschits and Oeming, eds, *Judah and the Judeans in the Persian Period*.

——. *The Fall and Rise of Jerusalem: Judah under Babylonian Rule*. Winona Lake, IN: Eisenbrauns, 2005.

——. "Demographic Changes in Judah between the Seventh and the Fifth Centuries B.C.E." Pages 323–76 in Lipschits and Blenkinsopp, eds, *Judah and the Judeans in the Neo-Babylonian Period*.

——. "The Rural Settlement in Judah in the Sixth Century B.C.E.: A Rejoinder." *PEQ* 136 (2004): 99–107.

——. "The History of the Benjaminite Region under Babylonian Rule." *TA* 26 (1999): 155–90.

—— and Manfred Oeming, eds. *Judah and the Judeans in the Persian Period*. Winona Lake, IN: Eisenbrauns, 2006.

—— and Joseph Blenkinsopp, eds. *Judah and the Judeans in the Neo-Babylonian Period*. Winona Lake, IN: Eisenbrauns, 2003.

—— and David Vanderhooft. "Yehud Stamp Impressions: History of Discovery and Newly-Published Impressions." *TA* 34 (2007): 3–11.

——, Yuval Gadot, Manfred Oeming, and Benjamin Arubas. "The 2006 and 2007 Excavation Seasons at Ramat Rahel: Preliminary Report." *IEJ* 59 (2009); 1–20.

——, Yuval Gadot, Manfred Oeming, and David Vanderhooft. "Seventeen Newly-Excavated Yehud Stamp Impressions from Ramat Rahel." *TA* 34 (2007): 74–89.

Machinist, Peter. "The First Coins of Judah and Samaria: Numismatics and History in the Achaemenid and Early Hellenistic Periods." Pages 365–79 in Sancisi-Weerdenburg, Kuhrt, and Root, eds. *AH*. Vol. 8, *Continuity and Change*.

Magen, Yitzhak and Benny Har-Even. "Persian Period Stamp Impressions from Nebi Samwil." *TA* 34 (2007): 38–58.

Mazar, Amihai. *Archaeology of the Land of the Bible: 10,000–586 BCE*. New York, NY: Doubleday, 1990.

Mazar, Benjamin. and Immanuel Dunayevsky. "En-Gedi, Third Season of Excavations." *IEJ* 14 (1964): 121–30.

Meyers, Eric M. "Exile and Restoration in Light of Recent Archaeology and Demographic Studies." Pages 166–73 in Grabbe and Knoppers, eds, *Exile and Restoration Revised*.

—— and Carol L. Meyers. "Demography and Diatribes: Yehud's Population and the Prophecy of Second Zechariah." Pages 268–85 in Coogan, Exum, and Stager, eds, Scripture and Other Artifacts: Essays on the Bible and Archaeology in Honor of Philip J. King.

Morrison, Cecile and B. Kluge, eds. *A Survey of Numismatic Research 1990–1995*. Berlin: International Association of Professional Numismatists Special Publication, 1997.

Na'aman, Nadav. "An Assyrian Residence at Ramat Rahel?" *TA* 28 (2001): 260–80.

Oded, Bustenay. "Where Is the 'Myth of the Empty Land' to Be Found? History versus Myth." Pages 55–74 in Lipschits and Blenkinsopp, eds, *Judah and the Judeans in the Neo-Babylonian Period*.

Pritchard, James Bennett. *Winery, Defences, and Soundings at Gibeon*. Philadelphia: University of Pennsylvania Press, 1964.

Rainey, Anson. "The Biblical Shephelah of Judah." *BASOR* 251 (1983): 10–22.

——. "Historical Geography: The Link between Historical and Archaeological Interpretation." *BA* 45 (1982): 217–23.

Rappaport, Uriel. "Numistics." Pages 25–59 in Davies and Finkelstein, eds, *CHJ*. Vol. 1, *Introduction*.

Reich, Ronny and Eli Shukron, "The Yehud Stamp Impressions from the 1995–2005 City of David Excavations." *TA* 34 (2007): 59–65.

——. "The Urban Development of Jerusalem in the Late Eight Century B.C.E." Pages 209–18 in Vaughn and Killebrew, eds, *Jerusalem in Bible and Archaeology*.

Sack, Ronald H. "Nebuchadnezzar II and the Old Testament: History versus Ideology." Pages 221–34 in Lipschits and Blenkinsopp, eds, *Judah and the Judeans in the Neo-Babylonian Period*.

Sancisi-Weerdenburg, Heleen. and Root Cool Margaret, eds. *Achaemenid History*. Vol. 8, *Continuity and Change: Proceedings of the Last Achaemenid History Workshop, April 6–8, 1990*. Leiden: Nederlands Instituut voor het Nabije Oosten, 1994. [=*AH*]

—— and Amelie Kuhrt, eds. *Achaemenid History*. Vol. 4, *Centre and Periphery*. Leiden: Nederlands Instituut voor het Nabije Oosten, 1990. [=*AH*]

Sauer, James A. "Transjordan in the Bronze and Iron ages: A Critique of Nelson Glueck's Synthesis." *BASOR* 263 (1986): 1–26.

Shiloh, Yigal. *Excavations at the City of David. I. 1978–1982, Interim Report of the first Five Seasons*. Qedem 19: Institute of Archaeology. Jerusalem: The Hebrew University of Jerusalem Press, 1984.

——. "The Population of Iron Age Palestine in the Light of a Sample Analysis of Urban Plans, Areas and Population Density." *BASOR* 239 (1980): 25–35.

Stern, Ephraim. "The Babylonian Gap: The Archaeological Reality." *JSOT* 28 (2004): 273–7.

——. "New Evidence on the Administrative Division Palestine in the Persian Period." Pages 221–6 in Sancisi-Weerdenburg and Kuhrt, eds, *AH*. Vol. 4, *Centre and Periphery*.

——. *Material Culture of the Land of the Bible in the Persian Period 538–332 B.C.* Warminster: Aris & Phillips, 1982.

——, Oded Lipschits, and David Vanderhooft, "New Yehud Stamp Impressions from En Gedi." *TA* 34 (2007): 66–73.

Valkama, Kirsi. *Judah in the Mid-Sixth Century BCE: Archaeological Evidence for a Post-Collapse Society*. Helsinki: Bookwell, 2012.

Vanderhooft, David. "Babylonian Strategies of Imperial Control in the West: Royal Practice and Rhetoric." Pages 235–62 in Lipschits and Blenkinsopp, eds, *Judah and the Judeans in the Neo-Babylonian Period*.

—— and Oded Lipschits. "A New Typology of the Yehud Stamp Impressions." *TA* 34 (2007): 12–37.

—— and Wayne Horowitz, "The Cuneiform Inscription from Tell en-Nasbeh: The Demise of an Unknown King." *TA* 29 (2002): 318–27.

Vaughn, Andrew G. and Ann E. Killebrew, eds. *Jerusalem in Bible and Archaeology: The First Temple Period*. SBL Symposium series 18. Atlanta: SBL, 2003.

Verhoef, Peter A. *The Book of Haggai and Malachi*. NICOT. Grand Rapids: Eerdmans, 1987.

Weinfeld, Moshe. "*Pelekh* in Nehemiah 3." Pages 249–50 in Galil and Weinfeld, eds, *Studies in Historical Geography and Biblical Historiography: Presented to Zecharia Kallai*.

Williamson, Hugh Godfrey Maturin. *Ezra, Nehemiah*, WBC. Vol. 16. Waco, TX: Word, 1985.

Wright, John W. "Remapping Yehud: The Borders of Yehud and the Genealogies of Chronicles." Pages 67–90 in Lipschits and Oeming, eds, *Judah and the Judeans in the Persian Period.*

——. "A Tale of Three Cities: Urban Gates, Squares and Power in Iron Age II, Neo-Babylonian and Achaemenid Judah." Pages 19–51 in Davies and Halligan, eds, *Second Temple Studies*. Vol. 3, *Studies in Politics, Class and Material Culture.*

Yezerski, Irit. "Burial-Cave Distribution and the Borders of the Kingdom of Judah toward the End of the Iron age." *TA* 26 (1999): 253–70.

Young, T. Cuyler Jr. "The Consolidation of the Empire and Its Limits of Growth under Darius and Xerxes." Pages 53–112 in Boardman, Lewis, Hammond, and Martin, eds, *CAH*. Vol. 4, *Persia, Greece and the Western Mediterranean c. 525–479 B.C.*

Zevit, Ziony. "Is there an Archaeological Case for Phantom Settlement in the Persian Period." *PEQ* 141 (2009): 124–37.

Zorn, Jeffrey Ralph. "Tell en-Nesbeh and the Problem of the Material Culture of the Sixth Century." Pages 413–50 in Lipschits and Blenkinsopp, eds, *Judah and the Judeans in the Neo-Babylonian Period.*

——. "A Note on the Date of the 'Great Wall' of Tell en-Nesbeh: A Rejoinder." *TA* 26 (1999): 146–50.

——. "Estimating the Population Size of Ancient Settlements: Methods, Problems, Solutions and a Case Study." *BASOR* 295 (1994): 31–48.

——, Joseph Yellin, and John Hayes. "The *m(w)sh* Stamp Impressions and the Neo-Babylonian Period." *IEJ* 44 (1994): 161–83.

CHAPTER 4

Judah in the Achaemenid Economy: Hag 1:1–15

Background

In this chapter, I will do an exegesis of Hag 1:1–15 in which I will examine how the province of Judah was constituted in the imperial economic structure implemented by Darius. In the second year of his reign (520 BCE), Darius charged Judah with rebuilding the Jerusalem temple. Through orders to rebuild the Jerusalem temple, Darius wanted to expand the imperial economy.

A quick reading of Hag 1:1–15 reveals that the text includes several types of prophetic words. In this investigation, I will not discuss the intricate questions of redactional layers on the Book of Haggai.[1] Rather, I shall

1 For a thematic perspective, see John Kessler, "Building the Second Temple: Questions of Time, Text, and History in Haggai 1.1–15," *JSOT* 27 (2002): 243–56; Kessler, *The Book of Haggai*, 108; Meyers and Meyers, *Haggai, Zechariah 1–8*, xliv–lxx; Verhoef, *The Book of Haggai and Malachi*, 47; Tim Meadowcroft, *Haggai: Reading* (NBC; Sheffield: Phoenix, 2006), 88–9; Rex Mason, *The Book of Haggai, Zechariah and Malachi* (Cambridge: Cambridge University Press, 1977), 13–7; Rex Mason, "Purpose of the 'Editorial Framework' of the Book of Haggai," *VT* 27 (1977): 413–21. Alternatively, for a psychological interpretation, see Elie Assis, "Composition, Rhetoric and Theology in Haggai 1:1–11," *JHS* 7 (2007): 1–14; Elie Assis, "To Build or not to Build: a Dispute between Haggai and His People (Hag 1)," *ZAW* 119 (2007): 514–27. For prophetic formulae, see Mark J. Boda, "Haggai: Master Rhetorician," *TB* 51 (2000): 297–9; Mark McEntire, "Haggai: Bringing God into the Picture," *RE* 97 (2000): 69–78; Paul L. Redditt, *Haggai, Zechariah, Malachi: Based on the Revised Standard Version* (NCBE; London: Marshall Pickering, 1995), 11–2. For other analyses of 1:4–11, see Hans Walter Wolff, *Haggai: A Commentary* (trans. M. Kohl; Minneapolis: Augsburg, 1988), 33–9; Klaus Koch, "Haggais unreines Volk," *ZAW* 79

investigate the historical perspective that Haggai communicates. My exegesis of the text will emphasise the political alliance established by Darius with Judah to expand and consolidate the Achaemenid Empire.

An Exegesis of Hag 1:1–15: Crop Failure and Temple Rebuilding

Hag 1:1

בשנת שתים לדריוש המלך בחדש הששי ביום אחד לחדש
היה דבר יהוה ביד-חגי הנביא[2] אל זרבבל בן שאלתיאל פחת יהודה
ואל יהושע בן יהוצדק הכהן הגדול לאמר

[In the second year of Darius the king, on the first day of the sixth month, the word of YHWH came through the prophet Haggai to Zerubbabel the son of Shealtiel, the governor of Judah, and to Joshua the son of Jehozadak, the high priest saying]

The opening verse, beginning with the regnal year of Darius, gives the month and the day of month. The text is set in the second year of Darius the king, on the first day of the sixth month.[3] In Haggai, Darius is commonly

---

(1967): 52–66; Odil Hannes Steck, "Zu Haggai 1:2–11," *ZAW* 83 (1971): 372–3; James William Whedbee, "A Question-Answer Schema in Haggai 1: The Form and Function of Haggai 1:9–11," in *Biblical and Near Eastern Studies: Essays in Honour of William Sandford Lasor* (ed. Gary A. Tuttle; Grand Rapids: Eerdmans, 1978), 188–9; William S. Prinsloo, "The Cohesion of Haggai 1:4–11," in "*Wünschet Jerusalem Frieden*": *Collected Communications to the XIIth Congress of the International Organization for the Study of the Old Testament, Jerusalem, 1986* (ed. Mattias Augustin and Klaus D. Schunck; BEATAJ 13; Frankfurt am Main: Peter Lang, 1988), 339.

2 According to the apparatus of BHS, the LXX adds le,gwn eivpo.n (saying) after הנביא ביד חגי (cf. Hag 2:1–2). Other Greek versions inserted only dh. (also). However, this adjustment is unnecessary because the Hebrew text makes grammatical sense as it is.

3 The date, being both the first of the month and a Sabbath (Amos 8:5; Isa 1:13, 14) may point to a wordplay between Haggai's name גגח and the Hebrew word festival (חג).

understood as referring to Darius I (522–486 BCE), therefore, the year described by the opening verse of Haggai can be identified as circa 520 BCE.[4] The importance of this specific date is that it emphasises the historical and social context in which Haggai should be understood: the second year of Darius's reign.

Widespread uprisings surrounded the rise of Darius and extended into the first and second years after Darius acceded to the throne, characterising the historical and social setting of Haggai. Among the rebellions, Babylon's and Egypt's repeated revolts posed the greatest threats to Darius. Babylon was the centre of the Empire, and Egypt occupied the key role position on the western border of the Empire. Accordingly, their uprisings could strongly affect their immediate environs.[5]

During this time of unrest, Darius realised the importance of securing the allegiance of subordinate provinces, however economically and politically small or weak. Darius allied with small provinces nearby for the control of Babylon.[6] He also asked Judah to be loyal to the empire when faced with another more dangerous uprising in Egypt, which was to play a crucial role in the western border of the empire. This request from Darius of Judah corresponded with the divine command that Judah rebuild the temple.

Precisely in the second year of Darius (520 BCE), the issue of the Jerusalem temple reconstruction came through the prophet Haggai to

Petersen, *Haggai, Zechariah 1–8*, 44–5; Verhoef, *The Book of Haggai and Malachi*, 49–50; Kessler, *The Book of Haggai*, 114–5.

4 Barstad, "Haggai Among the Prophets," 265; Lipschits, "Achaemenid Imperial Policy," 32–4; Peter Runham Ackroyd, "The Written Evidence for Palestine," in Sancisi-Weerdenburg and Kuhrt, eds, *AH*, Vol. 4, *Centre and Periphery*, 207–8; Peter Runham Ackroyd, "Problems in the Handling of Biblical and Related Sources in the Achaemenid Period," in *AH*, Vol 3, *The Root of the European Tradition* (ed. Heleen Sancisi-Weerdenburg and Amelie Kuhrt; Leiden: Nederlands Instituut voor het Nabije Oosten, 1988), 33–54.

5 See Chapters 1 and 3 above.

6 Hoglund, "The Achaemenid Context," in Davies, ed., *Second Temple Studies*. Vol. 1, *Persian Period*, 62–4.

Zerubbabel the governor (פחה) and Joshua the high priest (הכהן הגדול).[7] It employed the prophetic formula ...היה דבר יהוה ביד חגי הנביא אל, which is commonly used to introduce the word of YHWH delivered by a prophet to an audience. As one can see, three important elements of this introductory formula are an addresser, an addressee and a commissary (also Mal 1:1).

With regard to the formula, of particular interest are imperial letters, which gave administrative instructions and royal commands to local authorities. It is likely that in the imperial communication system, the great king (addresser) conveyed his orders through his commissioners, the satraps (commissary), to every representative (addressee) of every region in the satrapy (Esth 3:8, 12).[8] This is likely because a regular and trustworthy flow of communication from the royal centres to the local administrative centres would have been done with consideration for the economic and military implications.[9]

Given this application, the introductory formula in the Book of Haggai may demonstrate a connection to that of imperial administrative letters. In

7 On question toward the rebuilding of the Jerusalem temple, see Grabbe, *A History of the Jews and Judaism in the Second Temple Period*. Vol. 1, *Yehud*, 355–6.

8 For a survey of works on administrative letters from Mesopotamian Empires, see Robert Francis Harper, *Assyrian and Babylonian Letters*. 5 Vols (Reprint; Chicago: The University of Chicago Press, 1977), 301, 338, 403, 518; Otto Schroeder, *Keilschrifttexte aus Assur verschiedenen Inhalts* (Leipzig: Hinrichs'sche, 1920), 113; Steven William Cole and Peter Machinist, *Letters from Priests to the Kings Esarhaddon and Assurbanipal* (SAA XIII; Helsinki: Helsinki University Press, 1999), 40; Robert Henry Pfeiffer and Robert Francis Harper, *State Letters of Assyria: A Transliteration and Translation of 355 Official Assyrian Letters Dating from the Sargonid Period (722–625 B.C.)* (AOS Vol. 6; New Haven: American Oriental Society, 1935), 80–1; Simo Parpola, *Letters from Assyrian and Babylonian Scholars* (SAA X; Helsinki: Helsinki University Press, 1993), 357; Simo Parpola, *Letters from Assyrian Scholars to the Kings Esarhaddon and Assurbanipal*. Part I: Texts (AOAT 5/1; Winona Lake, IN: Eisenbrauns, 2007), 287.

9 Hayim Tadmor, "Monarchy and the Elite in Assyria and Babylonia: The Question of Royal Accountability," in *The Origins and Diversity of Axial Age Civilizations* (ed. Shmuel N. Eisenstadt; Albany, NY: State University of New York Press, 1986), 203–24; Meadows, "The Administration of the Achaemenid Empire," in Curtis and Tallis, eds, *Forgotten Empire*, 186.

a Darius administrative letter, Haggai's promulgation has a political affiliation, which further functions to convey YHWH's assurance to Darius's work.

These verses demonstrate that YHWH summoned Darius to rebuild the Jerusalem temple. Without giving information regarding the date of their imperial commissary, Darius formally sanctioned Zerubbabel as the governor (פחה)[10] and Joshua as the high priest (הכהן הגדול) for the temple rebuilding work.[11] Likewise, YHWH only revealed the strategy for restoring the temple to his chosen builders, Darius, Zerubbabel the governor and Joshua the high priest, by means of a prophet's promulgation.

Archaeological evidence of royal building inscriptions indicates that generally temple-building or rebuilding was a responsibility assigned to kings by their gods. Once a temple was dedicated, the king's status as his god's earthly vice-regent would be reaffirmed, and a long and prosperous reign would be promised to him by his god.[12]

However, with a slight variation, this verse indicates that in the name of YHWH Darius commissioned Zerubbabel the governor and Joshua the high priest to accomplish the temple reconstruction that Cyrus had granted to rebuild. In this context, Darius is to be seen as YHWH's earthly partner and the beneficiary of a prosperous reign. In a similar vein, both Zerubbabel and Joshua become authorised co-operators or assistants of Darius as secondary beneficiaries.

10 *DCH*, Vol. 6, 676. Pedaiah is a son of Jekoniah in 1 Chr 3:19, whereas Zerubbabel is a son of Jekoniah in Hag 1:1, 12, 14; 2:2; Ezra 3:2, 8; 5:2 and Neh 12:1. Japhet, "Sheshbazzar and Zerubbabel: Against the Background of the Historical and Religious Tendencies of Ezra-Nehemiah," 71; Avigad, *Bullae and Seals*, 9–31.

11 *DCH*, Vol. 2, 364–70. The term הכהן הגדול appears in Lev 21:10; Num 35:25, 28, 32; Josh 20:6; 2 Kgs 12:11; 22:4, 8; 23:4, and 2 Chr 34:9. These passages refer to the pre-exilic period, but the dating of these texts is problematic. Mostly, they would be considered to be a postexilic term that replaces the earlier הכהן (priest) and הדאש הכהן (the chief priest). Berquist, *Judaism in Persia's Shadow*, 64.

12 Diana Edelman, *Origins of the 'Second' Temple Persian Imperial Policy and the Rebuilding of Jerusalem* (Equinox: London, 2005), 91–8.

Zerubbabel, a son of Shealtiel is in the Davidic line with monarchic aspirations.[13] In view of his royal heritage, Zerubbabel's authority to exercise leadership in the Jerusalem temple rebuilding project is sufficient for recognition by his people. As an imperial administrator, Zerubbabel's task is to seek and secure loyalty from the province by taking advantage of locally royal status.[14]

The function and the status of Zerubbabel may demonstrate a correspondence with that of Nehemiah, the governor appointed by the empire in the following century (Neh 5:14, 15, 18; 12:26). As Nehemiah showed his faithful loyalty to the Jerusalem wall rebuilding (Neh 1–6), so Zerubbabel, in all probability as a representative of Darius, should serve to facilitate the temple rebuilding. When viewed from this parallel with Nehemiah (Neh 5:3–4), it is evident that Zerubbabel should also steward the imperial taxation system.

The other representative is Joshua. All references to Joshua in the Book of Haggai identify him as a son of Jehozadak being sent into exile and as הכהן הגדול (Hag 1:1, 12, 14; 2:2, 4).[15] Among the usages of the term הכהן הגדול in the Hebrew Bible,[16] one strikingly interesting case can be found in

13 Zerubbabel appears in Haggai without the title פחה (Hag 1:12; 2:23), as פחה of Judah (Hag 2:21) and by his name alone (Hag 2:4). Jeconiah, Judah's last king has seven sons including Shealtiel and Pedaiah (1 Chr 3:16–19). Pedaiah's lineage receives further mention in Chronicles, where Zerubbabel is listed as Pedaiah's son.

14 Bongenaar, *The Neo-Babylonian Ebabbar Temple*, 40; Berquist, *Judaism in Persia's Shadow*, 52–8; Lipschits, "Achaemenid Imperial Policy," 19–29.

15 The genealogy in 1 Chr 5:29–41 lists Joshua as a descendant of Aaron and as the grandson of Seraiah, chief priest (הכהן הראשׁ) during the fall of Jerusalem. His title in Haggai is the same as in Zech 3:1, 8; 6:11. The title is omitted in Zech 3:3, 6, and 9. Ezra and Nehemiah mention him simply as a priest (Ezra 3:2, 8; 5:2; 10:18; Neh 7:7; 12:26; probably also 12:1).

16 The regulations for the cities of refuge use הכהן הגדול rather than in an official sense (Lev 21:10; Num 35:25, 28, 32; Josh 20:6). These passages indicate that הכהן הגדול is singled out from among equals but is not given a special title. On the other hand, the corresponding regulations in Deut 19:4–13 never refer to the priesthood. This indicates that the references to הכהן הגדול probably reflect the priestly writers' wish to emphasise the priests' importance. Janet E. Tollington, *Tradition and Innovation in Haggai and Zechariah 1–8* (JSOTSup 150; Sheffield: Sheffield Academic Press,

הכהן הגדול Hilkiah from the time of the reign of Josiah in the monarchic period (2 Kgs 12:11; 22:4, 8; 23:4; 2 Chr 34:9). Hilkiah as the high priest was in charge of financial tasks with regard to the repair of the temple of YHWH. In addition, Hilkiah had a responsibility for teaching the book of Law which was found in the time of restoring the temple (2 Kgs 22). Consequently, the application of the term to Joshua might represent a continuation of this understanding: there is little doubt that the repair and maintenance of the temple were central responsibilities of Joshua as the high priest in the Book of Haggai.

In the temple administration of the financial strategy of the empire, also, it is undeniable that the high priest was appointed as the temple administrator. In the Jerusalem temple, which was to be restored, his duties could include the management of the temple properties and the supervision of temple personnel. In the time of Nehemiah, Eliaship the high priest took charge of properties and people in the Jerusalem temple, although Nehemiah re-sorted out the temple organisation (Neh 13:6–31).

Sometimes, the temple administrator would act in the company of the governor as the general manager of the temple.[17] In this capacity, the high priest was the other representative with administrative authority in the temple. This did not mean, though, that the authority of the high priest in the Jerusalem temple would assume a theocratic governing structure in the province Judah.[18] Rather, the status of Joshua the high priest was no

---

1993), 125–31. For a pre-exilic dating of cities of refuge, see Jacob Milgrom, *Leviticus 1–16: A New Translation with Introduction and Commentary* (AB, Vol. 3; New York: Doubleday, 1991), 9–13. For a post-exilic dating of cities of refuge based on linguistic evidence, see Avi Hurvitz, *A Linguistic Study of the Relationship between the Priestly Source and the Book of Ezekiel: A New Approach to an Old Problem* (Paris: Gabalda, 1982), 10–56; Robert Polzin, *Late Biblical Hebrew: Toward an Historical Typology of Biblical Hebrew Prose* (HSM 12; Missoula, MT: Scholars Press, 1976), 85–115.

17 See Chapter 2 above. See also Bongenaar, *The Neo-Babylonian Ebabbar Temple*, 6–33.

18 On whether Judah should be described as theocratic, see Jeremiah W. Cataldo, *A Theocratic Yehud?: Issues of Government in a Persian Period* (LHB/OTS 498: New York; London: T & T Clark, 2009). On the hierarchy of status of the temple in Achaemenid Judah as compared with monarchical Judah, see David L. Petersen,

more than an imperial delegate to efficiently serve the authority of the imperial political structure.

From Hag 1:1, one should note that, in his second year of Darius the Jerusalem temple reconstruction was assigned in Judah, in the name of YHWH. For this work, Darius employed Zerubbabel the governor and Joshua the high priest as the helpers. This task of rebuilding the Jerusalem temple needed to be expedited. For the rebuilt Jerusalem temple would then enable the production and storage of the substantial provisions required by Darius's campaign against Egyptian revolts. Judah was forcibly committed to display its reliable allegiance. In doing this well, Judah would receive the guarantee from Darius.

Hag 1:2

כה אמר יהוה צבאות לאמר: העם הזה אמרו לא עת בא עת בית יהוה להבנות

[Thus said YHWH of hosts, "this people say the time has not come yet for the house of YHWH to be rebuilt."]

This verse certainly reflects the response of the people in Judah although there is no description of the prophet proclaiming the word of YHWH to the people. However, it is unquestionable that the people had been called upon to rebuild the temple, though indirectly. The people here mean the rest of the people, all unnamed except Zerubbabel and Joshua. They said that this was not the time to rebuild the temple. Irrespective of the command being supported by the name of YHWH, the people neglected the edict of Darius to rebuild the temple (also Ezra 6:1–12).

It is informative to reflect back on the charge given by Darius to Zerubbabel and Joshua to rebuild the temple. In light of the genealogies of both leaders their inherited authority was evident to the people, but their responsibility to exercise their leadership over the temple rebuilding was questioned. Hag 1:2 clearly establishes the dramatic conflict that runs

---

"The Temple in Persian Period Prophetic Texts," in Davies, ed., *Second Temple Studies*. Vol. 1, *Persian Period*, 125–45.

through the Book of Haggai: the people neglect to rebuild the temple in disobedience to the word of YHWH.

Concerning the phrase "the time has come" (עת בא, a recent eschatological viewer has reworked the old concept of the monarchical ideology, adapting motifs from the monarchical period Zion psalms and the מלך יהוה Psalms.[19] He argues that, although the Book of Haggai does not make any messianic claims, it certainly advances a theological compromise to acknowledge the realities of the demolition of the Empire and YHWH's control on Judah (Hag 2: 6–9). In support of this position, he notes one case in the Cylinder inscription of Merodachbaladan[20] in which a date for restoration is already set at the time of destruction (עת בא). He further argues that at the time when a deity is pacified, some sorts of signs are revealed to instruct the selected king to restore the destroyed temple (Hag 2:20–23).[21]

In this argument, the time to rebuild the Jerusalem temple should be delayed because the dissipation of YHWH's anger is not yet evident nor is his return to Jerusalem imminent. However, no support for the idea that the reconciliation of YHWH is pertinent to the temple restoration can be found in the Book of Haggai. The item עת in Haggai should be understood within the context of the contemporary events as violent crises prompted the intervention of the prophet.[22]

19 Bedford, *Temple Restoration in Early Achaemenid Judah*, 183–240.

20 Cyril John Gadd, "Inscribed Barrel Cylinder of Marduk-apla-iddina II," *Iraq* 20 (1953), 123–34.

21 Peter Ross Bedford, "Discerning the Time: Haggai, Zechariah and the 'Delay' in the Rebuilding of the Jerusalem Temple," in *The Pitcher Is Broken: Memorial Essays for G. W. Ahlström* (ed. Steven W. Holloway and Lowell K. Handy; JSOTSup 190; Sheffield: Sheffield Academic Press, 1995), 71–3.

22 Barstad, "Haggai Among the Prophets," 273. With regard to the sixth month, Edelman stresses that it marked the beginning of the final month of the first half-year. It was intended to set the tone for activities that would need to have been undertaken in the remaining half of the year. Edelman, *Origins*, 92–3. see also Yehezkel Kaufmann, "Das Kalendar und das Alter des Priesterkodex," *VT* 4 (1954): 307–13; Judah Ben-Zion Segal, "Intercalation and the Hebrew Calendar." *VT* 7 (1957): 250–307. Apparently, the Hebrew Bible has absolutely nothing to do with a biennial calendar. See James C. Vanderkam, "Ancient Israelite and Early Jewish," in Freedman, ed., *ABD*, 1:814–20; Ephraim Jehudah Wiesenberg, "Calendar," in Cecil Roth, ed., *EJ*, 43–50.

Focusing on the sixth month of the year should take into consideration the actual agricultural calendar. In relation to the early Israelite calendar, the Gezer Calendar,[23] the sixth month appears to have extended from the middle of August to the beginning of September, when grapes, olives, figs and pomegranates were being harvested.[24] Chronologically, the produce of grains, such as wheat and barley, would already have been reaped and the harvest of fruits would be approaching.[25]

It would have been difficult for the people to furnish the temple rebuilding with the required wood and bricks, not to mention forced labour during a harvest time. Yet, from an economic point of view, this intermediary season would not have been the appropriate time to rebuild the temple either. Instead, it would have been the very time to reap the harvest which might be used to pay their mandatory taxes in the newly established imperial administration, not to mention to meet their needs for daily provisions.[26]

In this view, the understanding of the appropriate time or sapiential reasoning for the reconstruction is revealed by the reflection of the phrase לא עת בא in which the word עת is followed by a genitival infinitive construct (Hag 1:2, 4), such as: "it was still day, it was not the time to gather in the flocks" (Gen 29:7; see also Eccl 3:2–8).[27] This grammar suggests that the agricultural community, which is mainly composed of the non-exiled, is

23 This calendar has been dated as early as around 925 BCE. Young, "The Style of the Gezer Calendar," 362–75.

24 The agricultural seasons correspond to the solar year and depend on temperature, precipitation, and similar factors, all of which influence the daily life of the Israelite farmer (Gen 45:6; Exod 34:21; Ruth 2:23; Num 13:20; 2 Sam 16:1; Isa 24:13; Jer 40:10). Borowski, *Agriculture in Iron Age*, 33–7.

25 The major festivals are linked to the agricultural cycle. See Hinckley Gilbert Mitchell, J. M. Powis Smith, and Julius A. Bewer, *A Critical and Exegetical Commentary on Haggai, Zechariah, Malachi and Jonah* (New York: Scribner, 1912), 58; Elie Assis, "A Disputed Temple (Haggai 2, 1–9)," *ZAW* 120 (2008): 582–3; Philippe Guillaume, *Land and Calendar: The Priestly Document from Genesis 1 to Joshua 18* (New York; London: T & T Clark, 2009), 84–124.

26 Kessler, *The Book of Haggai*, 123–7.

27 Kessler, "Building the Second Temple," 243–56; Kessler, *The Book of Haggai*, 125–6.

responsible for rejecting YHWH's calls to rebuild the temple. The reason for their resistance seems to be that, as landowners, they already take charge of the land's economy (Hag 2:4). Thus they prioritise economic profits over rebuilding the Jerusalem temple.[28]

The above argument supposes the conflicts over land tenure issues or political allegiances between the exiled and the non-exiled. However, the Book of Haggai is never intended to incite conflict between the two groups. Moreover, Haggai accuses the people of being more obsessed with their desired project than their agricultural harvest.

According to Hag 1:3–4, the people enjoyed the panelled houses which were provided during the construction of the temple and palace in Jerusalem. At the specific moment of temple rebuilding, their main leader, Zerubbabel, who was fundamentally involved in the political, economical, and cultural systems, called up a dazzling promise for Judah. The people positively expected that YHWH would restore the Davidic dynasty and ensure its political stability and economic prosperity, as had been the case with David. However, the Judean political reality under the Achaemenid power was nothing but a rebellion, which threatened the destruction of Judah.

Opposing the people's argument, Haggai exhorts them to rebuild the house of YHWH. The use of the Niphal infinitive construct form להבנות in Hag 1:2 also appears in Zech 8:9: "the temple might be built" (להבנות היכל).[29] Both verses highlight the building process in which the people themselves are now engaged. This further supports the view that the people are surely being commissioned to be the work force for the temple project.

It is particularly important to note that there are many cases in which the word בנה is linked with one verb זרע (Jer 35:7) and another verb נטע to

28 Haggai intentionally underplays divisions within the community in order to present a vision of a community unified in its opposition to the rebuilding of the temple. Kessler, *The Book of Haggai*, 140–8, 164, 203–6.

29 *DCH*, Vol. 2, 226–8. People build cities (Gen 4:17; 1 Kgs 9:17), alters (Exod 17:15; 1 Kgs 18:32), walls and gates (2 Kgs 15:35; Neh 2:17), and homes and families (Gen 16:3; Deut 25:9).

describe agricultural activities (e.g., Deut 28:30; Isa 65:21–22; Jer 1:10; 18:9; 24:6; 29:5, 28; 31:28; 35:7; 42:10; 45:4; Ezek 28:6; 36:36; Amos 9:14; Eccl 2:4). Obviously, this formula emphasises that the people should "build" or "restore" ("rebuild") the temple in order to live well, as grains or vegetables are sown or planted to enjoy food. Thus the temple rebuilding involves the people in a nourishing and fostering process. Some cases among of the numerous texts indicating that the reconstruction of the temple by the words of YHWH would bring posterity include 1 Sam 2:35; 2 Sam 7:5–16 and 1 Kgs 1:37–39. Therefore, to ensure a bountiful harvest, this is the very time to rebuild the temple.

As I have shown above, Hag 1:2 accuses the people of neglecting YHWH's command to rebuild the Jerusalem temple. The people were definitely being commissioned to rebuild the temple. Nevertheless, those surrounding Zerubbabel had the very different idea of restoring the Davidic dynasty concomitantly with the temple. Their desire was caused by their faulty understanding of the title of Zerubbabel and their misconception of the importance of rebuilding the Jerusalem temple. Thus, this verse includes a warning against the two leaders, Zerubbabel and Joshua, for not raising their voices in favour of the temple reconstruction, despite having been authorised by YHWH to manage that project.

Hag 1:3

ויהי דבר יהוה ביד חגי הנביא לאמר

[Then the word of YHWH came through Haggai the prophet saying.]

The clause ויהי דבר-יהוה ביד-חגי הנביא (Hag 1:3) is nearly identical to Hag 1:1, differing only in that the perfect verb היה has been converted into the imperfect form due to the ו consecutive conjunction. The leading item is likewise the word ביד which means "by the hand of," "on behalf of," or "for the sake of," indicating an instrument: for example, "YHWH spoke through Moses" (Exod 9:35); "YHWH spoke through Jeremiah" (Jer 37:2). Subsequently, the use of the word ביד gave the authority to the messenger in the sentence of … היה … דבר by denoting the source of the word (Hos 1:1; Jer 1:1–2; Zeph 1:1; Zech 1:1).[30]

Also, this verse shows the role of intercession between the recalcitrant people and YHWH's commandment. Such intercession is one of the most important tasks of prophets during difficult situations. Now, Haggai actively participates in criticising the people's neglect to rebuild the Jerusalem temple. It is likewise the case that in disputes arising within a region or between regions, a royal commissioner should intervene to settle the contentious issue (Ezra 4–5).[31]

Hag 1:4

העת לכם אתם לשבת בבתיכם[32] ספונים-והבית הזה חרב

["Is it the time for you yourselves to dwell in your panelled houses while this house is in ruins?"]

The people certainly did not consider it time to rebuild the house of YHWH and they had not begun the temple rebuilding. In a similar way to that by which the people expressed their disobedience to the word of YHWH, Haggai raised this rhetorical question to the people: "is it the time for you yourselves to dwell in your panelled houses while this house was in ruins?" It is worthwhile to note that Haggai emphasises the discrepancy between YHWH and the people with the word "the house" (הבית), a kind

30 *DCH*, Vol. 2, 89–91.

31 See Chapter 2 above.

32 BHS suggests correcting בבתיכם ("in your houses") to בבתים ("in houses"), based on the LXX ἐν οἴκοις οφ. The LXX is followed by Targum, and the Vulgate. בבתיכם following two other pronouns is syntactically unusual. The correction is probably right, in light of the word's relationship with the adjective ספונים, and as it avoids unnecessary redundancy. Yet בבתיכם may be seen as intentional, highlighting the contrast between the people's houses and YHWH's house. Therefore, I will not make the emendation.

of word play.[33] The vital word tybh obviously has a contrastive effect in that it intensified the sense of inconsistency between YHWH and the people.

One key point of this verse is that people's houses are panelled (ספונים). The word ספונים is a Qal passive participle masculine plural absolute form of the verb ספן, which means "to make level," "to roll down to cover," or "to lay a table." This form is only used in this verse but the root ספן appears six times in the Hebrew Bible. This term is consistently used as a verb except in 1 Kgs 6:15, where it is used as a noun referring to the ceiling: for example, "for there the ruler's portion was reserved" (Deut 33:21); "he covered the house with beams and planks of cedar" (1 Kgs 6:9); "it was panelled with cedar" (1 Kgs 7:3, 7; Jer 22:14).[34] In each case, it literally signifies "structured" or "constructed" in the context of the luxury construction of the temple and the palace in Jerusalem. With these usages in mind, I would rather interpret the word ספן in this verse to be well "governed," "administrated," or "managed."

This interpretation makes evident the similarities between 2 Sam 7:2 and Hag 1:4. When David dwelled in a luxurious house of cedar unlike YHWH, he had a strong desire to build the house of YHWH (2 Sam 7:2//1 Chr 17:1). His passion for the Jerusalem temple building brought about the establishment of the Davidic dynasty (2 Sam 7:5–16) although YHWH did not allow him personally to build the temple as a qualified builder (1 Chr 22:6–10). Inasmuch as the Davidic house was panelled with cedar from floor to ceiling (1 Kgs 7:7) the people in Judah are making a veiled allusion to what they read about David, which demonstrates their strong focus on restoring the Davidic dynasty through Zerubbabel.[35]

From a historical perspective, the hope of the people for a Davidic dynasty could also be supported by the Jerusalem resettlement. In the

33 The following Hebrew words designate the temple in the book of Haggai: הבית הזה (Hag 1:4; 2:3, 7, 9), בית יהוה (Hag 1:2, 14), הבית (Hag 1:8), הביתי (Hag 1:9), המקום הזה and הבית זה (Hag 2:9), and היכל־יהזה (Hag 2:15, 18). Meanwhile, הבית הזה in Hag 2:7 represent the Davidic house. I will explain this in Chapter 5.

34 *DCH*, Vol. 6, 181–2; Steck, "Zu Haggai," 362; Petersen, *Haggai, Zechariah 1–8*, 48–9; Verhoef, *The Book of Haggai and Malachi*, 57–9; Wolff, *Haggai*, 30.

35 Petersen, "Zerubbabel and Jerusalem Temple Reconstruction," 366–72.

Achaemenid period, continuous settlement occurs in Jerusalem although most settlements are confined to the southeastern spur and the temple mount.[36] The settlements accord with the Achaemenid policy to revive Jerusalem as Judah's provincial nucleus for the empire's economic and military benefits. Indeed, once erected on its specially prepared site within the capital city, the Jerusalem temple, with its palace, constitutes a crucial part of the economic, political, and administrative life of the people.[37] Notwithstanding this, the people in Haggai regarded the new settlements in Jerusalem as a part of the attempt within Judah to create an independent sub-province (ספן).

In contrast to the people's concept of the term "panelled" (ספנים), it is informative to ponder Jeremiah's association between the panelled house and Jehoahaz's (or Shallum's) tragic life (Jer 22:11–14). This figure of tragedy is also alluded to by the major re-painting of the signet ring (כחותם) given to Zerubbabel in Hag 2:23.[38] Informed by this reading, the people's efforts are revealed to be a delusory hope that will literally amount to no more than their panelled houses.

The other key is that the house of YHWH is still in ruins (חרב). The word חרב here is an adjective and describes "a dry state," (Lev 7:10; Prov 17:1, Ezek 36:35) "desolate," or "in ruins" (Hag 1:9; Jer 22:5; 33:10; Ezek 5:14).[39] Notably, where the temple is mentioned, this word occurs only three times (Hag 1:4, 9; Jer 33:10). So, the reader might wonder, what is the point in using the word חרב to refer to the temple status?

The Jerusalem temple had to be in use even in the Neo-Babylonian period. Mourning the fall of Jerusalem, the people coming from peripheral

36 See Chapter 3 above. See also Stern, "The Persian Empire," 71–2; Tadmor, "Judah," 261–96; Widengren, "The Persian Period," 489–538; Avnimelech, "Influence of Geological Conditions," 24–31; Carter, *Emergence*, 294.

37 Barstad, "Haggai Among the Prophets," 268–9.

38 See the exegesis of Hag 2:23 in Chapter 5.

39 The verb חרב in the Hebrew Bible is generally used in relation to devastations resulting from drought, punishment, or war (Isa 44:27; 50:2; 51:10; Jer 25:9; 51:3; Ezek 6:6; 12:20; 25:19; 26:2; 30:7). Also, this word as noun, חרב, which occurs 9 times, can be translated "dry land" (Hag 2:6; Gen 7:22; Exod 14:21; Ezek 48:21). *DCH*, Vol. 3, 306–11.

parts of Judah performed religious rituals in the desolate Jerusalem temple (Jer 41:5).[40] The record of Haggai supports this description that the temple is not completely destroyed (Hag 1:9; 2:3), but is still the location for sacred rituals (Hag 2:10–14). While the temple is still standing among the people living in Jerusalem, it is at least partly damaged or destroyed (Ezek 11:15).[41] Resonances with Malachi are apparent, for in both passages the people despise the house of YHWH (Mal 1:7–8). Thus, Haggai's exhortations function as an attack on the performance of sacrifices within the temple, while it remained in such an inappropriate state (Hag 2:12–14).

Supporting the view that the temple is not at all in ruins, an interesting translation proposes that the term חרב be understood as "desolate" rather than as "in ruins."[42] This translation is based on the dissimilarity between the inhabited dwellings of the human population and the uninhabitable residence of YHWH. One fine case in which this term is indeed used to mean "desolate" can be seen in Jer 26:9, "this house should be like Shiloh, and this city should be desolate without an inhabitant" (also Jer 33:10, 12).

However, this emendation might not be necessary because of the relationship between "desolate" and "in ruins." The usage may be understood as hyperbolic, citing Isa 25:2 "for you made the city a heap, the fortified city was in ruins."[43] Though the word חרב is not used, yet, the use of similar term מפלה certainly never means that the city becomes an actual stone heap that is never rebuilt. Likewise, the use of the term חרב may be an example of the poetic reservoir found in the prophetic language. What the text conveys is that the temple is not still in a repaired condition.

This exegesis of Hag 1:3–4 has demonstrated that Haggai brought charges against the people who communally neglected any activities at the Jerusalem temple. To emphasise this, Haggai expresses the crucial contrast

40 For their religious aspect, see Smith, *The Religion of the Landless*, 75–83; Albertz Rainer, *A History of Israelite Religion in the Old Testament* 2 Vols (OTLS; Louisville: Westminster; John Knox, 1994).

41 See Chapter 3 above.

42 Meyers and Meyers, *Haggai, Zechariah 1–8*, 24; Robert P. Carroll, *Jeremiah: A Commentary* (OTL; Philadelphia: Westminster, 1986), 635–6.

43 Barstad, "Haggai Among the Prophets," 270–1.

between YHWH and the people wherein the phrase "the house" (הבית) reveals the dichotomy between houses being panelled (ספנים) and the temple being in ruins (חרב). With the word ספנים, which recalls the Davidic dynasty, the people focus on the royal lineage of Zerubbabel in an attempt to restore Judean royal dynasty. Meanwhile, Haggai advocates the restoration of the Jerusalem temple, which is being used in its state of desolation for the benefit of the efficient imperial administration.

Hag 1:5

ועתה כה אמר יהוה צבאות: שימו לבבכם על-דרכיכם

[Now therefore, thus said the Lord of hosts, "Consider your ways"]

This verse strongly urged the people to change their course of action, in the name of YHWH, while repeating the prophetic messenger form כה אמר יהוה צבאות (also Hag 1:2 and 7) with the particle adverb עתה. The expression עתה is very commonly used for rhetorical effect: "I see him, but not now" (Num 24:17; see also Josh 11:8; Isa 33:10; Ezek 27:34); "and now, lest he stretch out his hand" (Gen 3:22; see also Isa 5:3, 5; Amos 7:16; Ezek 27:34); "but now take courage" (Hag 2:4).[44] As one can see from the above passages, the adverb עתה indicates the present moment, explains a new subject or prompts a conclusion drawn from the preceding statement. Focusing on the events concurrent with the discourse, "just now" the prophet Haggai enjoins the people to consider their course of action.

In connection with the word עתה, which concludes the preceding instruction and implies that what follows is consequentially related, the imperative formula using שימו (Hag 1:5, 7; 2:15) draws immediate attention to the present contrasting situation.[45]

44 *HALOT*, Vol. 2, 1483–6; Bill T. Arnold and John H. Choi, *A Guide to Biblical Hebrew Syntax* (Cambridge: Cambridge University Press, 2003), 139–40; Verhoef, *The Book of Haggai and Malachi*, 121.

45 Richard J. Coggins, *Haggai, Zechariah and Malachi* (OTG; Sheffield: Sheffield Academic Press, 1987), 33–4.

The verb שׂים followed by the noun לֵב (לבב) represents "to have regard for" or "to pay attention to," which places importance on focusing the people's hearts towards the issue in question: for example, "give attention to all that I was going to show you" (Ezek 40:4; see also 44:5; Isa 41:22; Hag 1:7; 2:18; Exod 9:21; Judg 19:30; Job 1:8; 23:6). Therefore, this phrase should be interpreted as "consider or concern yourselves with your chosen way," in the form of an imperative expression that encourages the people towards self-reflection.

As it happens, the people try to establish the Davidic governance for the prosperity of the people through restoring the Davidic kingdom. However, YHWH asks the people to reflect upon the consequences of the way that they have chosen since it is not YHWH's way. Exhorting the people to reconsider their actions indicates YHWH's negative response to the choice the people have made. In the rift between the way of YHWH and the way of the people, Haggai plays the prophetic role of intervening to encourage the people to act rightly.

Hag 1:6

זרעתם הרבה והבא מעט אכול ואין לשבעה שתו ואין לשכרה לבוש, ואין לחם לו;
והמשתכר משתכר[46] אל-צרור נקוב

["You have sown much, but bring little. You eat, but there is no satiety. You drink, but there is no quenching. You clothe yourselves, but no one is warm. And one who earns wages puts wages into a bag with holes."]

Once the circulation of agricultural knowledge reached the people of Judah, they sowed grains and fruit trees in abundance.[47] However, when it came to the harvest, they reaped little. Considering how much they sowed, the diminutive yield starkly contrasted their expectations. To emphasise this,

46 BHS notes that two Hebrew manuscripts correct the participle מִשְׂתַּכֵּר to imperfect יִשְׂתַּכֵּר (since the sentence lacks a finite verb). Yet the sentence does not require a finite verb to be grammatically correct. This is particularly true in Hag 1:6, because the second מִשְׂתַּכֵּר designates all money or benefits that the people are aiming to earn or create. Therefore, I will keep the text as it is.

47 Borowski, *Agriculture in Iron Age*, 47–84; Hopkins, *Highlands*, 213–34.

Haggai employs two contrast words "much" (רבה) and "little" (מעט) in this sentence. Due to the crop failure, the people ate their meals but never felt full, and their thirst unquenchable. Further indicating the unsatisfying nature of choosing a course of action contrary to the will of YHWH, the people put on clothes without receiving any warmth.

Naturally, when they have their meals (אכול) the people expect to be satiated (לשׂבעה). Along with drinking (שׁתו) and being clothed (לבושׁ), they expect to have their thirst quenched (לשׁכרה) and to be warm enough (לחם). Yet, in reality, they experience disappointment as their daily provisions fail to satisfy their needs. To emphasise this discrepancy, comparable phrases are turned into contrasting phrases with a negative-particle adverb אין.

All three phrases become polar structures, in which expectations stand in opposition to reality. What one finds in the text is a description of the real crop failure: the grains have been largely destroyed and the vines render very little produce, leading to the near decimation of Judah's significant wine industry. Furthermore, the people fail in their wool industry. Thus every component in Judah's agricultural system is broken.

Much less surplus from the yield diminished provisions for daily life and resulted in a scarcity of trade commodities. So while workers wanted to enjoy the benefits of their work, it was impossible, for it was as if they were putting their wages into a bag with holes in it.[48] Thus, the last sentence of this verse further accentuates the contrast between expectations and reality.

The word משׂתכר, which is the Hithpael participle masculine singular absolute form of the verb שׂכר, appears once in this verse. The basic meaning of the verb שׂכר is the granting of payment for labour, services or any type of benefit received from someone. The word שׂכר in a reflexive mode appears to represent to "hire oneself out" or "take oneself into paid service." So, the word משׂתכר with the particle article ה denotes "one who worked for something" as a relative pronoun phrase. In this interpretation, the noun משׂתכר designates all the people who were doing their best to make a living.

With this context, it is interesting to note that Haggai uses the word צרור to reference a purse, with holes, containing wages. The noun צרור

48 The province of Judah would mint coins after the period of Nehemiah. Verhoef, *The Book of Haggai and Malachi*, 62–3; Gilter, "The Levant," 101–13.

indicates "a pouch that is being wrapped up" in the form of a leather bag, which could be tied up at the top. One very plausible use for such a purse would be to store minted coins used as wages or collected as profits through the agricultural pursuits.[49] In which case, the people would imagine big pouches of silver such as in Gen 42:35 and Prov 7:20. However, in this instance, their money simply disappears as if the purse they put it in is full of holes. The people find that the wages they have earned in such a manner are of no avail to their well-being.

Within the context of the larger imperial market, Judah's role as a commissary should have been jeopardised. What is worse, any shortage of daily provisions leads to increased demand, and subsequently a rise in value. Hence, the people would have been forced to pay a high price, which, in turn, would have led to a high cost of living. No economic benefits would have been created whilst there was a shortage of basic products.[50] The agricultural economic system would have been distressingly ruined.

On this point, it is worthwhile to look at the key word in this verse, זרע. This word occurs 245 times in the Hebrew Bible, in 44 different forms (Hag 2:19; Num 20:5; Deut 14:22; 28:38; Isa 5:10; 30:23; 32:20; 55:10; Jer 35:7; 50:16; Ps 10:37; 126:6; Job 4:8). Within the agricultural cycle, all kinds of seeds would have been sown on the fields.[51] And, in time, the people would have pruned all the different plants they had sown. Then, they would have expected to gather their harvest. So, the item זרע would have been linked to words such as נור or חרשׁ (plough), נטע (plant, Isa 17:10; Jer 35:7; Ps. 10:37), זמר (prune, Lev 25:4), אסף (gather, Exod 23:10; 23:16; Lev 25:4, 22; 26:16; Deut 22:9), בוא (bring, Gen 46:6; Hag. 1:6), or קצר (reap, Lev 25:11, 20; Jer 12:13) in the context of agricultural activities.

49 Verhoef, *The Book of Haggai and Malachi*, 62. Coins minted in gold and silver were generally used to settle business transaction, though Judah also continued to use Greek coins. Rappaport, "Numistics," 25–6.

50 See Chapter 1 above.

51 The term זרע is also used to designate human seed, offspring, and descendants (Gen 3:15; 4:25; 9:9; 12:7; 13:15–16;15:3, 5, 13–16, 18; 16:10; 17:7–10, 12, 19; 19:32, 34; 21:12–13; 22:15–18; 24:7; 28:13–14; 38:8–9; 1 Sam 1:11; 2:20; 2 Sam 7:12). *DCH*, Vol. 3, 139–44; *HALOT*, Vol. 1, 282–3.

It is noteworthy that the agricultural activities of seeding and harvesting rely entirely on YHWH's blessing. Demonstrating that dependence is the following verse from Genesis: "Isaac sowed in that land, and reaped in the same year a hundredfold because YHWH blessed him" (Gen 26:12).

YHWH apportioned crucial blessings in relationship to how the people responded to YHWH himself, his temple or his commandments, in the forms of successful sowing and a high yield: "if you show reverence for my temple ... the ground will yield its crops and the trees of the field their fruits. Your threshing will continue until the grape harvest and the grape harvest will continue until the planting, and you will eat all the food you want and live safely in your land" (Lev 25:2–5; see also Gen 26:12; Deut 6:11; 11:13–17; 2 Kgs 19:29; Job 31:8; Ps 107:37–38; Isa 30:23; 37:30; Ezek 23:16). The blessing of YHWH is that his people should reap their harvest lavishly, eat well and be satisfied.

Quite an opposite state of affairs is found in this verse and similar situation texts, for example: "because you forget YHWH your saviour ... in the day you will make your plant grow, and in the morning you will see your seed flourish, but the harvest will be a heap of ruins..." (Isa 17:10–11); "if you do not obey YHWH your God ... you will sow many seeds in the field but you will harvest little ... you will not drink ..." (Deut 28:15, 38–39); "if you reject my decrees ... when I cut off your supply of bread ..." (Lev 26:15, 26; see also Jer 12:13; Hos 8:7; Mic 6:14–15; Eccl 11:6). Correspondingly, YHWH's curse is that the people eat their meals but never feel full due to the lack of harvest (Isa 23:18; 56:11; Ezek 16: 28; 39:19).[52]

In the agrarian society of the ancient Near East, the deities not only provided prosperity, but, contrariwise, they could also inflict famine.[53] In essence, Judah is an agrarian economy. Thus, whenever the people violate

52 In other contexts, rhetorical antonyms of זרע or נטע include: נתשׁ, "root up," "remove" or "drive out," (Jer 12:14; 31:26–27); נתץ, "break down" or "throw down"; רים, "take away" (Jer 18:7; 31:28; Ps 9:7; 52:7); אבד, "destroy" (Jer 9:12); רעע, "afflict," "beat" or "smash" (Isa 26:21; Jer 25:6; Ps 105:15); נסח, "forcibly remove" or "tear down" (Deut 28:63; Ps 52:7); נצה, "be in ruins" (2 Kgs 19:25; Isa 37:26; Jer 2:15; 4:7; 9:11; 46:19); שׁמה, "be desolate" (Isa 64:10–11; 54:1; Jer 19:8; Ezek 32:38).

53 Barstad, "Haggai Among the Prophets," 276.

YHWH, his punishment is mainly manifested in the agricultural areas of Judean life. Furthermore, YHWH stops prophets from intervening and rejects the people's offerings (Jer 14:11–12). Then, the punishment culminates in a war or a famine being inflicted on them (Jer 14:15–16).

As I have shown in Hag 1:2 and 4, the people were obviously reluctant to look after the house of YHWH. Their reluctance caused YHWH to duly withdraw his blessing from their agricultural endeavours. As a result, the agricultural yield was unquestionably a failure, with which none of the people could have been pleased. Thus, the adverse agricultural circumstances that were manifested in the Judean agricultural reality should be understood as YHWH's punishment.

The exegesis of Hag 1: 5–6 that I performed above demonstrates that there should be little doubt of a relationship between the temple and agriculture. Retrospectively questioning the preference of the people, Haggai clearly indicates that their crops failed as a result of the temple remaining in ruins. The people devoted themselves to sowing in plenty, with expectations of a bountiful harvest: yet they reaped no benefits from their efforts. Their provisions were inadequate to meet even the necessities of eating, drinking, and being clothed. Nor could they appropriate any benefits from interregional trade, because they lacked marketable products. As a result of defying YHWH's command, Judah's agricultural economic network was destroyed.

Hag 1:7

כה אמר יהוה צבאות: שימו לבבכם על דרכיכם[54]

[Thus said the Lord of hosts, "Consider your ways"]

54 BHS suggests that שימו לבבכם על דרכיכם ("consider your way") is a scribal addition in view of the exact repetition in Hag 1:5. Yet, in a way of letting the people reflect back on the severe crop failure, this verse serves as the confirmation of YHWH for the people to build the temple sooner than later in the following verse. I see no reason to change the text here.

Once again, this unit starts with the introductory formula כה אמר יהוה צבאות that was used to announce the prophetic messages in Hag 1:5. In Hag 1:5–6, the people were called to reflect upon the agricultural failure that their choice had provoked. Now, the people are invited again to reflect upon the temple restoration. While considering the frustration of their agricultural results, it is important for the people to ponder how they should progress towards something better.[55] Progress will begin with the people moving from their inactivity to active reconstruction of the temple (Hag 1:8).

By highlighting the relationship between the temple remaining in desolation and the severe agricultural difficulties, the prophet Haggai faithfully acts on behalf of the people and encourages them to restore the Jerusalem temple. As we will see, the people should respond by committing themselves to the establishment of the temple governance for the vast economic affluence, rather than Davidic governance.

Hag 1:8

עלו ההר והבאתם עץ, ובנו הבית; וארצה בו ואכבד (ואכבדה)[56] אמר יהוה

["Go up to the mountain, bring wood and rebuild the house, that I may be pleased in it and be glorified," said YHWH.]

With the prophetic messenger formula אמר יהוה, the prophet Haggai lets the people recall what they are charged to do. That charge consisted of these three imperative phrases: "Go up (עלו) to the mountain, bring (בא) wood and rebuild (בנו) the temple." I will now explore each of these commands, beginning with the first word, עלו, which is a Qal imperative masculine

55 Kessler, *Haggai*, 133.

56 *Qere* has a cohortative form ואבדדה for *Ketib* ואכבד. If one reads the imperfect form with the *Ketib*, it would be most logical also to do the same with the preceding verb ארצה. As it is, the nuance is one of simple temporal succession, indicating the response promised by YHWH. Adopting the *Qere*, however, the phrase reads as a final or consecutive clause: "I will let myself be glorified." So, the adjustment to *Qere* would be better in Haggai's messages.

plural form of the verb עלה, which means "to ascend," "to go up" or "to make one's way up."[57]

The word עלה appears many times in the Hebrew Bible and, remarkably, is used in two different patterns. One pattern is used to describe going up to a geographical high place, for example: "So Abram went up from Egypt to the Negev" (Gen 13:1; see also 45:25; Num 32:11; Isa 14:14; Amos 3:5; Song 4:2). The other pattern is used to describe going up toward the Jerusalem temple, Zion, as a technical meaning for instance: "come, let us go up to the mountain of YHWH, to the house of the God of Jacob" (Ps 122:4; see also 47:6; 48:3; Exod 34:24; 1 Sam 1:13; 10:3; Isa 2:3; Jer 31:6). Given its two usages, in this verse עלה could not designate a definite location for the people to ascend. Rather, it urges the people to go up into the mountains (ההר), indicating the hill-country of the Hebrew Bible (Gen 31:21; 1 Sam 31:1, 8). It is worth noting that in general these high places were heavily forested (Josh 17:14–18), and the trees in the mountains could have been readily used for building, which leads to the second of the three commands issued in verse 8.

The second command is to bring wood, which is one of the required building materials.[58] The use of a Hiphil perfect form הבאתם suggests that the people have been given absolute responsibility not only to secure wood but also to rebuild the temple. Yet the duty of the people to bring wood, as a building material, seems to contradict this reference to the temple in Hag 2:15: "one stone is laid upon another in YHWH's temple." Wood, thus, appears not to literally refer to actual building materials. So, the reference to bringing wood would have been seen as a call to undertake preparatory measures for the stonework required in the temple's reconstruction. Preparation and erecting scaffolding would have been one such measure, since the woodwork in the first temple had been burned.[59] This kind of

57 *DCH*, Vol. 6, 400–8.

58 Meyers and Meyers, *Haggai, Zechariah 1–8*, 28.

59 When the Jerusalem temple was destroyed in 586 BCE, all the timber had been burned. However, there remained an ample supply of stones for building. See Verhoef, *The Book of Haggai and Malachi*, 65–6; Kessler, *The Book of Haggai*, 133–4; Lisbeth S. Fried, "The House of the God Who dwells in Jerusalem," *JAOS* 126 (2006): 100.

argument is supported by the fact that only the cedar (1 Kgs 5) that had to be imported from Lebanon could provide suitable timber for the construction of a temple.[60] Beams of cedar, stretching from floor to ceiling, provided structural support to the temple of Solomon (1 Kgs 6:15).

Though cedar was one material for the temple construction, it does not follow that the temple was built of cedar. The prophet Jeremiah called down judgement on those kings who had panelled their houses with cedar (Jer 22:14), because of the extravagance of their buildings. Even so, unlike the other temple building passages that consistently refer to a range of materials (i.e., wood, stone, and metal) this passage identifies wood alone as a material to be procured. To reconcile this apparent contradiction, one should recall that the temple is still in use (Hag 1:4; 2:10–14), and only needs to be repaired. It seems, thus, that this temple rebuilding has never been intended to produce an extravagant building like Solomon's temple.

The importance of wood within the temple structure is increasingly evident in view of the Jerusalem temple's function within the imperial temple administration. For, one major asset of the Jerusalem temple is its large storehouse for grains, wine, oils, and other commodities. The presence of this storehouse is indicated through the use of the word לשכה, which is used to describe temple storerooms (Neh 10:4; 13:4). Within the storehouse, columns and pilasters, which are basic and necessary features of granaries and silos would have been built with timber. That is why, in the third and central command, YHWH simply commands to build the house of YHWH, without giving any details regarding what is required and how it has to be done unlike the first temple (1 Kgs 6; 1 Chr 21–29; 2 Chr 2).

As for the process of fulfilling this third command, to rebuild the temple, trees of the Judean forest would have been adequate to re-structure

60 Judah is granted permission by Cyrus to negotiate with Lebanon for a new shipment of cedar to restore the temple (Ezra 3:7). See Liphschitz and Biger, "The Timber Trade," 121–7.

the Jerusalem temple.[61] Indeed trees from the local forest were even used in the first Jerusalem temple building. Among the local trees, cypress (Isa 41:19; Eccl 24:13) was one kind that Solomon had used to build the temple (1 Kgs 5:22; 2 Chr 3:5).[62] Sycamore (1 Kgs 10:27; 2 Chr 1:15) and pine (1 Kgs 5:22; Isa 41:19; Ezek 31:8; Ps 104:17)[63] were also used in Solomon's temple, for flooring, doors, and ceilings. Additionally, local palm trees provided a motif for the ornaments adorning King Solomon's temple (1 Kgs 6:29, 32, 35; Ezek 41:18–20). The command to bring wood, therefore, is enough to rebuild the Jerusalem temple.

After commanding that the temple be rebuilt, YHWH proclaims that once it is rebuilt (בנה), he will take pleasure (רצא) in it and he will be glorified (כבד). The first verb רצא, which means to take pleasure in, appears with YHWH as subject twenty-eight times. Of these instances, occasionally the preposition ב is included, for example: "for YHWH took pleasure in his people" (Ps 49:14); "did YHWH take delight in thousands of rams" (Mic 6:7).[64] In each case, a person or a thing (thousands of rams) is the object of YHWH's delight and is described within a temple (Isa 60:7; Jer 14:12; Hos 8:13; Amos 5:22; Mic 6:7).

The other verb, כבד, which is used in its Niphal form, denotes "to be considered weighty," "to be honoured," "to enjoy honour," or "to behave with dignity."[65] The cases in which the glory of YHWH appears in the passive form were quite limited, for example: "YHWH was glorified" (Isa 26:15); "and I would be glorified in the midst of you" (Ezek 28:22); "on

61 About agricultural buildings, such as silos and barns (מגודה Hag 2:19; Jer 50:26; Joel 1:17, מגדל, Isa 5:2; or סכה, Isa 1:8), see Banning, Edward Bruce "Towers," in Freedman, ed., *ABD*, 6:622–4.

62 Cypress was also used for manufacturing ships. In the story of Noah's ark (Gen 6:14); furniture; lances; musical instruments and doors. Jacob and Jacob, "Flora," 805.

63 Sycamore could not be used for larger buildings, which require longer and stronger beams. Pine would also have been utilised in shipbuilding and musical instruments. Meyers and Meyers, *Haggai, Zechariah 1–8*, 27–8; Jacob and Jacob, "Flora," 806.

64 The verb רצה with the *person* (an individual or the people) appears in 2 Sam 24:23; Isa 42:1; Jer 14:10, 12; 42:1; Ezek 20:40, 41 and Hos 8:13. And the verb רצה accompanied by the *thing* is used in Deut 33:11 and Prov 16:7. *HALOT*, Vol. 2, 1280–1.

65 *DCH*, Vol. 4, 349–52.

the day that I glorified myself" (Ezek 39:13). In every case, the reflexive use of כבד with YHWH as subject implicitly conveys YHWH's honouring of himself by means of the very desirable and precious resources that the people offer.[66]

One should here recall the purpose of rebuilding the Jerusalem temple. A built temple would facilitate the management of agriculture, and would result in the blessing of an abundant harvest. Since the rebuilt temple promises significant economic benefits, it would follow that the rebuilding process would be an important investment that should be well financed with numerous resources. Upon reaping the blessings of restoring the temple, the temple's treasuries would be handed over to the imperial king in the name of taxation. This would improve Judah's position within the empire. Also, the people of Judah would be able to enjoy the benefits of their affluence. Thus, YHWH should rejoice in the prosperous economic resources of the temple.

This exegesis of Hag 1:7–8 has demonstrated the importance of quickly rebuilding or restoring the Jerusalem temple. In contrast to the people's indifference, as their intercessor during the economic disaster, Haggai incessantly and determinedly exhorts them to restore the Jerusalem temple. He confidently assures the people of the prosperity that YHWH has promised once the temple is restored. With this affluence, the Jerusalem temple could even obtain the role of imperial fiscal centre. Furthermore, the restored Jerusalem temple would regain its reputation as an economic thriving centre. This is how YHWH would be glorified in his house. Accordingly, Haggai compels the people to pay great attention to restoring the Jerusalem temple restoration.

66 This glorification is upheld both through the actions of YHWH himself and through the actions of others on YHWH's behalf. The glory is associated more closely with a tangible sense of the presence of YHWH. For this reason, the glory of YHWH is fulfilled through the act of rebuilding the temple on YHWH's behalf, rather than by the temple structure itself. Tim Meadowcroft, "A desolate Land, People and Temple: Haggai and the Environment," *Colloq* 40 (2008), 152.

Hag 1:9

פנה אל הרבה והנה[67] למעט והבאתם הבית ונפחתי בו: יען מה
נאם יהוה צבאות יען ביתי אשר הוא חרב ואתם רצים איש לביתו

["You have looked for much but it turns out to be little. And you bring it into the house. However, I blow it away. Why?" YHWH of hosts declared. "Why is it my house, which is still in ruins while you run quickly to his house."]

This verse reiterates the hope placed on agriculture, and the disappointment of that hope, as depicted in Hag 1:6. The combination of the first verb, פנה, with the preposition אל highlights the definite object.[68] So, I could further interpret this phrase as "you have eagerly looked for much" or "you have undoubtedly expected much," in order to emphasise their expectant hope for object. Undoubtedly, the people expect much harvest.

However, the result of their harvest turns out to be "little." To draw attention to the word following והנה, this verse employs its opposite before והנה (Gen 15:17; 31:51).[69] The parallel between the two words אל הרבה , meaning "many," and למעת, meaning "only a little," emphasises the difference between the expected yield and reality. The vital point is conveyed by the second word: it is the small amount of harvest remaining.

There is an analogous syntactical use of a preposition in Jer 8:15, "for a time of healing, but behold, terror." This passage similarly incorporates contrasting words before and after והנה, through its use of "healing" or "cure" in opposition to "terror" or "dismay." These examples syntactically emphasise the contrast between Judean reality and the Judean expectations.

Despite their meagre yield, the people bring their produce home in order to store it. However, YHWH blows even that away (נפה). The intensity of this violation against YHWH is emphasised through the verb נפחתי,

67 Based on the evidence of the LXX, the Syriac and Targum, BHS suggests correcting והנה to והיה. Yet, this emendation definitely weakens the emphasis on contrast between the words preceding and following והנה. Therefore, I will keep the MT as it is.

68 *DCH*, Vol. 6, 705–7.

69 *DCH*, Vol. 2, 574–8.

which refers to YHWH in the first person to communicate: "I blow on you with my fiery wrath" (Ezek 22:21).[70] In this sentence, YHWH sets the implied definite object, that I identified as being the harvest, aflame and melts it away in his anger (Ezek 22:20).

In this interpretation, Haggai's reference to YHWH in the first person should be viewed as communicating that YHWH is the one fiercely breathing the strong wind, in essence a storm. As a result, the modest harvest is completely blown away. This might occur during threshing or transportation. The distinctive lack of YHWH's blessing over the sowing and reaping certainly demonstrates YHWH's punishment. Judean agriculture is getting worse.

Concerning the word הבית, it has been claimed that it refers to the house of YHWH, based on Mal 1:13,[71] where the people disdainfully offer their sacrifices in the temple. They themselves undervalue the cult to YHWH (הפחתם אות). Subsequently, rejection and displeasure is present at the house of YHWH. In the same way, in Haggai's text, the people have brought their little produce as an offering to the temple, but YHWH has blown away their sacrifice. By correspondence we can conclude that this is because he detests and disregards their action.

There is no doubt that the house (הבית) in Malachi's text indicated the temple. However, the house (הבית) in Haggai's text should be recognised as an agricultural storage facility. This is indicated by the question "is the seed still in storage?" in Hag 2:19. Additionally, for Malachi's use of the verb נפח, YHWH is not the subject while in Haggai YHWH is the subject of the verb נפח. The word נפח certainly represents the force or power in YHWH's judgement.

YHWH then puts forward the reason why he blew away even the rest of their modest harvest. This further tragedy happened because, in contrast to the fervour for Zerubbabel's house, the people are still not concerned for the house of YHWH being in ruins (Jer 33:10, 12; Ezek 36:35, 38; Neh 2:3, 17). For the present purpose, to demonstrate its point, one should consider a man (איש) Zerubbabel of the Davidic lineage in connection to the following

70 *DCH*, Vol. 5, 714.

71 Petersen, *Haggai, Zechariah 1–8*, 29; Redditt, *Haggai, Zechariah, Malachi*, 21; Meyers and Meyers, *Haggai, Zechariah 1–8*, 29; Kessler, *The Book of Haggai*, 137.

word "his house" (לביתו). In the Hebrew Bible, only the house of David is paralleled by or comparable to the house of YHWH. Therefore, I should translate the phrases יען ביתי אשר-הוא חרב ואתם רצים איש לביתו like this: "you run quickly to his house" rather than "each of you runs quickly to his own house."[72] The use of "his house" (לביתו) could be a concrete expression of the panelled house in Hag 1:4.

In contrast to the people's fervour for Zerubbabel's house, they remain unconcerned that the house of YHWH remains in ruins (Jer 33:10, 12; Ezek 36:35, 38; Neh 2:3, 17). The verb רצים gives credence to this interpretation. When this verb is accompanied by an object, it generally means to "be busy with something" (2 Sam 18:21–24, 26; 20:36; 2 Kgs 1:5; Isa 40:31; Jer 12:5; 23:21).[73] The people are preoccupied with Zerubbabel's house only. There is a similar case in Hab 2:2, where the phrase מען ירוץ קורא בו means to take the required measures "so that the person could concentrate on reading the record while he was running." Likewise, the people are described as only being eager to establish the Davidic dynasty through Zerubbabel.

Hag 1:10

על כן עליכם[74] כלאו שמים[75] מטל;[76] והארץ כלאה יבולה

["Therefore, because of you, heavens have withheld the dew and the earth has also withheld her yield."]

72 לביתו recalls בתיכםin verse 4. Meyers and Meyers, *Haggai, Zechariah 1–8*, 3, 30; Kessler, *The Book of Haggai*, 106, 138; Verhoef, *The Book of Haggai and Malachi*, 44, 72.

73 *HALOT*, Vol. 2, 1207–8.

74 Based on the evidence of the LXX, BHS suggests taking out עליכם. This might be taken as a clerical error by dittography from the preceding על כן. As I have discussed above, however, the suffix of עליכם is a very important element of the argument. Therefore, I will keep the MT.

75 BHS suggest the possibility that שׁמים should be emended to השמים, following a Kennicott variant. This adjustment would be grammatically right but it does not give any different meaning. So, I will keep the MT.

76 BHS suggests correcting מטל to טלָם ("their dew") or מָטָר ("rain"), for מטל does not make sense. Similar grammatical usage of מטל is found in elsewhere; for example, "many waters shall be stopped" (יכלאו מים, Ezek 31:15). To assume an implicit object to the verb כלא however is not difficult. Therefore, the emendation is unnecessary.

The people continue to attend to their own interests through attempting to establish the Davidic dynasty. YHWH's reaction to the people's neglect for his house is truly negative. The particle adverb על כן expresses the sort of the punishment that he threatened and which seems to have already been happening.

A threat of punishment is further emphasised through reiterating the word על. The combination of the preposition על followed by the word על-כן only appears 3 times in the Hebrew Bible: "because of the instructions in this letter" (Esth 9:26); "therefore YHWH did not take pleasure in their young men" (Isa 9:16); "therefore I wailed for Moab" (Jer 48:31). These verses each indicate definite objects through the use of the preposition על. Therefore, the preposition על of עליכם should be understood to mean "because," and it should be understood as clarifying the cause of the judgment. Thus, the people's failure to reconstruct the temple can be understood as the cause for YHWH's verdict (Jer 14:22).

YHWH is described as determinedly sending the agents of the "heavens (שׁמים) and the earth (הארץ)," which causes the people to be in trouble.[77] The heavens are asked to stop (כלא) dew (טל) and the earth is asked to withdraw (כלא) its produce (יבולה). In this description of YHWH's judgement, the vital word is the verb כלא which means "to restrain," "to shut up," or "to hinder" (Num 11:28; 1 Sam 6:10; Jer 32:3; Ps 59:14).[78] This is the only case in which the word שׁמים is used as the subject of the verb כלא. This irregular use of שׁמים suggests the interpretation that the heavens are prevented from giving any more dew.

In an agricultural cycle, the quantity and timing of the rains is fundamental to the harvest. So, the main blessings of the Hebrew Bible repeatedly echo a promise of "the dew of the heavens" (Gen 27:28; Deut 33:28). This is because an abundant harvest of grains, wine, and oil could only be secured in land where the heavens are withholding the dew: a situation of severe drought.

77 For more on YHWH's agency through natural phenomenon, see John Joseph Collins, *Daniel* (Hermeneia; Minneapolis: Fortress, 1993), 229–30.

78 *HALOT*, Vol. 1, 476–7; *DCH*, Vol. 4, 416–18.

As a result, the land is described as having withheld its produce (יבולה). This description is the only case in which the word הארץ is used as the subject of the verb כלא, as the word שמים was in the first clause. The word יבולה, meaning "product," "produce," or "yield" of the soil, is usually used to describe arable land, vineyards and orchards (Lev 26:4, 20; Deut 11:17; 32:22; Judg 6:4; Ezek 34:27; Zech 8:12). Yet its use in this sentence indicates a severe crop failure. The lack of rain for extended periods has led to a breakdown of the agricultural economy, ultimately resulting in famine, a much worse circumstance.[79] The severe punishment meted out by YHWH is agricultural.

Hag 1:11

ואקרא חרב על הארץ ועל ההרים ועל הדגן ועל התירוש ועל היצהר[80]
ועל[81] אשר תוציא האדמה; ועל האדם ועל הבהמה ועל כל יגיע כפים

["I summoned a drought on the arable land and the mountains, and on the grain, the fresh wine, the fresh oil, and all things the ground would produce, and on the men and cattle, and all the toil of their hands."]

This verse describes how YHWH brought (קרא) a drought upon the earth. The verb קרא appears many times to describe a human action and, much more rarely, as יהוה (75 times, Gen 27:1; 41:8, 14; Isa 13:3; 41:4). Even among divine actions, this is the only case in which YHWH is the subject of the

79 Barstad, "Haggai Among the Prophets," 275.

80 BHS suggests that the phrase ועל היצהר would have been added to the text. The reason for this is that grain, wine, and oil are the main agricultural industries in Judah, and they are quite often referred to together in the Bible (Num 18:12; Deut 7:13; 11:14; 12:17; 14:23; 18:4; 28:51; Jer 31:12; Hos 2:10, 24; Joel 1:10; 2:19; Neh 5:11; 10:40; 13:5, 12; 2 Chr 31:5; 32:28). However, a vat (פורה) in Hag 2:16 was commonly used to draw both fresh wine juice and fresh oil. Also, in this verse Haggai firstly put the list of all that was affected by the drought in general terms of the arable lands, the vineyards and orchards, and then identified these effects more specifically. Therefore, ועל היצהר cannot be seen as an additional phrase.

81 Many Hebrew manuscripts inserts כל before על אשר תוציא האדמה. This reading makes better sense, emphasising "all" produce from the land. So, I will change the MT and put כל into the Hebrew text.

imperfect first person verb קרא. The use of the first person underlines that YHWH is responsible for the drought oהֹרֶב (2 Kgs 8:1; Ps 105:16).[82]

Then there is the play on words between חָרֵב ("the ruin") of the temple (Hag 1:4 and 9) and חֹרֶב ("the drought") of the land (Hag 1:11). When the people give careful thought to what happened to them, they might consider the relationship between חָרֵב and חֹרֶב, which share the same root חרב.

As I have mentioned in Hag 1:5, according to the ruling principle in an agrarian society YHWH addresses judgment to his recalcitrant people. His judgement stands in direct opposition to the blessing he had promised as a reward for obedience. The fields (ארץ) are described as having become too sterile to yield anything. The mountains (הר) have also become desolate.[83]

The cases of the word ארץ followed by הר appear several times in the Hebrew Bible. For example: "thus Joshua struck all the land, the hill country and the Negev and the lowland and the slopes ..." (Josh 10:40) and "Thus Joshua took all that land, the hill country and all the Negev, all that land of Goshen, the lowlands, the Arabah, the hill country of Israel and its lowlands" (Josh 11:16). Except in Ps 48:3 "beautiful in elevation, the joy of the whole earth, was Mount Zion," where the word הר means the Jerusalem temple, it indicates areas marked by internal topographical difference. Generally, such high places were heavily forested and needed clearing before they could be inhabited. So, Joshua had told the people to "go up to the forest and clear the ground for yourselves ... the hill-country could be yours ..." (Josh 17:14–18).[84]

82 The word חֹרֶב, is used in relation to skin or bone (Job 30:30) but also in relation to climate in order to describe the heat of the desert (Gen 31:40; Isa 4:6; 25:4; 36:30).

83 The word ארץ implies general land and the earth (Gen 18:2; Exod 34:8; Ps 74:7; 89:40). The word הר is often used to refer to a "mountainous region" (Josh 10:40; 11:16), such as the mountains of Yehud (Josh 21:11), the mountain of Ephraim (Josh 17:15), and a hill-country of the Amorites (Deut 1:7). It can also be employed to designate an individual mountain, though, such as Mount Sinai, Mount Horeb or Mount Hermon. Finally, the term also refers to "the whole land of designated regions" such as in the land of Moriah (Gen 22:2), the mountains around Jerusalem (Ps 125:2). Aharoni, *The Land of the Bible*, 414–19.

84 Judean farmers developed runoff agriculture in the Negev in the tenth century BCE with the help of water catchment systems. This technological development was a

In relation to the produce of the land, the phrase "on the land and on the mountains" is used to describe both the arable land producing cereals and the highly terraced hill-country, which produced fresh fruit and fresh oil. Therefore, the term ארץ should be understood as referring to the arable lands which were producing grains, while the term הרים should signify the hill-countries (the vineyards and orchards) which were yielding grapes and olives.[85] Even in alluding to these distinctions, the writer of the Book of Haggai emphasised the extent of the areas that had been seriously affected by the drought. Indeed, there seems to have been no Judean soil unaffected by the drought.

The list of all that had been affected by the drought initially proceeds in general terms, mentioning that it was the arable lands, the vineyards and orchards. The list progresses to identify these effects more specifically, naming grains (דגן), wine (תירוש), and olives (יצהר). These categories would have been understood with further specification. The category of grains would have included wheat and barley. Also, the next word תירוש which derives from the verb ירש meaning "to drive out" or "to press out," would have been understood to denote "an unfermented wine," meaning new wine or fresh wine. Lastly, the word יצהר refers to "olive oil" and is derived from the root צהר, meaning "to press out oil." Thus the three agricultural products of utmost importance in the Judean economy were described as having come to ruins.

A situation similar to this can be found in the accounts of the drought and the famine in the concurrent Book of Joel. These descriptions include: "the fields were laid waste, the ground mourned because the grain was destroyed, the wine failed, the oil languished" (Joel 1:10). Here we see the recurring triad of grains, wine, and olives (דגן, תירוש, יצהר). Indeed this exact formulation of the triad is found throughout the Hebrew Bible: "grains, wine, and olives (דגן, תירוש, יצהר)" (Deut 11:13–17; Jer 31:12; Hos 2:8–9; Joel 2:24). Further texts referring to the triad of grains, wine, and olives through slight semantic variations include: גנה ... זית ... כרם (Amos

response to the lack of land suitably hydrated for cultivation. Faust and Weiss, "Judah, Philistia and the Mediterranean World," 71–92.

85 Borowski, *Agriculture in Iron Age*, 101–34.

4:9; Isa 17:10–11; Jer 3:3; 5:24; 12:13; 14:7–22; Ezek 34:26–27; Zech 8:12; 10:1; 14:17). By using this triad, verse 11 thus indicates that the commodities in Judean agricultural industries—the commodities on which the society depends in order to flourish—have been undoubtedly destroyed.

Haggai firmly proclaimed that "all things the ground produced" had completely perished. Nothing had escaped the severe drought. Legume and vegetable farming thus would have also been undermined. Nor would animal husbandry have been exempted. The Judean agricultural economic system had broken down.

Indeed, the famine resulting from the drought is described as having been experienced by "the people" and "the cattle" alike. The word אדם describes the whole of mankind as a collective noun, but indicates a particular emphasis on the people of Judah (Jer 47:2; Job 36:25).[86] Similarly, the following word בהמה refers to animals in general, but indicates a particular emphasis on domestic animals such as cattle and sheep (Jer 36:29; Deut 28:26; Isa 18:6). The parallel use of the word האדם together with the word הבהמה appears 8 times in the Hebrew Bible. There are four noteworthy examples of this combination. Firstly, it is used in creation (Jer 27:5) and once in relation to paying tax (Num 31:47). Secondly, other uses of this combination are used to convey YHWH's wrath: "my anger and my wrath would be poured out on this place, upon man and beast" (Jer 7:20); "I smote the inhabitants of this city, both man and beast" (Jer 21:6); "the fate of the sons of men and the fate of beasts was the same" (Eccl 3:19). In YHWH's judgement, both the people and the cattle in Judah were totally struck by the famine.

It is worth briefly exploring the impact of famine on agriculture. One impact would have been that the cereal stalks, which would have been used as fodder for domesticated animals, would have been spoiled. The spoiled fodder would inevitably have affected the quality of animal products such as milk, cheese, yoghurt, wool, and hair. The quantity of such products would

86 This reference to creation recalls the dynamics of the relationship between human beings and the soil from which they are created, so powerfully evoked in Gen 2:7. Tim Meadowcroft, "A Desolate Land, People and Temple: Haggai and the Environment," *Colloq* 40 (2008), 58; Verhoef, *The Book of Haggai and Malachi*, 77.

have also been impacted, as animals died from malnutrition. Animal death would lead to a decrease in available manure, which was used to fertilise the arable land and fields. The farming of the series became in sequence undermined. Therefore, Haggai depicts all of the people's agricultural efforts (יגיע) as having been in vain (Hag 2:14; Isa 55:2; Ps 78:39).

The above exegesis on Hag 1:9–11 has shown that the temple's bad state resulted in agricultural and economic disaster for Judah. Instead of obeying YHWH's command to rebuild the temple, the record of Haggai reveals that the people insistently attended to their interests in the establishment of the Davidic dynasty. By way of punishment, YHWH sent storms (נפח) down even upon their meagre harvest (Hag 1:9). Yet, since the temple remained in ruins (חָרֵב), YHWH brought drought (חֹרֶב) to the land (Hag 1:10). The drought then destroyed all possible agricultural activities not only within the arable land but within mountains (Hag 1:11). Grain, wine, and olives (דגן, תירוֹשׁ, יצהר), which were the luxury goods of Judah, proved no exception. The Judean agricultural labour was completely futile. Indeed, the Judean economy, which was based on agricultural success, was completely broken down.

Hag 1:12

וישמע זרבבל בן שלתיאל ויהושע בן יהוצדק הכהן הגדול וכל שארית העם
בקול יהוה אלהיהם ועל דברי חגי הנביא כאשר שלחו יהוה אלהיהם;[87]
וייראו העם מפני יהוה

[Then Zerubbabel the son of Shealtiel, and Joshua the son of Jehozadak, the high priest, and all the remnant of the people should obey the voice of YHWH their God and the words of Haggai the prophet, as YHWH their God sent him. And the people should fear in the presence of YHWH.]

The individuals addressed and referred to in Hag 1:2 are now addressed in combination with Zerubbabel and Joshua; now they are all expected

87 The Greek version reads pro.j auvtou,j (=אֲלֵיהֶם) to avoid dittography. This is reflected also in Peshitta, Targum, and the Vulgate. Yet, the use of repetition in Haggai is frequent (e.g. שִׂים לבב and נאם יהוה). Therefore, this adjustment is unnecessary.

to respond positively to the proclamation of Haggai the prophet. Here Zerubbabel is again mentioned first, yet this time without his official title within the empire. In contrast, Joshua is listed with his official title. As I have already mentioned, the absence or presence of the official title in designating Zerubbabel indicates very careful and intentional alternation. This change indicates the unstable position of Zerubbabel as the governor of Judah, under Darius.[88] The official title of Zerubbabel would be preserved only insofar as he showed unwavering loyalty to Darius. Therefore, the non-appearance of the official title should be read as indicating the prepared intention of the writer of Haggai to suggest the increasingly precarious nature of Zerubbabel's political position.

Furthermore, the remnant of the people has also been invited to respond positively to the prophet's promulgation. Due to the problematic word "remnant" (שארית),[89] scholars have debated whether or not the remnant should be read to mean the non-exiled people or the returning exiles.[90] In the Hebrew Bible, however, the use of the word שארית indicates a single unity of the genitive noun that follows. So, for example, we see the phrase "remnant of Jerusalem" used in reference to those remaining after the 597 deportation (Jer 24:8//Ezek 5:10; 9:8; 1:13) and "remnant of Judah," which describes the Judeans who left their country at the fall of the kingdom but who returned under Gedaliah (Jer 40:11, 15). Therefore, the phrase "the remnant of the people" of Judah in Haggai should not be taken only as a single designation for the Babylonian exiles. Also, Haggai never intends to suggest a contrast between the exiled and the non-exiled people of Judah.[91]

88 For the incipient ascendancy of the high priest, see Petersen, *Haggai, Zechariah 1–8*, 55–6; Wolff, *Haggai*, 51; Meyers and Meyers, *Haggai, Zechariah 1–8*, 50.

89 *HALOT*, Vol. 2, 1380–1.

90 The view that "remnant" refers to the initial return of exiles from Babylon to Yehud is based on the opposition to the temple reconstruction in Ezra 1–4. See Bedford, *Temple Restoration*, 36–148; Hanson, *The Dawn of Apocalyptic*, 32–380; Hugo (Haim Dov) Mantel, "The Dichotomy of Judaism during Second Temple," *HUCA* 44 (1973): 56–87.

91 Further on the understanding of "remnant" in the exilic period, see Sara Japhet, "The Concept of the 'Remnant' in the Restoration Period: On the Vocabulary of

Similar usages to that of "remnant" in Haggai can be found in Jeremiah. There we find, for example: "Ishmael took captive all the remnant of the people who were in Mizpah, the king's daughters" (Jer 41:10), and "all the leaders of the forces with him took all the rest of the people whom Ishmael the son of Nethaniah had carried away captive from Mizpah" (Jer 41:16). These parallel uses support my interpretation that "the remnant of the people" represents the rest of the people, apart from the aforementioned leaders or royal family members. So I have argued that the "remnant" in Haggai represents all the unnamed people, with Zerubbabel and Joshua as the only exception.

The other dominant interpretation of "the remnant of the people" seems less compelling when applied to Haggai. The phrase has been taken to refer to a faithful group: for example, "if it was too difficult in the sight of the remnant of this people in those days, would it also be too difficult in my sight?" (Zech 8:6), and "I will not treat the remnant of this people as in the former days" (Zech 8:12; see also Isa 10:20; 28:5; Jer 31:7–9; Mic 7:18). In those cases, "the remnant of the people" describes the population being saved from YHWH's judgement. In this light, "the remnant of the people" in the Haggai text would be understood as a simple designation of Haggai's faithful audience. While they have been distinctly called to heed the word of YHWH to rebuild the temple, the people have not been obedient. This claim focuses too much on the people's obedience, which was expected but had not yet been evident. So this interpretation would seem to misconstrue the text.

Amidst the people's recalcitrance to rebuilding the Jerusalem temple, the role of Haggai as an intermediary from YHWH is significant. The formula חגי הנביא כאשר שלחו יהוה אלהיהם ("upon the word of Haggai the prophet as YHWH their God has sent him") clearly provides an implied authority to Haggai (Isa 6:8; Zech 2:12–13). It shows that Haggai as the messenger of YHWH should undertake to exhort the disobedient people of Judah.

In response to the proclamation of Haggai, all individuals are expected to adhere loyally to YHWH's will. The first verb וישׁמע is the Qal imperfect

---

Self-Definition," in *Das Manna fällt auch heute noch: Beiträge zur Geschichte und Theologie des Alten, Ersten Testaments: Festschrift für Erich Zenger* (ed. Frank-Lothar Hossfeld and Ludger Schwienhorst-Schönberger; Freiburg; New York: Herder, 2004), 340–61.

third person masculine singular form of the root שׁמע. It means "to listen to" carefully or "to hear and accept a request" from YHWH or a person. In particular, the verb שׁמע which is constructed with the phrase בקול ... על denotes "to be obedient" or "to act in accordance with the will of" something that the prophet commands (Jer 26:5; 35:18; 38:20).[92] The phrase שׁמע ... על ... בכול is usually viewed in the Deuteronomy and Deuteronomistic traditions. Thus, it has often been claimed that this expression refers to a positive response to the revealed word of YHWH that both traditions share.[93] However, Haggai's text does not show that the people and their leaders eventually obey the messages delivered in the name of YHWH. Instead, they are again asked to heed the words of YHWH.

In the context, the subject of the verb שׁמע should be Zerubbabel, Joshua, and the people. Yet, the verb שׁמע is a third masculine singular form. This might highlight that they should all with one mind respond favourably to the central theme of Haggai's message.

The following verb is וייראו, which is the Qal imperfect third person masculine plural form. It means "to fear" or "to be afraid." Now, the people are being enjoined towards an experience of fear in the presence of YHWH (מפני יהוה). In the Hebrew Bible, the word ירא mainly represents terror and worship.[94] Terror and worship are, in one sense, polar opposites for the former is characteristic of utter torment (Neh 6:9, 13, 19) whereas the latter suggests trust (Jer 4:26; 17:8).

Nevertheless, in the Hebrew Bible both senses are associated with each other, for a worshipful fear is manifested by the wrath of YHWH against the people's guilt. An interesting case demonstrating this is found in Jonah 1:5. Jonah, attempting to flee from YHWH, has set sail for Tarshish and has been caught in the midst of a terrible storm. All the sailors onboard with Jonah have been struck with fear. After having been identified as the

92 The phrase שׁמע בקול and the verb ירא are key parts of Deuteronomy and Deuteronomistic vocabulary. Kessler, *The Book of Haggai*, 142–5, 147; Kessler, "Building the Second Temple," 243–56.

93 Kessler, *The Book of Haggai*, 142–5, 147; Kessler, "Building the Second Temple," 243–56; Verhoef, *The Book of Haggai and Malachi*, 80.

94 *DCH*, Vol. 4, 276–83; *HALOT*, Vol. 1, 432–3.

cause of this storm, Jonah acknowledges himself as the one who should take the act of fearful obedience to YHWH (Jonah 1:9).

To expand upon this analogy, one should recall the mode of the establishment of Judean independence with Zerubbabel in Hag 1:3–4 and 9. With the phrase בקול ... שׁמע ... ירא, the people were instructed to acknowledge their sinfulness in the midst of YHWH's wrath. Then, they were instructed to obediently rebuild the temple. The people's rebellion against the word of YHWH has aroused the wrath of YHWH, evident through the terrible economic catastrophe, and in response YHWH has called for an immediate transformation in them.

A similar emphasis on the phrase בקול ... שׁמע ... ירא ... is found in Isaiah. Isa 50:10 says, "who is among you that fears YHWH, that obeys the voice of his messenger, and that walks in darkness and has no light? Let him trust in the name of YHWH and rely on his God."[95] This verse commands steadfast obedience to the words of YHWH as proclaimed by the prophet.[96] The prophetic intervention should bring about a radical movement by the people towards obediently what the prophet proclaimed.

Hag 1:13

ויאמר חגי מלאך יהוה במלאכות יהוה[97] לעם לאמר: אני אתכם נאם יהוה

[Then Haggai, the messenger of YHWH, through YHWH's mandate, said to the people, "I am with you, declares YHWH."]

95 The expression בקול ... שׁמע ... ירא ... alludes to the commandments of YHWH given through Moses. Kessler further states that this phraseology is used to describe a positive response to the word of YHWH delivered in specific situations by his messengers. Kessler, *The Book of Haggai*, 143–4.

96 Meyers and Meyers, *Haggai, Zechariah 1–8*, 34–5; Kessler, *The Book of Haggai*, 122–3, 147, 241–7; Joyce Baldwin, *Haggai, Zechariah, Malachi: An Introduction and Commentary* (TOTC; London: Inter Varsity, 1972), 6.

97 BHS suggests that the terminology מלאך יהוה במלאכות יהוה is a substantial reiteration, since the Greek version has ἄγγελος κυρίου. The omission of במלאכות יהוה is understandable. However, in this particular verse, the preposition ב gives a causal, attributing the idea of charge to במלאכות. It is literally translated as "in the work of YHWH." Therefore, the adjustment is unneeded.

In this verse, Haggai introduced himself as מלאך יהוה (the messenger of YHWH) for YHWH's work to rebuild the Jerusalem temple. This introductory phrase communicates both the authority of Haggai as an agent of YHWH and the authority of the message he conveys (Isa 44:26; Mal 2:7; 2 Chr 36:15).[98]

It is worthwhile to note that there are some cases described with similar terms in the Hebrew Bible in which human leaders sent messengers (מלאכים) on business or diplomatic missions. For example: "the king of the people of Ammon answered the messengers of Jephthah" (Judg 11:13; see also 2 Sam 3:12–14; 1 Kgs 20:2–4).[99] Actually, the proclamation of Haggai to rebuild the Jerusalem temple is also associated with Darius's economic and military decree. This is one case in which the prophetic commission thus reflects the idea of diplomatic protocol. In this respect, Darius's decree is undeniably intertwined with YHWH's commandment, which demonstrates YHWH's full affirmation of Darius's temple rebuilding project.

The following clarification במלאכות יהוה (in YHWH's work) gives credence to Darius's work. The noun מלאכה can be translated under "business work" or "administrative work,"[100] as seen in these examples: "for YHWH of hosts had work to do in the land of the Chaldeans" (Jer 50:25); "What is your commission?" (Jonah 1:8) and "I rose and went about the king's business" (Dan 8:27). Important building projects (Neh 4:15) and any work done by the people for a ruler could be referred to as the ruler's work (1 Kgs 7:51; 2 Chr 16:5). All of the passages quoted above either refer to specific work projects or to the routine of a particular business endeavour of any class of labour from menial to royal.

Quite a similar text to Hag 1:13 is Ezra 6:22, which says, "YHWH turned the heart of the king of Assyria toward the Israelites to encourage them in the work of the house of God (בית האלהים במלאכת), the God of

98 Petersen, *Haggai, Zechariah 1–8*, 56–7; Kessler, *The Book of Haggai*, 148–9; Meadowcroft, *Haggai*, 138–9.

99 *DCH*, Vol. 5, 284–8. It is sometimes difficult to distinguish between human messengers and angelic messengers (Isa 14:12; Ezek 9:1–8; Mal 3:1; Zech 1:14; 2:3; Hos 12:14; Dan 7:9–14; 12:5; Gen 16:7–14, 18, 22; Judg 13:20).

100 *DCH*, Vol. 5, 288–90.

Israel." There is no doubt that the temple work is itself the work of YHWH. The prophet Haggai firmly proclaims that the project of rebuilding the Jerusalem temple is definitely YHWH's work.

In Hag 1:13, Haggai declared to the people that YHWH was present among them (אני אתכם). Throughout the Hebrew Bible the clause "I am with you" is the prevailing assurance of YHWH's supporting presence.[101] The people's resistance to the temple reconstruction is now no longer a consideration.[102] The only criteria for YHWH's blessing and presence is that the people, together with Zerubbabel and Joshua, accept their responsibility for doing YHWH's work.

From this exegesis of Hag 1:12–13, I have demonstrated how the people and their leaders should have responded to the commandment of YHWH to rebuild the temple. Haggai had anticipated the people's response (שמע ירא) to YHWH's command to rebuild the temple (Hag 1:12). To bring about the transformation within the people that he required, YHWH sent (שלח) Haggai as his messenger (מלאך יהוה). Haggai was charged with carrying out the work (במלאכות) of ensuring that the people accepted Darius's project of rebuilding the temple as YHWH's work (Hag 1:13).

Hag 1:14

ויער יהוה את רוח זרבבל בן שלתיאל פחת יהודה
ואת רוח יהושע בן יהוצדק הכהן הגדול ואת רוח כל שארית העם;
ויבאו ויעשו מלאכה בבית יהוה צבאות אלהיהם

[And, YHWH stirred up the spirit of Zerubbabel the son of Shealtiel, governor of Judah, and the spirit of Joshua the son of Jehozadak, the high priest, and the spirit of all the remnant of the people. Thus, they should come and set to work on the house of YHWH of hosts, their God.]

101 Meyers and Meyers, *Haggai, Zechariah 1–8*, 35. The expression "YHWH is with you" indicates the military power associated with the presence of YHWH.

102 The declaration of the presence of YHWH certifies that YHWH will be actively present with the people to make their work fruitful, no matter whether the temple has been completed or the actual work has not yet begun. Kessler, *The Book of Haggai*, 149–50.

YHWH eventually aroused (עור) the רוח of Zerubbabel, Joshua and all the people in order to initiate the rebuilding of the temple. The basic meaning of the verb עור is "to be awakened" or "to stir up." So, this is one example of its use: "awake, sword, against my shepherd and against the man" (Zech 13:7; see also Isa 51:9; Hab 2:19).[103] It asks a self-conscious sense. Meanwhile, the causative sense (יער) of the verb עור means "to wake up," "to be excited," "to wake someone up," "to put into motion," or "to start to work." This use of עור is for instance, evident here: "Who arouses one from the east whom he calls in righteousness to his feet?" (Isa 41:2; see also Jer 50:9; Ezek 23:22).

The causative use of this verb, עור marks the condition of being capable of being influenced. The use of verb עור in Hag 1:14 should be interpreted causatively since YHWH is enlightening the apathetic people regarding the rebuilding of the Jerusalem temple. The people and their leaders are not only in a state of being capable of being influenced, but they are expected by YHWH to be moved to obey him. Namely, YHWH intends to prompt the people and their leaders to work on the rebuilding of the temple.

Normally, the word רוח is used as the object of the verb עור to describe the political context for a given activity. So, for example, it is used for descriptions of the following: YHWH stirring up the kings of Medes against Babylon (Jer 51:11); the spirit of a destroyer against Babylon (Jer 51:1); the spirit of the king of Assyria against several Israelite tribes (1 Chr 5:26); the spirit of the Philistines and the Arabs against Jehoram and Judah (2 Chr 21:16); and the spirit of Cyrus to make a proclamation regarding the building of the Jerusalem temple (2 Chr 36:22). Therefore, YHWH's rousing of the people's spirit is not completely devoid of political significance.

Due to this connotation of the phrase רוח ... עור, it has been suggested that the Jerusalem temple reconstruction has a political role in Judah. So, although the Jerusalem temple rebuilding was initiated through Darius's policy, through managing the agricultural economy of Judah and controlling the provincial annual budget, the rebuilt Jerusalem temple could

103 *DCH*, Vol. 6, 314–6.

form a local self-determining institution.[104] This interpretation suggests that the rebuilding of the Jerusalem temple would eventually lead to the semi-autonomy of Judah. However, this is not how the rebuilding project in fact functioned for Judah.

Rather, the rebuilding of the Jerusalem temple functioned to establish a strengthened administrative base for imperial armies.[105] Through the temple work, Darius sought the increased centralisation of power within the territories (see Chapter 2 above).[106] For that purpose, Zerubbabel and Joshua were deputed to governor and high priest, respectively, in the imperial bureaucratic structure. Their titles required Zerubbabel and Joshua to consider the temple reconstruction to be their own responsibility. Therefore, neglecting the work of rebuilding the temple was an act against the empire. At this point, I would suggest that Haggai was very keen to communicate the political implications of rebuilding the temple.

There are other examples of Judah's commitment to the empire. In 488 BCE and also in 459 BCE, again while Egypt was revolting against the Achaemenids, the Achaemenids took a more active role in their administration of the western territories, which included the province of Judah. What was worse was that the Achaemenids were also wary of the Greek threat against which they began to build a series of forts and ports along the eastern coast.[107] This crisis within the empire resulted in the missions of Ezra and Nehemiah to Judah, to function as mediating authorities like Zerubbabel. Ezra provided the codification of Judean laws in the service of imperial policies (see Chapter 2 above), and Nehemiah built the walls of Jerusalem which remained in ruins. Jerusalem, and its walls, would later become a battlefield for conflicts between a resurgent Egypt and

104 Some critics argue that the reconstruction of the temple would inaugurate a new messianic age. See, for example: Wolff, *Haggai*, 52–3; Weinberg, *Citizen-Temple Community*, 115–21; Meyers and Meyers, *Haggai, Zechariah 1–8*, 35, 41–3, 220–1.

105 The recovered Jerusalem temple economy would facilitate the creation of food supplies. Berquist, *Judaism in Persia's Shadow*, 57–8, 65–8; Berquist, "Constructions of Identity in Postcolonial Yehud," 53–66.

106 Assis, "To Build or Not to Build," 522.

107 Hoglund, "The Achaemenid Context," 62–4; *Achaemenid Imperial*, 29–36, 54–68, 208–25.

the Achaemenids (Neh 1–2). Both Ezra and Nehemiah truly show their devoted loyalty towards the empire facilitating an ideal, faithful alliance between the Achaemenids and the province of Judah.

Against this hostile context, YHWH invoked all the people to participate in the Jerusalem temple restoration. The people along with Zerubbabel the governor and Joshua the priest were to come (ויבאו) and to begin working (יעשו) on the house of YHWH. Everyone was to be involved in the compulsory task of rebuilding the temple: this was the result towards which YHWH was working. Haggai, as his messenger, was actively encouraging the people to take part in a variety of affairs to rebuild the Jerusalem temple.

The noun מלאכה, which is connected with the two verbs (בא, עשה), describes a variety of domains for work, such as "handiwork" or "craftsmanship."[108] As, for example, it is used here: "you should not bring a load out of your houses on the sabbath day nor do any work" (Jer 17:22; 18:3; see also Exod 20:10; Deut 5:14; Judg 16:11). The word מלאכה is also used in reference to "services or objects or possessions of all types." As, for example, it is used here: "who are the singers for the service of the house of YHWH" (Neh 11:22; 2:16; see also Exod 22:7, 10; Ezra 10:13). In Hag 1:14, though, the word מלאכה refers to various stages of the rebuilding work, even the preparatory work, which would have consisted of removing debris from the construction site and acquiring the necessary building materials. The people should be motivated to begin "work in the house of YHWH" (מלאכה בבית יהוה).

From Hag 1:14, one may conclude that the people and their leaders were enjoined to submit themselves to reconstructing the temple. When left ignored, this command was soon re-emphasised by the activity of YHWH himself. YHWH stirred up the spirits of Zerubbabel, Joshua, and the people to take responsibility for the Jerusalem temple restoration. Their important transition towards the temple rebuilding was a source for great hope.

108 The verb עשה appears 4 times in the Hebrew Bible together with the noun מלאכה (Jer 18:3; 2 Chr 34:13; 1 Kgs 11:28).

Hag 1:15

ביום עשרים וארבעה לחדש בששי[109] בשנת שתים לדריוש המלך

[This was on the twenty-fourth day of the sixth month in the second year of Darius the king.]

The closing verse of the first chapter of Haggai is solely composed of the adverbial description of time. The manner of dating occurs with the sequence of year-month-day thereby inverting the sequence of day-month-year from Hag 1:1.[110] Identifying the regnal year first certainly draws attention to the designated time period, which was in 520 BCE. By emphasising the historical situation of this moment, Judah was reminded of the importance that they be ready to supply all necessary supplies for imperial campaigns attempting to suppress the recurring rebellion in Egypt and to expand the imperial territories. It was to facilitate these imperial acts that Darius empowered the Jerusalem temple restoration, which would secure economic and military support from Judah.

However, the Judean reality was just the opposite. What the text demonstrates is that a drought resulted in a terrible economic drain in Judah, so the province was unable to provide the requested support and taxes. This turn of events threatened Judah with political crisis. Facing such a grave predicament caused the people to reflect on what they should do. Haggai's resounding response was that they should commit themselves to restoring the Jerusalem temple. The immediacy of this demand is indicated in that

109 BHS suggests that יום עשרים וארבעה לחדש בששי should follow in Hag 2:15–19. This suggestion would come from the consensuses: the double dating between Hag 2:15a and Hag 2:15b–2:1; the lack of dating of Hag 2:15–19 as a separate unit. However, one should note that both Hag 1:1 and Hag 1:15 actually happens on the same month. Also, Hag 1:15b does not reiterate Hag 1:15a. Therefore, there is no need to adjust the text.

110 The definite date formula at both the beginning and the end of this chapter is exceptional. Normally, such dates are only placed at the end of a textual unit. This suggests that the verse was intended to be read in relation to the following chapter of Haggai. Meyers and Meyers, *Haggai, Zechariah 1–8*, 36; Mason, *The Book of Haggai, Zechariah and Malachi*, 44.

no time seems to pass between the temporal descriptions in the opening and closing verses of the chapter. Since Judah was such a small province, it depended on political alliances with neighbouring powers.[111] This is why Haggai puts his promulgations within this historical agenda.[112]

Concerning the temple building or rebuilding story, it is true that Biblical accounts of temple building draw on conventional literary patterns which were common to the ancient Near East at that time. Though similarities to these literary patterns pervade the royal building inscriptions, these inscriptions also modified the patterns for functionality.[113]

In regard to Haggai's account of the temple rebuilding, there is one particularly important reference to a restoration account of the temple of the Ebabbar at Sippar in the second year of Nabonidus (554–553 BCE). This reference shows how signs from Shamash and Adad to the king Sennacherib in Neo-Assyria were vital for the repair of the temple.[114] Nabonidus seemed to have been engaged in a process of religious and political revision, promoting

111 James M. Trotter, "Was the Second Jerusalem Temple a Primarily Persian Project?" *SJOT* 15 (2001): 276–93; Barstad, "Haggai Among the Prophets," 266–8.

112 Hans M. Barstad, "History and the Hebrew Bible," in *Can a "History of Israel" Be Written* (ed. Lester L. Grabbe; JSOTSup 245; Sheffield: Sheffield Academic Press, 1997), 37–64; Michael H. Floyd, "The Nature of the Narrative and the Evidence of Redaction in Haggai," *VT* 45 (1995): 470–90; Sara Japhet, "'History' and 'Literature' in the Persian Period: The Restoration of the Temple," in *Ah, Assyria ... Studies in Assyrian History and Ancient Near Eastern Historiography Presented to Hayim Tadmor* (ed. Mordechai Cogan and Israel Eph'al; Jerusalem: Magnes, 1991), 174–88.

113 Hurowitz studies literary accounts of the temple-building and highlights six key elements, although they do not necessarily occur in every account. He also demonstrates some parallels between building stories of the ancient Near East. Drought and crop failure in Haggai (Hag 1:3–10) may be cautiously compared with a letter by Ili-ipšara. Temples as residences for deities parallel verses Hag 1:4 and 9. In Nabonidus's inscription, two passages contain commands in synonymous languages of Hag 1:8: "to gather building materials" and "to build a temple." Furthermore, Nebuchadnezzar's inscriptions may be compared to the phrase "YHWH stirs up the spirit" in Hag 1:14. Victor Hurowitz, *I Have Built You an Exalted House: Temple Building in the Bible in Light of Mesopotamian and Northwest Semitic Writings* (JSOTSup 115; Sheffield: Sheffield Academic Press, 1992), 32–64, 131–62, 209–15, 220.

114 Barstad, "Haggai Among the Prophets," 274.

the moon god, Sin, at the expense of Marduk.[115] Then Nabonidus, who had been commanded to rebuild the temple, sought the aid of master-builders and canny architects, and successfully rebuilt the temple.

It is true that variations in religious policy and in official appointments within the empire serve as clues to the history of the king's reign, especially those distinctive descriptions of the state of the economy and the deployment of the army.[116] In the second year of his reign, as with Nabonidus, in the second year of Darius the Jerusalem temple reconstruction happened in the name of YHWH. Particularly, it happened on the eve of both repression of the Egyptian revolt and further territorial expansion to strengthen the political and economic power of Darius, not to mention the reinforcement of his authority. And Darius commissioned the imperial officers Zerubbabel and Joshua as the master-builders to accomplish and administer this imperial temple reconstruction.

This study of Hag 1:15 has confirmed that Haggai's proclamation of the Jerusalem temple reconstruction should be understood within the historical context of the second year of Darius. It was in 520 BCE that Darius accredited the reconstruction of the temple in Jerusalem, in order to provide economic support for the empire through the temple fiscal administration. Being a small province, Judah would benefit most through compliance with the Jerusalem temple restoration project.

This exegesis on Hag 1:1–15 has further shown that, in the second year of Darius (520 BCE), Zerubbabel the governor and Joshua the high priest were commissioned to rebuild the Jerusalem temple (Hag 1:1). Notwithstanding this commission, both leaders expressed disapproval of Darius's policy of rebuilding the temple. Along with their leaders, the people strongly resisted that it was the time (עת) to rebuild the temple (בית, Hag 1:2). Instead, the people applied themselves to rebuilding the Davidic dynasty (בתי ספנים) with Zerubbabel, who was of a local royal lineage (Hag 1:3–4). Evidently, the temple remained in disrepair (חָרֵב).

115 Henry William Frederick Saggs, *The Greatness that was Babylon* (London: Sidgwick, 1988), 313.

116 Kuhrt, *The Ancient Near East*, 598–603; Briant, *From Cyrus to Alexander*, 70–6; Dandamaev, *Political History*, 103–77.

The people's failure to obey YHWH's word and rebuild YHWH's temple undoubtedly resulted in their crop failure (Hag 1:5–6). Their obstinate passion for the restoration of the Davidic dynasty caused the drought (חֹרֶב) as punishment for their refusal to obey YHWH's command. The high value of crops of grapes and olives was spoiled, which was detrimental to the Judean agricultural economy (Hag 1:9–11).

The current economic catastrophe could be stopped by the work of rebuilding the temple (Hag 1:7–8). Haggai, as YHWH's messenger, enjoined the people to respond positively, proclaiming that the work of rebuilding the temple was YHWH's work (Hag 1:12–13). YHWH then stirred up all the individuals' spirits to begin working on the house of YHWH (Hag 1:14). In accordance, they were to promptly and subserviently engage in the temple rebuilding work (Hag 1:15). Moreover, Haggai emphasised the strong relationship between the temple reconstruction and Judean agriculture.

Conclusions

This reading of Hag 1:1–15 has revealed the following: Zerubbabel and Joshua were administrative leaders of Achaemenid Judah (Hag 1:1); the people in Jerusalem responded negatively to the temple rebuilding command (Hag 1:2); YHWH's temple remained in ruins whereas the Davidic palace was being panelled (Hag 1:3–4); there was catastrophic crop failure (Hag 1:5–6); the people were instructed that rebuilding the temple was absolutely necessary (Hag 1:7–8); drought and famine were caused by the people's neglect of the temple restoration work (Hag 1:9–11); YHWH anticipated the people's acknowledgement of the importance of rebuilding the temple (Hag 1:12–13); rebuilding the temple required the people's obedience to YHWH (Hag 1:14); and the temple rebuilding was of utmost importance for the wider Achaemenid economy (Hag 1:15).

Furthermore, this study also reveals several interesting features of chiastically rearranged parallelisms in the structure of the chapter. Some of the structural parallels emphasise similarities in content (e.g., Hag 1:1// Hag 1:15, Hag 1:5–6// Hag 1:9–11) while others show differences in content (e.g., Hag 1:2// Hag 1:14, Hag 1:3–4// Hag 1:12–13). Hag 1:7–8 functions as the culmination, or as the centralised symmetrical mark, in the chiasmus construction. In addition to this, the writer of Haggai uses word play including different "root" meanings like "drought" or "desolate" (חֹרֶב and חָרֵב, Hag 1:4, 9, 11). Moreover, the recurrence of key words such as "time" (עת, Hag 1:2 and 4), "house" (בית, Hag 1:2, 4, 8, 9), and "build" (בנה, Hag 1:2 and 8) underlines YHWH's command to rebuild the temple.

Above all, Hag 1:1–15 highlights the command to rebuild the Jerusalem temple. This task was proclaimed in the name of YHWH during the second year of Darius (Hag 1:7–8). For this task, Darius commissioned Zerubbabel as governor and Joshua as high priest both as overseers (Hag 1:1). It was assumed that their authority would motivate the people to rebuild the temple. However, none of the inhabitants of Judah regarded the command to repair the temple as mandatory (Hag 1:2). Instead, they worked hard to change the political situation in Judah through investing in the rise of Zerubbabel who was of Davidic lineage (Hag 1:3–4). As a result, the temple remained in a state of disrepair.

In an agrarian ancient Near Eastern society like Judah, drought and famine were regarded as punishment from the deity. Expecting a bountiful harvest, the people sowed a lot but they reaped little (Hag 1:5–6): crop failure could neither provide the people's requisites of their life nor reap the benefits they had expected from their yields. The worse scenario, drought, led to famine (Hag 1:9–11): the yields of grains, wine, and olives were severely depleted. The Judean agricultural economy was completely ruined.

In this economic catastrophe, YHWH led the people to consider the relationship between the agricultural failure and the temple that remained in ruin (Hag 1:5 and 7). This was the very time to rebuild the Jerusalem temple (Hag 1:8). Haggai affirmed that the Jerusalem temple rebuilding project was definitely YHWH's work (Hag 1:12–13). Also, Haggai ensured that YHWH himself stirred up the spirits of Zerubbabel, Joshua, and the people in favour of the work of rebuilding the temple (Hag 1:14). Judah was to be faithfully committed to obeying YHWH's commandment (Hag 1:1 and 15).

Bibliography

Ackroyd, Peter Runham. "The Written Evidence for Palestine." Pages 207–20 in Sancisi-Weerdenburg and Kuhrt, eds, *AH*. Vol. 4, *Centre and Periphery*.

——. "Problems in the Handling of Biblical and Related Sources in the Achaemenid Period." Pages 33–54 in Sancisi-Weerdenburg and Kuhrt, eds, *AH*. Vol. 3, *The Root of the European Tradition*.

Aharoni, Yohanan. *The Land of Bible: A Historical Geography*. Translated by Anson F. Rainey. Philadelphia: Westminster, 1967.

Arnold, Bill T. and John H. Choi. *A Guide to Biblical Hebrew Syntax*. Cambridge: Cambridge University Press, 2003.

Assis, Elie. "A Disputed Temple (Haggai 2, 1–9)." *ZAW* 120 (2008): 582–96.

——. "To Build or not to Build: A Dispute between Haggai and His People (Hag 1)." *ZAW* 119 (2007): 514–27.

——. "Composition, Rhetoric and Theology in Haggai 1:1–11." *JHS* 7 (2007): 1–14.

Augustin, Mattias and Klaus D. Schunck, eds. *"Wünschet Jerusalem Frieden": Collected Communications to the XIIth Congress of the International Organization for the Study of the Old Testament, Jerusalem, 1986*. BEATAJ 13. Frankfurt am Main: Peter Lang, 1988.

Avigad, Nahman. *Bullae and Seals from a Post-Exilic Judean Archive*. Qedem 4: Institute of Archaeology. Jerusalem: The Hebrew University of Jerusalem Press, 1976.

Avnimelech, Moshe A. "Influence of Geological Conditions on the Development of Jerusalem." *BASOR* 181 (1966): 24–31.

Baldwin, Joyce. *Haggai, Zechariah, Malachi: An Introduction and Commentary*. TOTC. London: Inter Varsity, 1971.

Banning, Edward Bruce. "Towers." Pages 622–24 in Freedman, ed., *ABD*. Vol. 6.

Barstad, Hans M. *History and the Hebrew Bible: Studies in Ancient Israelite and Ancient Near Eastern Historiography*, FAT 61. Archaeology and Biblical Studies 5. Tübingen: Mohr Siebeck, 2008.

——. "Haggai Among the Prophets: An Example of Prophetic Continuity in the Hebrew Bible." Pages 265–83 in Bar-Asher, Rom-Shiloni, Tov, and Wazana, eds, *Shai le-Sara Japhet: Studies in the Bible, its Exegesis and its Language*.

Bedford, Peter Ross. *Temple Restoration in Early Achaemenid Judah*. JSJSup 65. Leiden: Brill, 2001.

——. "Discerning the Time: Haggai, Zechariah and the 'Delay' in the Rebuilding of the Jerusalem Temple." Pages 71–94 in *The Pitcher Is Broken: Memorial Essays for Gösta. W. Ahlström*. Edited by Steven W, L. Holloday, and Lowell K. Handy. JSOTSup 190. Sheffield: JSOT, 1995.

Berquist, Jon L. "Constructions of Identity in Postcolonial Yehud." Pages 53–66 in Lipschits and Oeming, eds, *Judah and the Judeans in the Persian Period.*

——. *Judaism in Persia's Shadow: A Social and Historical Approach.* Minneapolis: Fortress, 1995.

Bongenaar, A. C. V. M. *The Neo-Babylonian Ebabbar Temple at Sippar: Its Administration and its Prosopography.* Leiden: Nederlands Historisch-Archaeologisch Instituut Te Istanbul, 1997.

Borowski, Oded. *Agriculture in Iron Age Israel: The Evidence from Archaeology and the Bible.* Winona Lake, IN: Eisenbrauns, 1987.

Briant, Pierre. *From Cyrus to Alexander: A History of the Persian Empire.* Translated by Peter T. Daniels. Winona Lake, IN: Eisenbrauns, 2002.

Carroll, Robert P. *Jeremiah: A Commentary.* OTL. Philadelphia: Westminster, 1986.

Carter, Charles E. *The Emergence of Yehud in the Persian Period: A Social and Demographic Study.* JSOTSup 294. Sheffield: Sheffield Academic Press, 1999.

Cataldo, Jeremiah W. *A Theocratic Yehud? Issues of Government in a Persian Province.* LHB/OTS 498; New York; London: T & T Clark, 2009.

Cogan, Mordechai and Israel Eph'al, eds, *Ah, Assyria ... Studies in Assyrian History and Ancient Near Eastern Historiography Presented to Hayim Tadmor.* Jerusalem: Magnes, 1991.

Coggins, Richard J. *Haggai, Zechariah and Malachi.* OTG. Sheffield: Sheffield Academic Press, 1987.

Cole, Steven William and Peter Machinist. *Letters from Priests to the Kings Esarhaddon and Assurbanipal.* SAA 13. Helsinki: Helsinki University Press, 1999.

Collins, John Joseph. *Daniel,* Her. Minneapolis: Fortress, 1993.

Curtis, John E. and Nigel Tallis., eds. *Forgotten Empire: The World of Ancient Persia.* London: The Trustees of the British Museum, 2005.

Dandamaev, Muhammad A. *A Political History of the Achaemenid Empire.* Translated by W. J. Vogelsang. Leiden: Brill, 1989.

Davies, Philip R. ed. *Second Temple Studies.* Vol. 1, *Persian Period.* JSOTSup 117. Sheffield: Sheffield Academic Press, 1991.

Edelman, Diana. *Origins of the 'Second' Temple: Persian Imperial Policy and the Rebuilding of Jerusalem.* London: Equinox, 2005.

Eisenstadt, Shmuel N., ed. *The Origins and Diversity of Axial Age Civilizations.* Albany, NY: State University of New York Press, 1986.

Faust, Avraham and Ehud Weiss, "Judah, Philistia and the Mediterranean World: Reconstructing the Economic System of the Seventh Century B.C.E." *BASOR* 338 (2005):71–92

Floyd, Michael H. "The Nature of the Narrative and the Evidence of Redaction in Haggai." *VT* 45 (1995): 470–90.

Freedman, David Noel, ed. *Anchor Bible Dictionary*. 6 Vols. New York; London, Doubleday, 1992. [=ABD]

Fried, Lisbeth S. "The House of the God who dwells in Jerusalem." *JAOS* 126 (2006): 89–102.

Gadd, Cyril John. "Inscribed Barrel Cylinder of Marduk-apla-iddina II." *Iraq* 20 (1953): 123–34.

Gilter, Haim. "The Levant." Pages 101–13 in Morrison and Kluge, eds, *A Survey of Numismatic Research 1990–1995*.

Grabbe, Lester L. *A History of the Jews and Judaism in the Second Temple Period*. Vol. 1, *Yehud: A History of the Persian Province of Judah*. LSTS. London; New York: T & T Clark, 2004.

_____, ed. *Can a "History of Israel" Be Written*. JSOTSup 245; Sheffield: Sheffield Academic Press, 1997.

Guillaume, Philippe. *Land and Calendar: The Priestly Document from Genesis 1 to Joshua 18*. New York; London: T & T Clark, 2009.

Hanson, Paul D. *The Dawn of Apocalyptic: The Historical and Sociological Roots of Jewish Apocalyptic Eschatology*. Philadelphia: Fortress, 1975.

Harper, Robert Francis. *Assyrian and Babylonian Letters*. 5 Vols. Reprint. Chicago, IL: The University of Chicago Press, 1977. [=*ABL*]

Hoglund, Kenneth G. *Achaemenid Imperial Administration in Syria-Palestine and the Missions of Ezra and Nehemiah*. SBL Dissertation Series 125. Atlanta, GA: Scholars Press, 1992.

——. "The Achaemenid Context." Pages 54–72 in Davies, ed., *Second Temple Studies*. Vol. 1, *Persian Period*.

Hopkins, David C. *The Highlands of Canaan: Agricultural Life in the Early Iron Age*. SWBA 3. Sheffield: Almond, 1985.

Hossfeld, Frank-Lothar, and Ludger Schwienhorst-Schönberger, eds. *Das Manna fällt auch heute noch: Beiträge zur Geschichte und Theologie des Alten, Ersten Testaments: Festschrift für Erich Zenger*. Freiburg; New York: Herder, 2004.

Hurowitz, Victor. *I Have Built You an Exalted Housed: Temple Building in the Bible in Light of Mesopotamian and Northwest Semitic Writings*. JSOTSup 115. Sheffield: Sheffield Academic Press, 1992.

Hurvitz, Avi. *A Linguistic Study of the Relationship between the Priestly Source and the Book of Ezekiel: A New Approach to an Old Problem*. Paris: Gabalda, 1982.

Jacob, Irene and Water Jacob. "Flora." Pages 803–17 in Freedman, ed., *ABD*. Vol. 2.

Japhet, Sara. "The Concept of the 'Remnant' in the Restoration Period: On the Vocabulary of Self-Definition." Pages 340–61 in Hossfeld and Schwienhorst-Schönberger, eds, *Das Manna fällt auch heute noch: Beiträge zur Geschichte und Theologie des Alten, Ersten Testaments: Festschrift für Erich Zenger*.

——."'History' and 'Literature' in the Persian Period: The Restoration of the Temple." Pages 174–88 in Cogan and Eph'al eds, *Ah, Assyria ... Studies in Assyrian History and Ancient Near Eastern Historiography Presented to Hayim Tadmor.*

——. "Sheshbazzar and Zerubbabel: Against the Background of the Historical and Religious Tendencies of Ezra-Nehemiah, Part II." *ZAW* 95 (1984): 218–29.

——. "Sheshbazzar and Zerubbabel: Against the Background of the Historical and Religious Tendencies of Ezra-Nehemiah." *ZAW* 94 (1982): 66–98.

Kaufmann, Yehezkel. "Kalendar und das Alter des Priesterkodex." *VT* 4 (1954): 307–13.

Kessler, John. *The Book of Haggai: Prophecy and Society in early Persian Yehud.* VTSup 91. Leiden: Brill, 2002.

——. "Building the Second Temple: Questions of Time, Text, and History in Haggai 1.1–15." *JSOT* 27 (2002): 243–56.

Koch, Klaus. "Haggais unreines Volk." *ZAW* 79 (1967): 52–66.

Kuhrt, Amelie. *The Ancient Near East c. 3000–330 B.C.* Routledge History of the Ancient World 2. London: Routledge, 1995.

Liphschitz, Nili and Gideon Biger. "The Timber Trade in Ancient Palestine." *TA* 22 (1995): 121–7.

Lipschits, Oded. "Achaeological Imperial Policy, Settlement Processes in Palestine, and the Status of Jerusalem in the Middle of the Fifth Century B.C.E." Pages 19–32 in Lipschits and Oeming, eds, *Judah and the Judeans in the Persian Period.*

McEntire, Mark. "Haggai: Bringing God into the Picture." *RE* 97 (2000): 69–78.

Mantel, Hugo (Haim Dov). "The Dichotomy of Judaism during Second Temple." *HUCA* 44 (1973): 56–87.

Mason, Rex. *The Book of Haggai, Zechariah and Malachi.* CBC. Cambridge: Cambridge University Press, 1977.

——. "The Purpose of the 'Editorial Framework' of the Book of Haggai." *VT* (1977); 413–21.

Meadowcroft, Tim. "A Desolate Land, Environment, People and Temple: Haggai and the Environment." Colloq 40 (2008): 54–74.

Meadows, Andrew R. "The Administration of the Achaemenid Empire." Pages 181–209 in Curtis and Tallis, *Forgotten Empire.*

Meyers, Eric M. and Carol L. Meyers. *Haggai, Zechariah 1–8.* AB. Vol. 25B. New York: Doubleday, 1987.

Milgrom, Jacob. *Leviticus 1–16: A New Translation with Introduction and Commentary.* AB. Vol. 3. New York: Doubleday, 1992.

Mitchell, Hinckley Gilbert Thomas, J. M. Powis Smith, and Julius A. Bewer. *A Critical and Exegetical Commentary on Haggai, Zechariah, Malachi and Jonah.* New York: Scribner, 1912.

Parpola, Simo. *Letters from Assyrian and Babylonian Scholars*. SAA 10. Helsinki: Helsinki University Press, 1993.

Petersen, David L. "The Temple in Persian Period Prophetic Texts." Pages 125–45 in Davies, ed., *Second Temple Studies*. Vol. 1, *Persian Period*.

——. *Haggai, Zechariah 1–8: A Commentary*. OTL. London: SCM, 1985.

——. "Zerubbabel and Jerusalem Temple Reconstruction." *CBQ* 36 (1974): 366–72.

Pfeiffer, Robert Henry and Robert Francis Harper, *State Letters of Assyria: A Transliteration and Translation of 355 Official Assyrian Letters Dating from the Sargonid Period (722–625 B.C.)*. AOS. Vol. 6. New Haven: American Oriental Society, 1935.

Polzin, Robert. *Late Biblical Hebrew: Toward an Historical Typology of Biblical Hebrew Prose*. HSM 12. Missoula, MT: Scholars Press, 1976.

Prinsloo, William S. "The Cohesion of Haggai 1:4–11." Pages 337–43 in Augustin and Schunck, eds, *"Wünschet Jerusalem Frieden": Collected Communications to the XIIth Congress of the International Organization for the Study of the Old Testament, Jerusalem, 1986*.

Rainer, Albertz. *A History of Israelite Religion in the Old Testament* 2 Vols. OTLS; Louisville: Westminster; John Knox, 1994.

Rappaport, Uriel. "Numistics." Pages 25–59 in Davies and Finkelstein, eds, *CHJ*. Vol. 1, *Introduction*.

Redditt, Paul L. *Haggai, Zechariah, Malachi: Based on the Revised Standard Version*, New Century Bible Commentary. London: Marshall Pickering, 1995.

Saggs, Henry William Frederick. *The Might That Was Assyria*. London: Sidgwick, 1984.

Sancisi-Weerdenburg, Heleen, ed. *Achaemenid History*. Vol. 3, *The Root of the European Tradition*. Leiden: Nederlands Instituut voor het Nabije Oosten, 1988. [=*AH*]

—— and Amelie Kuhrt, eds. *Achaemenid History*. Vol. 4, *Centre and Periphery*. Leiden: Nederlands Instituut voor het Nabije Oosten, 1990. [=*AH*]

Schroeder, Otto. *Keilschrifttexte aus Assur verschiedenen Inhalts*. Leipzig: Hinrichs' sche, 1920. [=*KAV*]

Segal, Judah Ben-Zion. "Intercalation and the Hebrew Calendar." *VT* 7 (1957): 250–307.

Smith, Daniel L. *The Religion of the Landless: The Social Context of the Babylonian Exile*. Bloomington: Meyer-Stone, 1989.

Steck, Odil Hannes. "Zu Haggai 1:2–11." *ZAW* 83 (1971): 355–79.

Stern, Ephraim. "The Persian Empire and the Political and Social History of Palestine in the Persian Period." Pages 7–87 in Finkelstein and Davies, eds, *CHJ*. Vol. 1, *Introduction*.

Tadmor, Hayim. "Judah." Pages 261–96 in Boardman, Lewis, Hornblower, and Ostwald, eds, *CAH*. Vol. 6, *The Fourth Century BC*.

——. "Monarchy and the Elite in Assyria and Babylonia: The Question of Royal Accountability." Pages 203–24. In Eisenstadt, ed., *The Origins and Diversity of Axial Age Civilizations.*

Tollington, Janet E. *Tradition and Innovation in Haggai and Zechariah 1–8.* JSOTSup 150. Sheffield: Sheffield Academic Press, 1993.

Trotter, James M. "Was the Second Jerusalem Temple a Primarily Persian Project?" *SJOT* 15 (2001): 276–93.

Tuttle, Gary A, ed. *Biblical and Near Eastern Studies: Essays in Honour of William Sandford Lasor.* Grand Rapids, MI: Eerdmans, 1978.

Vanderkam, James C. "Ancient Israelite and Early Jewish." Pages 814–20 in Freedman, ed., *ABD.* Vol. 1.

Verhoef, Peter A. *The Book of Haggai and Malachi.* NICOT. Grand Rapids: Eerdmans, 1987.

Weinberg, Joel P. *The Citizen-Temple Community.* Translated by Daniel L. Smith-Christopher. JSOTSup 151. Sheffield: Sheffield Academic Press, 1992.

Whedbee, James William. "A Question-Answer Schema in Haggai 1: The Form and Function of Haggai 1:9–11." Pages 184–94 in Tuttle, ed., *Biblical and Near Eastern Studies: Essays in Honour of William Sandford Lasor.*

Widengren, Geo. "The Persian Period." Pages 489–538 in Hayes and Miller, eds, *Israelite and Judean History.*

Wiesenberg, Ephraim Jehudah. "Calendar." Pages 43–50 in *EncJud.* Vol. 5.

Wolff, Hans Walter, *Haggai: A Commentary.* Translated by M. Kohl. Minneapolis: Augsburg Publishing House, 1988.

Young, Ian. "The Style of the Gezer Calendar and Some 'Archaic Biblical Hebrew' Passage." *VT* 42 (1992): 362–75.

CHAPTER 5

A Judean Revolt and its Results: Hag 2:1–23

Background

Hag 2:1–23 contains the responses of Zerubbabel the governor, Joshua the high priest, and the people in Judah to the Jerusalem temple rebuilding claim in the second year of Darius (520 BCE).[1]

According to Hag 1:1–15, Judah had been ordered to restore the Jerusalem temple's economy for supporting the empire (Hag 1:1, 7–8, 15). However, along with their two leaders, Zerubbabel and Joshua, the people of Judah rejected Darius's command. Instead, they were engaged with their own hope of re-establishing a Davidic dynasty through Zerubbabel (Hag 1:2, 4, 9). According to Haggai, the messenger of YHWH, Judah's disobedience to YHWH had been punished (Hag 1:12–14). YHWH caused crop failure (Hag 1:5–6), drought and famine (Hag 1:9–11). Nevertheless, the Jerusalem temple remained derelict (Hag 1:9).

Zerubbabel and Joshua were commissioned by Darius in the name of YHWH specifically for the work of rebuilding the Jerusalem temple (Hag 1:1, 15). Working as imperial administrators, they were to do their best for the Jerusalem temple restoration. However, they never carried out their responsibility. This was a violation against YHWH and a revolt against

1 For literary analyses of Hag 2:1–23, see Boda, "Haggai," 295–304; Wolff, *Haggai*, 73, 78–9, 99; Kessler, *The Book of Haggai*, 161–3, 201–2, 220–1; Meyers and Meyers, *Haggai, Zechariah 1–8*, xliv–lxx; McEntire, "Haggai," 69–78; Assis, "A Disputed Temple," 582–96; Floyd, "The Nature of the Narrative," 470–90; Verhoef, *The Book of Haggai and Malachi*, 22–5; Meadowcroft, *Haggai*, 146–209; Redditt, *Haggai, Zechariah, Malachi*, 11–2; Petersen, *Haggai, Zechariah 1–8*, 36–9; Mason, *The Book of Haggai, Zechariah and Malachi*, 13–7; Mason, "The Purpose of the 'Editorial Framework,'" 413–21.

Darius. As a result, Zerubbabel the governor, Joshua the high priest, and the people had to be punished. What follows is an exegesis on Hag 2:1–23. Here, I will touch on some of the problems in relation to the actions against YHWH and Darius.

An Exegesis of Hag 2:1–23: Davidic Rebuilding versus Temple Rebuilding

An Uprising to Institute the Royal Authority (Hag 2:1–9)

Hag 2:1

בשביעי בעשרים ואחד לחדש היה דבר-יהוה ביד-חגי[2] הנביא לאמר

[In the seventh month, on the twenty-first day of the month, the word of the YHWH came through the prophet Haggai, saying,]

This unit duly starts with the prophetic language ... היה דבר-יהוה ביד-חגי הנביא (the word of YHWH came through the prophet Haggai, Hag 2:1–2), as in Hag 1:1 and Hag 1:3. The leading point of this form is the word ביד or אל which emphasises Haggai's role as a representative for both the word of YHWH and the commands of Darius. Generally Darius's government was facilitated through the satrap, who functioned as an intermediary and managed the satrapal administration. The satrap would preside over the regions within his satrapy, resolving internal conflicts within his provinces and dealing with the disputes that would break out between the provincial governors.[3] Like these imperial satraps, the prophet Haggai continued to

2 BHS marks that the Mur corrects ביד to אל. However, in Haggai's text, both ביד (Hag 1:1, 3) and אל (Hag 2:10, 20) introduce the intermediary through whom the word comes. Therefore, this adjustment is unnecessary.

3 See Chapter 2 above. See also Harper, *ABL*, 359, 391, 586, 691; Parpola, *Letters from Assyrian and Babylonian Scholars*, 57, 68, 302, 315.

function as a prophetic intermediary throughout the disasters both of the failure to rebuild the Jerusalem temple and the breakdown of the agricultural economic system.[4]

The word of YHWH came again in the seventh month.[5] Around one month had passed since the prophet Haggai had called Zerubbabel, Joshua, and the people to restore the Jerusalem temple. According to the Gezer Calendar, it was towards the end of the festival of Tabernacles in Tishri which begins on the fifteenth day of the seventh month and continues for seven days. This festival primarily celebrates the gathering of grains, new wine, and oil into storage for the coming year, the ultimate goal of all the preceding agricultural activities (Exod 23:16–17; Lev 23:34–39; Num 29:12–38; Deut 16:11–15).[6] Then, on the next day of the festival, YHWH would assemble the people. It was generally blessed with an adequate supply of rain for the forthcoming ploughing and sowing season. It seems to follow that those attending the festival must have been extremely keen to receive blessings responding to their needs and desires.

This designated month is also associated with the dedication of the first temple (1 Kgs 8: 2, 63; 2 Chr 7:8–10).[7] Solomon, with the people, had held large numbers of sacrifices to celebrate the dedication of the first temple. On

4 Verhoef, *The Book of Haggai and Malachi*, 94–5.

5 Meyers and Meyers state that, because of the lack of date, it would be more appropriate for the year to be part of the end of Hag 1 than the beginning of Hag 2. Meyers and Meyers, *Haggai, Zechariah 1–8*, 49.

6 See Steven L. McKenzie, *1–2 Chronicles* (AOTC; Nashville: Abingdon, 2004), 251–2; William Johnstone, *First and Second Chronicles*. Vol. 1, *1 Chronicles 1–2 Chronicles 9: Israel's Place among the Nations* (JSOTSup 253; Sheffield: Sheffield Academic Press, 1997), 352–7; Raymond B. Dillard, *2 Chronicles* (WBC, Vol. 15; Waco, TX: Word books, 1987), 57–9.

7 See Jeffrey H. Tigay, *Deuteronomy* (JPSTC; Philadelphia: The Jewish Publication Society, 1996), 157–8, 469; Jacob Milgrom, *Leviticus: A Book of Ritual and Ethics* (CC; Minneapolis: Fortress, 2004), 282; Jacob Milgrom, *Leviticus, 23–27: A New Translation with Introduction and Commentary* (AB, Vol. 3B; New York: Doubleday, 2001), 207; Baruch A. Levine, *Leviticus* (The JPS Torah Commentary; Philadelphia: The Jewish Publication Society, 1989), 326–33; Erhard S. Gerstenberger, *Leviticus: A Commentary* (OTL; Louisville, KY: Westminster John Knox, 1996), 436–47; Martin Jan Mulder, *1 Kings*, Vol. 1, *1 Kings 1–11* (HCOT; Leuven: Peeters, 1998), 379, 449.

the eighth day, then, the people had returned to their homes joyful and glad of heart for all the goodness that YHWH had shown to David and his people (1 Kgs 8:64; 2 Chr 7:10). YHWH's blessings to Solomon were guaranteed because Solomon and the people remained loyal to him and kept YHWH's commandments (1 Kgs 6:6, 11–13, 59, 61; 8:57–58; 2 Chr 7:17–33), which demonstrates that Solomon successfully accomplished the Jerusalem temple. Clearly, Solomon's good fortune is contingent upon obedience to YHWH's commandment and not to the building of the temple itself. Solomon could expect nothing as a reward merely for the temple construction.

As with this instruction to Solomon, in the case of building the second Jerusalem temple YHWH's blessing could only be expected through submission to YHWH's word. So, regarding both the Judean economic and political crises, Haggai highlights the importance of submission to YHWH's order for rebuilding the Jerusalem temple. It is highly unlikely that dynastic establishment and prosperity were assured as rewards for building the temple or any kind of buildings in the ancient Near East.[8]

The people, as recorded in the book of Haggai, nevertheless, seem to have had some sense that the temple building would facilitate the formation of dynasty as it did David. They recall that David's desire to build the house of YHWH led to the establishment of the Davidic dynasty and the prosperity of the Davidic kingdom (2 Sam 7). This miscalculation never inspires the people to devote themselves to actually restoring the Jerusalem temple. They steadfastly stick to their conspiracy for renewing the Davidic kingdom with the Judean governor Zerubbabel, who is of Davidic lineage.

Hag 2:2

אמר-נא אל-זרבבל בן-שלתיאל פחת יהודה ואל-יהושע בן-יהוצדק הכהן הגדול
ואל-שארית[9] העם לאמר

["Speak to Zerubbabel the son of Shealtiel, governor of Judah, and to Joshua the son of Jehozadak, the high priest, and to the remnant of the people," saying,]

8 Edelman, *Origins*, 91; Hurowitz, *I Have Built You*, 304.

9 BHS mentions that the LXX has πάντας (כל in Hebrew) before שארית and this is supported by the Syriac version. This reading would make better sense but I am not sure that this addition is necessary.

In spite of the temple's desolation, it seems quite probable that the people enjoyed gathering there for the feasts of the festival of Tabernacles. Since the royal leader Zerubbabel is clearly of some significance in this celebration, one can imagine that the assembly associated with this festival was a great affair.

In the records from this gathering, in Hag 2:2, Zerubbabel's name precedes Joshua's. This denotes that Zerubbabel has retained the primary administrative position. Also, the phrase "the remnant of the people" clearly refers to all the people of Judah except the leaders, Zerubbabel and Joshua, as Haggai's audience, which is likewise the case in Hag 1:12 and 14.

One should be careful to distinguish the people's response towards rebuilding the Jerusalem temple from their fervour for Zerubbabel which is indicated in Hag 1:12 and 14. Though they had been urged to pledge themselves to the temple restoration with the assurance of YHWH's blessing the people seemed uncommitted to the task. The people were instead caught up with excitement that Zerubbabel, who was of royal lineage, and charged with the task of the temple reconstruction, was now with them.[10] Thus, they devoted themselves to the building of the Davidic house to demonstrate their support for Zerubbabel.

This course of action was based on the understanding that the establishment of a dynasty would require an accompanying temple building (2 Sam 7). The Davidic lineage of the governor Zerubbabel instilled into the people a false sense of entitlement to him and to an independent dynasty of Judah. At the end of feasts, then, their attention was squarely focused on the blessings of YHWH that had been historically associated with the dynastic status Zerubbabel seemed to hold.

The people were clearly seized by the fancy of restoring the Judean kingdom remembered from the time of David. This notion, though, was very different from YHWH's commandment to rebuild the temple. Therefore, in the seventh month, the month associated with the temple dedication

10 Kessler, *The Book of Haggai*, 164; Meyers and Meyers, *Haggai, Zechariah 1–8*, 49; Verhoef, *The Book of Haggai and Malachi*, 95; Redditt, *Haggai, Zechariah, Malachi*, 24; Petersen, *Haggai, Zechariah 1–8*, 62–3.

of Solomon's temple, Haggai invoked the people to obey YHWH and rebuild the temple.

From Hag 1:1–2, it is evident that in the seventh month, against YHWH's demand for the temple reconstruction, the attention of the people is instead directed to a probable concomitant blessing through Zerubbabel (1 Kgs 8:64; 2 Chr 7:10). That is the restoration of the Davidic kingdom. Meanwhile, in the same month, Haggai puts tremendous emphasis on the importance of obediently fulfilling YHWH's command to rebuild the Jerusalem temple, as was demonstrated by Solomon (1 Kgs 6:6, 11–13, 59, 61; 8:57–58; 2 Chr 7:17–33). Viewed within this sharp tension, there is cause to doubt the people's expectation of blessing. Moreover, critical attention from YHWH and Darius to the people and the leaders will become increasingly pronounced.

Hag 2:3

מי בכם הנשאר אשר ראה את-הבית הזה בכבודו הראשון; ומה אתם ראים אתו
עתה הלוא כמהו כאין בעיניכם

["Who is left among you that saw this house in its former glory? How do you see it now? Does it not appear in your sight as nothing?"]

Following on from the prophetic introductory form in Hag 2:1–2, this verse develops the dramatic issue which leads the narrative forward, from a rhetorical point of view. In a series of three sentences, YHWH raises questions to the people; "who saw this house in its former glory?" "How do you see it now?" and "Does it not seem, in your sight, nothing?" These queries seem to rhetorically connect what this house did in the past with what it should be doing in the present. In particular, by recapitulating the second question, the third emphatically asks all the people including Zerubbabel and Joshua to assess the temple's current function with retrospective awareness.

At the start of this passage, YHWH alludes to the great splendour of the first Jerusalem temple that is at the heart of the people inquiring "who has seen this house in its former glory?" From this understanding, some scholars have argued that the focus of the passage is a comparison between the past and the present states of the same temple.[11] In such arguments, the word כבוד simply implies the "heaviness," "glory," or "splendour" of the appearance of the building itself (Ezek 31:18; Esth 1:4; Isa 4:2; Ps 102:17). Here כבוד is exclusively understood to highlight the striking appearance of the temple. Subsequently, Haggai's proclamation at the temple site would make the people pay tremendous attention on the temple building, because the temple in ruins lets them reflect on the first Jerusalem temple in a time of great prosperity.

However, the term הראשון does not modify the temple הבית but the glory כבוד of the temple. Therefore, the comparison is not of the difference between the past splendid state and the present shameful state of the temple. Rather, this verse asks the people to reflect upon the first glory of the Jerusalem temple. "What does the first glory of the temple represent?" This interpretation is supported by the use of the word כבוד in Hag 1:8. The past glory כבוד of the temple denotes that the rebuilt Jerusalem temple will be full of very desirable and precious resources.

From this understanding, it is worthwhile to examine the preposition ב in the phrase "the temple in its former glory" (בכבודו). The preposition leads to an adverbial phrase indicating a condition. This suggests an important shift in focus to what the temple did in the kingdom period, when the glory of the temple was associated with the wealth of Solomon and the breadth of his kingdom. Along with the affluent cash commodities of wheat, wine, and olive oil, Solomon developed commercial trades with Egypt that extended eastward to Arabia (see Chapter 1 above). This shift in focus is intended to invoke the people to consider what role the temple should play in the period of Darius and the Achaemenids.

In the comparison between the monarchical state and the current state, the word נשאר has also been identified as the people who have actually

11 See Kessler, *The Book of Haggai*, 162–6; Meyers and Meyers, *Haggai, Zechariah 1–8*, 49–50; Assis, "A Disputed Temple," 583; Verhoef, *The Book of Haggai and Malachi*, 95–7; Meadowcroft, *Haggai*, 148–54; Redditt, *Haggai, Zechariah, Malachi*, 24; Petersen, *Haggai, Zechariah 1–8*, 63–4.

seen the Solomonic temple.[12] However, it does not refer to those who have lived longer than seventy years and have memories of the glory of the Jerusalem temple in the kingdom period. It quite simply indicates all the people who are summoned for the Jerusalem temple reconstruction. Keeping the Jerusalem temple of the monarchical time in their minds, they are now called to profoundly consider what this temple should do in the Achaemenid reign, especially in relation to Darius's policy.

As a committed builder, Solomon finished the construction of the Jerusalem temple as YHWH had ordered and David had asked from him. For the continuous security and prosperity of the kingdom, Solomon had adhered to all the commandments of YHWH, as the conditions for divine blessing.

In similar manner, Zerubbabel, Joshua, and the people should be obedient to the command of YHWH to rebuild the Jerusalem temple for the benefit of his blessings. Towards this end, the prophet Haggai continued to encourage the people, including both leaders, to serve the word of YHWH to rebuild the temple in service to YHWH and as well to Darius. YHWH's command to rebuild the Jerusalem temple seems to have played a crucial role in assuring the survival of Judah under Achaemenid rule.

Nevertheless, the people and their leaders remained derisive of the temple rebuilding. Without concern for the actual building, they seemed certain that the pretense of rebuilding the temple would be sufficient to restore the Davidic kingdom. They continued to look down upon the temple itself; it was "like nothing" (אין) to them.

The neglect of the temple building by the people received censure in the phrase "is the building not like nothing (אין) at all." Haggai's rhetorical question contrasts the current desolate condition of the temple with the monarchical glorious state of the temple. Indeed, when the word אין is accompanied by the particle כ, it could indicate a comparison referring to the same object.[13] The combination of כאין alongside the comparative

12 See Meyers and Meyers, *Haggai, Zechariah 1–8*, 49; Verhoef, *The Book of Haggai and Malachi*, 95–7; Wolff, *Haggai*, 57; Petersen, *Haggai, Zechariah 1–8*, 64; Kessler, *The Book of Haggai*, 164–5.

13 *DCH*, Vol. 1, 213–20; *HALOT*, Vol. 1, 41–2.

particle appears 6 times in the Bible, for example: "is my lifetime as nothing in your sight" (Ps 39:6; 73:2), "all the nations are as nothing before YHWH" (Isa 40:17), or "you will be as nothing" (Isa 41:11–12). Accordingly, this syntax seems intended to prompt the audience to reflect on the function of YHWH's command to rebuild the Jerusalem temple, such as in Solomon.

This exegesis of Hag 2:3 has demonstrated through a series of three questions that the rejoicing of the people in expecting the restoration of Davidic kingdom is not only premature, but undermined by the temple's continued state of ruins. For, the people completely fail to reflect on the importance of both YHWH's word and Darius's command to rebuild the Jerusalem temple—the importance of which can be seen in Solomon, during the monarchical period. There is no doubt that the people should comply with YHWH's command to rebuild the Jerusalem temple: this would ensure the economic affluence of Judah.

Hag 2:4

ועתה חזק זרבבל נאם-יהוה וחזק יהושע בן-יהוצדק הכהן הגדול וחזק כל-עם הארץ
נאם-יהוה ועשו: כי-אני אתכם נאם יהוה צבאות[14]

[Now, thus, "have courage, Zerubbabel," said YHWH; "be courageous, Joshua, son of Jehozadak, the high priest; be courageous, all people of the land," said YHWH; and "they are, for I am with you," said YHWH of hosts.]

With the adverbial particle עתה which accentuates the present moment, Haggai draws attention to exactly what Zerubbabel and Joshua together with the people have set about doing. That is, they decisively persevere in establishing a royal authority through Zerubbabel in the Davidic lineage. After referring to the word of YHWH, they have undertaken the restoration of the Davidic kingdom without attending to the restoration of the temple building.

14 BHS suggests that נאם יהוה and נאם יהוה צבאות are additions. In Haggai, however, each prophetic messenger formula represents the delivery of the word of YHWH. Here, they are used for underlining Zerubbabel, Joshua, and all the people actions. The text should not be changed.

From the start, the words of YHWH in this verse give credence to the purpose of the people with the use of the verb חזק. The verb חזק is the masculine single form of a Qal imperative, meaning "to be strong," "to be confident," or "to devote oneself to something" depending on the context.[15] Also noteworthy is the expression "I am with you" (אני כם). This phrase might remind the people of the assurance "I am with you," that YHWH gave to David when he had desired to build the Jerusalem temple. This assurance convinced David that YHWH had cut off his enemies and established high on the earth (2 Sam 7:9). Therefore, חזק of this verse is nothing to the interpretation as denoting emotional strength to correspond with the call to fearlessness in the following verse is pointless.[16] Obviously, the word חזק with "I am with you" (אני כם) certainly suggests divine blessing in the form of military triumph. In this sense, the restoration of a royal dynasty as a benefit of obeying YHWH is also firmly assured to the people and their leaders, and all individuals that do (עשׂה) so.[17]

The next phrase noteworthy for explication is עם הארץ("all people of the land"). In the kingdom period, the term עם הארץ stood for any social class with a small number holding political power.[18] In the Judean kingdom period, however, the expression עם הארץ cannot be understood as synonymous with all the people of Judah, instead, עם הארץ describes the agrarian social class which had very limited political power. With their political

15 *DCH*, Vol. 3, 184–90; *HALOT*, Vol. 1, 302–4.

16 Kessler, *The Book of Haggai*, 167–9; Meyers and Meyers, *Haggai, Zechariah 1–8*, 50–1; Assis, "A Disputed Temple," 588–90; Verhoef, *The Book of Haggai and Malachi*, 98; Redditt, *Haggai, Zechariah, Malachi*, 24–5.

17 About the imperative verb עשׂו, Kessler notes that it should be seen as an exhortation to continue the work which has been started in Hag 1:12. Kessler, *The Book of Haggai*, 169. Meanwhile, Meyers and Meyers note the word עשׂו is related to its following object דברי ברית in Hag 1:5. Meyers and Meyers, *Haggai, Zechariah 1–8*, 51–2.

18 For a wide range of meanings of עם הארץ, see Tomoo Ishida, *History and Historical Writing in Ancient Israel: Studies in Biblical Historiography* (SHCANE16; Leiden: Brill, 1999), 81–96. On עם הארץ in Ezra 4:4, see also Lisbeth S. Fried, "The ʿAm Hāʾres in Ezra 4:4," in Lipschits and Oeming, eds, *Judah and the Judeans in the Persian Period*, 123–45.

power and economic abilities, עם הארץ participate in the restoration of Davidic line in the crisis of the Davidic kingdom.

Certainly, עם הארץ played a particular role in determining the succession of the Davidic throne, in events such as these: the overthrow of Athaliah and the enthronement of Joash (2 Kgs 11; 2 Chr 23), the execution of the conspirators against King Amon and the enthronement of Josiah (2 Kgs 21: 23–24; 2 Chr 33:24–25) and the ordination of Jehoahaz after Josiah's death in battle (2 Kgs 23:30; 2 Chr 36:1). The intervention of עם הארץ in political crises secured the succession of David's dynasty under the name of the whole people of Judah. Reminding his audience of this political history, Haggai intentionally employed the technical term עם הארץ instead of the general term "the people." The use of עם הארץ aims to promote the ascendancy of Zerubbabel's position and to restore the Judean monarchy.[19] This is particularly appropriate to the situation, for the people themselves were self-assured as if they believed themselves responsible for the monarchical restoration.

Haggai's audience seems to intertwine the terms of חזק and אני כם, confusing Solomon's temple building with the political purpose of restoring the dynasty. Instead, the phrase חזק ... אני כם should be understood as describing the situation when David charged Solomon with building the temple (1 Chr 22:13; 28:20). It was in this context that Solomon quickly applied himself to building the temple. It was with this in mind that, in Hag 1:13, Haggai prompted the people to work on the house of YHWH with the assurance that YHWH is with them. Indeed, it was with this in mind that Haggai expected the people to rebuild the Jerusalem temple with confidence, reminiscent of Solomon.

In light of the people's swelling aspirations for restoring the Davidic dynasty, Haggai again addressed Zerubbabel first, though this time without his title. This change indicates his diminished position in Achaemenid Judah, as can be seen in Hag 1:12. Meanwhile, the high priest designation can be consistently found alongside Joshua's name. This evidence has been claimed to signify the ascent of the high priest to a place of power over the

19 Meyers and Meyers, *Haggai, Zechariah 1–8*, 51.

governor in Judean society.[20] Such claims appear to be unlikely, though, in light of the historical records describing the Judean administration system. At most, Joshua's consistent designation as high priest indicates the stable position of the high priest in Judean social structure.

The names of at least three governors (פחה) in Achaemenid Judah can be seen in the Hebrew Bible. In the early Achaemenid period, the governors, Sheshbazzar (Ezra 5:15) and Zerubbabel (Hag 1:1, 14), were of a local royal lineage and appointed to the province of Judah to ensure each region's administrative efficiency. In 445 BCE, another governor Nehemiah organised task forces to rebuild the walls of Jerusalem and to forcibly repopulate the city by resettling a tenth of the inhabitants of other Judean cities (Neh 2:7–9; 7:4; 11:1–2).

Through extra Biblical materials, two more governors can be listed. According to the Elephantine papyri, in 410 BCE, the Judean people that had been stationed as imperial garrisons at Elephantine in Egypt were confronted with a religious problem.[21] The governor of Syene, a city on the shore opposite Elephantine was bribed by the priests of an Egyptian temple adjacent to the temple of the Elephantine Judeans. This governor then ravaged the Judean temple and disrupted their rituals.[22] For three years, starting in 407 BCE, the temple was neither rebuilt nor restored, so the Judean people sought help from the governor of Judah, Bagohi. Additionally, they wrote to Darius II (423–405 BCE), pleading for his intervention.

It is worth noting that there was no longer any development of authorisation, nor any investigation into, either Bagohi or Yehizkiyah as local representatives of the Davidic lineage. Only the first two governors, Sheshbazzar and Zerubbabel, were clearly shown to be of royal families. Indeed one might deduce that Darius emphasised the royal lineage of Zerubbabel

20 For Joshua's ascendancy in Zechariah's visions (Zech 3:1–10; 6:9–15), see Meyers and Meyers, *Haggai, Zechariah 1–8*, 50.

21 Cowley, *Aramaic Papyri of the Fifth Century B.C.*, # 30. See also Young, "Persian," 298; Grabbe, *A History of the Jews and Judaism in the Second Temple Period*. Vol. 1, *Yehud*, 148–9.

22 Brosius, *Persians*, 71.

to increase imperial income through the temple's fiscal administration. Incorporating Zerubbabel's royal image into the imperial policy seems to have been an attempt by Darius to strengthen Judah's political allegiance.

Hag 2:4 has shown what the people along with Zerubbabel and Joshua did. Three repetitions of the verb "be strong" (חזק) in the imperative form entreat all of Judah to persevere in the restoration of the Davidic house. The phrase אני אתכם is also used to indicate divine support of their dream of restoring the Davidic monarchy. The specific expression כל עם הארץ also indicates the fervour with which the people desired to restore the Davidic kingdom with the royal lineage of Zerubbabel. However, this emphasis on the royal lineage of Zerubbabel is also consistent with imperial policy and financially beneficial to Darius.

Hag 2:5

את-הדבר[23] אשר-כרתי אתכם בצאתכם ממצרים[24] ורוחי עמדת בתוככם אל-תיראו

["According to the word that I gave to you when you came out of Egypt, my spirit is among you, do not fear."]

Haggai charges the people of Judah to persist in the restoration of Davidic dynasty, which has been impeded by rebuilding the temple. Haggai reminds the people of their obligation to obey the commandments imposed through the Sinai covenant tradition, as is indicated by the phrase, "the word that I made you when you came out of Egypt." In general, the phrase את ... כרת[25] implies the covenant context between YHWH and his people. The phrase is used to indicate reciprocal agreements between YHWH and his people within the covenantal commandments, and it generally assumes

23 BHS suggests את־הדבר to be read זאת הברית or צבאות. However, את here functions as a preposition. Therefore, את should not be seen as a partly deleted form.

24 BHS suggests the removal of את־הדבר אשר־כרתי אתכם בצאתכם ממצרים because the LXX omits this phrase. However, Haggai's appeal to the Sinai covenant tradition serves the function of obedience to YHWH's commands. Therefore, the text should be kept.

25 *DCH*, Vol. 4, 463–7; *HALOT*, Vol. 1, 500–1.

the accompanying word ברית to any Biblical scholars.[26] Haggai is keen to stress these as the covenant terms, and these terms become the backdrop for understanding the repercussions of Judah's disobedience to YHWH.

Yet the terms remain vague because this verse uses the word דבר not the term ברית.[27] Here, one can see one parallel passage "YHWH made *a covenant* with the children of Israel when they came out of the land of Egypt" (1 Kgs 8:9), which followed the clause "the two tablets of stone that Moses placed in the ark at Horeb." This passage clearly describes the Mosaic covenant at Sinai and stipulates complete obedience to the commandments of YHWH. Instead of the technical term ברית Haggai alternately uses the term "word" (דבר), which might allude to the word of YHWH that is proclaimed to the people.

As befits Haggai's intentions, this passage focuses on the word of YHWH to rebuild the Jerusalem temple in the seventh month. As I have argued in Hag 2:1–2 in relation to the temple building, in the seventh month, Solomon finished the construction of the Jerusalem temple in accordance with YHWH's word and he was assured Davidic royalty and economic prosperity in Judah by YHWH. If the people of Judah expect the same blessings from YHWH in the same month they have to obediently fulfill YHWH's command to rebuild the Jerusalem temple, as was demonstrated by Solomon.

This paper has argued that the beginning of this verse, in which the particle את is without its proper verb, should be read as part of previous verse 4.[28] In support of this position, this argument stresses that the distance between verb and object can be seen to emphasise the authority of YHWH's commandment. Precedence for this interpretation is found in the case of Amos 6:14, "behold, I will raise up against you a nation, the house of Israel, said YHWH, the God of hosts" (... קום ... גוי). While the

26 Kessler, *The Book of Haggai*, 169–73; Meyers and Meyers, *Haggai, Zechariah 1–8*, 51–2; Assis, "A Disputed Temple," 588–92; Verhoef, *The Book of Haggai and Malachi*, 99–101; Redditt, *Haggai, Zechariah, Malachi*, 24–5.

27 On the background for the phrase דבר ... כרת, see Petersen, *Haggai, Zechariah 1–8*, 69–70; Baldwin, *Haggai, Zechariah, Malachi*, 47.

28 Meyers and Meyers, *Haggai, Zechariah 1–8*, 51–2.

ordinary function of the particle את is to denote the direct object of the verb, this use of word את without its accompanying verb requires careful consideration.

This use of the term את could function as the preposition with[29] or to mark an adverbial accusative, given the context.[30] Without its corresponding verb, the word את, in this verse, can be interpreted as "according to" or "concerning," while emphasising the nominative.[31] As such, this clause "according to the word that I gave to you when you came out of Egypt" strongly implies the requirement of decisive obedience to YHWH's call to rebuild the temple, as well as confirming YHWH's protection through the bilateral character of the clause.

This interpretation finds corroboration through examining the following phrase: "my spirit is among you." Taken literally, "my spirit" (רוחי) is another reference to YHWH's manifestation: for example, "come near to me, hear this: from the beginning I have not spoken in secret, from the time it came to be I have been there. And now YHWH has sent me and his spirit" (Isa 48:16; see also 32:1–15; 44:3; 59:21; 63:7–14; Zech 4:6).[32] YHWH's presence invariably provides protection (עמדת) and indeed allows human fear to be removed. Because the phrase "my spirit is among you" implied these provisions, it can be understood as YHWH's reassurance to his people regarding the temple rebuilding process. This phrase, and the associated provisions, also testifies to the ongoing validity of the covenant.[33] Therefore, the people and their two leaders need not be afraid of rebuilding the temple, the fiscal administrative centre within the imperial structure. Rather, the people of Judah should be confident, for the presence of YHWH will accompany the reconstruction of the Jerusalem temple.

In Hag 2:5, Haggai reminds the people around Zerubbabel of the commandments imposed from the Sinai-covenantal tradition, commandments

29 Wolff, *Haggai*, 70–1.

30 Verhoef, *The Book of Haggai and Malachi*, 98–9.

31 For further arguments on את, see Max Rogland, "Text and Temple in Haggai 2,5" *ZAW* 119 (2007): 410–15.

32 Wolff, *Haggai*, 71.

33 Kessler, *The Book of Haggai*, 170.

that run contrary to the desires of the people. These commandments include obedience to the word of YHWH—obedience that Solomon demonstrated in his own building of the temple. Reiterating the covenantal tradition, Haggai appeals to the recalcitrant people to reconsider and fearlessly obey the command of YHWH to build the temple.

Hag 2:6

כי כה אמר יהוה צבאות עוד אחת מעט היא;[34]
ואני מרעיש את-השמים ואת[35]-הארץ ואת-הים ואת-החרבה

[For, thus, said YHWH of hosts: "in a little while, I will shake the heavens, the earth, the sea and the dry land"]

Despite Haggai's rebuke of the people for their lack of obedience to YHWH's demand that they rebuild the Jerusalem temple, the people carried out entirely in their own desire to rebuild the Davidic dynasty. It is interesting that their preference for rebuilding the Davidic dynasty is also described with the prophetic formulae of אמר יהוה צבאות (thus YHWH of hosts said) and יהוה צבאות (YHWH of hosts said). This denotes that, in the presence of YHWH, they implicitly trusted in the concomitant splendour of rebuilding the Davidic lineage at the pretense of the Jerusalem temple rebuilding.

Applying the hope associated with the temple building to the Davidic royalty, the people become increasingly preoccupied with Zerubbabel. By reworking of the monarchical ideology, the people come to believe that Zerubbabel will be the source of their good fortune.[36] Focusing on the

34 BHS notes that the LXX suggests to be read ἔτι ἅπαξ, which reflect only words עוד אחת. The Syriac version and a Hebrew manuscript read the phrase to תוב חוא זבן. This adjustment might come from difficult translations of the rest words מעט היא. As I have discussed below, however, Haggai utilises the repetitive sense to emphasise the impending matter. Therefore, מעט היא should not be omitted.

35 BHS suggests the addition of the particle conjunction ו. Even if this is grammatically possible, it is not necessary to delete ו because the text itself makes sense.

36 Meyers and Meyers, *Haggai, Zechariah 1–8*, 52; Verhoef, *The Book of Haggai and Malachi*, 104; Redditt, *Haggai, Zechariah, Malachi*, 25.

phrase עוד אחת מעת היא, I will demonstrate that this is indeed their perspective. In this phrase עוד אחת מעת היא, the expression עוד מעת can be identified as commonly occurring in the Bible. Here are some examples: "for in a very little while my indignation will come to an end" (Isa 10:25) and "a little while and the time of her harvest will come" (Jer 51:33; Isa 29:17; Ps 37:10; Exod 17:4). In each case, עוד מעת denotes "soon" or "in a little while."

Also, the phrase עוד מעת demonstrates some interesting similarities with the repetitive sense of the adverb עוד. Here is one example in which the adverb עוד is used in this repetitive sense: "again I will build you, and you shall be built, again you shall adorn yourself with tambourines ... again you shall plant vineyards on the hills of Samaria" (Jer 31:4–5, 23; see also 23:15). Here, one sees the phrase describing an eschatological context, and each use indicates that YHWH will act in favour of his people. The adverbial insertions of אחת and היא into the phrase עוד מעת can be understood to emphasise the impending future events.[37] And then, this phrase becomes translated through the phrase "once again, it will be soon." With the support of prophetic form אמר יהוה צבאות , the audience is assured that YHWH will carry out great deeds for his people in the eschaton, even though the time of at which these deeds will take place remains unknown. It seems likely that the people expected their eschatological hopes to be realised upon the completion of the temple.

Within this eschatological perspective, an unspecified date would not have suggested expectation about the very remote future, but rather a belief that very soon YHWH would intercede to rectify the dire condition of his people. This should therefore deter any sustained eschatological interpretations of the verse. The addition of אחת and היא to the phrase ... עוד מעת is nothing but repetition of words with the same meaning. Rather, the recurring expression עוד אחת מעת היא should be interpreted as suggesting a sense of immediacy. It seems evident that the people and their two leaders are confident that their hopes will come to pass soon after their attempt to restore the Davidic dynasty (Hag 2:4).

37 On grammatical discussion in the phrase עוד אחת מעת היא, see Kessler, *The Book of Haggai*, 173–5; Meyers and Meyers, *Haggai, Zechariah 1–8*, 52–3; Wolff, *Haggai*, 51, 70.

This perspective emphasises the importance of the word כי. From a textual understanding of Hag 2:1–9, the use of this conjunction כי is parallel to the use of כי in Hag 2:4, wherein the people, together with Zerubbabel and Joshua, confidently expect military victory, based on the example of David (2 Sam 7:9).[38] Reassured by the expression "I am with you," all individuals develop momentum and perseverance.

Another critically vital word is מרעיש, a Hiphil participle form of the root רעשׁ (also Hag 2:21).[39] The verb רעשׁ is generally used in two different ways. One of which describes historical battles or destructions undertaken for the sake of YHWH's judgement; for example "the snorting of their horses was heard from Dan, at the sound of the neighing of their stallions the whole land quakes. They came and devoured the land and all that filled it, the city and those who dwelled in it" (Jer 8:16; 10:10; Ps 77:18–19).[40]

The other use is even more prevalent, wherein the verb רעשׁ describes the theophanic presence of YHWH, when YHWH roars and the heavens and the earth shake. For example, "the fish of the sea, and the birds of the air, and the beasts of the field, and all creeping things that creep on the ground, and all the men that are upon the face of the earth, shall quake at my presence, and the mountains shall be thrown down, and the cliffs shall fall, and every wall shall tumble to the ground (Ezek 38:20) and those who see you will stare at you, and ponder over you. Is this the man who made the earth tremble, who shook kingdoms?" (Jer 51:29). This use of the verb emphasises the doomed fate of YHWH's enemies while conveying comfort to his people.

In Hag 2:6, the subjects of this verb רעשׁ are cryptically the heavens, the earth, the sea, and the dry land which initially appears to be a description of nature's cosmic response to YHWH's eschatological theophanic presence. This eschatological interpretation is quite unlikely, though, considering

38 About connecting יכ to ארית־לא of Hag 1:5, see Kessler, *The Book of Haggai*, 173. However, in my reading of Hag 2:1–23, I connect Hag 1:6 to Hag 1:4.

39 *HALOT*, Vol. 2, 1171–2.

40 Kessler, *The Book of Haggai*, 176–8; Meyers and Meyers, *Haggai, Zechariah 1–8*, 52–3; Verhoef, *The Book of Haggai and Malachi*, 104; Redditt, *Haggai, Zechariah, Malachi*, 25.

David's victories against his historical enemies in the succession of wars that took place during the monarchical period (2 Sam 8–10). So, when relating this verse to the phenomenon of wars, one might consider that charging cavalry, chariots, and wagons also cause the nature to shake. Hence, it could be seen as a sort of euphemism, since the actual enemies cannot be directly mentioned for Judah is under Achaemenid rule and restoring the Davidic dynasty would require a political coup.

Hag 2:7

והרעשתי את-כל-הגוים ובאו חמדת[41] כל-הגוים;
ומלאתי את-הבית הזה כבוד אמר יהוה צבאות

["Also, I will shake the nations, so that the treasures of all nations shall come in, and I will fill this house with splendour," said YHWH of hosts.]

The people along with their leaders, Zerubbabel and Joshua, assumed that YHWH would first restore the Davidic throne and then defeat all enemies of the Davidic house. This is soon followed by the nations' coming to Jerusalem.[42] The objects of רעשׁ are foreign political entities within the atmosphere of war. However, eschatological interpretations of Haggai's vision have understood this verse to describe not merely Judean enemies, but a transcendent, universalistic dimension over which YHWH rules supreme.[43] This paper, though, interprets the verb רעשׁ exclusively as a literal description of the response of the nations to YHWH's acts of judgement.[44] This interpretation is corroborated in the following use of רעשׁ in Isa 14:16: "those who see you will stare at you, and ponder over you. Is this the man who made the earth tremble, who shook kingdoms?" (see also

41 BHS suggests the plural reading of חמדה because the LXX shows the plural form τὰ ἐκλεκτὰ. This would agree with the following plural verb ובאו. However, a single word which may carry a collective sense would usually lead the plural verb. Therefore this emendation is unnecessary.

42 Meyers and Meyers, *Haggai, Zechariah 1–8*, 53.

43 Meyers and Meyers, *Haggai, Zechariah 1–8*, 53.

44 Kessler, *The Book of Haggai*, 177–8; Verhoef, *The Book of Haggai and Malachi*, 101–2.

Ezek 26:10–16; 31:15–16). As Isa 14:16 demonstrates, the nuance of רעש represents the awesomeness of him who causes the shaking of kingdoms and the earth.[45]

The use of euphemism in Hag 2:7 does obscure the identity of the Judean enemies, but this should not throw their existence into question. For political reasons, the actual enemies could not be specified. It seems appreciate to understand the Judean revolt against Darius and his empire in light of concurrent, repeated Egyptian revolts (see Chapter 2 above).[46] During this time of unrest in Darius's reign, Judah is clearly looking forward to the beneficial consequence of political independence.

In the eschatological view, Judah expected to become at least as an independent sub-province once YHWH had destroyed all the nations postured against Judah. They believed that this independence would in turn be accompanied by economic prosperity since the treasures (חמדה) of the nations would eventually be brought (בא) to this house (הבית הזה), that is the house of Judah.[47] The people of Judah hoped for a recurrence of the fortunes from the monarchical period, a connection which is indicated by the word play of "the house" (הבית). The use of הבית הזה here certainly refers to the Davidic house in the context of the military victory of the previous verse. Likewise, the people of Judah truly believed that YHWH would definitely restore their economic activities through the establishment of her self-governance, as had happened in the Judean kingdom period.

There is also feasible interpretation on Judean wealth in relation to Darius's building project. Darius gave orders for the continuation of the building of the temple in Jerusalem to the governor Zerubbabel, with the promise of assistance from the district's revenues (Ezra 6:6–12). Because Zerubbabel is a member of the Davidic line and appointed as a chief political

45 Walther Zimmerli, *Ezekiel 2: A Commentary on the Book of the Prophet Ezekiel Chapters 25–48* (Hermeneia; Philadelphia: Fortress, 1983), 29, 37.

46 On the imperial campaign led by Darius in 519 in response to rebellion in Egypt, see Berquist, *Judaism in Persia's Shadow*, 65–8.

47 See Clines, "Haggai's Temple Constructed, Deconstructed and Reconstructed," 63–4; Kessler, *The Book of Haggai*, 179–81; Meyers and Meyers, *Haggai, Zechariah 1–8*, 53–4; Verhoef, *The Book of Haggai and Malachi*, 102.

authority within the former kingdom of Judah, this new influx of fiscal support from the imperial government is anticipated as the beginning of the restoration of Judah in the book of Haggai (Hag 2:6–9).[48] However, Haggai, throughout his messages, makes certain the affluent harvest once the Jerusalem temple is rebuilt, not the future restoration of Judah.

The term חמדה essentially indicates a "desire" or "precious" object. It was used to describe valuable items whose primary importance was commercial. One parallel use of the term חמדה can be seen in Ezek 26:12: "they will steal your riches (חמדה), plunder what you have won by trade, tear down your walls, destroy your luxurious houses, and throw your stones, your timber ...." From Solomon's time onwards, in addition to the three major agricultural industries of wheat, wine, and olive oil, Judah acquired precious commodities such as oaks, cypresses, and cedars as well as all kinds of precious stones from surrounding nations. This flourishing trade even extended through Neo-Assyria and Neo-Babylonia.

Judah's desire for the return to this earlier prosperity is evident in the use of Piel form of the verb מלא. The noun כבוד is followed by the verb מלא 6 times in the Hebrew Bible, including this phrase; "so that the priests could not stand to minister because of the cloud, for the glory of the YHWH filled the house of YHWH" (1 Kgs 8:11; see also 2 Chr 5:14; 7:2; Ezek 43:5; 44:4). Most of these occurrences describe the highly symbolic glory that indicates the presence of YHWH upon the completion of the temple.[49] However, each case that uses the Piel first person form of the root מלא with YHWH, as the subject seems to be a reference to material items rather than a reference to a theophanic phenomenon. Take for example, "I will come in after you and confirm your words" (1 Kgs 1:14), "I will fill the valleys with your refuse" (Ezek 32:5), and "I will fill its mountains with its slain" (Ezek 35:8). In these verses, the word כבוד would be understood to describe the abundance of the desirable and precious things that fortune will bring to the house of David, through their renewed commercial activities.

This exegesis of Hag 2:6–7 has proffered that at the moment of the temple building, the figure Zerubbabel had all the political, economical,

48 See Hoglund, *Achaemenid Imperial Administration*, 25–6.

49 Kessler, *The Book of Haggai*, 181; Meadowcroft, *Haggai*, 169–70.

and cultural strength necessary to establish Judean self-governance. As a result, the people surrounding Zerubbabel rose up against Darius and tried to restore the Davidic dynasty. The people of Judah anticipated that upon obtaining political independence Judah's glory would be restored to the levels it had reached in the Davidic kingdom.

Hag 2:8

לי הכסף ולי הזהב-נאם, יהוה צבאות

["The silver is mine, and the gold is mine," said YHWH of hosts.]

In contrast to the actions of the people, YHWH strongly emphasises that the Jerusalem temple's economic role of increasing the affluence of Judah during the Achaemenids. This verse demonstrates that YHWH is very supportive of the Jerusalem temple rebuilding that Darius has ordered. It also indicates how the restored Jerusalem temple should function in the political and economic context of Achaemenid Judah. It further indicates that between YHWH and all the people, as well as between Darius and the province of Judah, there is a vast difference in opinion concerning the function of the temple building.

Eschatological interpretations of this verse view it as predicting that, like the aforementioned precious metals of silver and gold, the treasures of the nations will come to the rebuilt temple as booty from war or gifts offered to a suzerain (Hag 2:7).[50] So for example, "the wealth of Damascus and the spoil of Samaria would be carried away before the king of Assyria" (Isa 8:4; 10:13–14; 30:6; Jer 15:13; 17:3; Mic 11:3). This interpretation is quite contrary to the association between the plunder and the destruction of the Jerusalem temple. An association demonstrated for example, in this phrase: "it shall strip his treasury of every precious thing" (Hos 13:15; Dan 11:8; 2 Chr 36:10). This eschatological interpretation, though, evinces the belief that YHWH has a right over all that the nations.

50 Meyers and Meyers, *Haggai, Zechariah 1–8*, 54; Kessler, *The Book of Haggai*, 181–2; Verhoef, *The Book of Haggai and Malachi*, 105.

However, in the Achaemenid political system, the Jerusalem temple no longer functioned as a shrine which underpinned the royal ideology of the monarchical period. So, this verse should not be understood as a supplementary explanation for the eschatological interpretation of Hag 2:6–7, as a description of the function of the rebuilt temple. Rather, this verse, together with Hag 2:9, demonstrates the practical function for the rebuilt temple. With this in mind, it is important to examine what the silver and the gold symbolise.

The foremost consideration in interpreting this symbolism is an account of the minting of silver and gold as coinages according to an Achaemenid economic standard.[51] Darius introduced a universal currency known as the daric which resulted in a significant increase of international business (see Chapter 2 above).[52] For, expanded interregional networks led to the advancement of commercial trade and a common market economy, which subsequently revolutionised the standard monetary denomination for these interregional trades (see Chapter 1 above). In addition to which, imperial taxation was normally paid in coins, on top of that which was paid as grain. The coins would then be melted down again and stored as bullion in large jars in the treasury, which would be broken again and made into coins whenever the kings were in need of money.[53]

On this point, the use of the phrase "the silver and the gold" with the particle article, rather than "silver and gold" might be evidence of this standard currency. YHWH can be seen to have promised that Judah will accrue great trade benefits through their international commerciality. This

51 For the relative availability and value of silver and gold, see Kessler, *The Book of Haggai*, 182; Meyers and Meyers, *Haggai, Zechariah 1–8*, 54, 348.

52 Croesus of Lydia first introduced the concept of gold and silver coins as state currency. Later on, Cyrus introduced the Lydian innovation among the Achaemenids. See, Sancisi-Weerdenburg, "Darius I," in Sasson, ed., *CANE*, Vol. 2, 1035–9, 1042–3; Farrokh, *Shadows in the Desert*, 65; Herodotus, *Hist.* VIII. 98.

53 Coinage was first introduced in ancient Israel during the sixth and fifth centuries BCE through Phoenician merchants trading with Greece. Later on, in the fifth and mainly in the fourth centuries, Judean coins came into circulation. However, Greek coins continue to be in use. Uriel Rappaport, "Numistics," in Davies and Finkelstein, eds, *CHJ*, Vol. 1, *Introduction: The Persian Period*, 25–6; Gilter, "The Levant," 101–13.

can be seen as the cause of Judah's increased bounty of agricultural produce. Darius ordered assistance to the Jerusalem temple rebuilding from imperial revenues (Ezra 6:6–12), demonstrating that the rebuilt temple is no longer exclusively a place of ritual. Instead, the Achaemenids are supportive of the temple rebuilding because of its potential for generating wealth.

Hag 2:9

גדול יהיה כבוד הבית הזה האחרון מן-הראשון אמר יהוה צבאות;
ובמקום הזה אתן שלום נאם יהוה צבאות[54]

["The splendour of this house will be greater in the latter than in the former" said YHWH of hosts and "in this place I will give peace," said YHWH of hosts.]

The prophet Haggai confirms once again that the splendour of the Jerusalem temple in the Achaemenids will be much greater than that of this temple in the kingdom period. Nevertheless, eschatological interpreters, focusing on the word שׁלם, persistently stress that Judah will be elevated and that the house of YHWH will be filled with riches from nations stripped of their treasures.[55] In their view, prophetic messages against the nations are also messages for the kingship of YHWH, indicating that YHWH is returning to Jerusalem to rule over his people and the nations.[56] For this to come to pass, the temple must be restored from which the divine king will rule. Therefore, eschatological interpreters understand this verse to mean that as the house of YHWH (הבית הזה) was filled with the splendour of YHWH's universal sovereignty so the word מקום also describes the house of YHWH.

54 BHS notes that the LXX has a long supplemental description after נאם יהוה צבאות. It remains καὶ εἰρήνην ψυχῆς εἰς περιποίησιν παντὶ τῷ κτίζοντι τοῦ ἀναστῆσαι τὸν ναὸν τοῦτον ("and peace of soul as a possession for all who build this temple reconstruction"). However, the people of Judah still disregard building the Jerusalem temple reconstruction. Therefore, the addition is superfluous.

55 Kessler, *The Book of Haggai*, 182–3; Verhoef, *The Book of Haggai and Malachi*, 105–6; Petersen, *Haggai, Zechariah 1–8*, 69–70; Redditt, *Haggai, Zechariah, Malachi*, 25.

56 Kessler, *The Book of Haggai*, 182–3; Verhoef, *The Book of Haggai and Malachi*, 106; Petersen, *Haggai, Zechariah 1–8*, 70.

In the Hebrew Bible, however, the word מקום is generally followed by a local nomination, which is understood by a determinative term like *KUR* in the Akkadian language.[57] Although this kind of determinative word would not be seen in Hebrew, phrases meaning "the place Topheth" (Jer 19:13) and "the place Shechem" (Gen 12:6) seem to perform the same function. When viewed alongside the parallel passage in Jeremiah, "you shall not see the sword nor shall you have famine because I will give you assured peace in this place" (Jer 14:13), the place in Hag 2:9 does not necessarily represent the Jerusalem temple as the promised place of peace described by the eschatological interpretation.

Rather, "the place" (מקום) indicates the whole land. The Hebrew Bible included three appearances of the noun שלם with the verb נתן, in the other two of which are: "I shall also grant peace in the land" (Lev 26:6) and "I will give you lasting peace in this place" (Jer 14:13). In each case, the word שלם refers to the real peace within the land. If the people respond with obedience to YHWH's word to rebuild the Jerusalem temple, he promises peace in the land. This interpretation also accords with the commandment of Darius to rebuild the temple through which YHWH assures the political security of Judah as well. Complete peace will therefore fill all the land of Judah.

In the economic administration of the Achaemenids, the temple project at Jerusalem came to function as the imperial economic and administrative centre, managing the agricultural economy and controlling the annual budget of Judah.[58] The temple's responsibilities in fiscal administration were to oversee both land economy and tax collection in the Judean region.[59]

57 Williamson, *Ezra, Nehemiah*, 112; Myers, *Ezra, Nehemiah*, 64.

58 See Chapter 2 above. See also Bongenaar, *The Neo-Babylonian Ebabbar Temple*; Vargyas, "Agrarkrisen und Umfang," 189–96; Pastor, *Land and Economy*, 82–6, 115–27.

59 On the theme of YHWH's landownership, see Peter Diepold, *Israel's Land* (BWANT 95; Berlin: Kohlhammer, 1972), 76–104; Moshe Weinfeld, *The Promise of the Land: The Inheritance of the Land of Canaan by the Israelites* (TLJS 3; Berkeley: University of California Press, 1993); Bedford, "Economic Role," 4–7; Weinberg, *Citizen-Temple Community*, 103–4.

By rebuilding the temple to fulfil these responsibilities that is, enhancing the local economic circumstances and fiscally supporting the Achaemenids, Judah is ensured peace and survival under the Achaemenid rule. In this sense, Haggai's insistence that the people should rebuild the temple despite the unfavourable conditions is seen not so much as an attempt to vindicate YHWH as a realistic appreciation of the potential economic importance of the temple.[60]

From the advent of centralised government in the ancient Near East, it is evident that the economic affairs of temples have been developed for the financial gain of the central government (see Chapter 1 above). Records of royal inscriptions and temple building inscriptions in the Neo-Assyrian and Neo-Babylonian periods indicate the pervasive importance of whether the temple is blessed and cursed.[61] For example, when the temple has been neglected and lies in ruins, the kings engaged in the rebuilding the temple have been guaranteed military power and have had their territories extended.[62] As a result, fields are enlarged, the harvest prospers and abundance ensues.[63] Eventually, even the dynastic stability and eternity are guaranteed.

According to the record of Solomon's temple construction (1 Kgs 6–8), which is literarily very similar to that of Haggai, Solomon's obedience to YHWH's command to build the Jerusalem temple also preserved the political stability and the economic prosperity of Judah (1 Kgs 6:11–13; 8:57–58). The blessings and curses described in YHWH's response to Solomon remained contingent on how the kings and their people would respond to YHWH's words. This is one reason that the Jerusalem temple rebuilding should have been the people's most pressing

60 Renger, "Interaction of Temple," 249–56; Dandamaev, "State and Temple," 589–96.

61 Saggs, *Greatness*, 233–53, 311–38; Hurowitz, *I Have Built You*, 84–5, 146, 208–9, 258, 291, 296–7, 299, 303, 307.

62 Jerrold S. Cooper, *The Curse of Agade* (Baltimore; London: The Johns Hopkins University Press, 1983), 5; Arvid S. Kapelrud, "Temple Building, A Task for Gods and Kings." *Or* 32 (1963): 56–62.

63 Henry William Frederick Saggs, *The Might That Was Assyria* (London: Sidgwick, 1984), 162–79, 271–3.

concern, and one reason that the temple rebuilding proved pivotal to the imperial economy.

In this exegesis of Hag 2:8–9, I have demonstrated that YHWH was very concerned for reconstruction of the Jerusalem temple. YHWH promised that the rebuilt temple would function economically and politically for the Achaemenids (also Hag 2:3, 5) and that the rebuilt Jerusalem temple would generate the Judean wealth. These two promises were connected, for if the temple successfully supported imperial fiscal gains, then Judah would be assured reliable patronage. The splendour of the Jerusalem temple would be unparalleled. From YHWH's blessing of the temple reconstruction, it also follows that the enduring poor condition of the temple resulted in subsequent punishments (Hag 2:10–23).

To sum up, this exegetical description of Hag 2:1–9 has shown that Haggai, as the spokesman of YHWH's word, called up the people together with Zerubbabel and Joshua to the task of rebuilding the temple (Hag 2:1–2). Yet the people ignored YHWH's command to rebuild the temple. Rather, they eagerly concerned themselves with rebuilding the Davidic dynasty through Zerubbabel (Hag 2:4). They expected the political independence of Judah and its restored economic splendour to result from rebuilding the Davidic dynasty (Hag 2:6–7). However, their efforts were in violation of YHWH's command.

Subsequently, YHWH's messenger, Haggai, clarifies the importance of the temple rebuilding (Hag 2:3). He emphasises that it will create economic prosperity in Judah and then reminds them of the requirement for obedience to YHWH's commandments given in the Sinai-covenantal tradition (Hag 2:5). He emphasises the blessings associated with rebuilding the temple: it will be the central location of imperial fiscal administration and Judah will finally become a reliable partner (Hag 2:8–9). It follows that, between YHWH and all the people, there is a vast difference in opinion concerning the temple building project, which is emphasised through the play on the word "house" with a different meaning (Hag 2:3, 7, 9).

Upgraded Priests' Status (Hag 2:10–14)

Hag 2:10

בעשרים וארבעה לתשיעי בשנת שתים לדריוש היה דבר-יהוה אל-חגי הנביא לאמר

[On the twenty-fourth day of the ninth month, in the second year of Darius, the word of YHWH came to Haggai the prophet, saying,]

The word of YHWH came to Haggai on the ninth month. It came two months after the festivals of the harvest and Tabernacles, where Zerubbabel and Joshua together with the people keenly expected to celebrate their conniving restoration of the Davidic dynasty. However, this did not happen. The temple reconstruction work that Haggai incessantly pronounced remained of no concern to the people of Judah. So, as a result, their reality unfolded in stark contrast to their desires and expectations. YHWH confronted the people with their derelictions of duty by re-commissioning their charge to rebuild the temple.

The people's response to Haggai's invocation of the temple rebuilding causes YHWH's judgement upon them. His judgement is introduced with the formula היה דבר-יהוה אל-חגי הנביא (the word of YHWH comes to the prophet Haggai). This iteration of the formula demonstrates a small variation from prior uses in Hag 1:1, 3; 2:1 through its use of preposition אל in place of the term ביד. This variation seems to indicate the relatively restricted audience for this word from YHWH.[64] However, there is no difference in denoting an intermediary or a recipient in the shift between ביד and אל.[65] This variation is very common in the Hebrew Bible, and can be seen in these examples; "YHWH spoke to Moses ..." (Exod 6:10); "... spoke to Pharaoh, the king of Egypt" (Exod 6:11, 28–29; see also Lev 4:1–2; Num 5:5–6).

64 Petersen, *Haggai, Zechariah 1–8*, 72.

65 Kessler, *The Book of Haggai*, 203; Meyers and Meyers, *Haggai, Zechariah 1–8*, 55; Verhoef, *The Book of Haggai and Malachi*, 115; McEntire, "Haggai," 70–1.

Now, Haggai is commissioned to deliver YHWH's judgement regarding the people's conspiracy for the Davidic dynasty. For, although they created the pretence of obeying Darius's commandment to rebuild the temple, the people did not attend to the temple rebuilding as their primary concern. Haggai now declares that, as far as YHWH would permit it, Darius could punish Judah for the disobedience to his commands. This clearly indicates that the temple rebuilding project, which is undeniably related to the imperial financial policy, is not merely the work of the Achaemenids but also the work of YHWH.

Hag 2:11

כה אמר יהוה צבאות: שאל-נא את-הכהנים תורה לאמר

[Thus said YHWH of hosts, "ask the priests a law" saying,]

With the authority that כה אמר יהוה צבאות (YHWH of hosts says thus), Haggai is commanded to inquire of the priests. Demonstrating the manner of YHWH's judgement against the general apathy towards rebuilding the Jerusalem temple, YHWH first summons the priests. He wants to interrogate them as if they need to be censured for betraying their duty to teach, in accordance with the word תורה. The word תורה is derived from the root ירה, which in the Hiphil form means "to teach."[66] It is used, for instance, in this phrase: "you are to teach the people of Israel all the statutes which YHWH has spoken to them by Moses" (Lev 10:11).

In many usages of the word תורה in the nomination, it indicates the law itself. Here is one such example: "this is the law of the guilt offering. It is most holy" (Lev 7:1; Num 6:21). Especially, in post-exilic texts, the term תורה describes the Pentateuch, as distinct from the rest of the scriptures; for example, "they built the altar of the God of Israel, to offer burnt offerings upon it, as it is written in the law of Moses the man of God" (Ezra 3:2; 7:6; 8:1, 8; Mal 3:22).[67] The underlying meaning of "teaching" that the

66 *HALOT*, Vol. 1, 1710–12.

67 Meyers and Meyers call תורה "a rabbinic text" which emerges from the legal texts of the Pentateuch. Meyers and Meyers, *Haggai, Zechariah 1–8*, 55.

word תורה itself implies is common to both usages. With this in mind, in Hag 2:11 the term תורה should be understood as emphasising the teaching role of the priests.[68]

The closest parallel to this use of the term תורה can be seen in Mal 2:7, "the lips of a priest should keep knowledge and people should seek the law from his mouth." Malachi's text includes the word בקשׁ instead of the accompanying verb שׁאל alongside the word תורה. Also, the word דעת is parallel to the word תורה. These syntactical features clearly emphasise that the priests are destined to instruct the people and that the people should be instructed by their teaching.

It has been considered that Haggai utilises the priestly teaching position as a tool for his prophetic message.[69] He even consults with the priests on the matter of iniquities of the people. This consideration has resulted in claims that the ruling leadership of prophet and the priests alike in the post-exilic Judean society was greatly emphasised.

It is quite true that the priests were clearly qualified for any activities described by YHWH through the term תורה. It was the very matter of teaching, however, on which the priests were judged by YHWH, and questions as to whether they remained deserving to be chosen for teaching the people. For, the association with the verb שׁאל demonstrates Haggai's commitment to ask the priests about the word תורה.

The teaching responsibility of the priests can be understood as being administered by them (Deut 33:10; Ezek 7:26; 22:26; Mal 2:6–9). In relation to the temple fiscal administration for the Achaemenids, on top of their cultic practices, under the leadership of the high priest all priests administered a variety of agricultural activities, supervised the agricultural calendar, and assessed the potential harvest for the next year before fixing taxes. Thus, the priests were obliged to administer the land tenure, to collect and deliver taxes, and to arrange the corvee labourers for both the military and construction work. With this understanding, the priests can be understood to have presided over all sorts of affairs, even the rebuilding of

68 See, Kessler, *The Book of Haggai*, 203; Verhoef, *The Book of Haggai and Malachi*, 115–16; Redditt, *Haggai, Zechariah, Malachi*, 26.

69 Meyers and Meyers, *Haggai, Zechariah 1–8*, 55.

the Jerusalem temple. Therefore, Haggai does not distinguish between the ordinary priests and the high priest in voicing the judgements of YHWH.

From the point of view of the temple administration, similar cases can be seen in the Neo-Babylonian period. Imperial officers, the *šatammu* managed temple finances in a similar way as the priests. Like the priests, the *šatammu* were associated with the temples and usually took charge of temple economic affairs for political entities (see Chapter 2 above). This relationship between the imperial economy and the temple household continues and consolidates in the Achaemenid period. Judah does not prove an exception in this regard.

Hag 2:12

הן ישא-איש בשר-קדש בכנף בגדו ונגע בכנפו אל-הלחם ואל-הנזיד ואל-היין
ואל-שמן ואל-כל-מאכל היקדש; ויענו הכהנים ויאמרו לא

["If one carries holy flesh in the fold of his garment, and touches with that fold bread, pottage, wine, oil or any kind of food, does it become holy?" The priests answered, "No."]

YHWH once again acknowledges the priests' authority on matters concerning instruction associated with the word תורה. Then, YHWH confronts them with the problems resulting from the current circumstances. The question concerns an instance when sacred meat, that is, the flesh of an animal offered on the altar, is transported outside the sacred enclosure, carried within the fold of a garment.

It has been understood that the holy flesh would have been dedicated to the altar as a sacrificial offering.[70] As a result, it would consecrate anything that it touches—in this case the fold of the garment in which it is carried (Lev 6:20; 1 Sam 21:4; Jer 11:15; Ezek 40:43). The sacrificed meat is carried (נשׂה) but there is no function of atonement indicated by the text. Therefore, it does not indisputably relate to the effect upon the communication of holiness through indirect contact.

70 Verhoef, *The Book of Haggai and Malachi*, 117–8.

This passage has been interpreted as describing an offering that has been brought as a special sacrifice for well-being (שְׁלָמִים).[71] This interpretation is based on the consumption of consecrated foodstuffs outside the temple.[72] Such consumption would have been permissible in the case of peace offerings, which involved involuntary and indirect contact between the consecrated meat and other common foods. So this verse can be seen to describe the securing of YHWH's blessing on the produce of the land, the flocks and herds, and the people of Judah. By way of eschatological hopes, the verse can be seen to celebrate YHWH's universal sovereignty.

Also, the query would have been referred to an activity that should not have been undertaken because of the current state of impurity of the existing altar.[73]

What can be ascertained about the ritual is found in examining the word בְּשַׂר־קֹדֶשׁ (holy flesh). The terminology קֹדֶשׁ is used in its noun form, which designates holy sacrifices being dedicated to YHWH. Every offering that has touched the altar of YHWH is presumably designated as holy, and any kind of cult is thus typified by the nominative (Lev 23). In this context, no matter which explanations are exposited in relation to both the word אִישׁ and the word בִּכְנַף בִּגְדוֹ, it is feasible that they would refer to the carrying of an offering by the people or in the ritual ceremony by the priests.[74] The term בְּשַׂר־קֹדֶשׁ accordingly denotes the cultic activities that the people have participated in.

It is worth noting that the sacrifice in the ninth month is linked to the forthcoming ploughing and sowing season. It is the time to urgently request the blessing of an adequate supply of rain. With this hope, the people would reflect back on the most recent harvest: though they had sown much but they had harvested little due to the drought (Hag 1:6, 10); YHWH had even blown away their modest harvest (Hag 1:9). The Judean agricultural economic system had broken down (Hag 1:11). All mentioned

71 See Meyers and Meyers, *Haggai, Zechariah 1–8*, 55–6.

72 Kessler, *The Book of Haggai*, 203–4.

73 Petersen, *Haggai, Zechariah 1–8*, 76–8.

74 Meyers and Meyers, *Haggai, Zechariah 1–8*, 55–6.

agricultural products, such as bread, pottage,[75] wine, oil, or any kind of food, would have been linked to these agricultural activities (Hag 1:5–6, 9–11). Certainly, YHWH's blessings had not been manifested in Judah's agriculture that year.

In this context of disappointment with the previous harvest, the priests answered YHWH's question without hesitation, and their answer is apodictically negative. This negative answer of the priests has been argued that Haggai's request for a priestly ruling makes the prophet emerge into clearer focus as a participant in the narrative and explicitly take the priestly ruling, for the priests do not discern between holy and unholy.[76] Thus, as the word תורה itself will perish from the priests (Ezek 7:26; 22:26; Mal 2:8–9) the prophet is emerging into clearer focus as a participant in the narrative.

Through the inquiry, however, what YHWH seeks to confirm from the priests is whether they remain qualified to teach the words of YHWH. YHWH never meant that תורה itself will perish from the priests. Rather, through the correct answer, they demonstrate that, although they have not carried out their duty towards the people, the priests do indeed remain qualified to teach.

This exegesis of Hag 2:10–12 has shown that YHWH reminded the priests of their role of teaching the people to carry out the commands of YHWH. In essence, YHWH has tested whether the priests are still qualified to teach the recalcitrant people to obey YHWH's commands. They realise that sacrifices that might be connected with an affluent harvest currently provoke no blessing from YHWH. This realisation is supported by the ongoing agricultural disaster in Judah. With this new understanding, the priests can be understood as having renewed their eligibility to exhort the people to be obedient to YHWH's commandment.

75 נזיד ("consecrated") is never used explicitly within a ritual context. It refers to cooked food including vegetables such as lentils and legumes (Gen 25:29, 34; Lev 25:5, 11). *HALOT*, Vol. 1, 683.

76 See Kessler, *The Book of Haggai*, 204–5.

Hag 2:13

ויאמר חגי אם-יגע טמא-נפש בכל-אלה היטמא; ויענו הכהנים ויאמרו יטמא

[Then asked Haggai, "if one who is unclean makes a sacrifice with any of these, does it become unclean?" The priests answered "it does become unclean."]

The request for a priestly ruling alerts the priests somewhat to the ongoing reality that urgently needs to be examined. The issued query is related to the sacrificial conduct of one who has become impure, so it is worth commenting on the phrase טמא־נפש. The word טמא is an adjective in the construct form and confines the nominative נפש to its meaning "unclean of." The following noun נפש initially means to "be breath" in the Bible, further denoting the living being itself (Lev 4:2; Josh 11:14).[77] The phrase טמא־נפש accordingly could represent a state of being defiled.

However, it has been claimed that the word נפש is identified with a corpse, as in this verse: "he shall not go in to any dead body (נפשת מת), nor defile himself, even for his father or for his mother" (Lev 21:11). Yet it has also been understood as describing a case of defilement which results from literally touching a corpse; for example, "I will make my abode among you, and my soul shall not abhor you" (Lev 26:1).[78] A person who touches a corpse is himself unclean (Lev 21:11; 22:4; Num 5:2; 6:6–7; 9:6) and anything that an unclean person touches becomes unclean (Num 19:22). So, the defiled person is ceremonially excluded from celebrating the festival and is sent away from the camp (Num 5:2; 9:6).[79]

77 *DCH*, Vol. 5, 724–34; *HALOT*, Vol. 1, 711–13.

78 Lena-Sofia, Tiemeyer, "The Question of Indirect Touch: Lam 4,14; Ezek 44,19 and Hag 2,12–13," *Bib* 87 (2006): 64–74; Kessler, *The Book of Haggai*, 204; Meyers and Meyers, *Haggai, Zechariah 1–8*, 56–7; Verhoef, *The Book of Haggai and Malachi*, 118; Redditt, *Haggai, Zechariah, Malachi*, 27.

79 Anyone who touches a corpse becomes unclean for a minimum of seven days. Such uncleanness could be overcome by cleansing rituals, using water (for impurity) on the third and seventh days of a person's impurity. Without such purification, a person defiles the tabernacle of YHWH and that person shall be cut off from Israel (Num 19:13). See Petersen, *Haggai, Zechariah 1–8*, 79.

This vein of interpretation further suggests that the absolute form of the noun נפש can be interpreted as a corpse. Such an interpretation is seen, for example, in these passages: "they put out of the camp every leper, and every one having a discharge, and every one that is unclean through contact with the dead (לנפש)" (Num 5:2); and "here were certain men who were unclean through touching the dead body of a man (לנפש)…" (Num 9:6–10). It is very worthwhile that, when describing a dead person, the word נפש employs the preposition ל. The noun נפש in Hag 2:12, though, is clearly defined by the construct state of טמא, and it denotes "one who is impure."

The contrasting application of the noun נפש, is particularly interesting for gauging the sense of the impurity of the defiled person. Haggai is doing very dramatic work here. One interesting verse comes to mind for its similar usage of the noun נפש. Isaiah identifies himself as a man of unclean lips (טמא־שפתים) who is not prepared to listen to the word of YHWH to make intercession of behalf of Israel (Isa 6:5). Likewise, the people now refuse to comply with the prophet's message to rebuild the temple. In this sense, it is quite right that this נפש טמא describes the people of Judah as disobedient to YHWH's word, for they have only focused on the restoration of the Davidic dynasty. They have violated YHWH's command to focus on rebuilding the Jerusalem temple, and that is sin.

A person who has become ceremonially unclean offers a sacrifice (נגע) with the same foodstuffs (בכל־אלה) referred to in Hag 2:12, such as grains, vegetables, wine, and oil. This verb נגע primarily means "to touch" or "to reach," implying some kind of physical contact, depending on the context.[80] In the context of the word טמא, the verb נגע might be intended to describe a sacrifice. Associated with the previous verse 12, Hag 2:13, the question is: if the recalcitrant people, in response to YHWH's command, would make a sacrifice with food offerings then would they be blessed?

Clearly, being ritually defiled disqualifies one from taking part in the organised worship, in all its functions and activities. That neither the people nor their offerings are clean, compels Haggai to ask his question.[81]

80 *DCH*, Vol. 5, 608–11; *HALOT*, Vol. 1, 668–9.

81 The binary semantic oppositions are קדש and חל or טהור and טמא. Thus the juxtaposition of קדש and טמא is somewhat unusual. The fourth term, however, can be

The priests subsequently answer in the affirmative: uncleanness in any sacrifice, due to the disobedience of the people, is indeed contagious. This answer quite evidently exemplifies the very situation of the people of Judah.

In this desperate reality, the priests are also faced with deciding what they should do regarding the issue of ritual fitness-defilement.[82] This is the very time for the priests to uproot the cause of this vicious cycle. As teaching authorities sanctioned by YHWH, they should do this by leading the people to recognise the priority of rebuilding the temple.

This does not indicate that the high priest Joshua should become the chief ruler of Judean society.[83] Though it is likely that the leadership of the community would be left in the hands of the priests (Hag 2:10–14). Indeed, in relation to the imperial temple administration, the priest Joshua should administer a temple economy utilising temples as a means of levying and gathering imperial taxes and tributes.[84] Therefore, the temple restoration and maintenance were primary responsibilities of Joshua as the high priest, as they were for Hilkiah the high priest in the time of restoring the temple (Hag 1:1).

From this reading of Hag 2:13, it can be concluded that the people of Judah were defiled by their rebellion against YHWH's word to rebuild the temple. Their disobedience likewise defiled any sacrifice that they would offer: they had become a ritually defiled people. The onus fell on the priests to redress these terrible circumstances. Haggai clearly entreats the priests to reflect upon the relationship between the current agricultural disaster and the disobedience to YHWH's command of temple rebuilding. This is the very time to confirm the role of the priestly rule over the people, especially in the temple rebuilding.

---

understood as constituting the continuous sequence (Deut 14:2–3, 21; Ezek 22:26). See Petersen, *Haggai, Zechariah 1–8*, 74.

82 Meyers and Meyers, *Haggai, Zechariah 1–8*, 56–7.

83 Grabbe, *An Introduction to First Century Judaism*, 34–6.

84 Carroll, "So What Do We Know about the Temple?" 41–3; Lipschits, "Achaemenid Imperial Policy," 32–4.

Hag 2:14

ויען חגי ויאמר כן העם-הזה וכן-הגוי הזה לפני נאם-יהוה וכן כל-מעשה ידיהם;
ואשר יקריבו שם טמא הוא[85]

[Then Haggai said "so is it with this people, and with this nation before me," said YHWH, "whatever they do and whatever they offer, there is unclean."]

Disobedience to the command of YHWH to rebuild the temple is the underlying reason for the resulting catastrophe. At the moment when the priests acutely recognised the need to heed YHWH, Haggai provided the application of the priests' instruction by asserting the importance of the temple project. In this context, it is very valuable to define the following phrases in this verse more closely. To whom does "this people" (העם־הזה) refer? Who is "this nation" (הגוי־הזה)? What does "all the work of their hands" describe (כל-מעשה ידיהם)? And what is it that "they offer there" (אשר יקריבו שם)?

The first phrase העם־הזה has already been used to designate the people, excluding Zerubbabel and Joshua, in Hag 1:2, where this people would rather build the Davidic dynasty than YHWH's temple. The preference evidently conflicts with YHWH's, and as a result YHWH calls this people ritually unclean before his presence.

With regard to the following term הגוי־הזה, there have been arguments wherein those who see an allusion to Samaria in the noun גוי or in the adverb שׁם.[86] However, it is quite unnecessary because Haggai at no point credits

85 BHS mentions that the LXX has an extensive addition after טמא הוא. It remains ἕνεκεν τῶν λημμάτων αὐτῶν τῶν ὀρθρινῶν ὀδυνηθήσονται ἀπὸ προσώπου πόνων αὐτῶν καὶ ἐμισεῖτε ἐν πύλαις ἐλέγχοντας ("and whoever shall approach them shall be defiled because of their early burdens; they shall be pained because of their toils; and you have hated him that reproved in the gates"). The addition would be taken from Amos 5:10 to pose a real threat to the presence of YHWH with all his people. Yet, this additional description is quite unnecessary because this verse, with impending calamity, rather prompt the people of Judah to rebuild the Jerusalem temple.

86 Verhoef, *The Book of Haggai and Malachi*, 118–20; Petersen, *Haggai, Zechariah 1–8*, 79–85; Redditt, *Haggai, Zechariah, Malachi*, 27–8.

Samaritan opposition with responsibility. When the term הגוי־הזה appears in the Hebrew Bible, at times it carries an overtone of reproach, which accords with this context, in which the people have disobeyed the voice of YHWH.[87] Here are two similar cases: "shall I not punish this nation for these things? says YHWH …" (Jer 5:29); and "this is the nation that does not obey the voice of YHWH their God, and does not accept discipline, truth has perished. This nation is cut off from their lips" (Jer 7:28).

There are also some fine cases where the unclean people are further addressed as a sinful nation. Here, for example, are two such instances: "sinful nation, a people laden with iniquity, offspring of evildoers, sons who deal corruptly …" (Isa 1:4); and "against a godless nation I send him, and against the people of my wrath I command him, to take spoil and seize plunder, and to tread them down like the mire of the streets" (Isa 10:6). There remains significant overlap between the use of "people" and "nation" together.

In Haggai's use of the term הגוי־הזה, it also seems to describe the whole community, including the two leaders that had been excluded from the term "this people," for the word "nation" generally refers to a political or an administrative unit. Unquestionably, the leaders have been as apathetic as the people in heeding the command of YHWH regarding the temple project. So, in spite of a slight expansion of semantic range, it is conceivable that "this nation" merely reiterates "this people," emphatically affirming the contagious state of impurity described above.

Obviously, this general iniquity affects all the work of their hands (כל-מעשה ידיהם). In the context of Haggai, where agricultural activities are taken for granted, the meaning of this expression should give reference to Hag 1:6, 9–11 or Hag 2:16–17. Among which, the most obvious contextual reference for this phrase is the meaning in Hag 1:11 which designates the comprehensive catastrophe befalling the agricultural produce. All the efforts that the people have made within the realm of agriculture have been in vain, since YHWH has not blessed the land.

87 Herbert G. May, "'This People' and 'This Nation' in Haggai." *VT* 18 (1968): 193.

This tragedy deservedly has implications for the cultic area. This connection is attested to by the verb קרב in the Hiphil form, which is frequently used to describe the presentation of sacrifices, especially at the altar. Here is one such example of this use: "he threw the blood round about against the altar (קרב) that was at the door of the tent of meeting" (Lev 1:5; 3:3–9; 9:7; Num 16:9–10).[88] The contagious nature of defilement of the people, their economic undertakings and all their sacrifices have become impure, and consequently, unacceptable to YHWH.

The impurity of the people prevents them from reaping benefits and poses a very real threat to whether the presence of YHWH will remain among them. One striking analogy can be found in Jer 14:10–11, "thus said YHWH concerning this people, they loved to wander and they did not restrain their feet. Therefore, YHWH did not accept them, now he will remember their iniquity and punish their sins." And YHWH said to me "do not pray for the welfare of this people" (also Jer 6:19–21). Similarly, in the context of the people's failure to restore the temple YHWH rejects them, their offerings and their economic activities. Obedience to YHWH's command to rebuild the temple is evidently crucial to his blessing.

This study of Hag 2:14 has demonstrated that the people failed to act in accordance with YHWH's word. Their disobedience ritually defiled them and especially their leaders. Their impurity subsequently defiled all other activities in which they engaged. Faced with impending calamity, prompt obedience to YHWH's command to rebuild the Jerusalem became crucial.

From the study of Hag 2:10–14, it has been clear that the people continued neglecting the command of YHWH to rebuild the temple. Instead, they preferred to attempt a rebuilding of the Davidic dynasty through Zerubbabel. Their disobedience made the people recalcitrant to YHWH and his word. As a result the people were ritually disqualified and the sacrifices of this ritually defiled people were rejected (Hag 2:10–12). YHWH withheld his blessings from their agriculture. In the ensuing catastrophe,

88 *HALOT*, Vol. 2, 1132–4; Kessler, *The Book of Haggai*, 205–6; Meyers and Meyers, *Haggai, Zechariah 1–8*, 57–8.

Haggai roused the authority of the priests to enlighten the people (Hag 2:13). The status of priest was infused with authority. Now, elevated, the priests were to promptly instruct the people to obey YHWH's command to rebuild the temple in order to overcome the current economic disaster (Hag 2:14).

Crop Failure (Hag 2:15–19)

Hag 2:15

ועתה[89] שימו-נא לבבכם מן-היום הזה ומעלה; מטרם שום-אבן אל-אבן בהיכל יהוה

["Now, consider the time from this day on when one stone is placed on another in the temple of YHWH."]

In this verse, YHWH exhorts the people to reflect upon what they have chosen in which YHWH refers to the people in the second person, as the object of his blame. It is unlikely that they are indirectly designated as the third personal plural by talking to the priests about "this people" in the previous unit (Hag 2:10–14), where the defilement of the people has already been claimed.

With the phrase שׂים לבב, this verse focuses on the people's heart towards the issue in question, as did Hag 1:5 and Hag 1:7. To demonstrate that, it is important to note the phrase מעלה מטרם. The word מעלה usually highlights the immediate context; for example "the spirit of the YHWH comes mightily upon David from that day forwards" (1 Sam 16:13). The term describes moving forward from a particular, defined moment.

Additionally, the term עתה provides a rhetorical marker that distinguishes a new speech with considerable force (Hag 2:15–19). It draws immediate attention to a textual transition, emphasising the different situation

89 BHS suggests posting עתה at the end of Hag 2:15–19, to connection it to the first half phrase of Hag 1:15. As I have discussed in the exegesis of Hag 1:5 above, עתה leads the unit of Hag 2:15–19, and lets the people consider the Jerusalem temple-rebuilding project. Therefore, I will keep the text as it is.

in situation such as in Hag 1:5. So, it can be translated as "now" focusing on time that is concurrent with the perspective of the discourse. Now (עתה), Haggai announces emphatically, "consider the time from this day on" (Hag 2:15a).

In connection with the following phrase, the people are exhorted to pay attention to the day "when one stone is set upon another stone in the temple of YHWH" (Hag 2:15b). The phrase "in the temple of YHWH" (בהיכל־יהוה) appears 6 times in the Hebrew Bible (Isa 3:3; 2 Kgs 24:13; 2 Chr 29:16; Zech 6:14, 15), each of which designates the spatial sense of the temple of YHWH. The recurring combination of verb שׂים with the word אבן means to "set up," "put," or "establish" in a physical sense of establishing or setting something up. So for example, "Samuel takes a stone and sets it up between Mizpah and Jeshanah, and calls its name Ebenezer" (1 Sam 7:12; also Josh 10:27).[90] Haggai, in contrast, strongly urges the people to note "this day" when one stone is supposed to be set upon another stone in the house of YHWH as a kind of watershed moment.

Therefore, it is unnecessary to extrapolate that the foundation for the temple has already been laid. Nonetheless, this phrase has generally been taken to indicate the time when the foundation stone of the second temple was laid. According to Ezra 3:8, 10–11, Sheshbazzar undertook preliminary work on the clearing of rubble and began reconstructing the foundations of the temple.[91] This interpretation depends on an alternative understanding of the phrase מעלה מטרם, though as describing a backwards movement from a defined moment.[92] However, focusing on

90 *HALOT*, Vol. 2, 1483–6.

91 On work on the Jerusalem temple reconstruction before Zerubbabel, see Grabbe, *A History of the Jews and Judaism in the Second Temple Period*. Vol. 1, *Yehud*, 276–7; Peter Runham Ackroyd, *Exile and Restoration* (Philadelphia: Westminster, 1968), 147–8; Petersen, "Zerubbabel and Jerusalem Temple Reconstruction," 366–72; Baruch Halpern, "The Ritual Background of Zechariah's Temple Song," *CBQ* 40 (1978): 171–2.

92 *HALOT*, Vol. 1, 379–80; Kessler, *The Book of Haggai*, 207; Meyers and Meyers, *Haggai, Zechariah 1–8*, 59; David J. Clark, "Problems in Haggai 2:15–19," *BT* 34 (1983); 432–9.

the concurrency, this verse lets the people picture the desirable contradiction to all that they have been experiencing up until this point once the Jerusalem temple is rebuilt.

To put it more directly, this phrase inspires the people to reflect on what they have done in relation to the temple rebuilding and whether they have had the requisite sense of urgency. Therefore, it is quite conceivable that Haggai employs a sort of rhetorical device to intentionally reinforce the link between the state of the people's mind and the state of the temple. This moment of reflection requires the renewed authority of the priests to guide the people.

When the need to rebuild the temple reaches a pinnacle, though, the people are with Zerubbabel, who is of the royal house of Judah and through whom they have persistently attempted to establish Judean independence (Hag 1:4, 9).[93] The people expect that all Judah's enemies will be defeated and that Judah will thrive with the plundered treasures, as is indicated in Hag 2:6–7 upon the restoration of the Davidic dynasty. However, the reality could not be in greater contrast: Judah remains under the Achaemenid rule and their agricultural industries are in ruins. This is the circumstance in which Haggai exhorts the people to contemplate their current experience and to compare this with the blessings that will accompany obedient work on the temple.

From the exegesis of Hag 2:15 YHWH summons the people who have been doing as their hearts desire back to obedience. Though they dreamt of the prosperity that the restoration of Davidic dynasty would bring, they were punished with severe agricultural distress. Haggai befittingly entreats the people to imagine the ensuing results of rebuilding the Jerusalem temple. The people are now challenged to turn towards the good way, towards obedience.

93 Meyers and Meyers, *Haggai, Zechariah 1–8*, xxxix, 1–8, 39–41, 195–6.

Hag 2:16

מהיותם[94] בא[95] אל-ערמת עשרים והיתה עשרה;
בא אל-היקב לחשף[96] חמשים פורה[97] והיתה עשרים

[Since they were, "when one has come to a pile of twenty measures, it only amounts to ten. And when one has come to the winepress to draw fifty measures from the vat it only amounts to twenty."]

The beginning word מהיותם is composed of an infinitive construct of the verb היה carrying a third person plural possessive suffix with the particle preposition מן. So, a literal translation would be "since they were." Haggai now comes back to the Judean reality and continues to push the people to reflect on their disobedience and the ensuing economic catastrophe.

Their attempt to restore the Davidic dynasty obviously has not led to YHWH's blessing on their agricultural industries, and their agricultural reserves are severely depleted. This reality demonstrates a striking difference from the harvest expected to result from obedience to the word of YHWH.[98] Therefore, the people should carefully consider how these days have been unfolding since they obstinately declined to build the house of David.

94 BHS suggests the emendation תם מה היי instead of מהיותם. This follows the LXX rendering τίνες ἦτε ("what state were you in?").This implies the people's discouraging state before they began work on the temple rebuilding. In the context that the people's attention is drawn to the previously mentioned days, this verse describes the people's misfortunes within the context of agricultural activities. So, the adjustment is unnecessary.

95 BHS proposes to read בֹּא instead of בָא. It would be grammatically right but the infinitive construct form is very frequent in Haggai.

96 BHS proposed the addition חשׂף. The word חשׂף means "to strip off" or "to skim off." With this meaning, the phrase can be literally translated into "one comes to a press installation to skim off fifty measures," which makes sense. Therefore, חשׂף is not an addition.

97 BHS regards פורה an addition for the word היקב. It means that the press is a wine press rather than an oil press. However, פורה is normally used for wine and oil. So, the suggestion is unnecessary.

98 Kessler, *The Book of Haggai*, 206; Meyers and Meyers, *Haggai, Zechariah 1–8*, 60.

Stemming from the imprudent choice of the people, their agricultural production has been ineffective and fruitless. The people come to granaries (ערמה) in order to store the harvest despite the paucity of their produce (Hag 1:6).

The word ערמה itself is a rare word and the verbal form from which it derives is used only once in quite a different context: "the waters are piled up" (Exod 15:8). Although Haggai does not mention anything about the type of produce, the granary would be used for storing cereals such as grains.[99] The verse describes people bringing their crops in twenty measures (עשׂרים) yet it only amounts to ten (עשׂרה) indicating that half of the amount in storage has frustratingly disappeared, as in Hag 1:9.

The people also bring their harvested grapes or olives to stone presses (יקב) to draw wine or to squeeze olive oil.[100] The term of יקב describes an installation hewn in a rock near or in the vineyard. Here are two other similar uses, for example: "he hews out a wine press in the vineyard" (Isa 5:2); and "presses (יקבים) shall overflow with wine and oil" (Joel 2:24). The people bring fifty measures (חשׂף) into the installation (יקב) yet it only amounts to twenty a vat (פורה).

The pressing installation פורה is normally used for wine and oil. This indicates that the worst decrease has appeared in both the wine industry and the oil industries. This paper has already shown that these industries were of particularly great significance to the Judean economy. All three crucial and competitive commodities throughout Judean economic history had come to complete ruin demonstrating the complete contrast between the people's desire and their reality.

One crucial point to this analysis is the difference between the proportions of the yield the people expected and the amount of produce they actually resulted. This difference of proportion also represents the actual decreased

99 Storage granaries are above ground. Normally they do not belong to individuals but to a large social organisation, such as the state. Borowski, *Agriculture in Iron Age*, 76–8.

100 There are at least three types of winepresses: (1) a press hewn in the rock within or next to the vineyard, (2) a press built of stones and mortar within the confines of a city and (3) a portable stone press. Borowski, *Agriculture in Iron Age*, 111.

amount of consumption by the people. The crop that they yielded fell by 50 per cent and 60 per cent, which was much short of that of their average year.

The reductions of 50 per cent and 60 per cent indicate the sheer scope of the problem, even though it does not represent exact amounts, because even a small decrease in supplies would have greatly endangered the livelihoods of many. Even in an average yield, the price difference of products could rise from previous financial years by 100 per cent.[101] In the shortfall of the harvest, however, the difference in price reached levels of up to 433 per cent. So, it certainly follows that the people were bitterly troubled by the severe economy.

Hag 2:17

הכיתי[102] אתכם בשדפון ובירקון ובברד את כל-מעשה ידיכם;
ואין-אתכם[103] אלי נאם-יהוה

["I have struck you and every work of your hands with blight, mildew and hail. Because you are not with me," YHWH declared.]

This verse puts forward the explanation for why the people yielded the terribly meagre harvest. As in Hag 1:9, where YHWH had explained the reasons why he blows even the modest harvest away, Haggai proclaims YHWH's strong judgement from the first person perspective. Certainly, YHWH has taken responsibility for the breakdown of the economy.

This description of this disastrous situation begins with the verb נכה, which is in the Hiphil form (Num 18:28; Judg 15:16; 2 Kgs 6:27; Jer 33:5; Ezek 22:13). It expresses "to strike" or "to smite" with a causative nuance which attributes a fatal disaster to the punishment of YHWH. So for example, in the case of this phrase: "I killed a thousand men" (Num 18:27).

101 Vargyas, "Agrarkrisen und Umfang," 190–2.

102 BHS suggests that הכיתי is an addition from Amos 4:9. However, the emphasis here lies on what YHWH has done in the current crop failure. So, the phrase does not seem to be taken from Amos 4:9.

103 BHS notes that the LXX has καὶ οὐκ ἐπεστρέψατε, followed by the Syriac version. BHS, therefore, suggests the correction ולא שבתם ("but you did not turn yourselves"). The Vulgate and Targum are support the LXX. The meaning is much the same either way. So, I will keep the text as it is.

With describing agricultural yields, the word נכה alludes to "poor harvest" or "malformed crops." There is an analogous expression with a preposition in Amos 4:9; "I smite you with scorching blight and mildew. And the caterpillar is devouring your many gardens and vineyards, fig trees and olive trees." In both verses, YHWH has summoned all sorts of diseases as a punishment through the form of agricultural catastrophe.

By this point in the textual record, blight, mildew, and hail have afflicted the crops. The resulting poor harvest and the malformed produce are unsurprising.[104] For, blight (שׁדפון) is a fungal crop disease that attacks mainly cereals on the eve of the harvest, and the effects of which are exacerbated by the hot desert winds. Mildew (ידקון) appears with the damp wind, and is active in the opposite context as blight in terms of the degree of humidity. It too is a fungal disease, which infects grains with paleness. Finally, the presence of mould in leaves intensifies and spreads in both moist and warm conditions.

These two diseases often appear together in the Hebrew Bible, and together they wreak havoc on the agricultural yield. As if that were not bad enough, the crops have also been struck by hail (ברד), which is also described as "stones of ice" in Josh 10:11. There was little way to protect crops against hail, and one can imagine the devastating effects of hail on Judah's ailing crops.

The Hiphil perfect first person of the verb נכה with the preposition את appears twice in the Hebrew Bible. The other case can be seen in Jer 2:30, "I have struck your sons." The verb נכה with the preposition את clearly highlights the definite object.[105] The objects that YHWH intends to inflict are the people and all work of their hands (מעשׂה ידיכם). The meaning of the item מעשׂה with the word ידיכם indicates every sort of "work," "labour," "accomplishment," or "achievement" that the people have done.[106] These are two corroborating examples: "because the sons of Israel have been only provoking me to anger by the work of their hands, declares YHWH"

104 Kessler, *The Book of Haggai*, 207–8; Verhoef, *The Book of Haggai and Malachi*, 127.

105 Waltke, Bruce Kenneth and M. O'Connor. *An Introduction to Biblical Hebrew Syntax* (Winona Lake, IN: Eisenbrauns, 1990), 433–6.

106 *HALOT*, Vol. 1, 889–93.

(Jer 32:30); and "they might provoke me to anger with all the work of their hands" (2 Kgs 22:17). Compared with Hag 1:11, Hag 2:17 clearly and concretely indicates which objects will be damaged: on account of the severe disaster caused by YHWH, nothing will grow.

A drought is then combined with hail and the crop diseases of blight and mildew. The addition of another affliction to the time of crisis results in unimaginable famine, even beyond the crop failure. For, drought causes extensive damage to the harvest as well as to animals. It leads to further big losses in the interregional trade. The textile industry becomes unexceptionally stricken. In this whole breakdown of the agricultural economic system, the survival of the people no longer seems possible. Furthermore, the extreme shortage of daily provisions causes the increased demand and a subsequent sharp rise in market prices. As a result the people of Judah have an extremely hard time in surviving no less paying their imperial taxes. Judah's failure to support imperial financial demands for the Achaemenid Empire could generate a political crisis of Judah.[107]

Nonetheless, the people of Judah remain disobedient to YHWH (אין־אתכם אלי). They obstinately reject Haggai's proclamations that persistently encourage them to rebuild the temple. Haggai beseeches the people to obey YHWH by twice using the phrase "I am with you" (1:13; 2:4) to encourage the people to work on the temple restoration. It is evident that the condition of the land comes to reflect the disobedience of the people to the word of YHWH concerning the temple project.

From Hag 2:16–17, it has been shown that YHWH sent judgement upon the people for leaving the temple in ruins by way of hail and crop diseases blight, mildew. This results in the scant harvest from which people suffered so severely. This breakdown emerges at first subtly (Hag 1:6) and then more explicitly (Hag 1:9; 2:16), finally leading to a catastrophe that greatly affects the people's lives. Agricultural structure is totally broke down as YHWH completely withdraws his blessing from the recalcitrant people and their every work.

107 Hoglund, *Achaemenid Imperial Administration*, 29–36, 54–68, 208–25; Berquist, *Judaism in Persia's Shadow*, 53, 57–8, 65–8.

Hag 2:18

שימו-נא לבבכם מן-היום הזה ומעלה; מיום עשרים וארבעה לתשיעי[108]
למן-היום אשר-יסד היכל-יהוה שימו לבבכם[109]

["Consider the time from this day on, from the twenty-fourth day of the ninth month. From the day when the temple of YHWH was founded, consider."]

The beginning phrase "consider the time from this day on" of this verse is the same as that of Hag 2:15, except for the first word עתה. This retrospective clause in the form of imperative expression indicates that the people's thoughts are not merely being directed back over all that they have been experiencing up until this point. Rather, they are being so directed with the developmental purpose of stimulating reflection about the contrasting blessings that will be given from the first day that they begin working on the temple project. Promptly, the people should shake off the vain deception and focus on what lies ahead.

Haggai emphatically entreats the people to look towards the newly opened future, in contrast to their forlorn reality. The turning point will be the day that the temple of YHWH begins to be laid, since, in doing so, the people are demonstrating obedience to YHWH. Indeed, the verb יסד used here in a Pual form confirms this as the turning point.[110] The intensive passive form of the verb יסד is used 4 times in the Hebrew Bible, including these verses: "the foundation of the house of YHWH was laid" (1 Kgs 6:37); "the foundation of the temple of YHWH is not yet laid" (Ezra 3:6); and "the day that the foundation of the house of YHWH of hosts is laid, that the temple might be built" (Zech 8:9). Each of these verses uses the term

108 BHS suggests that מיום עשרים וארבעה לתשיעי is a gloss, claiming that this is an attempt to harmonise the text with Hag 2:10. However, YHWH's judgement is announced to Joshua (Hag 2:10), the people (Hag 2:18), and Zerubbabel (Hag 2:20), on the same day. Therefore, the text gives very meaning

109 BHS suggests that the phrase למן-היום אשר-יסד היכל-יהוה שימו לבבכם is an addition. However, there is no reason to assume that the temple foundation is laid. This verse just indicates that temple rebuilding should be begun now. Therefore, BHS should not be taken.

110 *DCH*, Vol. 4, 232–3; *HALOT*, Vol. 1, 417.

יסד to describe the temple construction or reconstruction. The prophet Haggai now highlights the work of building that the people are to engage in through the passive form.

When read alongside Ezra 5:16, which uses the Sumerian loanword אשׁיא to describe "foundations or footings on bedrock,"[111] Sheshbazzar seems to be involved in the actual laying of the foundation stone or in the attendant ceremonies. Moreover, in Ezra 3:6, 10, 11 and Zech 4:9, the root יסד has been used in reference to the temple's foundation. On this view, this verse has been connected to a foundation-laying ceremony to establish continuity between the old and new temple: it is because of the opposition of Judah's enemies that the rebuilding of the temple has been frustrated (Ezra 4:1–5);[112] it is because of the removal of a brick or stone from a destroyed temple or building and its placement in the foundations of a new structure.[113] However, there is little additional reason to interpret this verse as describing the laying of the foundation of the temple. As in Hag 2:15, the temple project is still the compelling work that the people should be motivated to begin.

Haggai specifically clarifies that in "the twenty-fourth day of the ninth month" the temple rebuilding should be begun. Also, Hag 2:18 is a record from around the time of the season for sowing wheat and barley and then starting to plant legumes and vegetables. Mapping the relationship between the arrangement of the agricultural activities and the commencement of the temple rebuilding actual point demonstrates that, for an affluent harvest over the coming sowing season, an agricultural calendar should be supervised by the rebuilt temple. For the purpose, the Jerusalem temple reconstruction should be urgently begun.

Above all, Judah is compelled to rebuild the Jerusalem temple to govern and develop their agricultural activities, while trying to improve their economic relationships and advantages. With the last word, "consider," Haggai decisively exhorts the people to look forward to the time when both the

111 C. G. Tuland, "'uššayyā' and ʿuššarnâ: a Clarification of Terms, Date and Text." *JNES* 17 (1958): 269–75.

112 Verhoef, *The Book of Haggai and Malachi*, 129–30.

113 Kessler, *The Book of Haggai*, 208–9.

sowing will be sown and they will commence the temple reconstruction. This is the time for the people to act in a way that will precipitate blessings, and to live in the promise of the future.

Hag 2:19

העוד הזרע במגורה[114] ועד-הגפן והתאנה והרמון[115]
ועץ הזית לא נשא מן-היום הזה אברך

["Is the seed still in the storage? Even the vine, the fig tree, the pomegranate and the olive tree, has it not borne fruit? From this day I will bless you."]

Once again, speaking about the commencement of the temple reconstruction implicit in the previous verse, Haggai leads the people to the promise of divine blessing using these rhetorical questions: "is the seed still in the storage?" and "even the vine, the fig, the pomegranate, and the olive tree, has it not borne fruit?" In the queries, the rhetorical interrogative particle ה of the first word, עוד is used to emphasise the crop failure, which might suggest persuaded assent in the expression of the interrogator.[116] The answer to the question "is the seed still in the storage?" should be categorically no. Ordinarily seeds of grains in an individually-owned grain pit or storage room (מגורה) would be protected from spoilage once next year's seeds have been put aside, yet at this time the wheat and barley seeds would have been very scarce as a result of the scant harvest.[117]

The following enquiry is: "even the vine, the fig, the pomegranate, and the olive tree, has it not borne fruit?" alongside the interrogative first

114 BHS suggests correction מגדע or נגדע because of no verb. However, verb-less sentences are very common in Hebrew Therefore, this adjustment is unnecessary because the phrase itself makes sense as it is.

115 BHS suggests the addition ועד-הגפן והתאנה והרמון because the following verb is singular. However, a singular replacing a plural or a plural replacing a singular is very common in Hebrew.

116 Carroll Stuhlmueller, *Rebuilding with Hope: A Commentary on the Book of Haggai and Zechariah* (ITC; Michigan: Grand Rapids, 1988), 34.

117 Hopkins, *Highlands*, 213–34; Borowski, *Agriculture in Iron Age*, 71–3.

sentence, this second sentence renders a negative-declarative sentence linking to the negative answer inspired by the first question. Rhetorically these parallel questions function to emphasise the desperate economic situation of the people. Referring to fruit-bearing trees, the verb נשׂא designates the yield of their respective fruit. This verse demonstrates the same pattern: "the tree bears its fruit, the fig tree and vine give their full yield" (Joel 2:22). The answer to the second question in Hag 2:19 is obviously and repeatedly "no." None of the fruit-bearing plants named in Hag 1:11 has borne fruit. The agricultural reality is certainly deplorable insofar as everything, even into the next wave of production remains uncertain and unstable.

Then, the prophet Haggai abruptly announces YHWH's blessing: "from this day I will bless you." The word ברך is mainly used in the Piel form in the Hebrew Bible, though a first person expression of YHWH (אברך) is very rare—such as, "I will abundantly bless her provision" (Ps 132:15). This expression certainly denotes that the change from cursing to blessing is assured by YHWH himself. So, this expectation itself would have seemed very compromising, despite not distributing any immediate bounty of produce to make up for the previous reduction (Hag 2:16).

The inauguration of change is therefore noteworthy though it does not mention the exact day. The day is merely linked to the commencement of the temple rebuilding (Hag 2:18). The verb ברך does not even have any associated objects. However, there is little doubt that the object of YHWH's blessing should be connected with the blessings of the harvest, from the context. The object assured by the blessing could further spread far beyond the agricultural reality, though.[118] The people of Judah can be assured that the conditions of the present and recent past will not continue into the future.

This assurance recalls the leading principle that deities of the ancient Near East provide prosperity or adversity to agrarian areas depending on whether or not their people obey them. In a similar manner, the blessing of YHWH is certainly contingent upon the rebuilding of the Jerusalem temple. In an agricultural environment the link is especially evident between

118 Meyers and Meyers, *Haggai, Zechariah 1–8*, 65–6, 80–2; Kessler, *The Book of Haggai*, 210–18; Verhoef (*The Book of Haggai and Malachi*, 135–7.

the reconstruction of the temple and a resulting abundance of produce. At this historical moment, the land of Judah created a military buffer zone between the Achaemenids and Egypt, particularly during the Egyptian revolts against the Achaemenids.[119] This political context placed particular pressure on Judah to produce a huge amount of agricultural goods to provide for the Achaemenid army. This context added to the importance of Judah's restoration of the temple.

From Hag 2: 18–19, this paper has shown that YHWH assures Judah a bountiful harvest upon the start of temple reconstruction. To illustrate this, Haggai calls the people to reflect once again on what they have experienced while the temple remained in disrepair. Their disobedience resulted in a severe economic disaster in which even seeds for coming planting were not assured. This reflection should have emphasised to the people the vital importance of figuring out how Judah might survive under the reigning power while seeking a staunch alliance with the most suitable subordinate.

To sum up, this study on Hag 2:15–19 has depicted the people of Judah as accused by YHWH for disobeying his commandment to rebuild the temple (Hag 2:15). Even by the end of Hag 2:19, YHWH's temple remains in ruins. According to the common ruling principle of an agrarian society in the ancient Near East, YHWH subsequently summoned up adversity to punish the agrarian areas of Judah. In combination with a drought (Hag 1:10), hail, and crop diseases of blight and mildew undoubtedly led to crop failures. The agricultural productions were 50 per cent and 60 per cent lower than the expecting sum of the harvest. The Judean agricultural economy was completely devastated (Hag 2:16–17). Even seeds for the next year's grains and fruits were scarce in the dreadfully poor harvest. That experience was quite enough to make the people contemplate what they should now do. Indeed, as Haggai had been exhorting them, it was the very time for the people to rebuild the temple. The blessing of YHWH would then be given to the agriculture: rebuilding the temple was vital for agricultural prosperity (Hag 2:18–19).

119 Berquist, "Constructions of Identity," 53–66; Berquist, *Judaism in Persia's Shadow*, 57–8, 65–8; Trotter, "Was the Second Jerusalem Temple a Primarily Persian Project?" 276–93.

Deposed Zerubbabel's Status (Hag 2:20–23)

Hag 2:20

ויהי דבר-יהוה שנית אל-חגי בעשרים וארבעה לחדש לאמר

[The word of YHWH came to Haggai a second time on the twenty-fourth day of the month, saying,]

Another word of YHWH is announced to Zerubbabel, who is exposed as the object in the following verse. On that same day YHWH's judgement was also proclaimed to the priests and the people. Hag 2:20 starts with prophetic language that is nearly identical to the clause in Hag 2:1 and 10, ויהי דבר-יהוה שנית אל-חגי (the word of YHWH comes to Haggai). It differs only in that the perfect verb היה has been converted into the imperfect form due to the w consecutive conjunction.

In a sequence of YHWH's judgement following the formula in Hag 2:10, Haggai has already declared that the judgement extends to cover both the priests and the people. It seems unlikely, though, that Zerubbabel would be included in this new introductory formula. It would be reasonable to infer that the judgement of Zerubbabel is applied with a slight distinction from that pertaining to the priests and the people. For, the judgement of YHWH against Zerubbabel will be quite distinct from the previous two objects.

However, those interpreters favouring an eschatological view of this verse have claimed that the new starting form demonstrates the authority of Zerubbabel who is dealt separately from the two previous objects.[120] Eschatological interpreters have maintained that its own dateless form indicates a hazy future that, despite its lack of clarity, will be actualised in time.[121] It is because the prophetic discourse with Zerubbabel is to do

120 Meyers and Meyers, *Haggai, Zechariah 1–8*, 82; Kessler, *The Book of Haggai*, 222; Petersen, *Haggai, Zechariah 1–8*, 97; Verhoef, *The Book of Haggai and Malachi*, 141–2; Wolff, *Haggai*, 80.

121 Meyers and Meyers, *Haggai, Zechariah 1–8*, 82; Kessler, *The Book of Haggai*, 222; Verhoef, *The Book of Haggai and Malachi*, 142.

with questions of the political status of Judah and of his leadership in the changed Judean circumstance. This interpretation is dependent upon the traditions of Zion's pre-eminence and the perpetuity of the Davidic dynasty. However, this distinct rhetorical form should instead be understood within the context of YHWH's judgement in response to the periods of inaction in temple rebuilding.

On the "twenty-fourth of the month," indicated in previous textual units (Hag 2:10–14, 15–19), Haggai persuades the priests and the people to turn towards the temple rebuilding project with the phrase שׂים לב. When the priests encourage the people to rebuild the temple and the people become involved in the temple work, their agricultural and economic endeavours will be blessed soon after. Blessings for the future have been opened up to them.

Concurrently, on the very same date, Zerubbabel is included in the conviction. This suggests that Zerubbabel might have quite a different story. YHWH provides a great hope for the future, without evoking assumptions or assuring the ultimate destiny of Judah, as an independent political entity. These features distinguish the day when the temple rebuilding should commence as vital to the future of Judah. While it is not the day when the Davidic dynasty is established the very date will change the position of Zerubbabel.

Hag 2:21

אמר אל-זרבבל פחת-יהודה לאמר: אני מרעיש את-השמים ואת-הארץ[122]

["Speak to Zerubbabel, the governor of Judah," saying, "I will shake the heavens and the earth."]

By the virtue of the title, Zerubbabel of the Davidic line was misunderstood as conveying a more inclusive hope from which the people tried to establish a self-governing Davidic dynasty (Hag 1:4, 9; 2:4). They had expected all of

122 BHS notes that the LXX adds αὶ τὴν θάλασσαν καὶ τὴν ξηρὰν after את-השמים ואת-הארץ, in accordance with Hag 2:6. The text itself is enough to indicate YHWH's intervention. Therefore, there is no need to harmonise with Hag 2:6.

Judah's enemies to be swiftly defeated, allowing Judah to thrive and enjoy her riches (Hag 2:6–7). However, this desire to build the house of David is tantamount to revolting against the empire, and YHWH has responded in judgement against this duplicitous ambition of Judah's.

Endowed with the title governor of Judah, Zerubbabel fulfils an important role for how Judah should function within the political and the economic structure in the Achaemenids. Darius presumably conferred Zerubbabel's title as governor of Judah with the intention of maximising the usefulness of the existing Judean authority. It would be very useful to connect the Judean coalition with Darius in the context of his territorial expansion.

However, the restoration of the Judean tradition of Davidic lineage may readily have further exacerbated the political and cultural pressures on the Achaemenid Empire.[123] Particularly during the Egyptian revolts, the empire depended on a strong pledge of support from the existing ruling authority in Judah.[124] Indeed Zerubbabel, as the governor of Judah, was asked to show his loyalty to Darius. In contrast to fostering the intended affiliation, however, the assignment of Zerubbabel, a member of the Davidic line, simultaneously encouraged the autonomy of Judah. By meddling between Egypt and the Achaemenids, Judah defied Darius. Subsequently, Judah faced the very real possibility of extreme hostility from the Achaemenids.

The descriptions of trembling (מרעיש) of nature in Hag 2:21 cosmologically convey the violence and seriousness of YHWH's judgement against Zerubbabel on that actual historical day. The verb מרעיש in a Hiphil form clearly indicates YHWH's judgement on Zerubbabel. The term מרעיש describes Zerubbabel as trembling in terror, which signifies his complete submission. This interpretation stands in strong contrast to that of eschatological

123 The BHQ apparatus notes that the Greek version adds "son of Shealtiel." This is done in assimilation to Hag 1:1 and Hag 2: 2. However, this omission would be understood in the context of judgement towards Zerubbabel, so that his status is clarified with an imperial administrative officer. See Eugene Ulrich ed, *The Biblical Qumran Scrolls: transcriptions and Textual variants* (VTSup 134; Leiden; Boston: Brill, 2010), 619; Biblia Hebraica Quinta editione cum apparatus critico novis curis elaborato: *Introduction and Commentaries on the Twelve Minor Prophets* (ed, Anthony Gelston; Fascicle 13; Stuttgart: Deutsche Bibelgesellschaft, 2010), 117.

124 Briant, *From Cyrus to Alexander*, 70–6; Dandamaev, *Political History*, 103–77.

interpreters who attribute the ultimate and final deliverance of YHWH.[125] In their view, the expression מרעיש announces YHWH's intervention on behalf of his people and the mention of the heavens and the earth symbolises cosmic upheaval, resulting from which all powers will submit to YHWH.

The terrible judgement of YHWH against Zerubbabel is not the central issue in question. Certainly, the judgement מרעיש is not for Zerubbabel in a positive way but towards Zerubbabel in a negative way. In this usage, one can see the same play on words that Haggai quite often uses, indicating an unexpected meaning for the words or phrases. YHWH addresses Zerubbabel the Davidic figure with judgement using the same phrase that the soon to be restored Davidic dynasty expects in Hag 2:6–7, albeit applied differently—as judgement. In contrast to both the priests and the people, to whom new possibilities will be opened up, the outlook for Zerubbabel seems bleak.

This exposition of Hag 2:20–21 has shown that the hope based around Zerubbabel resulted in the judgement of YHWH, wherein Zerubbabel was distinguished from the priests and the people. With the revised formula of the prophetic message, Zerubbabel is sentenced to tremble with fear. It seems that both the priests and the people were persuaded and expected to join the temple rebuilding project. Zerubbabel was clearly treated in quite a different way though, which alludes to the closed future for Zerubbabel since the Davidic project is categorically subordinate to the temple project, which YHWH commands and the Achaemenids actively encourage.

Hag 2:22

והפכתי כסא ממלכות והשמדתי חזק ממלכות[126] הגוים;
והפכתי מרכבה ורכביה וירדו סוסים ורכביהם איש בחרב אחיו[127]

125 Meyers and Meyers, *Haggai, Zechariah 1–8*, 66, 82–3; Kessler, *The Book of Haggai*, 223; Verhoef, *The Book of Haggai and Malachi*, 142–3; Petersen, *Haggai, Zechariah 1–8*, 97–8.

126 BHS suggests deleting ממלכות. However, political and military power of enemies is emphasised in ממלכות הגוים of the parallelism. Therefore, I will keep the text as it is.

127 BHS deems איש בחרב אחיו to be a gloss because of the parallelism with והפכתי מרכבה ורכביה. However, this phrase denotes the means to suppress the enemies, rather than an extended parallelism. Therefore, BHS should not be accepted.

["I will overthrow the authority of the thrones of kingdoms and destroy the power of the kingdoms of the nations. I will overturn the chariots and their riders then the horses and their riders will go down, each by the sword of his brother."]

YHWH determinedly rejects the expected establishment of the Davidic kingdom and further rebukes the invocation of Judean power against Darius. The Judgement of YHWH eventually bears down upon the people's conspired hope for Zerubbabel's royal extractions. Also, his judgement will involve the destruction of any foreign domination that would rise up against Darius in his immediate succession to the Achaemenid throne, no matter how benign or minimal.

The phrase "thrones of the nations" (כסא ממלכות) and its parallel, "the kingdoms of the nations" (ממלכות הגוים), are placed as crowns for political and military power. The term כסא is in general found in conjunction with the royal throne ממלכה.[128] Its synonym חזק in the second clause denotes authority or honour. These words כסא and חזק refer accordingly to the nations' military power or ability to use force to attain their objectives.[129] Here, for example, are two phrases that use the terms in a similar manner: "have we not by our own strength taken Karnaim for ourselves?" (Amos 6:13); and "I will destroy the fat and the strong" (Ezek 34:16; Exod 13:2; 14:16).

In light of this, the thrones themselves represent the power of authorities in which the former word כסא might be seen as an emphasising reiteration. This would be as a collective expression of the word ממלכות, to emphasise there is no exception to this judgement. Thus, it would be understood that this phrase (כסא ממלכות) refers to every throne of every nation: any power that stands in opposition to the reign of Darius as YHWH's agent will be promptly and thoroughly destroyed.

To explain the connection of a plural construct noun to a single nominative it could be claimed that the thrones of kingdoms refer to the single Achaemenid dynasty, since the ruler of an empire represents many political entities. With this interpretation, the verse has been read to mean that any empire strongly opposed to Judah will be brought down, like the conspired

128 *DCH*, Vol. 5, 439–41; *HALOT*, Vol. 1, 487.

129 Kessler, *The Book of Haggai*, 223–4.

hope to restore the Davidic dynasty. YHWH's war is aimed at promising Judah's future prosperity exempted from the wrath of YHWH. On that day that YHWH will assuredly re-establish his world sovereignty, any foreign domination will be destroyed.[130]

However, YHWH's verdict is not against an empire composed of many political entities but against the many insubordinate subjects of an empire. Judah as one of many insurgent entities has not been entirely tolerated by Darius, for even a very small city in rebellion might gain a foothold in the imperial economy that could bring the empire's political structure into crisis.[131]

In fact, at the time of Darius's reign, beginning with the onset of rebellions in Elam and Babylon, subordinate rebellions of varying sizes were widespread, extending throughout Media, Assyria, Parthia, Margiana, Sattagydia, and Scythia (see Chapter 2 above).[132] Egypt also rose up against Darius, leading to Judah's attempt to benefit from the geopolitical tactics between Egyptians and the Achaemenids as she did throughout Neo-Assyrian and the Neo-Babylonian empires.

While the multiple uprisings against Darius posed severe threats to his power, he successfully suppressed them and rapidly regained control of his subordinates. Therefore, it seems quite probable that YHWH's judgement was not exclusively applied to Judah, which instigated but one of the revolts against Darius.

YHWH declares the commencement of quelling every revolt against Darius. The first verb הפך is frequently found with YHWH to be the subject in descriptions of his overthrowing or overturning, including the abasement of all nations which oppose YHWH (Amos 4:11; Jer 20:16).[133] Extending the description of this first verb, the second verb, שׁמר guarantees the complete destruction or abolition of political entities hostile to

130 See Meyers and Meyers, *Haggai, Zechariah 1–8*, 66–7; Kessler, *The Book of Haggai*, 223–6.

131 Barstad, "Haggai Among the Prophets," 279–80.

132 Briant, *From Cyrus to Alexander*, 114–22; Dandamaev, *Political History*, 114–31.

133 *DCH*, Vol. 2, 579–81; *HALOT*, Vol. 1, 253–4. Meyers and Meyers, *Haggai, Zechariah 1–8*, 66–7; Kessler, *The Book of Haggai*, 224–5.

the Achaemenids.[134] The repetition of the Hiphil form in verb variations highlights the terrible imagery that portrays what will take place in each situation.

To demonstrate this, Haggai employs the image of a decisive military victory. Armies of rebels represented by chariots and their riders as well as horses and their riders will, without exception, be overthrown and destroyed.[135] The means by which this suppression of each nation's power will be accomplished is the sword of "his brother." In most cases, the word אח does not refer to a blood brother but to a brother who is a partner in a treaty or engages in diplomatic relations, whatever equality or inequality.[136] In which, the pronoun "his" of the term "his brother" (אחיו) reassures the reality that each of insurgent states irrefutably remains subject of Darius.

To judge from the exegesis of Hag 2:22, YHWH ensures that any political and military power that confronts Darius will be completely overthrown and devastated. This is the result of YHWH's intervention on behalf of Darius: the strength of rebellious nations will be annihilated and the power of rebellious authorities will be destroyed. YHWH's volition in judging usurpers against Darius is very much determinate and he will accomplish his conviction on them.

Hag 2:23

ביום ההוא נאם-יהוה צבאות[137] אקחך זרבבל בן-שאלתיאל עבדי
נאם-יהוה ושמתיך כחותם: כי-בך בחרתי נאם יהוה צבאות

[On that day, said YHWH of hosts, "I will take you, my servant, Zerubbabel, the son of Shealtiel," said YHWH, "I will make you like a signet ring," "for I have chosen you" said YHWH of hosts.]

134 *HALOT*, Vol. 2, 1552–3.
135 Meyers and Meyers, *Haggai, Zechariah 1–8*, 67; Kessler, *The Book of Haggai*, 224–6.
136 *DCH*, Vol. 1, 173–9; *HALOT*, Vol. 1, 29.
137 BHS suggests the addition of נאם-יהוה צבאות because it is a repetition. However, repetitions are not uncommon.

The explicit and ultimate judgement of Zerubbabel is expressed with the prophetic formula נאם-יהוה צבאות (the word of YHWH of hosts). The use of this formula emphasises the determinate volition of YHWH's judgement. Furthermore, YHWH calls Zerubbabel his servant instead of using the title of governor, which gives a crucial hint of changes in the status of Zerubbabel.

YHWH proclaims that Zerubbabel will now be taken (לקח) as YHWH's servant (עבד) and will be given (שׂים) a signet (חותם). In many instances, the verb לקח with YHWH as the subject is used for the appointment to a new position or responsibility in ways both good or bad; for example, "I take you from the pasture, from following the sheep, that you should be prince over my people Israel" (2 Sam 7:8; Exod 6:7; Lev 8:2; Num 27:18, 22; Ps 78:70) and "YHWH takes me from following the flock ... do not prophesy against Israel, and do not preach against the house of Isaac" (Amos 7:15–16).[138]

In this instance, Zerubbabel is qualified as a servant of YHWH, which often expresses the position of a person before YHWH. When the noun עבד is accompanied with the word יהוה it is sometimes associated with leaders or officials of communities or nations (Gen 26:24; Judg 2:8; Josh 1:1, 7, 8; 2:3; 2 Sam 7:5, 8; Isa 41:8–9; Jer 25:9; 27:6), and their duty is always to perform tasks that are associated with the commandments of YHWH.[139] Therefore, the implications of this designation likely include that Zerubbabel as a Judean figurehead should make sure the Judean people heed YHWH's call to build the temple. Also, in historical reality, Zerubbabel as an official administrator should support imperial policies as much as possible.

Unfortunately, Zerubbabel had taken the side of hostility against the empire. After having participated in the wrong side, YHWH firmly declares that Zerubbabel is the YHWH's servant with a signet ring (חותם). This signet ring reminds us of the doom of Coniah (=Jeconiah = Jehoiachin, 1 Chr 3:16; Esth 2:6) who was taken to Babylon and died there when Nebuchadnezzar laid siege to Jerusalem (2 Kgs 24:8–17; 2 Chr 36:9–10;

138 *DCH*, Vol. 4, 564–75; *HALOT*, Vol. 1, 534–5.

139 *DCH*, Vol. 6, 215–25; *HALOT*, Vol. 1, 774–5.

Jer 22:24–27). As a result, he did not reign in Jerusalem, but was taken to Babylon and died there (2 Kgs 23:33–35).

It is true that the signet ring that Zerubbabel receives is nothing but the role that Coniah had (Jer 22:24, 28; 24:1; 27:20; 28:4; 29:2; 37:1; 2 Kgs 24:10–16).[140] He is demoted by the signet ring. For, the intended portrayal of Zerubbabel's life in light of the portrayal of Coniah's tragic life indicates that while new possibilities would be opened to the priests and the people, Zerubbabel is doomed.

It is highly likely that the people represented in the book of Haggai craftily tried to restore the house of David through Zerubbabel, conspiring for the legacy of the Davidic line. Therefore, it could be vital to consider the depiction of Coniah as a way of reviewing the past. The life of Coniah invokes the portrayal of a tragic life now that Zerubbabel is chosen to be the recipient of this signet ring.[141] Coniah as a despised and broken idol is cast out into a ruling country to die. His descendant, Zedekiah (Jer 32:4–5), in addition to Zerubbabel on the Davidic line are also completely excluded from any future political leadership.[142]

As noted above, with the perfect form of the verb בחר which represents an accomplished fact, two verbs לקח and שׂים in the imperfect form indicate that the state of affairs is currently in tentative progress. Subsequently, it cannot be over-emphasised that Zerubbabel may have been toppled and killed by Darius, which would have been common to usurpers who arose against him.[143] Indeed, after 520 BCE nothing more was recorded of Zerubbabel.

However, eschatological interpretations have strongly argued that this verse rather affirms YHWH's sovereignty and power over Judah's future, for the words of עבדי, לקח, בחר, and חותם are frequently used of Davidic monarch (2 Sam 7:5, 8; 1 Kgs 11:13; 14:8; 2 Kgs 19:34; 2 Chr 32:16).[144] All

140 Barstad, "Haggai Among the Prophets," 281–2.

141 Ishida, *History*, 93–4.

142 For an anti-Zerubbabel faction in relation to the Judean exile, see Carroll, *Jeremiah*, 441–3.

143 Barstad, "Haggai Among the Prophets," 282.

144 John Kessler, "Haggai, Zerubbabel, and the Political Status of Yehud: The Signet Ring in Haggai 2:23" in *Prophets, Prophecy, and Prophetic Texts in Second Temple*

terms are associated with important individuals and groups in Biblical traditions (Num 12:7–8; Jer 25:9; 2 Sam 7:8; 1 Kgs 21:8; Jer 22:24). In particular, they root the future activity of YHWH on behalf of Zerubbabel in YHWH's choice of him (כי-בך בחרתי). In their sense, Zerubbabel must be highly upheld in the favour of YHWH.

These interpreters recognise that Darius deliberately employed the dynastic model to promote imperial interests with his subordinates, whereby members of former ruling dynasties were placed in positions of authority.[145] Furthermore, interpreters with an eschatological orientation argue that the Davidic governor Zerubbabel would have somewhat elevated the political status of Judah through his own role, at least to the level of a vassal king in the Neo-Assyrian and Neo Babylonian periods, insofar as Judah remained subservient to Darius. The eschatological future will be introduced "at this time" (ביום ההוא), which would also be the day anticipated by the people when Judah would again achieve political independence and self-rule under the Davidic Zerubbabel.

Even in the eschatological view, the status of Zerubbabel is clearly of complete subordination to the imperial power. This subservient position of Zerubbabel is reaffirmed by the signet ring, which is just a re-painting of Coniah. As signet, Zerubbabel, like Coniah, is merely a tool for the Empire, which is validated by the choice (בחר) of Zerubbabel to be incorporated with imperial policies (1 Chr 15:2; 28:4; Ezek 20:5).[146] Notwithstanding this, the imperial appointment of Zerubbabel as governor very nearly revives the Davidic dynasty. Undeniably, it was wholly viable as a conspiracy. YHWH then comprehensively excludes the Judean kingship from the Davidic genealogy. The hope of the house of David is clearly terminated.

Judaism (ed. Michael H. Floyd and Robert Donel Haak; LHB/OTS 427; New York; London: T & T Clark, 2006), 111–12; Kessler, "Haggai, Zerubbabel, and the Political Status," 114–18; Kessler, *The Book of Haggai*, 226–7, 233–9; Meyers and Meyers, *Haggai, Zechariah 1–8*, 67, 69–70; Tollington, *Tradition and Innovation*, 135–44.

145 Eric M. Meyers, "The Persian Period and the Judean Restoration: From Zerubbabel to Nehemiah" in *Ancient Israelite Religion: Essays in Honor of Frank Moore Cross* (ed. Patrick D. Miller, Paul D. Hanson, and S. Dean McBride Jr; Philadelphia: Fortress, 1987), 512.

146 *DCH*, Vol. 2, 137–9; *HALOT*, Vol. 1, 119–20.

From Hag 2:23, it is evident that the choice of a governor who is a descendant of the former ruling elite is a deliberate and conscious political ploy by the policy of Darius. Zerubbabel, for Darius's benefit, is expected to be a loyal promoter of imperial interests and should be fully consistent with imperial policies. With this understanding, the imposition of the Davidic dynasty on Zerubbabel is clearly adduced as disloyalty and rightly incites the people to rebellion against Darius. As was the fate of other traitors, it is not unlikely that Darius would subsequently remove Zerubbabel.

To sum up the main points of this study on Hag 2:20–23, it has shown that the title of governor of Judah conferred on Zerubbabel by an imperial patron was taken for granted (Hag 2:21). In the second year of Darius, in particular, as a reliable supporter Zerubbabel should have facilitated the temple rebuilding that Darius had commanded. This temple rebuilding work was in essence associated with the commandment of YHWH (Hag 1:12, 14; 2:3, 5, 8–9).

Notwithstanding this, Zerubbabel involved himself in the conspired to rebuild the Davidic dynasty (Hag 2:4, 6–7). Zerubbabel was subsequently accused for this subordinate "rebuilding" (Hag 2:20–21). He not only violated YHWH's command but also rebelled against Darius's commandment. These failures result in the fatal judgement against him. Furthermore, YHWH definitely ensures that uprisings against Darius will be thoroughly overthrown and quashed (Hag 2:22). Amidst this judgement, it is no exaggeration to say that Zerubbabel is unequivocally doomed to be excluded from empirical history, as it is true of other usurpers (Hag 2:23)

Conclusions

In this chapter I have shown that Hag 2:1–23 provides a well-defined unified message delivered continuously by Haggai through several types of prophetic formulae. Hag 2:1–23 is a follow up of Haggai's announcement of the temple rebuilding in Hag 1:1–15. At the same time, it is a response to the actions of Zerubbabel the governor, Joshua the high priest, and the people of Judah (Hag 2:1–9). The behaviour of all these three groups leads to the judgement of YHWH against Judah (Hag 2:10–23).

The text of Hag 2 should be divided into two parts. The first part deals with causes for YHWH's judgement (Hag 2:1–9), and the second with consequences of YHWH's judgement (Hag 2:10–23). Hag 2: 10–23 could be divided further into three sections: Hag 2:10–14, 15–19, and 20–23. In these subsections, Joshua (Hag 2:10–14), the people (Hag 2:15–19), and Zerubbabel (Hag 2:20–23) respectively are sternly admonished.

Darius bestowed the title of governor of Judah on Zerubbabel. The title, therefore, carried the obligation of allegiance to Darius as a faithful patron (Hag 2:2). Irrespective of the requirement for such an administrative officer, Zerubbabel's Davidic lineage predisposed him towards the pursuit of an independent Judah, rather than to be loyal towards Achaemenid imperial policy. He did this through taking advantage of repeated Egyptian rebellions (Hag 2:4). The people, together with Zerubbabel and Joshua, never paid any attention to YHWH's command to rebuild the temple. Instead, focusing on Zerubbabel's royal Judean lineage, they involved themselves in rebuilding the Davidic dynasty. In their conspiracy to reestablish the Davidic dynasty, they worked for the political independence of Judah, to be followed by an economic boom for Judah (Hag 2:6–7).

However, their preferred building project became impossible to carry through. Moreover, it developed into a violation against YHWH. The inhabitants of Judah were commissioned to rebuild the temple, YHWH now calls out to them (Hag 2:1–2). Then he reminds them of the faithful obedience to YHWH's commandments required by the Sinai-covenantal tradition (Hag 2:5). The rebuilt temple will definitely create economic affluence in Judah. The temple will be the location of the empire's central fiscal administration in Jerusalem. In this way, Judah will become a worthy partner in the Achaemenid administrative system (Hag 2:8–9).

From an imperial, economic, and military point of view, Judah's food supply was crucial for the imperial army rations. To be able to conduct his campaign against Egypt, Darius had to depend upon sufficient food rations from Judah. For this purpose, the temple should be rebuilt promptly. YHWH referred to the teaching authority of the priests (Hag 2:10–14).

It was their task to enlighten the people about the temple rebuilding in order to increase agricultural surplus in Judah.

The people neglected the word of YHWH concerning the temple restoration. This led to ritual disqualification (Hag 2:10–12). The sacrifices of defiled people were subsequently rejected. YHWH's blessing was taken away. Along with drought (Hag 1:11), hail, and crop diseases like blight and mildew afflicted the harvest terribly (Hag 2:16–17). As a consequence, the whole Judean agricultural economic system collapsed. Even seeds for the next season were scarce. From within this spiral of disaster, Haggai insisted that it was the persistent rejection of the temple renovation project that provoked the agricultural catastrophe (Hag 2:17). People were beseeched to contemplate what they should do now (Hag 2:15, 18–19).

Equally bad was striving of the people for the political independence of Judah through the establishment of a Davidic dynasty. In reality, this was conspiracy and rebellion against Darius. A very important text is found in the story of the Signet Ring of Zerubbabel. Here, the allusion to Coniah reassured the people of the truth that YHWH had rescinded his authorisation for the Judean kingship from the Davidic lineage (Hag 2:20–23). However, YHWH's judgement was Zerubbabel's downfall; nothing more is recorded of him. Probably suffering the fate also of other traitors, Zerubbabel may have been overthrown and killed by Darius.

Bibliography

Ackroyd, Peter Runham. *Exile and Restoration*. Philadelphia: Westminster, 1968.

Assis, Elie. "A Disputed Temple (Haggai 2, 1–9)." *ZAW* 120 (2008): 582–96.

Baldwin, Joyce. *Haggai, Zechariah, Malachi: An Introduction and Commentary*. TOTC. London: Inter Varsity, 1971.

Bedford, Peter Ross. "The Economic Role of the Jerusalem Temple in Achaemenid Judah: Comparative Perspectives." Pages 3–20 in Bar-Asher, Rom-Shiloni, Tov, and Wazana, eds, *Shai le-Sara Japhet: Studies in the Bible, its Exegesis and its Language*.

Berquist, Jon L. "Constructions of Identity in Postcolonial Yehud." Pages 53–66 in Lipschits and Oeming, eds, *Judah and the Judeans in the Persian Period*.

———. *Judaism in Persia's Shadow: A Social and Historical Approach*. Minneapolis: Fortress, 1995.

Biblia Hebraica Quinta editione cum apparatus critico novis curis elaborato: *Intorduction and Commentaries on the Twelve Minor Prophets*. Edited by Anthony Gelston. Fascicle 13. Stuttgart: Deutsche Bibelgesellschaft, 2010. [=BHQ]

Boda, Mark J. "Haggai: Master Rhetorician." *TynBul* 51 (2000): 295–304.

Bongenaar, A. C. V. M. *The Neo-Babylonian Ebabbar Temple at Sippar: Its Administration and its Prosopography*. Leiden: Nederlands Historisch-Archaeologisch Instituut Te Istanbul, 1997.

Borowski, Oded. *Agriculture in Iron Age Israel: The Evidence from Archaeology and the Bible*. Winona Lake, IN: Eisenbrauns, 1987.

Carroll, Robert P. "So What Do We Know about the Temple? The Temple in the Prophets." Pages 34–51 in Eskenazi and Richards, eds, *Second Temple Studies*. Vol. 2, *Temple Community in the Persian Period*.

———. *Jeremiah: A Commentary*. OTL. Philadelphia: Westminster, 1986.

Clark, David J. "Problems in Haggai 2:15–19." *BT* 34 (1983): 432–39.

Clines, David J. A. "Haggai's Temple Constructed, Deconstructed and Reconstructed." Pages 60–87 in Eskenazi and Richards, eds, *Second Temple Studies*. Vol. 2, *Temple Community in the Persian Period*.

Cooper, Jerrold S. *The Curse of Agade*. Baltimore; London: The Johns Hopkins University Press, 1983.

Cowley, Arthur Ernest. *Aramaic Papyri of the Fifth Centuty BC*. Oxford: Clarendon, 1923. [=*AP*]

Dandamaev, Muhammad A. *A Political History of the Achaemenid Empire*. Translated by W. J. Vogelsang. Leiden: Brill, 1989.

———. "State and Temple in Babylonia in the First Millennium B.C." Pages 589–96 in Lipinski ed., *State and Temple Economy in the Ancient Near East*. Vol. 2.

Davies, William David and Louis Finkelstein, eds. *Cambridge History of Judaism*. Vol. 1, *Introduction; The Persian Period*. Cambridge: Cambridge University Press, 1984. [=*CHJ*]

Diepold, Peter. *Israel's Land*. BWANT 95. Stuttgart: Kohlhammer, 1972.

Dillard, Raymond B. *2 Chronicles*. WBC. Vol. 15. Waco, TX: Word, 1987.

Edelman, Diana. *Origins of the "Second" Temple: Persian Imperial Policy and the Rebuilding of Jerusalem*. London: Equinox, 2005.

Farrokh, Kaveh. *Shadows in the Desert: Ancient Persia at War*. Oxford: Osprey, 2007.

Floyd, Michael H. "The Nature of the Narrative and the Evidence of Redaction in Haggai." *VT* 45 (1995): 470–90.

—— and Robert Donel Haak, eds. *Prophets, Prophecy, and Prophetic Texts in Second Temple Judaism*. LHB/OTS 427. New York; London: T & T Clark, 2006.

Fried, Lisbeth S. "The ʿAm Hāʾres in Ezra 4:4." Pages 123–45 in Lipschits and Oeming, eds, *Judah and the Judeans in the Persian Period*.

Gerstenberger, Erhard S. *Leviticus: A Commentary*. OTL. Louisville, KY: Westminster John Knox, 1996.

Gilter, Haim. "The Levant." Pages 101–13 in Morrison and Kluge, eds, *A Survey of Numismatic Research 1990–1995*.

Grabbe, Lester L. *A History of the Jews and Judaism in the Second Temple Period*. Vol. 1, *Yehud: A History of the Persian Province of Judah*. LSTS. London; New York: T & T Clark, 2004.

_____. *An Introduction to First Century Judaism: Jewish Religion and History in the Second Temple Period*. Edinburgh: T & T Clark, 1996.

Halpern, Baruch. "The Ritual Background of Zechariah's Temple Song." *CBQ* 40 (1978): 167–90.

Harper, Robert Francis. *Assyrian and Babylonian Letters*. 5 Vols. Reprint. Chicago, IL: The University of Chicago Press, 1977. [=*ABL*]

Herodotus. *The Histories*. PCS. Translated by Aubrey de Selincourt. Harmondsworth: Penguin, 1954. [=*Hist.*]

Hoglund, Kenneth G. *Achaemenid Imperial Administration in Syria-Palestine and the Missions of Ezra and Nehemiah*. SBL Dissertation Series 125. Atlanta, GA: Scholars Press, 1992.

Hopkins, David C. *The Highlands of Canaan: Agricultural Life in the Early Iron Age*. SWBA 3. Sheffield: Almond, 1985.

Hurowitz, Victor. *I Have Built You an Exalted Housed: Temple Building in the Bible in Light of Mesopotamian and Northwest Semitic Writings*. JSOTSup 115. Sheffield: Sheffield Academic Press, 1992.

Ishida, Tomoo. *History and Historical Writing in Ancient Israel: Studies in Biblical Historiography*. SHCANE 16. Leiden: Brill, 1999.

Johnstone, William. *First and Second Chronicles*. Vol. 1, *1 Chronicles 1–2 Chronicles 9: Israel's Place among the Nations*. JSOTSup 253. Sheffield: Sheffield Academic Press, 1997.

Kapelrud, Arvid S. "Temple Building, A Task for Gods and Kings." *Or* 32 (1963): 56–62.

Kessler, John. "Haggai, Zerubbabel, and the Political Status of Yehud: the Signet Ring in Haggai 2:23." Pages 102–19 in Floyd and Haak, eds, *Prophets, Prophecy, and Prophetic Texts in Second Temple Judaism*.

——. *The Book of Haggai: Prophecy and Society in early Persian Yehud*. VTSup 91. Leiden: Brill, 2002.

Levine, Baruch A. *Leviticus*, JPSTC. Philadelphia: Jewish Publication Society, 1989.

Lipschits, Oded. "Achaeological Imperial Policy, Settlement Processes in Palestine, and the Status of Jerusalem in the Middle of the Fifth Century B.C.E." Pages 19–32 in Lipschits and Oeming, eds, *Judah and the Judeans in the Persian Period.*

—— and Manfred Oeming, eds. *Judah and the Judeans in the Persian Period.* Winona Lake, IN: Eisenbrauns, 2006.

McEntire, Mark. "Haggai: Bringing God into the Picture." *RE* 97 (2000): 69–78.

McKenzie, Steven L. *1–2 Chronicles.* AOTC. Nashville: Abingdon, 2004.

Mason, Rex. *The Book of Haggai, Zechariah and Malachi.* CBC. Cambridge: Cambridge University Press, 1977.

——. "The Purpose of the 'Editorial Framework' of the Book of Haggai." *VT* (1977); 413–21.

May, Herbert G. "'This People' and 'This Nation' in Haggai." *VT* 18 (1968): 190–7.

Meadowcroft, Tim. *Haggai: Reading, A New Biblical Commentary.* Sheffield: Phoenix, 2006.

Meyers, Eric M. "The Persian Period and the Judean Restoration: From Zerubbabel to Nehemiah." Pages 509–21 in Miller, Hanson and McBride, eds, *Ancient Israelite Religion.*

—— and Carol L. Meyers. *Haggai, Zechariah 1–8.* AB. Vol. 25B. New York: Doubleday, 1987.

Milgrom, Jacob. *Leviticus: A Book of Ritual and Ethics.* CC. Minneapolis: Fortress, 2004.

——. *Leviticus 23–27: A New Translation with Introduction and Commentary.* AB. Vol. 3B. New York: Doubleday, 2001.

Miller, Patrick D., Paul D. Hanson, and S. Dean McBride Jr, eds. *Ancient Israelite Religion: Essays in Honor of Frank Moore Cross.* Philadelphia: Fortress, 1987.

Mulder, Martin Jan. *1Kings.* Vol. 1, *1Kings 1–11.* Leuven: Peeters, 1998.

Parpola, Simo. *Letters from Assyrian and Babylonian Scholars.* SAA 10. Helsinki: Helsinki University Press, 1993.

Pastor, Jack. *Land and Economy in Ancient Palestine.* London: Routledge, 1997.

Petersen, David L. *Haggai, Zechariah 1–8: A Commentary.* OTL. London: SCM, 1985.

——. "Zerubbabel and Jerusalem Temple Reconstruction." *CBQ* 36 (1974): 366–72.

Rappaport, Uriel. "Numistics." Pages 25–59 in Davies and Finkelstein, eds, *CHJ.* Vol. 1, *Introduction.*

Redditt, Paul L. *Haggai, Zechariah, Malachi: Based on the Revised Standard Version,* New Century Bible Commentary. London: Marshall Pickering, 1995.

Renger, Johannes. "Interaction of Temple, Palace, and 'Private Enterprise' in the Old Babylonian Economy." Pages 249–56 in Lipinski, ed., *State and Temple Economy in the Ancient Near East.* Vol. 1.

Rogland, Max. "Haggai 2,17: A New Analysis." *Bib* 88 (2007): 553–7.

Saggs, Henry William Frederick. *The Might That Was Assyria*. London: Sidgwick, 1984.

Sancisi-Weerdenburg, Heleen. "Darius I and the Persian Empire." Pages 1035–49 in Sasson, ed., *CANE*. Vol. 2.

Stuhlmueller, Carroll. *Rebuilding with Hope: A Commentary on the Book of Haggai and Zechariah*. ITC. Grand Rapids: Eerdmans, 1988.

Tiemeyer, Lena-Sofia. "The Question of Indirect Touch: Lam 4,14; Ezek 44,19 and Hag 2, 12–13." *Bib* 87 (2006): 64–74.

Tigay, Jeffrey H. *Deuteronomy*, JPSTC. Philadelphia: Jewish Publication Society, 1996.

Tollington, Janet E. *Tradition and Innovation in Haggai and Zechariah 1–8*. JSOTSup 150. Sheffield: Sheffield Academic Press, 1993.

Trotter, James M. "Was the Second Jerusalem Temple a Primarily Persian Project?" *SJOT* 15 (2001): 276–93.

Tuland, C. G. "'uššayyā' and ʿuššarnâ: a Clarification of Terms, Date and Text." *JNES* 17 (1958): 269–75.

Ulrich, Eugene, ed. *The Biblical Qumran Scrolls: Transcriptions and Textual Variants*. VTSup 134. Leiden; Boston: Brill, 2010.

Vargyas, Peter. "Agrarkrisen und Umfang der Agrarproduktion im Babylonien des 1. Jahrtausends." Pages 189–96 in Klengel and Renger, eds, *Landwirtschaft im Alten Orient*.

Verhoef, Peter A. *The Book of Haggai and Malachi*. NICOT. Grand Rapids: Eerdmans, 1987.

Waltke, Bruce Kenneth and M. O'Connor. *An Introduction to Biblical Hebrew Syntax*. Winona Lake, IN: Eisenbrauns, 1990.

Weinberg, Joel P. *The Citizen-Temple Community*. Translated by Daniel L. Smith-Christopher. JSOTSup 151. Sheffield: Sheffield Academic Press, 1992.

Weinfeld, Moshe. *The Promise of the Land: The Inheritance of the Land of Canaan by the Israelites*. TLJS 3. Berkeley: University of California Press, 1993.

Williamson, Hugh Godfrey Maturin. *Ezra, Nehemiah*, WBC. Vol. 16. Waco, TX: Word, 1985.

Wolff, Hans Walter, *Haggai: A Commentary*. Translated by M. Kohl. Minneapolis: Augsburg Publishing House, 1988.

Zimmerli, Walther. *Ezekiel 2: A Commentary on the Book of the Prophet Ezekiel Chapters 25–48*. Her. Philadelphia: Fortress, 1983.

Conclusion

In my thesis, I discuss in some detail the relationship between temple and economy in ancient Jerusalem. My main approach is an exegetical study of the Book of Haggai. My text corpus consists of Hag 1:2, 5–6, 7–8, 9–11, 12–14; 2:3, 8–9, 15–19. In my reading of the text I put weight on historical and economic perspectives. I also make extensive use of archaeological reports.

In the introduction, I challenge the current consensus regarding the rebuilding of the Jerusalem temple. Scholars have, as a rule, disputed that the temple rebuilding project is twofold aims. In my work, I first show how the renovated temple should form a basis for a self-sufficient economy in Judah. Second, as a semi-autonomous political entity, the temple should strengthen ties between Judah and the Achaemenid Empire. Most scholars dealing with Judean economy pay too little attention to the economic implications of agriculture in Judah. Moreover, they also disregard to a large extent the Book of Haggai as an important agricultural text.

In Chapter 1, I discuss agriculture in the ancient Near East. My main point is that the ancient Near Eastern economy was, above all, agrarian. From very early on, these ancient societies devised wide-ranging and elaborate irrigation systems, maximising use of land for agricultural purposes. With regional specialisation, many of them later demonstrated highly advanced political and economic structures (urbanisation). Similarly, throughout the Iron Age, ancient Israel developed agriculture and produced a multitude of agricultural products. Judah, in particular, was renowned for the production of vine and olive. Judah's rich agricultural produce, as well as other commodities, led to a comprehensive trade through a web of interregional trade routes in the ancient Near East.

In my thesis, I also deal with the management of agricultural economy in the ancient Near East. In this area, ever since the rise of centralised states (around 3500 BCE), temples were vital instruments for economic and administrative power. Temples were used for both collection and distribution of agricultural resources. Furthermore, temples administered tenants, oversaw agricultural affairs, managed provincial agricultural production, and enjoyed trade privileges. The economic importance of temples throughout the regions can hardly be exaggerated. Darius attempted to consolidate temple-based fiscal administrations further by implementing temple rebuilding projects. He also invigorated interregional trade through the support of professional merchants. Foremost among them were the Egibi family of Babylon and the Murashu family of Nippur. The flourishing business led to economic boom throughout the Achaemenid Empire.

In Chapter 2, I discuss Darius's history, focusing primarily on how the empire was run. I show how Darius already very early in his reign was forced to suppress widespread rebellion against his rule. One important policy of Darius is his recognition of local deities. In this way, he "authorised" his own rule as religious and political leader in each province. This religio-political propaganda was soon followed up by temple-restoration projects. Building or rebuilding temples throughout the imperial territories was done purely for economic and political reasons. The strategy ensured the successful annexation of a province and its population into the empire. Darius also reorganised the provinces. Each province was assessed based on its political and territorial status. Judah, a politically small and weak province, was a tribute city-state because of her agricultural capacity.

Roughly at the same time (around 520 BCE), Darius launched a military campaign against the revolt in Egypt. It was for this campaign that Judah had to supply provisions. However, Judah not only produced plenty of agricultural products. As we see, she also functioned as a military buffer zone between the Achaemenid Empire and Egypt.

In Chapter 3, I examine how the agricultural importance of Judah continued to contribute to the Achaemenid Empire. Despite the demise in Judah that followed the Babylonian conquest of Jerusalem in 586 BCE, archaeological excavations have demonstrated the continued existence of a considerable material culture in Judah. The expansion took place in the area of Benjamin, but also in the Negev, and probably even in the Judean hills.

The Achaemenids further repopulated and resettled towns ruined by the Neo-Babylonians. This took place in particular between Jerusalem and its immediate environs, extending as far as Jericho and the Shephelah. This region became important for Jerusalem's agricultural economy. Above all, Judah has a surplus of vine and olive. Throughout the Achaemenid period, the population steadily increased, leading to further administrative districts across the territory.

The Jerusalem temple rebuilding was initiated to increase production and prosperity in Judah, and to promote the temple as an economic and administrative centre (Hag 2:8–9). However, the imperial command to rebuild the Jerusalem temple was disregarded by the people of Judah. Instead, the Judeans attempted to restore the Davidic dynasty through Zerubbabel (Hag 1:4, 9; 2:5). This could only be understood as a revolt against Darius.

To make matters worse, despite all efforts by the Achaemenids to increase Judah's agricultural produce, a severe famine occurred. The famine was a result of a series of droughts, storms, and crop diseases (blight and mildew). All disasters were interpreted as divine punishment following failure to rebuild the temple (Hag 1:5–6, 9–11; 2:15–18). As a result, not least when combined with imperial tax obligations on Judah, the province was stretched beyond its capacity. The decline in Judah's economy was not only detrimental to her agricultural economy, but also to trade.

In Chapters 4 (Hag 1:1–15) and 5 (Hag 2:1–23), I present an exegesis of the Book of Haggai. In my exegesis of Hag 1:1–15, I show how the command to rebuild the Jerusalem temple was proclaimed in the name of YHWH during the second year of Darius in 520 BCE (Hag 1:1 and 15). Darius commissioned two imperial administrators for the Jerusalem temple rebuilding project: the governor Zerubbabel and the high priest Joshua. Both officials were to work on the Jerusalem restoration, and administer temple economy (Hag 1:12–14, 15).

However, things did not go according to plan. Zerubbabel, who was of the royal house of David, had been appointed for the Jerusalem temple rebuilding task only. He was expected to use his influence as descendent of a local royal lineage. However, instead he engaged in a dynasty building project directly opposed to the imperial agenda (Hag 1:4 and 9).

The preference for rebuilding the Davidic dynasty led to YHWH's punishment. Expectations of a bountiful harvest were met with crop failure. The people neither enjoyed sufficient yields nor reaped other expected benefits (Hag 1:5–6). Strong winds destroyed the already meagre harvest (Hag 1:9), and drought ultimately resulted in famine (Hag 1:10). The harvests of grain, vine and olive were severely damaged (Hag 1:11). The Judean agricultural system was completely destroyed. All of this happened because the imperial administrators had failed to make the people start the temple rebuilding (Hag 1:7–8, 12–14).

In my exegesis of Hag 2:1–23 (Chapter 5), I highlight the nature of the Jerusalem temple rebuilding. The project was purely of an economic kind. It was, very much, similar to what the empire demanded of other subordinates (Hag 2:3, 8–9). Rebuilding the Jerusalem temple as an economic and administrative centre supported Darius's policy of strengthening local temple economies in order to increase imperial fiscal powers.

Despite Zerubbabel's position as temple administrator installed by Darius, Judah attempted to confront Darius with a conspiracy to restore the Davidic dynasty through Zerubbabel (Hag 2:4). The conspiracy was fuelled by hopes for economic prosperity and political independence for Judah (Hag 2:6–7). Instead, it led to the economic breakdown of Judah.

The stubborn desire of the people to restore the Davidic kingdom caused the crisis that led to Haggai's prophecies. As the temple rebuilding was necessary for restoring agriculture in Judah, YHWH aroused the teaching authority of the priests to enlighten the people (Hag 2:10–14). According to Haggai, speaking on behalf of the deity, it was the people's persistent rejection of the temple work that had provoked the agricultural catastrophe (Hag 2:17–19). Now was the time for the people to start rebuilding the temple for economic stability, and to ensure reliable patronage. As a prophet of YHWH, Haggai warned and judged Judah for numerous acts of disobedience. Among them we find conspiratorial rebellion, the endeavour to restore the Davidic dynasty through Zerubbabel, and the reference to Coniah through the use of a signet ring. Because of the latter episode, Zerubbabel was doomed to fail completely (Hag 2:20–23).

Index